Learning SAP BusinessObjects Dashboards

Create professional, stunning, and interactive visual dashboards for both desktop and mobile devices

Taha M. Mahmoud

[PACKT] enterprise 88
PUBLISHING
professional expertise distilled

BIRMINGHAM - MUMBAI

Learning SAP BusinessObjects Dashboards

First published: June 2015

Production reference: 1240615

Published by Packt Publishing Ltd.
Livery Place
35 Livery Street
Birmingham B3 2PB, UK.

ISBN 978-1-78528-662-9

www.packtpub.com

Credits

Author
Taha M. Mahmoud

Reviewers
Dmitry Anoshin
Sven van Leuken
Vinay Singh

Commissioning Editor
Dipika Gaonkar

Acquisition Editors
Harsha Bharwani
Greg Wild

Content Development Editor
Prachi Bisht

Technical Editor
Utkarsha S. Kadam

Copy Editors
Ameesha Green
Dipti Mankame
Vikrant Phadke

Project Coordinator
Shipra Chawhan

Proofreader
Safis Editing

Indexer
Rekha Nair

Graphics
Jason Monteiro

Production Coordinator
Manu Joseph

Cover Work
Manu Joseph

About the Author

Taha M. Mahmoud (PMP, TOGAF, ITIL, and CSM) is a senior BI consultant, BI project manager, and solution architect. He has a BS degree in computer science and automatic control from Alexandria University, Egypt. He has a great passion for new technologies, especially those related to business intelligence. Taha has more than 9 years of experience in working on, consulting for, and deploying successful BusinessObjects projects in the banking and telecom industries. He is the author of *Creating Universes with SAP BusinessObjects*. You can contact him on Twitter at @tahama_2000 or visit his blog (http://business-objects-xi.blogspot.com/).

About the Reviewers

Dmitry Anoshin is a data-centric technologist and a recognized expert in building and implementing business analytics solutions. He has a track record of successfully implementing BI/DWH projects in numerous industries, such as retail, telecommunication, finance, and e-commerce. He has in-depth knowledge of BI, ETL, DWH, and big data technologies.

Dmitry is experienced in the data integration process and is proficient in using various data warehousing methodologies. He regularly goes beyond expectations while working for various industries. Moreover, he is a certified Splunk engineer and has implemented several projects for big data analytics based on Splunk Enterprise.

In his free time, Dmitry likes to discover new technologies related to data analytics and compare similar tools among various vendors. He has reviewed *Creating Universes with SAP BusinessObjects* and *SAP BusinessObjects Reporting Cookbook*. He is also writing *SAP Lumira Essentials*, *Learning Hunk*, and *SAP Data Services Cookbook*. On the latter, he — as an experienced author — is helping a new author develop an outstanding book.

Sven van Leuken started his professional business career after completing his studies in 1996, securing a bachelor's degree in computer science. For the first 6 years of his career, he worked as a SAP ABAP developer. Then, he turned to SAP BI, where he nowadays combines his development and project management skills with profound BI knowledge within the broad spectrum of data extraction, modeling, architecture, and performance optimization.

Sven is a trusted advisor and has in-depth knowledge of implementing robust, sustainable data models and legitimate BI solutions.

He is a SAP-certified application associate in SAP HANA. He also has these certifications: Business Intelligence SAP NetWeaver 7.0, NetWeaver 2004s BI, Business Information Warehouse Certification 3.0, ABAP 3.x, and ABAP 4.0 Consultant. He frequently writes articles and blogs on SCN and on his own website, which can be reached at `http://www.svenvanleuken.com/`.

Since 2008, Sven has been working as a project manager / scrum master. In this role, he has successfully managed many projects to deliver the required (high) quality within the budget and on time. He is a certified Prince2, ITILF, and IPMA-D project manager and has also passed the Professional Scrum Master (PSM-I) and Scrum Fundamentals Certified Credential (SFC) certification tests.

His sound technical knowledge (over 19 years of hands-on SAP experience) and project management experience, combined with well-developed communication skills for coaching, motivation, and innovation, make him the ideal sparring partner.

Vinay Singh is a SAP analytics solution architect, with over 9 years of experience in the retail and manufacturing industries. He has published a number of white papers and blogs on various SAP forums. A technology enthusiast, he keeps visiting colleges and companies in Germany and the MENA region for guest lectures and workshops on topics related to SAP BI and SAP HANA.

I would like to thank my wife, Minal—who herself is a BO consultant—for her support and input on a few topics as I was reviewing this book.

www.PacktPub.com

Support files, eBooks, discount offers, and more

For support files and downloads related to your book, please visit www.PacktPub.com.

Did you know that Packt offers eBook versions of every book published, with PDF and ePub files available? You can upgrade to the eBook version at www.PacktPub.com and as a print book customer, you are entitled to a discount on the eBook copy. Get in touch with us at service@packtpub.com for more details.

At www.PacktPub.com, you can also read a collection of free technical articles, sign up for a range of free newsletters and receive exclusive discounts and offers on Packt books and eBooks.

![PACKTLIB logo]

https://www2.packtpub.com/books/subscription/packtlib

Do you need instant solutions to your IT questions? PacktLib is Packt's online digital book library. Here, you can search, access, and read Packt's entire library of books.

Why subscribe?

- Fully searchable across every book published by Packt
- Copy and paste, print, and bookmark content
- On demand and accessible via a web browser

Free access for Packt account holders

If you have an account with Packt at www.PacktPub.com, you can use this to access PacktLib today and view 9 entirely free books. Simply use your login credentials for immediate access.

Instant updates on new Packt books

Get notified! Find out when new books are published by following @PacktEnterprise on Twitter or the *Packt Enterprise* Facebook page.

Table of Contents

Preface   **vii**

Chapter 1: Getting Started with SAP BO Dashboards   **1**

Introduction to SAP BO Dashboards   **2**
  SAP BusinessObjects BI platform 4.x   2
  SAP BO Dashboards   3
  SAP BO Dashboards design history   3

Installing SAP BO Dashboards   **4**
  The dashboards prerequisites   4
  Downloading SAP BO Dashboards   5
  Installing SAP BO Dashboards   7

Exploring SAP BO Dashboards' capabilities   **10**
  Accessing and using dashboard samples   10
    Accordion menu dashboard sample   12
    Chart Drill Down dashboard sample   14
  Accessing and using dashboard templates   15
    US Sales Map   17

Getting to know the SAP BO Dashboards interface   **19**
  Understanding the SAP BO Dashboards panels   21
    The Properties panel   21
    The Components panel   22
    The Object Browser panel   25
    The Query Browser panel   26
    Mobile compatibility   27
  Understanding SAP BO Dashboards toolbars   27
    The Standard toolbar   28
    The Themes toolbar   28
    The Export toolbar   28
    The Format toolbar   28
    The Start Page toolbar   29

Understanding SAP BO Dashboards quick views	29
Summary	**30**
Chapter 2: Understanding the Dashboard Creation Process	**31**
Phases in the project	**31**
The initiation phase	32
The planning phase	32
The execution/implementation phase	33
The control/testing phase	33
The closing phase	33
Determining the needs	**33**
Gathering business requirements	35
The sales by state analysis	35
The sales trend analysis	36
The sales and quantity per product analysis	36
Determining the target audience and devices	36
Sketching our dashboard	38
Building the prototype	41
Dashboard creation process	**42**
Preparing the dashboard workspace	**43**
Summary	**47**
Chapter 3: UI Components	**49**
Before we start	**50**
Preferences	51
The Document tab	53
The Grid tab	53
The Excel options	54
Document properties	55
Adding our first chart component (pie chart)	**56**
Linking the chart with data	60
Configuring the main chart properties	62
Introducing other chart types	**65**
Line, column, bar, and column line charts	66
Bubble, scatter charts, and tree maps	73
OHLC and candlestick charts	76
Bullet charts	77
Radar charts	77
Adding a single value component to our dashboard	**78**
Gauge and dial	78
Progress bar and sliders	82
Value and spinner	82

Play	83
Summary	**84**
Chapter 4: Using Maps and Other Components	**85**
Maps	**85**
Using maps	**86**
Adding built-in map dashboard components	86
Installing, configuring, and using the CMap plugin	90
Using other SAP BO Dashboard components	**97**
Using a calendar dashboard component	100
Using the trend icon	103
Using a trend analyzer	104
Using the print, reset, and local scenario buttons	106
Using the history and source data dashboard components	107
Using other third-party plugins	**111**
Using a dash printer	111
Using Micro charts	113
Summary	**116**
Chapter 5: Interactive Analysis with Dashboards	**117**
Using traditional selectors	**118**
Using radio buttons	118
Orientation	123
Insert On	123
Insertion types	124
Selected item	127
Using comboboxes and list boxes	128
Using checkboxes	130
List builder	133
Displaying tabular data	**134**
List view	135
Scorecard	136
The hierarchical table	138
The spreadsheet table	138
Grid	139
Using advanced menus	**139**
Label-based menu	140
Sliding picture fisheye menus	142
Accordion Menu	144
Using other selectors	**145**
Using the icon	146
Using Filter	147

Using push and toggle buttons 149
Using third-party selectors **149**
Summary **150**
Chapter 6: Advanced Interactive Analysis with Dashboards **151**
Using the dynamic visibility feature **152**
Grouping components **156**
Using Containers **158**
Using Panel Container 159
Using Canvas Container 160
Using a Tab Set 165
Using Alerts **166**
Using Alerts with Charts 166
Using Alerts with the single-value component 173
Using Alerts with maps 177
Using Alerts with Selectors 180
Using Alerts with the Combo Box selector 180
Using Alerts with the Scorecard selector 181
Using the drill-down (Insertion) feature **184**
Linking a dashboard to a Webi or Crystal report document **187**
Summary **187**
Chapter 7: Styling Up **189**
Using text dashboard components **189**
Using Input Text Area 191
Using labels 191
Using Input Text 191
Dealing with colors and themes **192**
Using the Appearance tab 192
Color binding 196
Using the color scheme 197
Using Themes 200
Using art and background components **201**
Using basic art components 201
Using the image component 202
Formatting the dashboard components **205**
Summary **206**
Chapter 8: Exporting, Publishing, and Importing Dashboards **207**
Exporting the dashboards file **207**
Publishing dashboards **211**
Importing dashboards **215**
Summary **216**

Chapter 9: Retrieving External Data Sources	**217**
Using direct query	**218**
Using web services	**229**
Web service query	229
Web service connection	234
Using Live Office	**236**
Using XML data	**245**
Summary	**248**
Chapter 10: Managing Dashboard Security	**249**
Understanding the SAP BusinessObjects security model	**249**
Applying object level security	**251**
Applying application level security	**260**
Applying row level security	**263**
Creating a row level security data profile using IDT	264
Creating row level security access restrictions using UDT	267
Applying security best practices	**269**
Summary	**270**
Chapter 11: Creating Mobile Dashboards	**271**
Creating dashboards for smart devices	**273**
Developing a mobile SAP BO Dashboard	**274**
Using supported mobile components	274
Using the recommended canvas size for iPads	276
Using a supported mobile data connection	276
Publishing mobile dashboards	**277**
Previewing our mobile dashboard	277
Publishing our mobile dashboard	279
Adding our dashboard to the mobile category	279
Accessing and using mobile dashboards	**281**
Introducing the main features of the SAP BI application	**283**
Viewing document information and adding a document to favorites	284
Using the Annotation feature	285
E-mailing dashboards	285
Summary	**285**
Appendix: References	**287**
Index	**291**

Preface

Business Intelligence (BI) is one of the fastest growing fields in the market. The main goal of BI is to help us get good insights by utilizing the historical information that we have. Historical information helps us take the right decisions at the right time, based on the trends and patterns that occurred in the past.

BI is also concerned about delivering information to the right users in the right format. Operational users, for example, are more concerned about details and transactional information. This is why BI reports are the proper format for them. On the other hand, the top management and executives are more concerned about high-level information, enriched with indicators that can help them spot wrong or unusual behavior at first sight. This will then help them take corrective actions, which is why dashboards are the most proper format for them.

Why do we need dashboards?

"Dashboard" is not a new terminology. Actually, we use dashboards in many aspects in our life. A car's main dashboard is a good example, as we all know how to read a car's gauges and speedometers. You can see an example of a car's main dashboard in the following diagram:

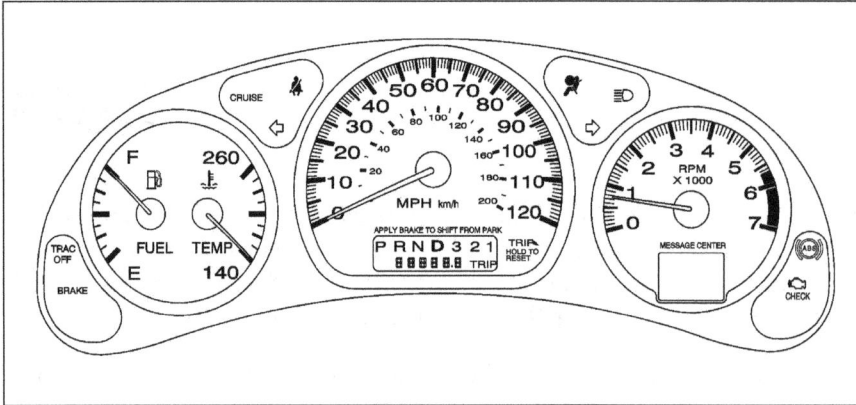

The speedometer is used to indicate the current speed of the car. As the speed changes, the speedometer's needle moves towards the actual current speed. The gauge, dials, and the speedometer are components that we will discuss in detail in *Chapter 3, UI Components*. We should also note that we have an indicator that starts when our speed reaches 120 km/hr to indicate that we are at high speed (risk) and so we need to slow down.

Fuel, heat, and RPM meters also work in the same manner. They are used to indicate the current value and also to indicate (highlight) the danger values. Danger values signal that we need to take some action. The main use of a dashboard is to help us decide when we should act, but it will not give us detailed information on what is going wrong. For example, when a car engine's heat reaches the red zone, we know that we need to stop and examine the car to find out what the problem is, but we will not get information on whether there is leakage of water or there is a damaged part that needs to be replaced.

Now we should have a good idea about why we need dashboards, so before we start talking about SAP BusinessObjects (SAP BO) Dashboard (formerly known as Xcelsius), we need take a moment first to define what a dashboard is.

What is a dashboard?

A dashboard is a visual representation of information that can help us spot a risk, or bad or wrong behavior. It also can help us monitor and track our performance. You can see a dashboard example in this screenshot:

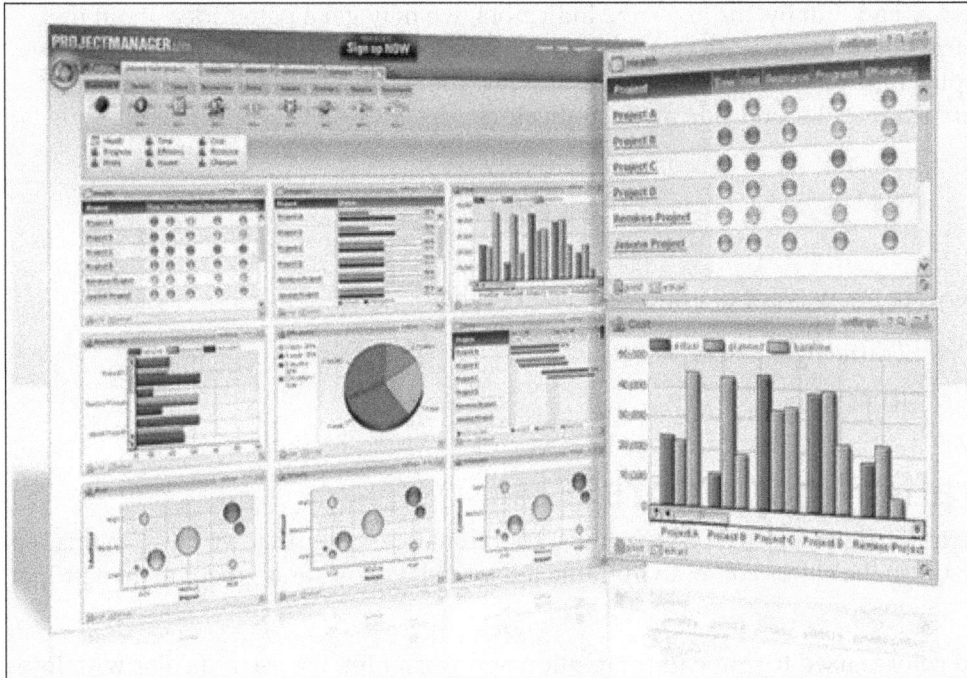

A dashboard is a container or view that can contain any number of the components listed as follows:

- Indicators
- Key performance indicators (KPIs)
- Key risk indicators (KRIs)
- Scorecards
- Reports

We will discuss each component in detail in the upcoming sections.

Indicators

An indicator is a visual effect that can add extra information that is not included in the original metric.

> A metric is a figure that measures something. Profit is our metric in the following example.

Let's have an example to help you understand this in a better way. Let's say our profit this month is $10. As you can see, you can't judge whether this number is good or bad. But by adding some indicators, we may get a better idea about this metric's performance. As you can see in the following screenshot, the first row display information without indicator while the second row display information with yellow color and side arrow indicators.

There are many types of indicators, such as these:

- Traffic light colors
- Icons

Traffic light colors

The traffic light colors type is the most traditional indicator that we have. In this type, we utilize the colors common in traffic lights (red, yellow, and green) to give proper indications.

Red color is used to grape user attention and warn him. we use red color with loses or bad performing KPIs. Red color indicates that immediate correction action should be taken.

Yellow will give the impression that we should be prepared to do something, such as slowing down our car and preparing to stop at the traffic lights, or trying to increase our sales to increase your net profit.

Finally, green will give the impression that everything is okay and we are performing well. We can use green color with profit metrics and well performing KPIs.

Icons

Icons are another type of indicators. We can use an icon to give the required impression to end users. For example, a trend-up icon beside a profit metric will give the impression that we are trending up. We can find some other types of icon indicators, as follows:

- Arrows, such as up, side, or down arrows
- Faces, such as a smiley, normal, or sad
- Progress bars

> Use icons if your dashboards will be printed in grayscale (black and white).

You also need to note the following:

- You can use more than one indicator type at the same time. For example, you can use traffic light colors and arrows to indicate your profit performance, as you saw in the previous screenshot.

- You can use more than three levels in the traffic light indicator type. For example, a five-color indicator may use the following colors: red, orange, yellow, light green, and dark green.

  You can see an example of sets of indicator types in the following screenshot:

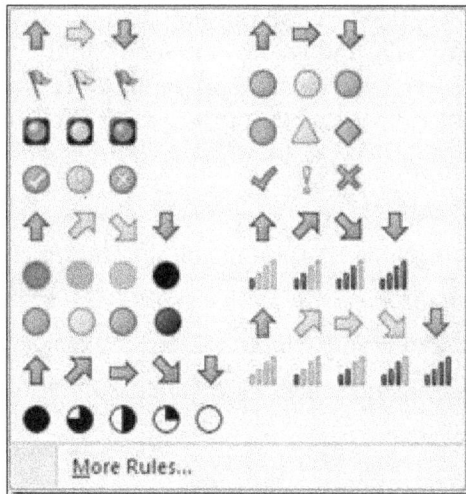

Key performance indicators (KPIs)

When we start working on something, we should first define our goals and objectives. After that, we should start trying to achieve our goals. Then, from time to time, we need to check how far we are from our goals and whether our performance with respect to achieving our goals is good or bad. The main purpose of a key performance indicator (KPI) is to show how close we are to our goals (target). Normally, we will need more than one KPI to indicate how far we are from our goals.

> Different industries will have different KPIs, even if they are related to the same goals, such as increasing profit, because the metrics are different.
>
> A KPI is a metric used to measure and monitor our performance in order to achieve our goal (or goals), and it gives us an indication of our performance.

Let's now look at a small example of a business case.

Let's suppose that we have a new website. There are many ways of income implemented in our site, such as advertisement, exam registration fees, products sold, and so on. First, we need to set our goals. Let's set a simple goal here: our net profit is $10 million, and our goal is simply to make it $15 million by the end of the fiscal year. So, the defined goal here is as follows:

Goal: Increase the net revenue of our website by 50 percent during this year.

Now we have a goal and we need to find out how to achieve it. There are many factors that will affect our goals, and we need to focus on the important ones. We call those factors metrics. A metric is usually a number that will affect our goal somehow, such as the number of sold products or Product price, so let's define our metrics here.

Net profit = Net income – Net cost

*Net income= Product income [Number of sold products * Unit price]*

> *+ Advertisement income [Number of visitors * AD revenue per view]*

> *+ Exam income [Number of scheduled exams * Exam fee]*

Net cost = Fixed monthly site maintenance

> *+ Product processing cost*

> *+ Exam setup*

> *+ Other expenses*

Now, as we can see, there are some variable metrics and some static metrics. For example, the number of visitors is a dynamic variable metric and monthly site maintenance fee is an example of a static metric. You should concentrate on dynamic metric in your KPIs.

We will use **# of visitors** as a metric in our KPI, but first we need to check whether this is enough of an indicator. Of course not! We need to link it somehow to our goal (achieving 50 percent growth in profit by the end of the year). To make it clearer, let's take a look at the # of visitors trend graph here:

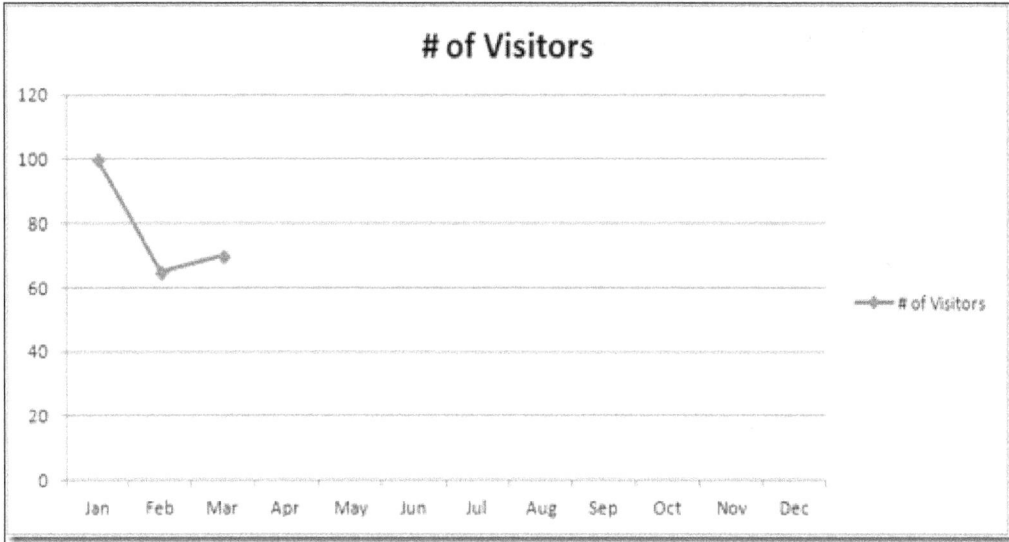

As we can see, the graph displays the number of visitors (in thousands) per month. It is clear that this is not enough to know whether those figures are good or bad. Let's try to answer this question using the previous graph: Does the count of 100,000 visitors in January mean that we will be able to achieve our goal by the end of the year or not?

As we can see, a metric is just a plain number, and all that we can indicate here is the number of visitors trend by linking our metric's values across time. We can get an idea on whether our number of visitors is increasing or decreasing over time. Also, as we already saw in our goal definition, we need to increase the number of visitors in general to get more advertisement income. So far, this is just a trend metric and there is something missing.

In order to gain $15 million, let's say that our strategy is to focus on advertisement profit this year. If we maintain constant values of the remaining factors, then we should get $10 million by the end of the year and, to increase our profit, we have to increase our average number of visitors per month. Let's say the old average number of visitors to our site was 60,000 per month. If we get an average of 60,000 visitors per month and everything else remains the same, then we should make a profit of $10 million by the end of the year. We need to calculate the new required average number of visitors (target), assuming that we will not change any other factors. Let's say that we need, on average, 90,000 visitors per month to achieve our target, which will somehow lead us to our goal. Now the graph should like this, after adding the calculated target:

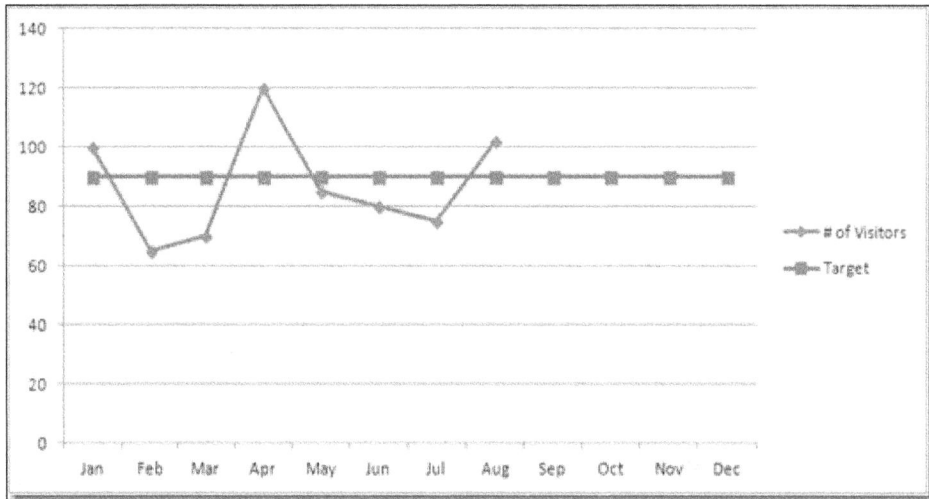

Now we have a KPI, as we can see after adding our monthly target that needs to be met in order to achieve our goal; we can indicate our performance month by month to achieve our goal. We can easily see that we performed well in **Jan**, **Apr**, and **Aug**. We nearly achieved our target in **May**, and performed badly in the remaining months.

How to define your KPIs

To define a KPI, we need to complete the following:

- **Define a goal**: First, we need to define our goals, or set of goals. Our goals should tell us what we want to achieve.

- **Define a metric**: The next step is to define our metrics. A metric is a number that will affect our goal.

- **Define a Target**: A target will help us understand how our metric should behave in order for us to achieve our goal.

- **Build your KPI**: A KPI will show us how our metric will behave against a preset target and will indicate our performance against our target.

Visual elements used to present KPIs (charts)

In the previous example, we had one measure (number of visitors) and one dimension (time), and this is why we selected the line chart—because it is the best visual element for showing a time trend. There are many other chart types, such as a pie chart for example, which can be used to show the relationship between one measure and one dimension. We can use a pie chart if we want to show, for example, sales by product. Also, we can use a combined chart (bar and line chart combined) to see the relationship between two measures and one dimension, such as the relationship between the communication channel, number of complaints, and average service time. We will discuss how to select the most proper chart components based on our metrics in *Chapter 3, UI Components*.

Key Risk Indicator (KRI)

A **Key risk indicator** (KRI) is mostly the same as a KPI but with a few differences, as listed in the following table:

Feature	KPI	KRI
Measuring	Performance	Risk
Against	Target	Threshold

In many cases, we may need to incorporate an alerting system with a KRI to send it immediately by mail or a warning SMS message to the risk owner. This is because, in most cases, we want to act immediately when the risk is triggered.

Scorecards

A scorecard is a group of related KPIs that contribute to achieve a major goal. There are two types of scorecards:

- **Balanced**: This is an equal-weight score card, which means that all KPIs under this goal have the same importance; when we calculate our achievement percentage for our goal, we simply take the average.

- **Not balanced**: This is a none equal-weight scorecard, which means that every KPI has it is own weight (importance); when we calculate our achievement percentage for our goal, we consider the KPI weight to calculate the average.

You can see a scorecard example in this screenshot:

	Actual	Benchmark	Apr 09 Trend	Peer Average	Peer Percentile
⊟ **Process - Creation**					
Average Call Answer Time	26.19	30.00 ●	⬆	32.98	63.00% ✓
% Calls Abandoned	5.89%	5.00% △	⬇	7.62%	75.00% ✓
% SRs Received by Chat	3.33%	5.00% △	⬇	6.04%	25.00% ✗
% SRs Received by Email	26.80%	25.00% ●	⇨	25.46%	44.00% ⁙
% SRs Received by Phone	45.71%	50.00% ●	⬆	50.07%	63.00% ⁙
% SRs Received by Web	0.60%	20.00% △	⬇	13.86%	19.00% ✗
⊞ **Process - Resolution**					
⊞ **Financials**					
⊟ **Satisfaction**					
Service Desk Customer Satisfaction	2.03	4.00 ✗	⇨	2.66	31.00% ⁙

Reports

A report is a summary or detailed information displayed in a simple table or chart format. An example of a detailed report is shown in the following screenshot:

Branches Summary

*** Query Name:Query 1 ***

Enter Customer Region [Level 1]: Central Region

Customer Region [Level 1]	Customer Branch City	Customer Branch Description
Central Region	Central Private	2
Central Region	Northern	17
Central Region	Not Used	4
Central Region	Qaseim	15
Central Region	Riyadh East	19
Central Region	Riyadh North	17
Central Region	Riyadh South	14
Central Region	Riyadh West	15

In this book, we will discuss all that you need to learn SAP BusinessObjects Dashboard Designer. This is a SAP tool that can be used to create stunning dashboards, KPIs, KRIs, and scorecards using the Flash and MS Excel technologies.

Congratulations for taking a step towards learning how to create dashboards using SAP BO Dashboard. Are you ready? Then let's go...

In this book, you will learn how to create a complete, interactive dashboard that contains charts, single-value components, selectors, and maps. You will learn how to apply advanced features,such asdynamic visibility, alerts, and color binding.

What this book covers

Chapter 1, Getting Started with SAP BO Dashboards, shows you how to download, install, and run SAP Dashboard Designer. After that, we explore this tool's capabilities and features by accessing SAP BO Dashboard designer templates and samples. We do this to demonstrate the capabilities of this tool and make you more excited to learn about it further. Then we discuss the SAP BO Dashboard Designer interface, menus, and panels.

Chapter 2, Understanding the Dashboard Creation Process, makes you familiar with the process of creating dashboards. We start by talking about the business requirement gathering phase. Then we discuss how important it is to sketch the initial requirements on a plain paper and think beyond data. After that,you get to learn how to create a prototype for our dashboard project,whichwe build step by step aswe progress through this book.

Importing data is the first step in the process of dashboard creation, so here you learn how to import data into your dashboard project. Then you learn how to maintain your Excel sheet and make it more readable. You also learn how to use imported data, which is meant for later chapters.

Chapter 3, UI Components, is where we start building the model by adding chart components to our dashboard project. Then you learn how to link this with the data that we imported in the previous chapter. After that, we see how to play with our charts' properties and how to handle missing data.

The single-value component is another visual element that we can use inside our dashboard, but because it is totally different from charts, we discuss it in detail.

Chapter 4, Using Maps and Other Components, teaches you how to add a map to your dashboard project. In this chapter, you also learn how to install, configure, and use third-party add-ons for Google Maps. Then youget to know the other available components in SAP BO Dashboard Designer.

Chapter 5, Interactive Analysis with Dashboards, explains selectors and shows you how to use them.

Chapter 6, Advanced Interactive Analysis with Dashboards, is the core of this book. In this chapter, we explain how to make our dashboard interactive using dynamic visibility. Also,you get to learn how to add alerts to your charts, single-value components, and selectors. After that, we see how to use data insertion and containers.

Chapter 7, Styling Up, demonstrates how to customize the look and feel of our dashboard by applying themes, changing colors, adding media and a logo, and so on.

Chapter 8, Exporting, Publishing, and Importing Dashboards, teaches you how to export your dashboard in different formats. Then you learn how to publish it to make it available for others.

Chapter 9, Retrieving External Data Sources, explains how to connect to data retrieved from other data sources.

Chapter 10, Managing Dashboard Security, illustrates how to manage dashboard security.

Chapter 11, Creating Mobile Dashboards, shows you how to create a dashboard for mobile applications.

Appendix, References, will include references for Supported excel functions, List of Built-in maps, and Supported mobile components and connections.

What you need for this book

You willneed SAP BusinessObjects Dashboards installed on your client machines by following the steps provided in the first chapter. You willalso need access to the BO server to implement the steps related to chapters 8 ,9, and 10. Finally, you will need a tablet to practice *Chapter 11, Creating Mobile Dashboards*.

Who this book is for

This book will help beginners to create stylish and professional looking dashboards in no time. It is also intended for business intelligence developers who want to use SAP BO to facilitate business intelligence in their organizations. No prior knowledge is required.However, you must have a basic knowledge of MS Excel and some analytical skills to build expressive business charts.

Conventions

In this book, you will find a number of text styles that distinguish between different kinds of information. Here are some examples of these styles and an explanation of their meaning.

Code words in text, database table names, folder names, filenames, file extensions, pathnames, dummy URLs, user input, and Twitter handles are shown as follows: "We can include other contexts through the use of the `include` directive."

New terms and **important words** are shown in bold. Words that you see on the screen, for example, in menus or dialog boxes, appear in the text like this: "Click on the **Installation and Upgrades** icon."

> Warnings or important notes appear in a box like this.

> Tips and tricks appear like this.

Reader feedback

Feedback from our readers is always welcome. Let us know what you think about this book—what you liked or disliked. Reader feedback is important for us as it helps us develop titles that you will really get the most out of.

To send us general feedback, simply e-mail `feedback@packtpub.com`, and mention the book's title in the subject of your message.

If there is a topic that you have expertise in and you are interested in either writing or contributing to a book, see our author guide at `www.packtpub.com/authors`.

Customer support

Now that you are the proud owner of a Packt book, we have a number of things to help you to get the most from your purchase.

Downloading the example code

You can download the example code files from your account at `http://www.packtpub.com` for all the Packt Publishing books you have purchased. If you purchased this book elsewhere, you can visit `http://www.packtpub.com/support` and register to have the files e-mailed directly to you.

Downloading the color images of this book

We also provide you with a PDF file that has color images of the screenshots/diagrams used in this book. The color images will help you better understand the changes in the output. You can download this file from `https://www.packtpub.com/sites/default/files/downloads/6629EN.pdf`.

Errata

Although we have taken every care to ensure the accuracy of our content, mistakes do happen. If you find a mistake in one of our books—maybe a mistake in the text or the code—we would be grateful if you could report this to us. By doing so, you can save other readers from frustration and help us improve subsequent versions of this book. If you find any errata, please report them by visiting `http://www.packtpub.com/submit-errata`, selecting your book, clicking on the **Errata Submission Form** link, and entering the details of your errata. Once your errata are verified, your submission will be accepted and the errata will be uploaded to our website or added to any list of existing errata under the Errata section of that title.

To view the previously submitted errata, go to https://www.packtpub.com/books/content/support and enter the name of the book in the search field. The required information will appear under the **Errata** section.

Piracy

Piracy of copyrighted material on the Internet is an ongoing problem across all media. At Packt, we take the protection of our copyright and licenses very seriously. If you come across any illegal copies of our works in any form on the Internet, please provide us with the location address or website name immediately so that we can pursue a remedy.

Please contact us at copyright@packtpub.com with a link to the suspected pirated material.

We appreciate your help in protecting our authors and our ability to bring you valuable content.

Questions

If you have a problem with any aspect of this book, you can contact us at questions@packtpub.com, and we will do our best to address the problem.

1
Getting Started with SAP BO Dashboards

The **SAP BusinessObjects (SAP BO)** Dashboards is a tool used to create interactive dashboards, which can be displayed on desktop and mobile devices. In this chapter, we will cover an introduction to this tool first, and then learn how to download, install, and run this tool. After that, we will see some sample and template dashboards in order to get an idea about what we can do using this tool. Finally, we will discuss the tool interface to get more familiar with the tool and understand the basic use of each panel, menu, and toolbar.

> There are many SAP BusinessObjects Business Intelligence tools, such as **Web Intelligence (Webi)**, Crystal Reports, Dashboards, Explorer, Lumira, and Design studio. Each tool targets a specific audience; for example, Lumira is the best selection for data and business analysts, while Webi reports is the right selection for normal users who want to see static reports, schedule reports, or do their own analysis.

In this chapter, we will learn the following:

- Introducing SAP BO BI platform and the Dashboard tool and an overview of SAP BO Dashboards' history
- Downloading, installing, and running SAP BO Dashboards
- Exploring SAP BO Dashboards' capabilities and features using dashboard samples and templates
- Discussing the main use of SAP BO Dashboards' panels, toolbars, and menus

Let's start with an introduction to SAP BO Dashboards.

Introduction to SAP BO Dashboards

In this section, we will discuss the following topics:

- BI tools included in SAP BusinessObjects BI platform 4.x
- An introduction to SAP BO Dashboards
- The history of SAP BO Dashboards

SAP BusinessObjects BI platform 4.x

Different customers have different reporting needs, presenting information in a different format to different users. These can't be met by one reporting/BI tool, so **SAP BusinessObject (SAP BO)** offers its customers a wide range of BI tools to choose from.

Customers can choose one of the following tools as per their needs:

- **SAP BusinessObjects Web Intelligence (Webi)**: This tool is used to provide normal tabular and simple detail operational reports, interactive reporting, and ad hoc queries.

- **Crystal Reports**: This tool is used to create pixel-perfect reports that are usually printed and shared with parties outside the organization, such as annual financial reports.

- **SAP BusinessObjects Explorer**: This powerful tool is used to explore the data. It is very fast and you can get fast answers to your business questions.

- **SAP BusinessObjects Lumira**: Lumira is a data discovery tool. It can be used to dynamically analyze your data with stunning visual representations. Quickly build beautiful visualizations with a few clicks, combine data sources, and get the big picture and granular details together. Visualize large volumes of data without having to sacrifice performance. Maximize data knowledge and drive immediate outcomes.

- **SAP BusinessObjects Dashboards**: This tool is used to create a flash-based visual dashboard. This is our main topic in this title, so we will talk about this tool in detail in the next section.

SAP BO Dashboards

SAP BO Dashboards, which was formerly known as Xcelsius, is a SAP tool used to transform raw data into flash-based dashboards. We can find the main features of this tool in the following list:

- Flash-based visual representation
- An easy way to link between components and data from the embedded MS Excel thread
- There are many available ways to establish a data connection, such as Live Office, Web services, and direct Universe query; the data connection is used to dynamically load the data into our dashboard
- The possibility to create a dashboard to be used on Mobile devices, such as iPad
- The Possibility to present the data on a map, either from a set of predefined maps or using the Google maps add-in
- An easy way to change style, colors, and themes

In the next section, we will talk about the SAP BO Dashboard history.

SAP BO Dashboards design history

SAP BO Dashboards was formerly known as Xcelsius. Xcelsius was a design tool created by "Informmersion" in 2002. Three years later, in 2005, the company was acquired by BusinessObjects. Live Office was used to integrate Xcelsius with other BusinessObjects tools, such as Crystal Reports, Webi, and Universes. Simplicity and visually stunning results were the most attractive features of Xcelsius at that time. After that, BusinessObjects was acquired by SAP, and the product was renamed to SAP BusinessObjects Dashboards in the latest SAP BI Platform release 4.x

> You can visit http://www.antivia.com/blog/?p=1081 for more information about the SAP BO Dashboards history.

Installing SAP BO Dashboards

In this section, we will learn about the prerequisites to install SAP BO Dashboards and how to download, install, and configure it.

In general, we would require the Windows operating system, MS Excel, and Flash Player as the minimum tools to support the SAP BO Dashboards environment.

The dashboards prerequisites

SAP BO Dashboards is a Windows client that can be installed on one of the following windows operating systems:

- Windows XP Professional SP2 and SP3
- Windows Server 2003 Standard or Enterprise Edition SP1 and SP2
- Windows Vista SP1 and SP2
- Windows 7

SAP BO Dashboards is integrated with MS Excel to hold the data in an intermediate layer, which acts as a data model for our dashboards. This is why MS Excel is a prerequisite for the installation. We should have one of the following MS Excel versions installed on our machine:

- MS Excel XP SP3 (or later)
- MS Excel 2003 SP1, SP2, and SP3
- MS Excel 2007 SP1 and SP2
- MS Excel 2010

SAP BO Dashboards uses a flash technology to display stunning visual charts, gauges, dials, and many other components that are bound (linked) to Excel or external data sources. This is why Macromedia Flash player is a prerequisite for the installations as well. We should make sure that we have installed: Flash Player 10 (or later).

SAP BO Dashboards can be used as a standalone tool, or it can be integrated with the SAP BusinessObjects BI platform. Dashboards can be exported to the SAP BO repository and can be accessed by many platform users. Also, we can dynamically export the data from the Webi report, Crystal report, and Universes instead of having fixed (static) data in the dashboard. This will allow us to have a complete dynamic BI solution.

We will use some features that will require you to have access to a SAP BO repository in the following chapters:

- *Chapter 8, Exporting, Publishing, and Importing Dashboards*
- *Chapter 9, Retrieving External Data Sources*
- *Chapter 10, Managing Dashboard Security*
- *Chapter 11, Creating Mobile Dashboards*

So, we should have access to the SAP BO BI Platform server to practice the materials presented in these chapters.

> Note that the SAP BusinessObjects BI platform version should be the same as the SAP BO dashboards version. Currently, there are two versions: 4.0, also known as 2011, and 4.1, also known as 2013.

We will introduce Live Office as one of the external data connections that we can use to populate our dashboard with data. Live office is a SAP plugin that can be installed on MS Office and used to retrieve data from the SAP BO BI platform repository, such as Webi report, Crystal report, and Universes. We need to install the SAP Live Office add-in as we will use it in *Chapter 9, Retrieving External Data Sources*.

Now, we are prepared to download and install the SAP BO Dashboards tool.

Downloading SAP BO Dashboards

To download SAP BO Dashboards, you should have an S-user ID for the sap service marketplace with download access. We can use the following steps to download the SAP BO Dashboards tool

1. Open this link to access the SAP Support website: `https://support.sap.com/software.html`

We can see SAP support webpage in the following screenshot:

SAP Software Download Center

Download SAP products that are associated with your S-User ID. You will require the Download Software authorization, which you can request via your company's SAP System Administrator.

What would you like to download today?

Installations & Upgrades	Support Packages & Patches	Files for your Databases

Choose **Installations and Upgrades** if you want to download a product that you currently do not have (but have a valid contract for), or if you wish to download a new version of the product.

Choose **Support Packages and Patches** if you want to download code-corrections for a specific version of a product.

2. Make sure that the **Software Downloads** tab menu is selected.
3. Click on the **Installation and Upgrades** icon.
4. Select the **A-Z Alphabetical List of my Products** block and then click on the letter **D**.

Installations and Upgrades

When downloading a product for the first time, download the **Installation**. If you want to upgrade to the next version of the product, download an **Upgrade**.

Find an Installation or Upgrade you are entitled to:

A-Z Alphabetical List of my Products	My Company's Application Components	Browse our download catalog

If you are looking for code-corrections to a particular version of your product, please find them in the Support Packages and Patches section.

Note: You can only download Installations and Upgrades you are entitled to (based on your S-User ID).

5. Select **SBOP Dashboards** (Xcelsius).

6. Select the latest available version. Currently, it is 4.1 SP05. Then, click on **Add to Download Basket**.

7. Open **SAP Download Manager**, and you will notice that the SAP BO Dashboards is added to the download list.

> If you don't have SAP Download Manager installed on your machine, then you can navigate to the **Download Manager** menu from the left panel and then select the version that suites your current OS.
>
> You can use the SAP Download Manager interface to pause, stop, and resume your download.

After downloading the file, unzip it, and then move to the next section..

Installing SAP BO Dashboards

The installation wizard for SAP BO Dashboards is a straightforward process, and doesn't need much user interaction. We need to perform the following steps to install the tool:

1. Navigate to the extracted folder and double-click on the Setup.exe file.

2. Choose a setup language; here, I will select **English**.

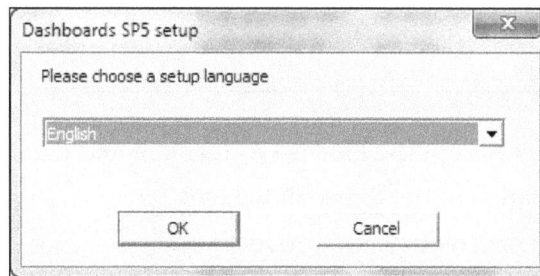

3. Click on **Next** after you read the information presented in the welcome screen.

4. Make sure that all prerequisite tests have succeeded, and then click on **Next**.

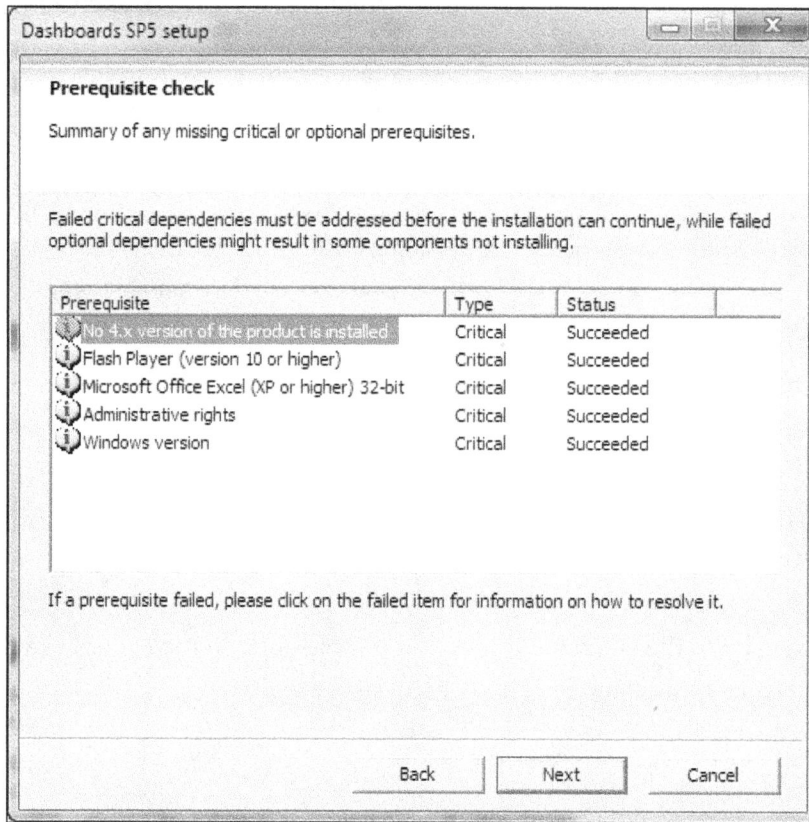

Dashboards SP5 setup

Prerequisite check

Summary of any missing critical or optional prerequisites.

Failed critical dependencies must be addressed before the installation can continue, while failed optional dependencies might result in some components not installing.

Prerequisite	Type	Status	
No 4.x version of the product is installed	Critical	Succeeded	
Flash Player (version 10 or higher)	Critical	Succeeded	
Microsoft Office Excel (XP or higher) 32-bit	Critical	Succeeded	
Administrative rights	Critical	Succeeded	
Windows version	Critical	Succeeded	

If a prerequisite failed, please click on the failed item for information on how to resolve it.

Back   Next   Cancel

5. Read and select **Accept the License Agreement** and then click on **Next**.
6. Select a destination folder to install the tool.
7. Enter the user information and product key.

8. Choose a language pack. By default, **English** is selected.

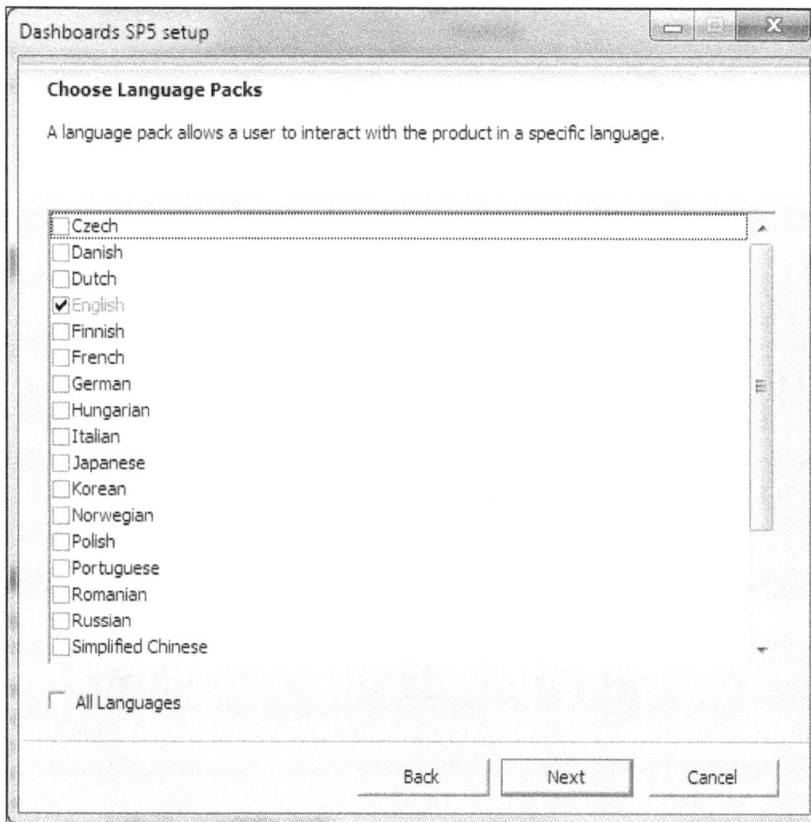

9. Select the installation type (**Typical/Custom**).

10. Click on **Next** to start the installation.

11. Wait until the installation is complete.

> **Setup language** will select the setup wizard language, while the language pack will define the language that you can use or display in your dashboards. The language pack can be installed separately, and is not mentioned here as it is not a part of our current scope.

Congratulations! We have completed the installation of the SAP BO Dashboards tool. In the next section, we will explore the tool's capabilities and features.

> You can refer to the following SAP website for more information about the installation, upgrade, deployment, application help, and additional information:
> http://help.sap.com/boxcel

Exploring SAP BO Dashboards' capabilities

After successfully installing SAP BO Dashboards, now we move to the most interesting section of this chapter, that is, the capabilities of SAP BO Dashboards. In this section, we will learn how to access and use:

- Dashboard samples
- Dashboard templates

Accessing and using dashboard samples

Dashboard samples are ready-to-use small dashboards that can be used to learn the usage of specific dashboard components and features. Each sample has its own dummy data, which can be directly previewed as the final output. In this section, we will select two dashboard samples to explore the tool's capabilities, but first, let's learn together how to access dashboard samples:

1. Navigate to the **File** menu.
2. Click on **Samples...**, as shown in the following screenshot:

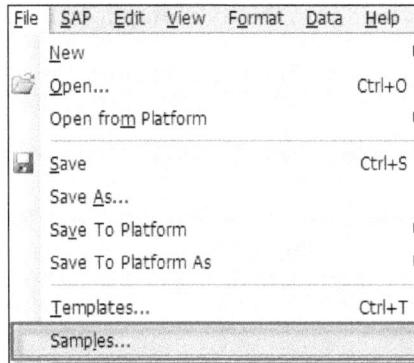

The **Samples** window will open, as displayed in the following screenshot:

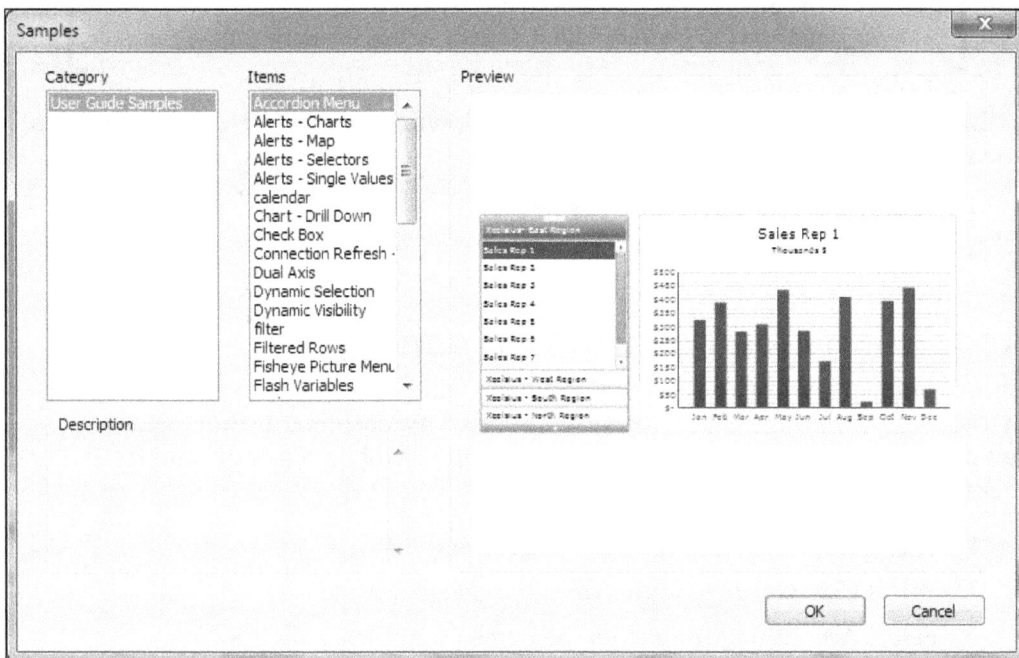

The samples window is divided into the following four main areas:

- **Category**: There is only one **User Guide Samples** category available by the default installation.

- **Items**: Here, we can select the required item or dashboard sample. There are around 38 items to select from. Each item will demonstrate a dashboard component or feature. You can use this sample to learn how to use a specific component, and to be familiar with how it will operate at runtime.

- **Description**: This is normally empty, but it should provide information about the selected item.

- **Preview**: This gives you a thumbnail view of this sample.

> The preview thumbnail is dynamic, as it is a flash component and you can interact with it directly in this window.

In this section, we will learn how to use the following two samples. I will leave it to you to explore the rest:

- Accordion menu dashboard sample
- Chart Drill Down

Accordion menu dashboard sample

Accordion menu is a two-level selector, which will be discussed in more detail in *Chapter 5, Interactive Analysis with Dashboards*. This dashboard component can maintain a two-level hierarchy. Let's open the dashboard sample and try to understand how it works:

1. Navigate to the **File** menu and select **Samples...**.

2. Select **User Guide Samples** from the category area.

3. Select **Accordion Menu** from the items list and click on **OK**.

4. The accordion menu dashboard sample will open.

5. Click on the **Preview** icon, as shown in the following screenshot:

6. This will open the **Preview** window displayed in the following screenshot. Preview is a simulator for what exactly we will see when we publish or export our dashboard.

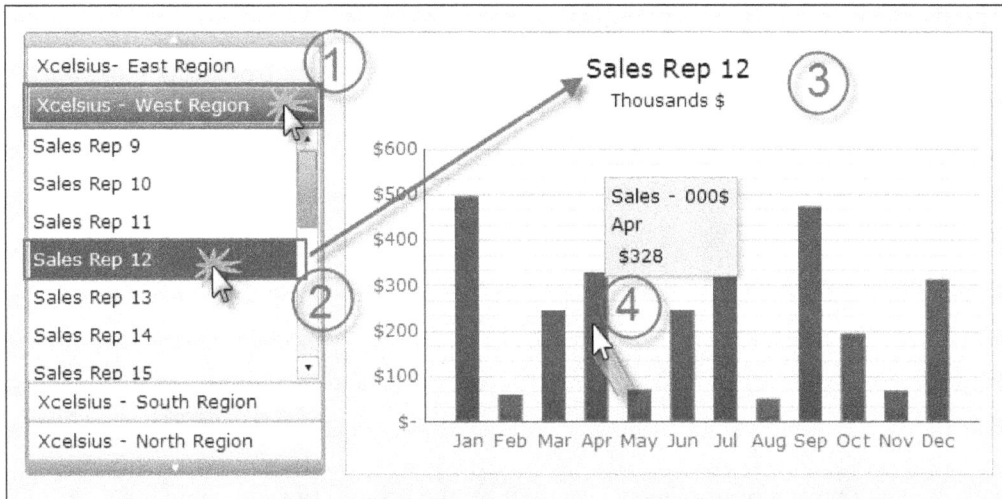

In this dashboard, we can see two main dashboard components:

- **Accordion Menu (left-hand side)**: This is a two-level dashboard selector.
- **Column chart (right-hand side)**: This chart will display sales in thousands $ by month.

Let's use this scenario to explore SAP BO Dashboards' capabilities, as follows:

1. Click on the **Xcelsius – West Region** category to expand sales repositories under this region.

2. Select **Sales Rep 12** to display the sales information in the chart on the right-hand side.

3. Notice how the data and chart title are changed in the column chart.

4. Hover your mouse pointer on the "Apr" sales to display a pop-up box that contains the following information:

    ° **Sales – 000$**: This is the measure name, as this chart displays Sales in Thousands.

    ° **"Apr" (x-axis value)**: Here, we have months on the x axis, so it will display "Apr" because we are hovering on an "Apr" column bar.

    ° **328 $ (y-axis value)**: This shows the exact sales achieved, 328 $ in our case. Remember that this number is thousands, as described in the chart subtitle.

We can see the steps highlighted in the previous screenshot. Try to repeat the scenario using other selections.

Chart Drill Down dashboard sample

In this section, we will explore the Chart Drill Down dashboard sample. This dashboard sample is different from the previous "Accordion Menu" because this sample will demonstrate a feature (drill down), rather than a component.

Drill Down is also known as **Master Detail**. The main idea of the Drill Down feature is that you can use one chart as a selector (Master) to update the data in the other chart (detail). Let's open the dashboard sample and explore how it works:

1. Navigate to the **File** menu and select **Samples....**.
2. Select **User Guide Samples** from the category area.
3. Select **Chart – Drill Down** from the items list and click on **OK**.
4. The dashboard sample will open.
5. Click on the **Preview** icon, as shown in the following screenshot:

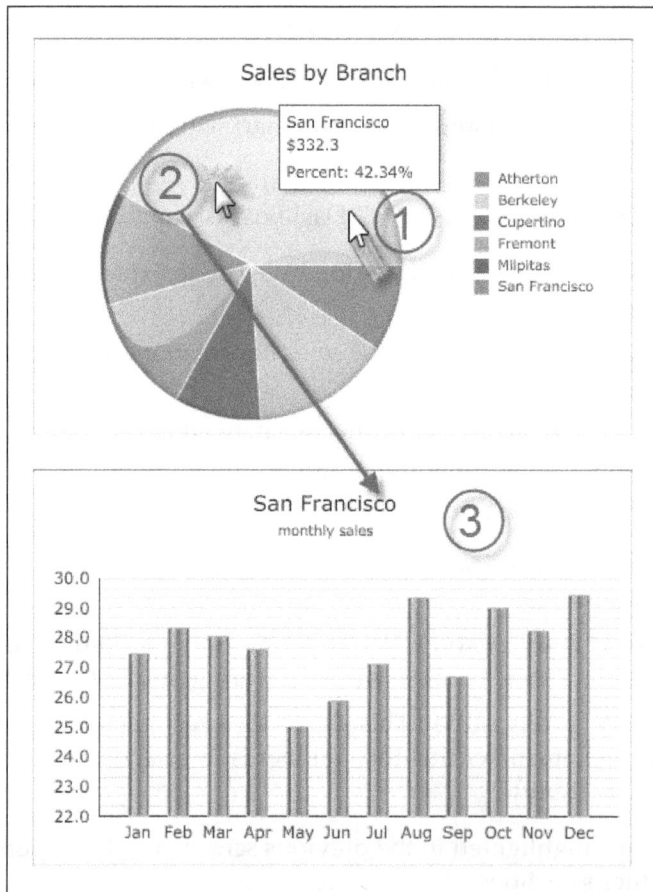

In this dashboard, we can see the following two main dashboard components:

- **Pie chart (the upper side)**: This chart will display sales by branch, and it will act like the Master component, as you can click on a specific branch to show the monthly sales trend in the bottom column chart (the detailed chart).

- **Column chart (the bottom side)**: This chart will display the sales trend per month for the selected branch. This is the detailed chart in the "Master Detail" model.

We will use this scenario to explore SAP BO Dashboards' capabilities:

1. Hover on the "San Francisco" branch to display the following information:
   - **San Francisco**: This is the branch name.
   - **332.3$**: This is the sales of the San Francisco branch.
   - **42.34 percent**: Sales percentage achieved by the San Francisco branch of the total sales achieved by all the branches.

2. Click on **San Francisco** to display the sales monthly trend on the column chart at the bottom.

3. Note how the data and chart title are changed in the column chart.

We can see the steps highlighted in the previous screenshot. Try the same scenario using other selections.

Accessing and using dashboard templates

Templates are complete dashboard projects that can be customized by sourcing real data to the right place in the Excel model, and we can directly start using it. Indeed, we can style it up to suit our organization's themes and colors. We can customize it as well, by adding or removing the dashboard components. In this section, we will select one dashboard template to explore the capabilities, but first, let's learn how to access the dashboard templates:

1. Navigate to the **File** menu.

2. Click on **Templates...** or press *Ctrl + T* to open the templates window, as shown in the following screenshot:

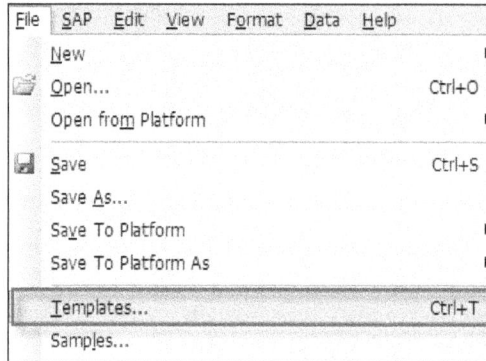

3. The **Template** window is exactly the same as the samples window. We have many categories to choose from: **Finance**, **Government**, **HR**, and so on. Under each category, we will see many related items.

4. The **New From Template** window will open, as displayed in the following screenshot:

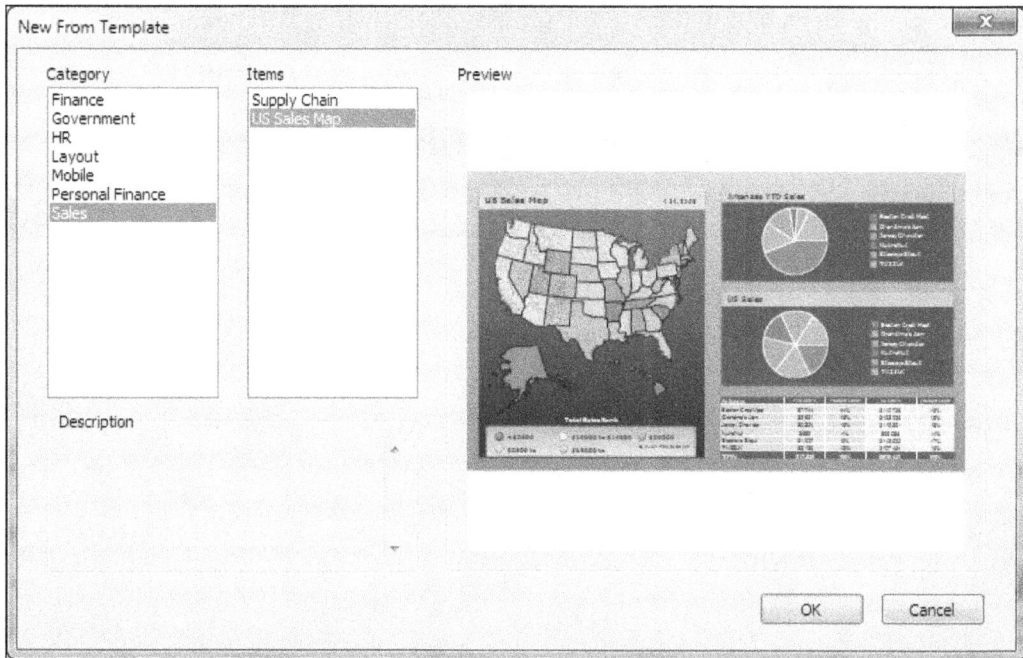

In this section, we will learn how to use the **US Sales Map** template under the **Sales** category.

US Sales Map

US Sales Map is a dashboard template that can be used to display the sales by states, divided by the product. We will discuss Maps in more detail in *Chapter 4*, *Using Maps and Other Components*. So, let's open the dashboard template and explore how it works.

1. Navigate to the **File** menu and select **Templates...**.
2. Select **Sales** from the category area.
3. Select **US Sales Map** from the items list and click on **OK**.
4. The **US Sales Map** dashboard template will open.

Before previewing, let's have a look at the Excel model inside this dashboard. As we can see in the following screenshot, there are three Excel sheets:

- **Setup**: This sheet will explain how to set up and customize this template.
- **How Do I**: This sheet will contain quick answers to many questions that you may have on how to use this dashboard.
- **Display**: This contains the current data displayed in the dashboard. Currently, this is static fixed data. However, you may use one of the external data sources to populate this dashboard and make it dynamic.

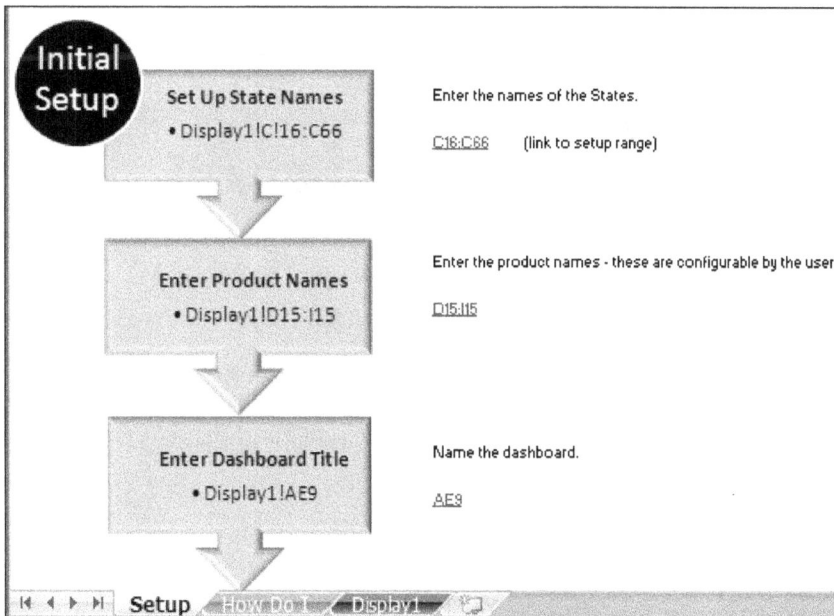

Now, after we have had a look at the Excel model inside this template, let's continue to preview it.

> The best practice is to include one or two sheets in any dashboard you have developed in order to explain how to use this dashboard, customize it, answer the frequent questions, and add a legend for colors used in the Excel model.

1. Click on the **Preview** icon, as shown in the following screenshot.
2. This will open the **Preview** window, as displayed in the following screenshot:

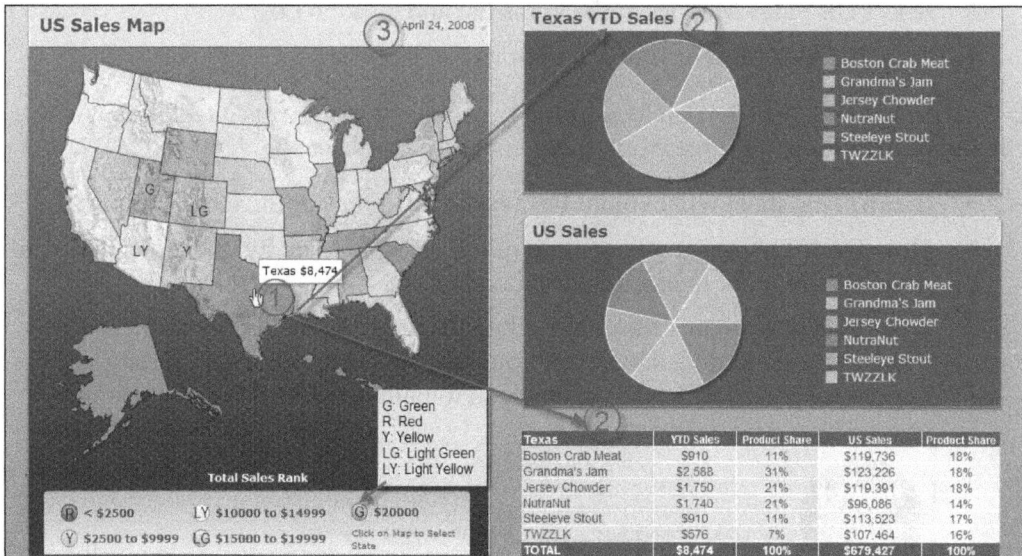

In this dashboard, we can see the following as dashboard components:

- **US Map (the left-hand side)**: This map will display the sales by state, along with an alert indicator to indicate the sales performance
- **State YTD Sales by product (Pie chart)**: This chart will display the sales by product for the selected state
- **US Sales (Pie chart)**: This chart will display the total US Sales by product
- **State summary (Table component)**: This table will display the sales and product share for the selected state

Let's try this scenario to explore SAP BO Dashboards' capabilities:

1. Hover on the **Texas** state to display the sales information.

2. Click on **Texas** to display the YTD sales by product and state sales summary.

3. Note that **US Sales** is a fixed pie chart and will only change if we change the date. The date in this template is static but can be customized to be an input to this dashboard.

> I added color coding on the previous screenshot to help you imagine the alerts implemented on the map, as this book will be printed in grayscale. You will be able to see colored images if you purchase the PDF version of this book.

We can see the steps highlighted in the previous screenshot. Try to repeat this scenario using other selections.

Now, after we have an idea about what we expect to create using SAP BO Dashboards, let's try to be more familiar with the tool interface.

Getting to know the SAP BO Dashboards interface

In this section, we will discuss the main interface panels, toolbars, and views. Let's have a look at the following screenshot, which describes the main interface areas in SAP BO Dashboards:

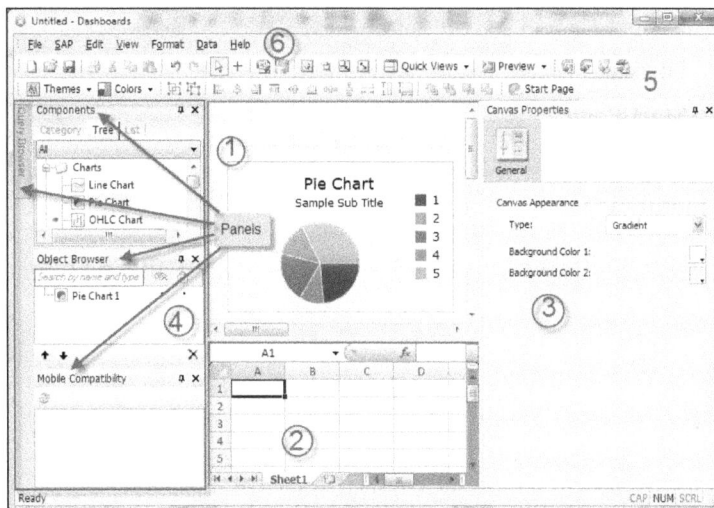

The main interface areas are:

- **Canvas**: We will use this area to place our dashboard components, such as charts, maps, and selectors.

- **Excel model**: We will use this embedded Excel model as a data container. Then, we will link our dashboard components to corresponding data cells in that Excel model. We can use this area exactly like a normal Excel file. We can add multiple sheets, use formulas, and use any Excel feature or option.

- **Properties panel**: This is a special panel, so it is located on the right-hand side, without any other interfering panels, by default. This panel will be the most used panel once you start working with Dashboards. The properties panel will display the properties for the currently selected component.

- **Panel's area**: We can access the remaining dashboard panels from this area. We can change the layout and order of these panels as we wish. We can also use the auto hide/pin feature to give us more space while working on the canvas and Excel model side. We have the following panels, which we will discuss in detail later:
  - **Object Browser**
  - **Components**
  - **Mobile Compatibility**
  - **Query Browser**

- **Toolbars**: We have the following toolbars:
  - **Standard**
  - **Themes**
  - **Export**
  - **Format**
  - **Start Page**

- **Menus**: We can apply the same functions that are available through toolbars, using menus as well.

Here, we will focus on the dashboard panels, toolbars, and quick views.

Understanding SAP BO Dashboards panels

We have five main dashboard panels that we will use to facilitate our dashboard creation process. These panels are:

- **Properties**
- **Component**
- **Object Browser**
- **Query Browser**
- **Mobile compatibility**

Let's explore them one by one.

The Properties panel

The **Properties** panel, as we mentioned before, is the most important panel that we will use while creating our dashboards. We can use this panel to control the currently selected dashboard components' properties. For example, we can see the **Properties** panel for line chart component. I selected the line chart properties panel because it has almost all possible properties for a dashboard component. We should note that properties are common for many objects, and we can use them in the same way. So, we will try to understand how to configure each property, and this should work in the exact same way if you find this property in another component:

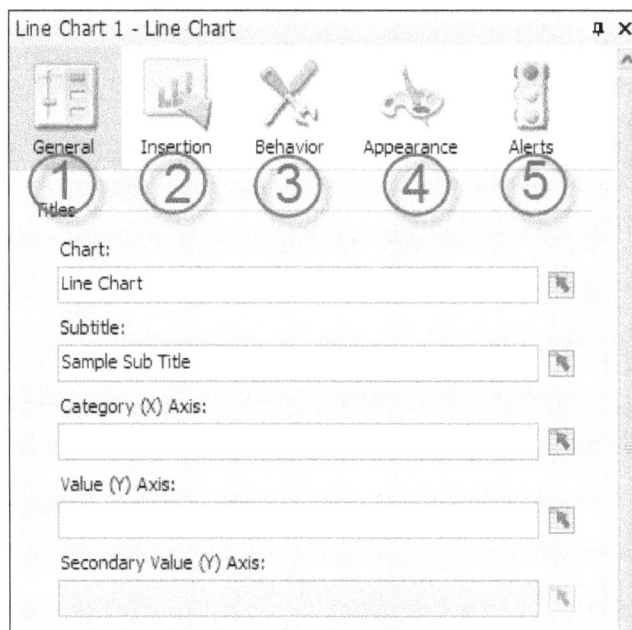

As we can see, properties are classified in tabs. Each tab contains some related properties, the **Appearance** tab for example, which contains all properties related to the layout, colors, size, and font. We will work through all the properties as we progress through the chapters. But for now, let's try to understand the main use of each property tab:

- **General**: We can set the general component properties from this tab, such as a chart title. We can also use this tab to link our component with the data presented in an Excel model. We will talk about this tab in detail in *Chapter 3, UI Components*.

- **Insertion**: This is an important feature that is available for some dashboard components. We can use this feature to interact with the dashboard and use one chart to drill to another. We already saw an example, while we were discussing the chart-Drill Down dashboard sample early in this chapter. We will talk in detail about this tab in *Chapter 6, Advanced Interactive Analysis with Dashboards*.

- **Behavior**: We can use this tab to control the selected component behavior, such as dynamic visibility, chart scale properties, and animations and effects. We will cover this tab in detail in *Chapter 6, Advanced Interactive Analysis with Dashboards*.

- **Appearance**: We can use this tab to control the look and feel of the selected components, such as the text color, background, and borders. We will discuss this tab in more detail in *Chapter 7, Styling Up*.

- **Alerts**: We can use this tab to set and configure the **Alert** feature for the selected dashboard components. We can use alerts to add more insight to our dashboard by comparing the currently achieved value against the targeted value. The comparison result will be compared against **Alert Threshold** and based on that, we can use an alerting mechanism, such as traffic light colors or icons. We will cover **Alerts** in more detail in *Chapter 6: Advanced Interactive Analysis with Dashboards*.

Next, we will discuss the **Components** panel.

The Components panel

We can consider the **Components** panel as our dashboard components library. Here, we will find all the available components that we can use.

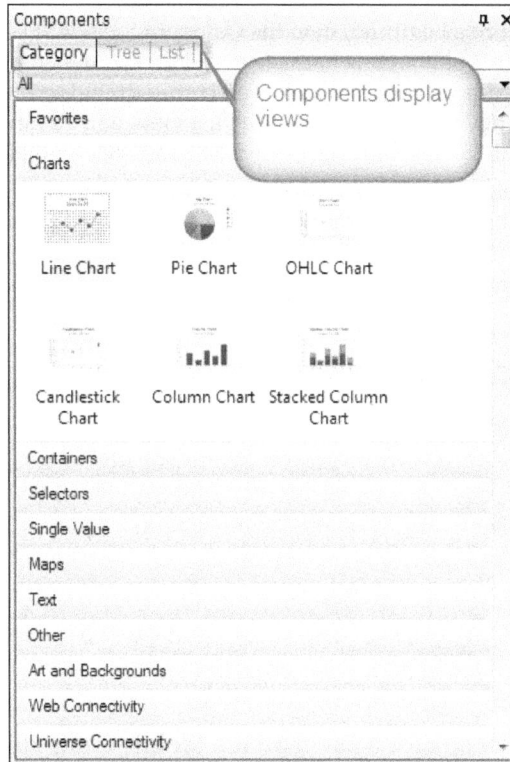

There are three main display views for the dashboard components library:

- **Category**: The **Components** panel will display Dashboard components by category such as **Charts**, **Selectors**, and **Maps**. When you click on a category, it will expand to show the components under this category. A thumbnail will be displayed for each dashboard component, to give an idea about what that component is. This is the main advantage of this display view. On the other hand, thumbnails will take a larger space to display on the screen, and hence we can see a fewer number of components at the same time.

- **Tree**: This display view is exactly the same as the previous one, but the dashboard components will be displayed in a **Hierarchical** folder tree structure. Each component will be displayed as an icon rather than a thumbnail. This view will give extra space to see more dashboard components at the same time.

- **List**: All dashboard components are sorted alphabetically in this view and presented like an icon. We can use this display view if we know the exact name of our dashboard components.

> If you are a beginner, then the Category view will be your favorite display view because it will give you a good idea about the Dashboard component, even before dragging it to the canvas. If you have experience, then the list view will be best for you, as you will be able to reach your dashboard component faster.
>
> You can use *Ctrl + 5* to open the **Components** panel or use the menu bar: **View | Components**.

We can use the component filter to display **All** components or **Mobile Only** components.

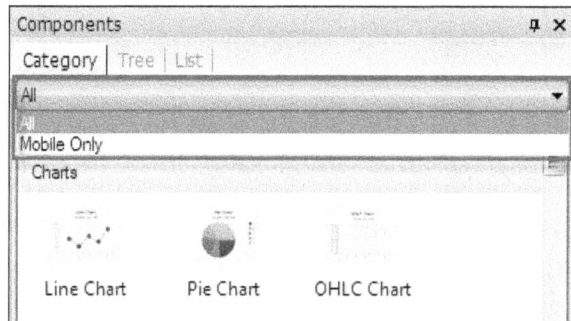

You can refer to the *Appendix* for a list of all the Mobile-compatible dashboard components.

> You can add the most frequent dashboard components to your **Favorite** folder or category for fast access for future use.

We can see the steps to add dashboard components to your favorites in the following screenshot:

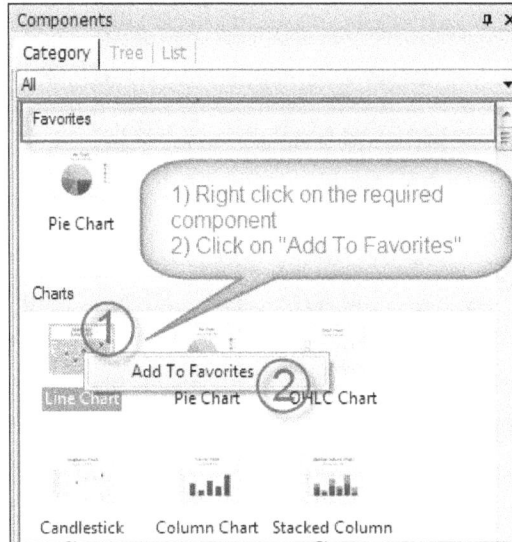

Next, we will discuss the Object Browser panel.

The Object Browser panel

We can use the **Object Browser** panel to manage a large number of canvas's dashboard components. This panel is very common in graphic design tools, such as Adobe PhotoShop, and it is used for the same purpose. We can use **Object Browser** to execute one of the following actions:

- To **Select/Rename** the dashboard components
- To **Delete** the dashboard components
- To **Show/Hide** a dashboard component at design time
- To **Lock/Unlock** a dashboard component at design time
- To change the dashboard components' display order

> We can use *Ctrl + 4* or navigate to **View** | **Object Browser** from the menu bar to open this panel.

We can see the **Object Browser** window in the following screenshot:

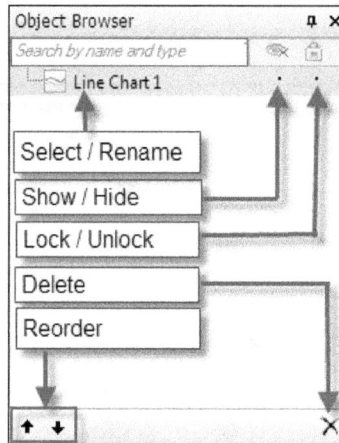

The Query Browser panel

This panel is used to manage direct Universe queries. Universe is a SAP BusinessObjects semantic layer, and it acts like an intermediate layer between database and business. We can use this panel to create a new query or manage existing queries, such as edit, delete, refresh, and reorder. We can see the **Query Browser** panel in the following screenshot:

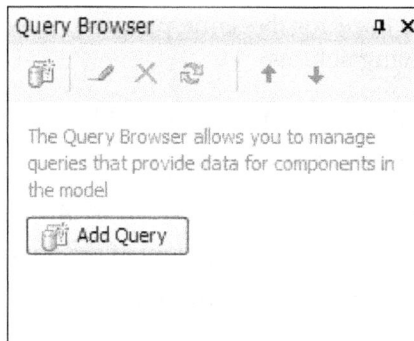

We will discuss this panel in detail in *Chapter 9, Retrieving External Data Sources*.

Mobile compatibility

We will use this panel to track our dashboard's compatibility with mobile devices. We need to note that "Mobile" here is not only referring to cell phones, but it is referring to all Mobile devices, especially tablets. We will cover this in detail in *Chapter 11*, *Creating Mobile Dashboards*.

We will use the **Mobile Compatibility** panel to get information and warnings on unsupported dashboard components, features, and connections.

We can see the **Mobile Compatibility** panel in the following screenshot:

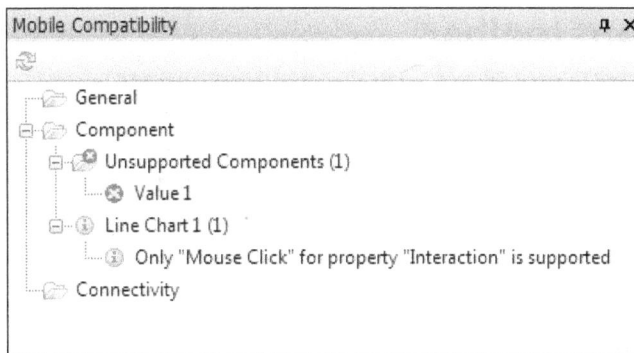

In the next section, we will talk about dashboard toolbars and menus.

Understanding SAP BO Dashboards toolbars

SAP BO Dashboards is a visual design program that contains many toolbars. A toolbar is a fast way to access different features and options, such as keyboard shortcuts. However, in toolbar's case, we don't need to remember the shortcuts. Also, keyboard shortcuts are not available for all options, and so toolbars are the easiest way to access options and features. We can show/hide a toolbar from the view menu, as shown in the following screenshot.

We have the following toolbars:

- **Standard**
- **Themes**
- **Export**
- **Format**

- **Start Page**

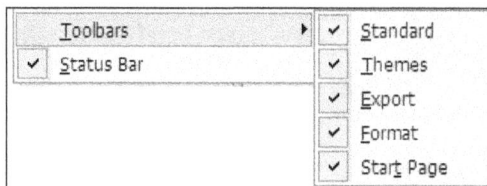

So, let's discuss each one in more detail.

The Standard toolbar

The **Standard** toolbars provide us with the standard options, such as new, open, and save. We can access the quick view menus from this toolbar as well. We will discuss the quick view menus in more detail later on. We can also use the **Preview** button to preview our dashboard. We can see the **Standard** toolbar in the following screenshot:

The Themes toolbar

We can use the **Themes** toolbar to change the current dashboard theme or color pallet. We can see the **Themes** toolbar in the following screenshot:

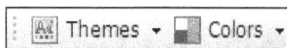

The Export toolbar

We can use this toolbar to export our dashboard to PowerPoint, Word, Outlook, or PDF file, as shown in the following screenshot:

The Format toolbar

We can use the **Format** toolbar to group or ungroup dashboard components, dashboard components' alignment, and control components' order.

> For those of you who have experience with Microsoft PowerPoint, this toolbar might look familiar.

We can see the toolbar in the following screenshot:

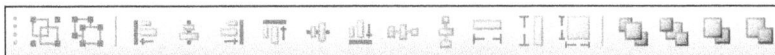

The Start Page toolbar

We can open the **Start Page** toolbar using the **Start Page** icon. Start page can be used to access recently opened documents, and access useful information about the main features of SAP BO Dashboards. We can see this in the following screenshot.

We can use a start page to access the recently opened documents, and to open the start page that contains much useful information about the main features of SAP BO Dashboards.

Understanding SAP BO Dashboards quick views

Quick Views are a very nice feature that can help the dashboard developer/designer focus on a specific area in the workspace. As we can see, we already have many panels, toolbars, and menus beside the Canvas and Excel model, which makes our workspace very crowded. In fact, you will not need to see all of them together most of the time. We can see the **Quick Views** menu in the following screenshot:

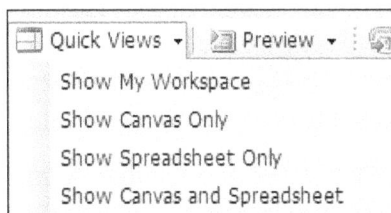

We have the following quick views in SAP BO Dashboards:

- **Show My Workspace**: This quick view will display **Canvas**, the **Excel model**, and the **Properties** panel on the right-hand side, and the **Components** panel on the left-hand side
- **Show Canvas Only**: This will display only the Canvas to help us focus on the design part, such as dashboard components place, alignments, and so on
- **Show Spreadsheet Only**: This view will help us focus on the Excel model, formulas, and data
- **Show Canvas and Spreadsheet**: This view will help us focus on both the Canvas and Excel model, and is a combination of the previous two options

Summary

We started the chapter with a general introduction to SAP BO BI platform 4.x and SAP BO Dashboards (formerly known as Xcelsius). Then, we walked through the process of downloading, installing, and configuring the tool, and finally, we worked on capabilities and features by accessing Dashboards samples and templates. We concluded the chapter with a discussion on toolbars, menus, and quick views.

In the next chapter, we will create a business use case to be used throughout the book as a project. Our focus will be to learn the process and best practice. After that we will go through the dashboard creation phases, and we will learn how to create dashboard prototypes in analysis phase. After that, we will prepare our environment to start building the eFashion dashboard (the project of the book).

2
Understanding the Dashboard Creation Process

One question that I always have to answer as a project manager is, "how can you achieve customer satisfaction?". With my experience, I think it's a very tricky question to answer. Let's try to build on our approach to answer this question by running through project life cycle.

There are two project life cycle approaches: classic waterfall and scrum/agile.

In this chapter, we will focus on the following topics:

- Determining our project need (initiation and planning)
- The dashboard creation process (the implementation phase)
- Preparing our workspace by importing data into our dashboard (the implementation phase)

Before that, let's quickly go through the phases in the project.

Phases in the project

The definition of a project (a planned set of interrelated tasks to be executed over a fixed period and within certain cost and other limitations) remains the same regardless of the industry, and so do the phases.

As per the PMI standard, the typical project phases are:

- Initiation
- Planning
- Execution/implementation

- Controlling/testing
- Closing

Here, we will discuss the project phases from the dashboard point of view.

The initiation phase

The initiation phase is the beginning of the project. In this phase, the idea for the project is explored and elaborated with the business user (Customer). It is in this phase that the project team aligns customer requirements with the deliverables(Dashboards). So, the successful execution of this phase will be a key factor in the success of the project.

In this chapter, we will work on how to have a better alignment with the customer so as to create informative, useful, and customer-centric dashboards.

The planning phase

Once the requirement is set with customer in the initiation phase, we move to the effort, time, and budget estimation. The planning phase helps us achieve this; for example, a typical dashboard end-to-end project would require the following resource:

Role	Numbers**
Project Manager	1
Business Analyst	1
Dashboard Designer	2
Universe Designer	2
ETL developer	2

**the number of resources will vary depending on the project size. The Author has taken the numbers just for illustration.*

- One of the major deliverables of this phase is design blueprint. The expected outcome of the blueprint is to have the following:
- Data mart design.
- Decisions on fact and dimension tables.
- Universe design/semantic layout.
- The complete dashboard design

The execution/implementation phase

In the implementation phase, we start the actual development work after completing the design in the planning phase based on the gathered business requirements. We will talk about the dashboard creation process in detail later in this chapter.

The control/testing phase

Once the Dashboard is created and implemented, it needs to be tested for end user acceptance. In the testing phase, the customer can accept or reject the dashboard. Acceptance will lead to project closure. If it is rejected with any defects, then we need to rework on the requirement.

The closing phase

Every project has its takeaways. **Project management office (PMO)** makes it mandatory (in most cases) that a project closure cannot happen until the documentation is complete. So, in the closing phase, the documentation related to best practices, lessons learned, and other factors affecting the project needs to be updated.

Determining the needs

We will start determining our dashboard requirements in the project initiation phase. Here, we will simulate the building of a dashboard based on the eFashion data. eFashion is a sample MS Access database installed with the SAP BuisnessObjects client and server installation for training purposes. There is also a ready-made universe that we can start to use immediately to query the data stored in the eFashion Access database and explore the features and capabilities of SAP BO Dashboards. The database contains around 89,000+ records in the fact table; so, it is a very good and rich example.

> Universe is the semantic layer that will translate the database tables and join business terms represented by business objects. For more information about Universe, refer to Creating Universes within SAP BusinessObjects.

We need to understand the data stored in eFashion before we start creating the dashboard on top of it, so let's try to introduce the eFashion company.

eFashion is a factory that produces many fashion-related products. There are many product lines in eFashion, such as accessories, leather, dresses, and jackets. The eFashion factory sells its products through many stores distributed across the US states. There is a quarterly target for eFashion sales. The quantity of each product sold is an important factor to achieve more sales.

Let's try to summarize what type of information we have.

We have the following *Dimensions*:

- **Time**: We can track our sales on a monthly basis; we can also track them quarterly and yearly as there's a hierarchical relationship between the month, quarter, and year.

- **Product line**: This is a dimension that can be used to analyze the information from the product's point of view. Products are accessories, leather, dresses, and jackets. For example, we can analyze our sales revenue with the product line to get the most profitable product. As with time, there's a hierarchical relationship between (multiple) products and their corresponding product line as well.

- **Geographical dimension (region)**: We can track our data using the state, city, and store. This dimension also has a hierarchical relation, that is, multiple stores in a city and multiple cities in a state.

We have the following *Measures*:

- Sales
- Quantity
- Target

> Dimension is an angle from which we can look at data. For example, Product Line is a dimension because we can analyze or look into our sales and the quantity sold from the product perspective.
>
> Measure is a metric number similar to sales and quantity.

Now, after we have a good idea about eFashion and the type of information they have, let's start determining their needs. To achieve this, we need to complete the following:

- Gathering business requirements
- Determining the target audience and devices

- Sketching dashboards
- Building a prototype

We will describe each topic in detail in the upcoming sections.

Gathering business requirements

The main target of businesses' requirements gathering sessions is to define the required KPIs and other dashboard components. As there are no real requirements, let's try to define our requirements based on the available information.

Here, we can define the following KPIs:

- The sales per state analysis
- The sales trend analysis
- The sales and quantity per product analysis

The sales by state analysis

Based on the available information, we can analyze our sales per states. We can also get more information by drilling down into the city and store level. We call the state, city, and store a hierarchy because they are related to each other. Each state consists of many cities, and each city can contain multiple stores under it in the geographical hierarchy. We can also incorporate the target and use the Alert feature to show a sales performance indicator for each state.

> Drilling is a common term in Business Intelligence, which refers to moving up and down in a specific hierarchy. We can drill down the time dimension to move from years to quarters, quarters to months, and so on. Drilling up will refer to the movement in the other direction from months to quarters, and so on.
>
> The mapping of the dashboard component is the best way to represent a geographical information.
>
> We usually use the Insertion feature to drill down into the next level of the hierarchy.

The sales trend analysis

Time is an important dimension that you will see in almost every dashboard. We will need to see our metric performance across a period of time. Trend analysis is another name for time analysis because it shows us the trend based on the history. We can predict whether we are trending up, trending down, or performing on the same rate (no trend, which means that we are performing at average). Time dimension in our example is a hierarchy of the year, quarter, month, and week. So, we will try to display the sales trend, and it will be very helpful if we can filter a specific product or state to empower our trend analysis.

> We usually use a line chart dashboard component to represent a trend.

The sales and quantity per product analysis

One of the most important sales analysis dimensions is the product. Everyone wants to know which is the best product that we are selling and which one is performing badly. This will help us know how the market responds to our products and how to create and enhance a successful product. The main analysis metrics that we will use to analyze our sales performance regarding products are sales and quantity. We also want to know how quantity can affect our product sales.

> Combined chart is the best dashboard component that can be used to show the relationship between two different metrics.

Next, we will try to determine the target users and devices.

Determining the target audience and devices

This is a very tricky part. We need to decide the target audience for our dashboard. We need to ask questions such as these: how will we use it? On what devices?

Our dashboard can be used by many categories of business users, and it is very important to know which business user category is the targeted user of our dashboard as the needs and focus of each category are totally different to the other. We have the following business user categories:

- **Executives and top management**: Usually, they are concerned about high-level information. They want to know whether they are performing nicely or badly using simple and informative charts. They don't have time to go into details, but they need to know whether they can make decisions and perform actions. Remember the example of the car from the *Preface*; and you just need to know whether you are okay, or whether you need to examine the car if the temperature indicator indicates a high temperature. The card dashboard will not tell you more details about why the car temperature is too high, but you know that you need to take action. If the executives and top management users need more information, they will ask the analysts and operation users for more information.

- **Analysts**: They need to have many filters, dimensions, and measures in order to be able to explore that data from different angles. They also need to drill up and down, and to see the data in different representations.

- **Operational**: They are concerned about details and leaf-level information. It is better to have this information in a report rather than a dashboard. However, in some cases, they may need a starter dashboard that can be used as an entrance for their detailed reports. We will learn how to call a Web Intelligence (Webi) report from a dashboard in *Chapter 3, UI Components*.

After determining the targeted users, we should also determine the target devices. We can use a SAP BO Dashboard designer to create dashboards for desktops or for Mobile devices. Desktop dashboards will be accessed later on from the BO repository using a PC or client machine. The smart devices dashboards will also be accessed from the BO repository, but using a smart device such as an iPad tablet, for example. We call these type of dashboards (smart devices) Mobile dashboards. The technology behind the generated desktop and Mobile dashboard is totally different. The desktop-exported dashboard is a .SWF file based on flash technology, while the mobile dashboard is an HTML5-based file. This is why there are many unsupported dashboard components in mobile dashboards.

This is the main reason why we need to determine the target device for our dashboard from the beginning. We will learn how to create a Mobile dashboard in *Chapter 11, Creating Mobile Dashboards*.

Sketching our dashboard

Sketching our dashboard is the next step after we gather all the requirements, and determine the target audience and devices. Here, we need to use a piece of paper and a pencil to sketch the dashboard based on the requirements. This is very important as it will act like the blueprint or design document for our dashboard. Then, we need to check with the customer whether the mock-up dashboard we created is what they are looking for and whether this satisfies their requirements.

> Using a pencil (not a pen) is very important as you will be able to erase and modify your sketches while discussing them with your customers or the targeted users.
>
> You can use modern drawing tools if you are comfortable with them.
>
> You may have more than one targeted business user category for your dashboard, as we already explained in the previous section, so you may need to discuss dashboard requirements with more than one business users to make sure that it will satisfy their need. Usually, you will need to create a separate view for each business user category as we will see in the eFashion dashboard project.

Here, we can find the sketches for the three dashboard levels that we agreed to implement based on the target audience.

We can see the executive and top management Dashboard sketch in the following screenshot (please don't laugh at my sketches).

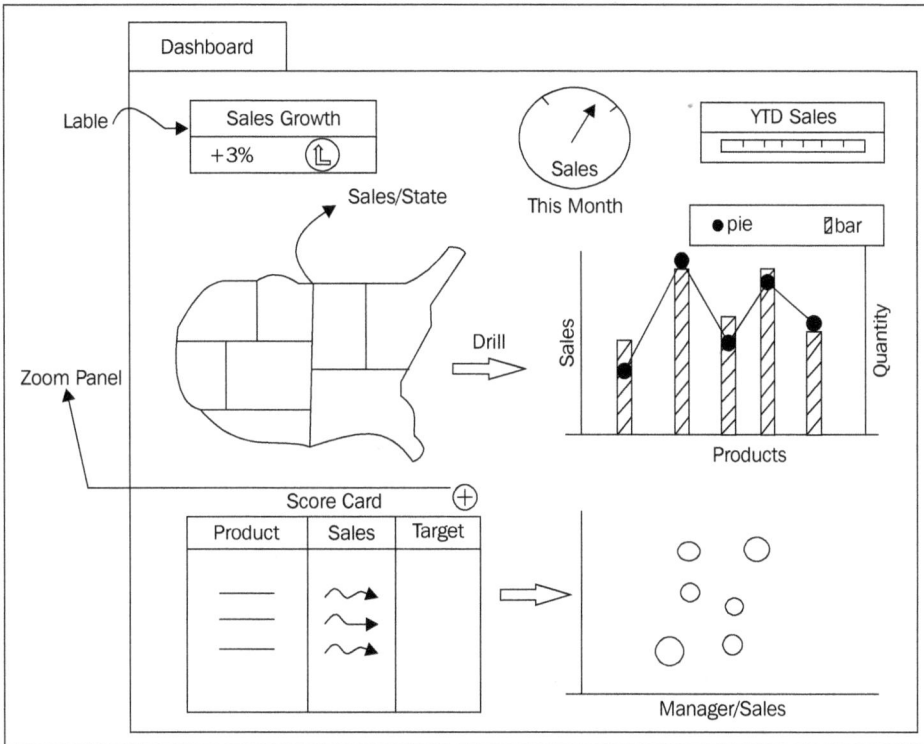

We can see the analysis dashboard sketch in the following screenshot:

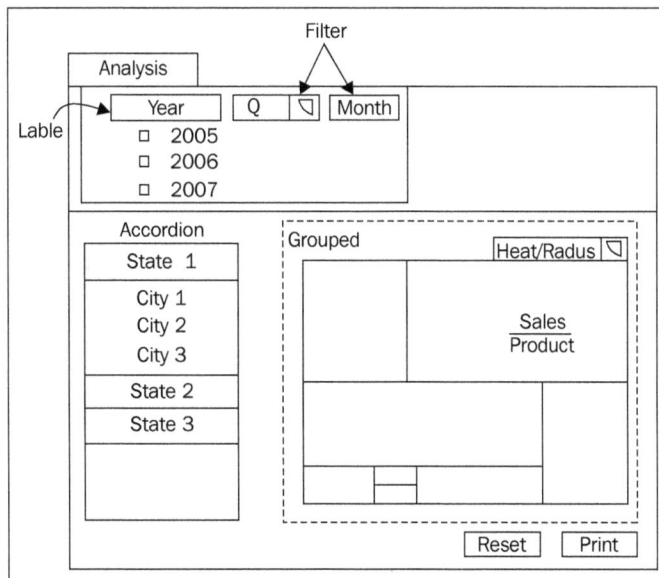

We can see the operation dashboard sketch in the following screenshot:

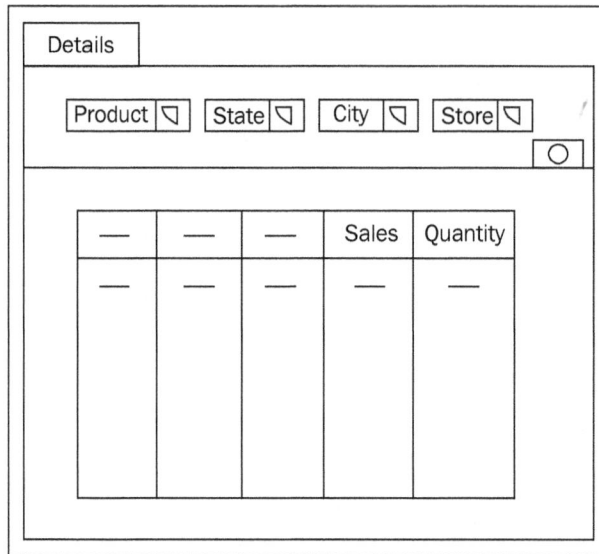

We can see the mobile dashboard sketch in the following screenshot:

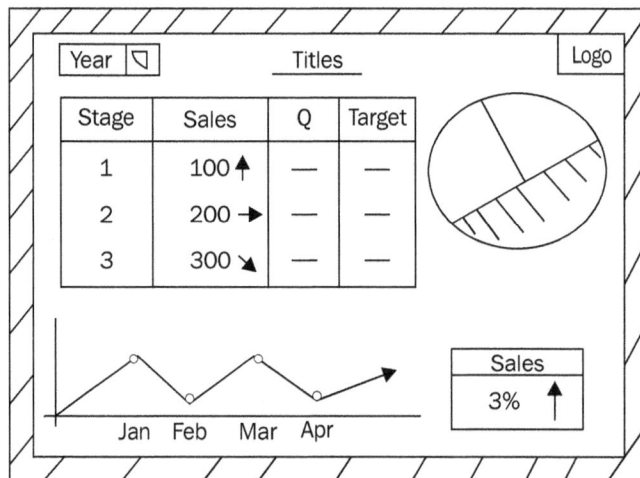

The next step is to create a final prototype based on the dashboard sketches (mock-ups) that we have.

Building the prototype

A prototype is a very effective and efficient way, across the industry, to agree with the customer on how we will deliver the requirements. A prototype is also a common practice in almost all industries. For example, a car factory will follow exactly the same steps that we already went through before they start producing a new car. They will agree on the requirements and car specification. Then, a car designer will sketch it, and finally, will create a prototype model before they start manufacturing it.

We will use a SAP BO Dashboard Designer to create the prototype, so it will look exactly the same as what we will deliver at the end. We can still modify the dashboard as per the requirements, and the target action from this process (building a prototype) is to finally agree and sign off the requirements before starting the implementation phase.

> A prototype is a simple dashboard based on a dummy data, but it will simulate the exact functionality expected from the dashboard.

As we didn't learn yet how to use the SAP BO Dashboards, we will not be able to create a prototype for our eFashion dashboard. We can see the basic prototype that I created for our dashboard based on the Executives and top management dashboard sketch in the following screenshot:

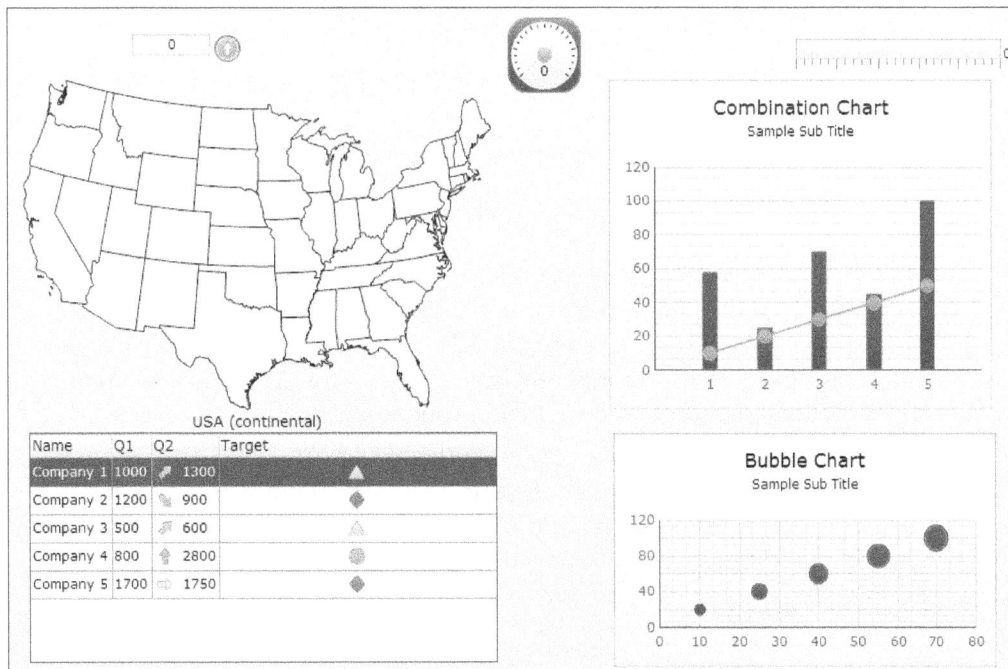

This completes the activities of the initiation phase. We start off with the dashboard creation process as the first step of the implementation phase.

> It is better if you use dummy data but with real dimension value to create the prototype. This will help the customer visualize the final dashboard.
>
> It is better also if you apply the styling up techniques that we will discuss in detail in *Chapter 7, Styling Up*; before showing it to your customer.

Dashboard creation process

We can start creating our dashboard once we complete the initiation phase.
The dashboard creation process is very simple, as we can see in the following diagram:

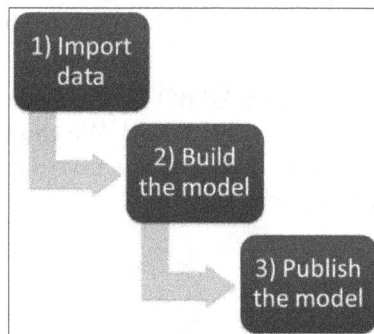

Now, let's discuss each step in more detail as follows:

- **Import data**: The first logical step in the dashboard creation process is to import data to your dashboard, which can be done by linking our dashboard MS Excel model with a dynamic data source, such as Live Office, Web service or Direct Universes query. This option will help us dynamically refresh the data in our dashboard after we publish it. On the other hand, we can also import the Excel raw data into our dashboard. In this case, our dashboard will depend on the data imported, and somehow it will be static.

- **Build the model**: We can start building the model after importing the data by adding dashboard components, and by linking them with the data we imported in the preceding section. We may link our dashboard objects directly to the source data, or we may need to use Excel formulas to shape the data and prepare it before linking it with the dashboard components.

- **Publish the model**: The last step after we complete the design of our dashboard is to publish it to the BO server to be used by the end users.

By now, you might be bored of reading a lot of theory. So, let's start implementing the eFashion dashboard as per the sketches and prototype that we have. We start with the workspace preparation and data import.

Preparing the dashboard workspace

We will use the raw data that has been exported to the Excel file and has been extracted from the eFashion database. The eFashion database is provided by SAP BO for training and practice purposes. We will learn how to connect directly with the eFashion Universe to dynamically refresh our data in *Chapter 9, Retrieving External Data Sources*. For now, we will just learn how to import and use the raw Excel data extracted from the eFashion database.

Before we start, we need to download the example code files from the Packt site. Then, we need to extract the downloaded file. The file contains the folders that we can see in the following screenshot:

Name	Date modified	Type	Size
Dashboards (Ready)	11/18/2014 7:27 PM	File folder	
Data	11/18/2014 7:27 PM	File folder	
Design	11/18/2014 7:27 PM	File folder	
Developemnt	11/18/2014 7:32 PM	File folder	
Side Examples	11/18/2014 7:28 PM	File folder	

Let's take a moment to describe each folder as follows:

- **Dashboards (Ready)**: This folder contains the .XLF file for each chapter. You can use this folder to open the final version of the dashboard that you should have if you followed all the steps mentioned in the chapter. You can use it to compare the dashboard file that you created with this one. You will find a .xlf file for each chapter.

- **Data**: This folder contains the Excel, CSV, XML, and any data files used in this book.

- **Design**: This folder contains all the logos, images, and icons that we will use to develop our dashboard project.

- **Development**: This folder will be empty, but you need to save the dashboard you create by the end of each chapter in this folder.

- **Side Examples**: At times, we will have some examples that are not a part of the main dashboard projects. We will use this folder to store them.

Now, let's try to import the data file that we will use in the next chapter.

1. Open **Dashboards** by a double-click on the desktop icon, or by navigating to the location **Start| SAP Business Intelligence | SAP BusinessObjects Dashboards 4 | Dashboards**.

2. The **Dashboards** start page will be displayed, as we can see in the following screenshot:

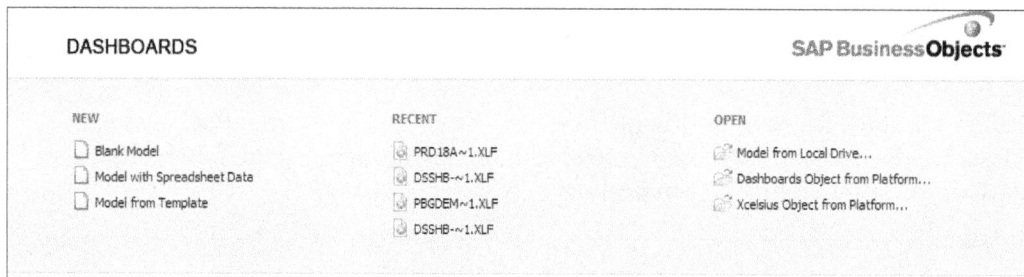

DASHBOARDS		SAP Business**Objects**
NEW	**RECENT**	**OPEN**
Blank Model	PRD18A~1.XLF	Model from Local Drive...
Model with Spreadsheet Data	DSSHB-~1.XLF	Dashboards Object from Platform...
Model from Template	PBGDEM~1.XLF	Xcelsius Object from Platform...
	DSSHB-~1.XLF	

We can create a new dashboard based on the following menus:

- **Blank Model**: This will open a new dashboard file with an empty Excel model. We can import the data from external files or data sources later on.

- **Model with Spreadsheet Data**: This option will open an empty dashboard file, but it will launch the import command immediately, which will ask you for the data file location to be imported as the first step.

- **Model from Template**: This option will open the dashboard templates that we discussed in *Chapter 1, Getting Started with SAP BO Dashboards*.

> You can always display the Start page by clicking on the Start icon.

To import the data file that we will need to follow, the steps are:

1. Select **Model with Spreadsheet Data** option from the **Start Page**.

2. Go to the example code files folder and navigate to the Data folder.

3. Open the `Chapter 2` folder.
4. Select the `Chapter2.xls` file.

> 💡 You can import the data into your Dashboard file at any time using **Data | Import**.

We can see the import dialog box in the following screen:

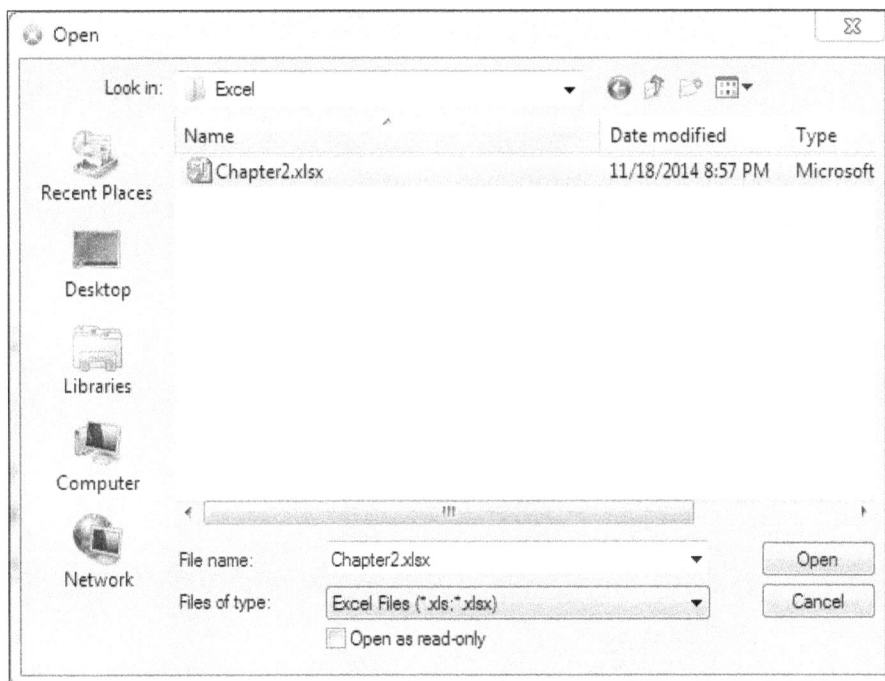

We also need to take care of the following warning.

> 💡 Caution: Importing data will overwrite the current data if your dashboard already contains data in the Excel file.

We can see the warning message in the following screenshot:

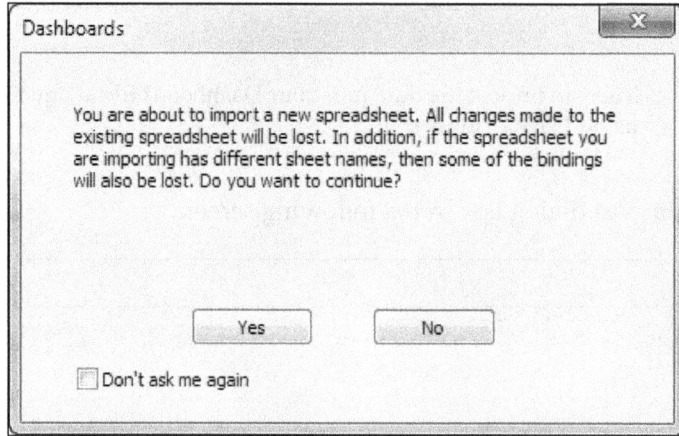

Dashboards X

You are about to import a new spreadsheet. All changes made to the existing spreadsheet will be lost. In addition, if the spreadsheet you are importing has different sheet names, then some of the bindings will also be lost. Do you want to continue?

Yes   No

☐ Don't ask me again

The dashboard file should look like the following screenshot after importing the data:

B	C	D	E
	Lines	Sum of Sales revenue	Sum of Quantity sold
	Accessories	1,899,404.70	12,572
	City Skirts	196,285.00	1,171
	City Trousers	66,531.10	511
	Dresses	1,408,594.90	9,477
	Jackets	304,680.40	1,871
	Leather	40,689.90	230
	Outerwear	25,616.30	259
	Overcoats	71,011.90	505
	Shirt Waist	1,654,358.50	9,223
	Sweaters	1,660,040.30	11,221
	Sweat-T-Shirts	3,232,135.10	19,203
	Trousers	272,436.30	1,476
	Grand Total	10,831,784.40	67,719

| Product | Map | ⊕ |

Finally, save the file as `dashboard _chapter2.xlf` under the `Developemnt` folder, and you can match it with `Dashbaord_chapter2.xlf` under the `Dashboards (Ready)` folder.

Summary

In this chapter, we briefly discussed the project life cycle. We walked through each phase and discussed the dashboard activity associated with that phase. For example, in the initiation phase, we aligned with the customer's need. It was followed by sketching dashboard components on paper and check with the customer whether this was what he expected from the project, and if this would fulfill his requirements. We also learned about the creation of prototype/models, data import, and publishing the model. We concluded the chapter with an example of the data import.

In the next chapter, we will use the mentioned case and learn how to add dashboard components. We will link it with the data, work around with charts, and add single values and some examples to make ourself comfortable with the topic.

3
UI Components

In this chapter, we will start to create our eFashion dashboard project using the data extracted from the eFashion database, as we explained in our previous chapter. In this project, we will follow the design and sketches that we already introduced in the previous chapter based on the requirements gathered during the business requirement gathering process in the project initiation phase.

We already learned how to import data to our dashboard, as this is the first step in the dashboard creation process. In this chapter, we will move to the next step, and we will start creating our model by adding charts and single value components to our dashboard canvas. Then, we will learn how to link them with the imported data. In the remaining chapters, we will learn how to add other dashboard components, such as maps, selectors, and so on. After this, we will learn how to export and publish our dashboards in *Chapter 8*, *Exporting, Publishing, and Importing Dashboards*.

Charts are the main dashboard components that we will use to create our dashboards. Selecting the chart is very important, and we need to select the right chart to help us get the maximum value of the presented information. The main idea of this book is to not only to help you learn how to create dashboards using SAP BusinessObjects Dashboards, but also to show you how to create informative and user friendly dashboards based on many best practices and design tips that we will present while progressing through this chapter.

Single value dashboard components are another type of components that we can use inside the dashboard to represent a single metric only, and this is why we call it single value component.

In this chapter, we will cover the following topics:

- Preparing our canvas and setting our document properties
- Adding our first chart dashboard component to our dashboard (pie chart)
- Linking chart with data
- Configuring main chart's properties
- Handling the missing data
- Introducing other chart types
- Adding our single value component to our dashboard
- Introducing other single value components

So, let's start working on our dashboard project.

Before we start

Before we start creating our dashboard, the canvas size needs to be set, as resetting it later would require a lot of rework for dashboard components, which will result in loss of time and resources. Similarly, the resolution of target devices needs to be considered. For example, if we are going to build desktop dashboard that we will display on desktop machines, we need to determine the most suitable dashboard resolution that will fit and be correctly displayed on all the business users' machines who will be using that dashboard. On the other hand, the dashboard resolution will be different if we are going to build a mobile dashboard that will be displayed on mobile devices, for example, and so we need to be precise about this option from the beginning.

> The recommended canvas size for Mobile dashboards that will be displayed on an iPad is 1024*768 pixel.

So, let's try to change our dashboard canvas size by performing the following steps:

1. Go to the **File** menu.
2. Select **Document** properties.
3. Select the **Preset Size** option under **Canvas size in pixels** area.
4. Then, select **1024*768** from the drop-down menu.
5. Click on **OK**.

The following image will make things easier for you.

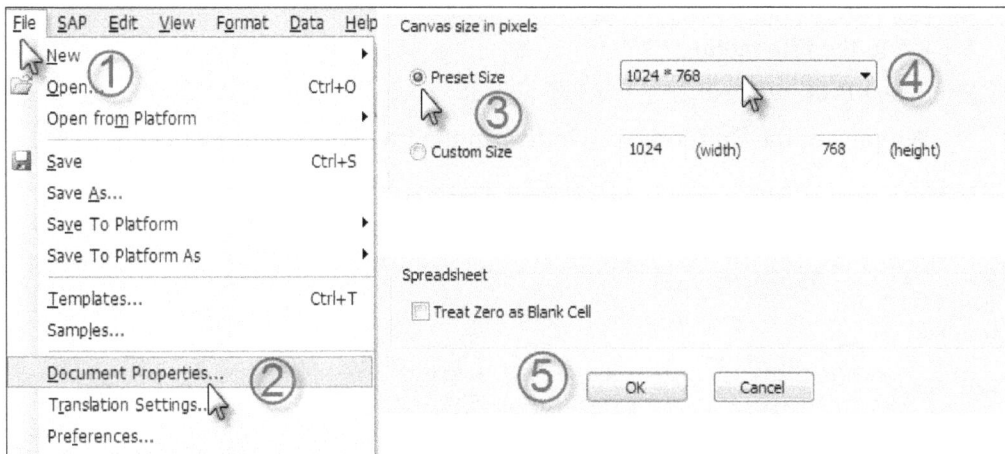

We can change the canvas size from the following two places, as we can see in the preceding screenshot:

- **Preferences...**
- **Document Properties...**

We will discuss them in more detail in the following sections.

Preferences

Preferences are used to control the application settings, such as canvas size, grid options, and MS Excel options. Any change to these settings will be automatically loaded whenever the application starts again. For example, if we change the canvas size to 800*600 and save it, then it will become the default canvas size value for any new dashboard, it will also be the default value to see in the canvas size even when we restart the dashboard application.

We have the following tabs under **Preferences...**:

- **Document**
- **Grid**
- **Open**
- **Languages**
- **Excel Options**
- **Accessibility**

However, let's learn how to open the **Preferences** window before diving into the details of each setting, as follows:

1. Go to the **File** menu.

2. Select **Preferences…**.

   We can see the **Preferences** window in the following screenshot:

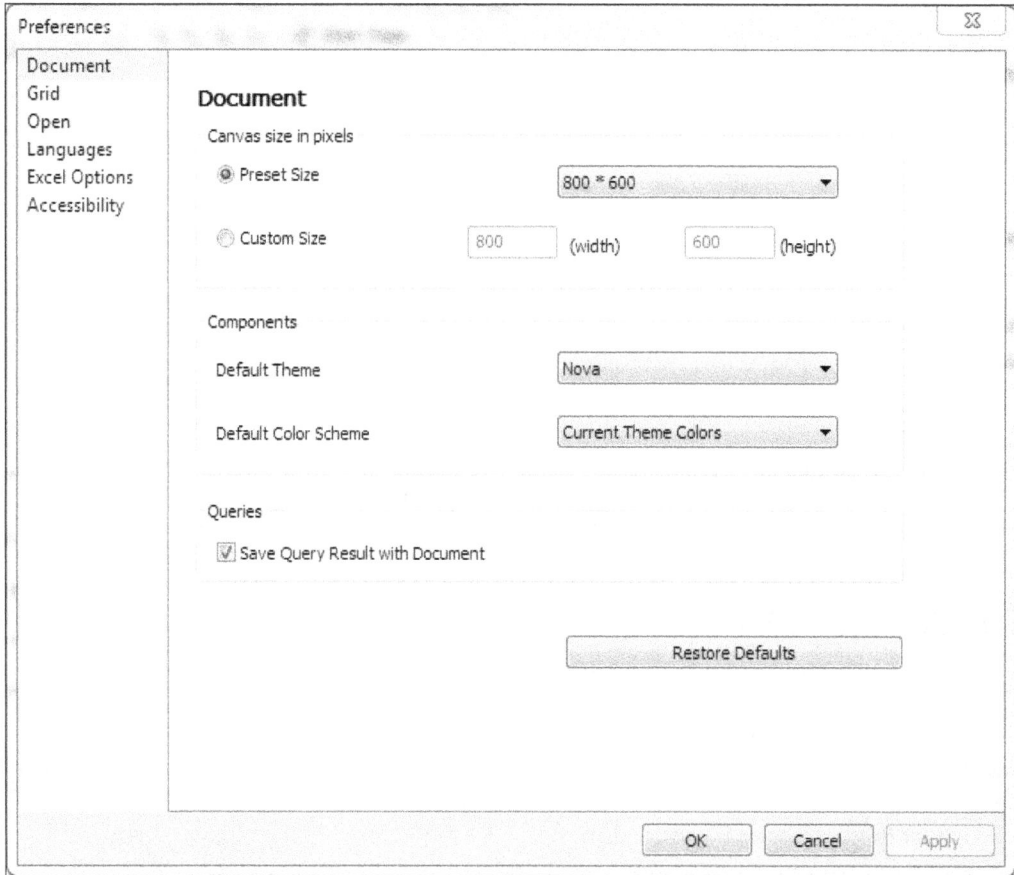

We will discuss document, grid, and Excel options as the remaining options are not very important.

The Document tab

In the **Document** tab, we can control the main document setting such as:

- **Canvas size in pixels**: We can use one of the preset canvas sizes or a customized canvas size by entering the canvas width and height in pixel.

> We recommend you to select your canvas size based on one of the preset options as it already contains most common and known canvas sizes that will fit perfectly on the corresponding screen resolution.

- **Default Theme** and **Default Color Scheme**: We will talk in detail on themes and color schemes in *Chapter 7*, *Styling Up*, but for now, all we need to know that we can change the default settings from here. The default settings will be used whenever we start creating a new dashboard. It will save you a few moments, as you can always change this from the document (dashboard) itself.

> The best practice is to build your color scheme that will be matching with your organization color scheme and use it from the beginning.

- **Save Query Results with document**: This option will help us save sample data retrieved from the Business Intelligence platform in the `.xlf` file. This is very useful if you want to demonstrate our dashboard in the offline mode.

> The `.xlf` file is the file extension for the dashboard document.

The Grid tab

Grids are small vertical and horizontal lines that will only be visible in the design mode but not at runtime. It will help us align our components easily and to have a more homogeneous design. As a best practice, we always recommend that you enable your grid. We can see the **Grid** tab in the following screenshot:

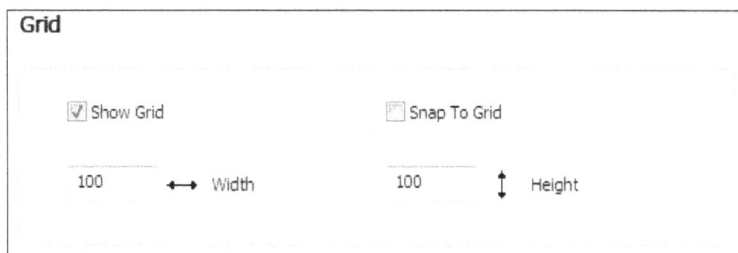

Grid	
☑ Show Grid	☐ Snap To Grid
100 ←→ Width	100 ↕ Height

In this tab, we need to enable **Grid** option to help us adjust our dashboard layout by performing the following steps:

1. Tick the **Show Gird** option.
2. Tick the **Snap To Grid** option.
3. Change **Width** and **Height** to 100.

The Excel options

Excel model is the core of any dashboard. It contains the data on which any calculation or logic would be applied before displaying it. The success of SAP BO Dashboards is also attributed to the fact that MS Excel is powerful, simple, and a widely known tool among end users.

We have many options here that we will revisit while progressing through our book, but we just need to take care of the **Maximum Number Of Rows** setting. Dashboards are usually built on the summarized data and the best practice is to do the aggregation behind the scenes and to bring the summarized aggregated data to the Excel model inside the dashboard. By default, the maximum number of allowed rows in Excel is 512.

> Increasing **Maximum Number Of Rows** in Excel will negatively affect the performance of our dashboard at runtime, and it will also affect the dashboard generation, exporting, and publishing time.

> **Downloading the example code**
>
> You can download the example code files from your account at http://www.packtpub.com for all the Packt Publishing books you have purchased. If you purchased this book elsewhere, you can visit http://www.packtpub.com/support and register to have the files e-mailed directly to you.

Here, we will just learn how to change it, but it is strongly recommended that you do not change that, unless you know that your data will go beyond 512 rows. You also need to avoid massive use of Excel calculations and formulas as it affects the performance. We can see the **Excel Options** window in the following screen:

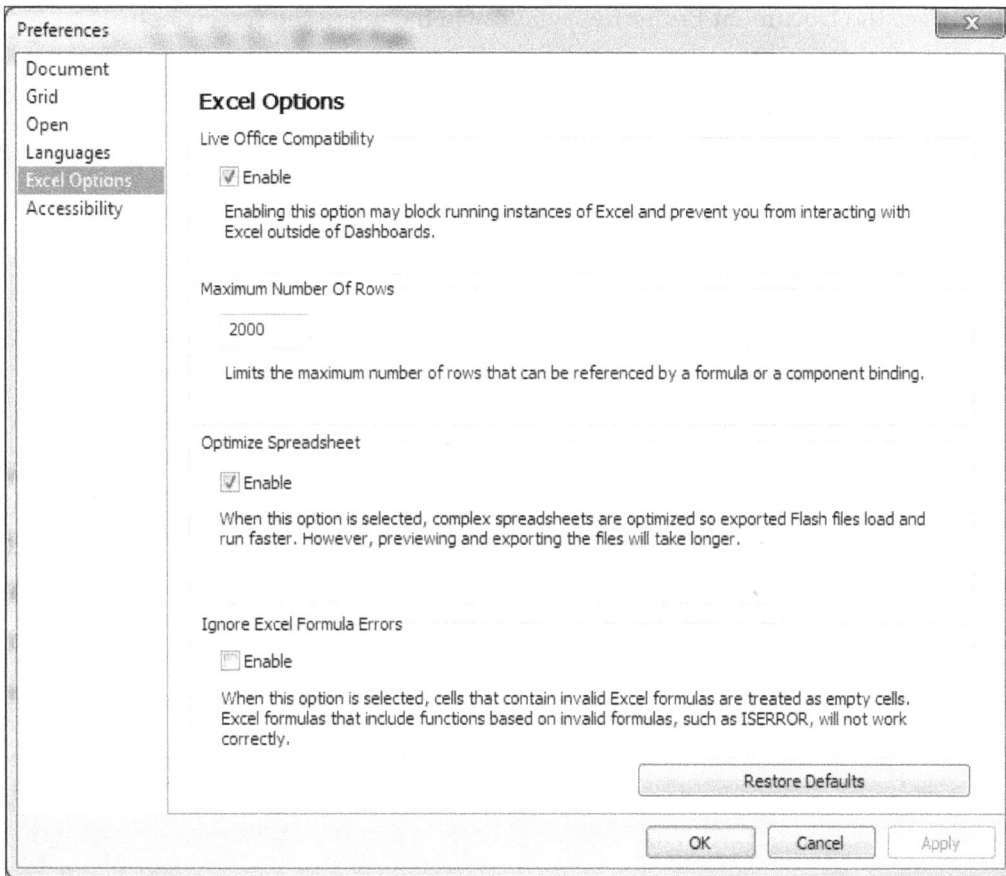

Document properties

Document properties can be used to control the current dashboard settings without the need to change the same setting in application preferences. Remember that changing preferences will affect all new dashboards, so it is more reasonable to change the dashboard settings that we need to change from **Document Properties** if we want these changes to be only applied on the current dashboard. The default values displayed in the **Document Properties** window are inherited from the **Preferences...** settings.

We can see the **Document Properties** window in the following screenshot:

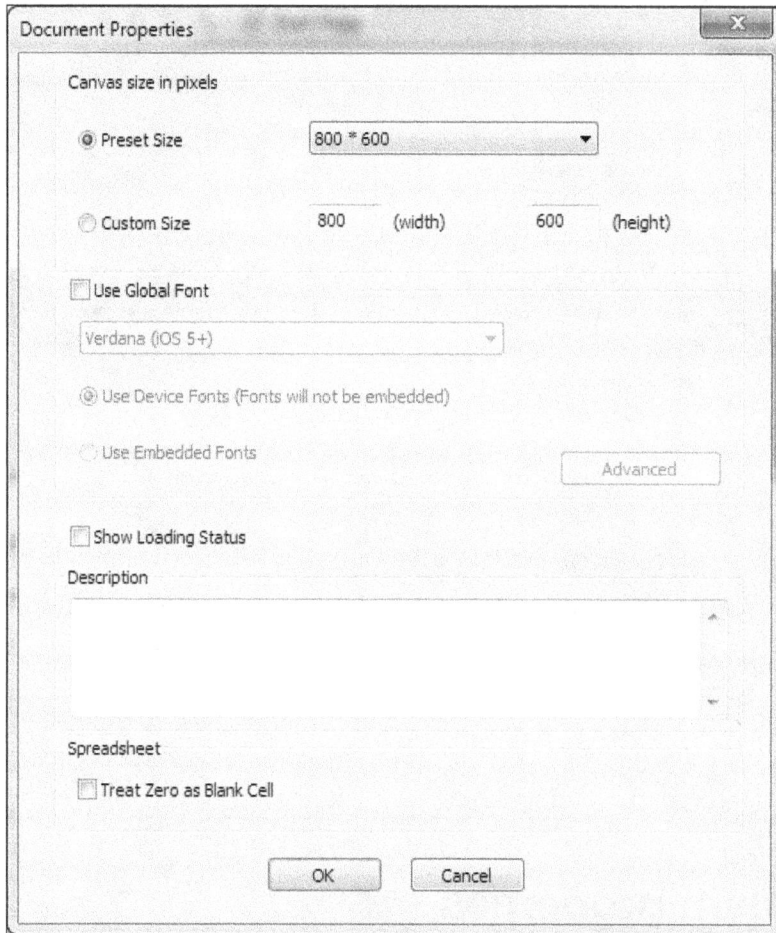

Adding our first chart component (pie chart)

Now, we are ready to build the model phase, as we have already imported the data and prepared our canvas. We will start by adding a pie chart to show the sales revenue per product line. We will learn how to add the pie chart component to our dashboard. Then, we will learn how to link it with the data in Excel model and how to change the pie chart properties. Finally, we will learn how to handle the missing data in our data ranges while displaying our chart. We can see the steps in the following screenshot:

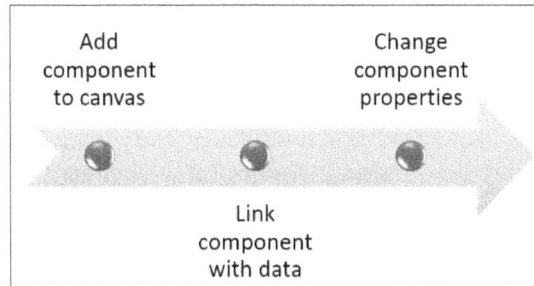

Pie charts can be used to show a relation between one dimension and one measure. The chart will show the measure distribution across dimension values. The arc size will normally be determined based on the metric quantity percentage.

We need to adhere to the following best practices while working with a pie chart:

- The total number of distinct values for your dimensions is less than or equal to five. The more distinct values you have for your dimension, the harder it is to read and understand the pie chart.

- Try to select simple colors, which are not only comfortable for the eyes, but can also be easily identified.

- Try to display the percentage, value, and category label in the pie chart because this will help if printed in a grayscale. This will also help if your pie chart arcs are very close in size, like the one given later.

- Don't use a pie chart if you have more than one dimension. For example, if you want to see products' sales by region, then use a column chart.

- Alerting feature is not available for a pie chart, so you can just use it for comparison but not for alerting and indication.

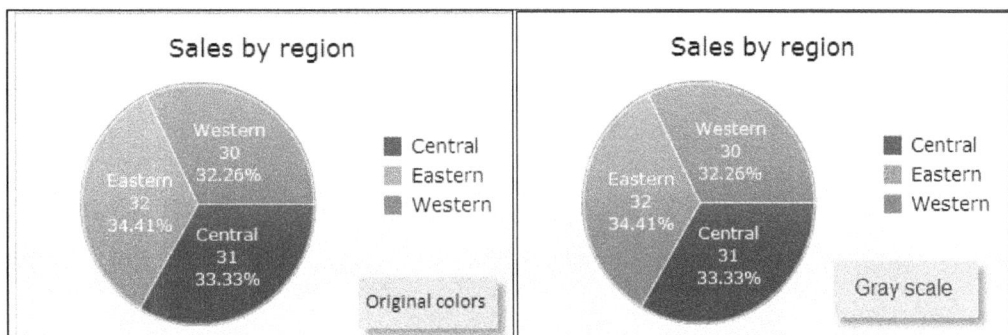

Let's perform the following steps to add a pie chart to our dashboard:

1. Open the dashboard .XLF file that we created together in *Chapter 2, Understanding the Dashboard Creation Process*. The file should be just an empty dashboard canvas, but the Excel model is already loaded with the data that we imported together. If you didn't work out this, then navigate to Example code folder | **Dashboards (Ready)** | **Chapter2.XLF**

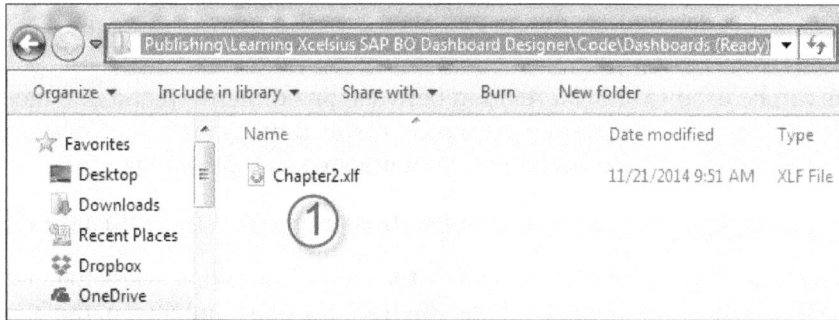

Before adding a component, we need to add a tab set container. Then, we need to create three tabs, as follows:

- **Dashboard**
- **Analysis**
- **Details**

The dashboard should look like:

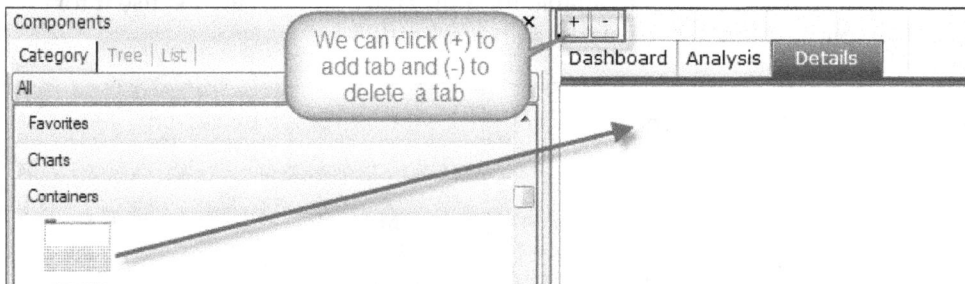

Activate the **Dashboard** tab, then we need to:

1. Activate the **Components** panel.
2. Drag and drop a **Pie Chart** component from the **Component** panel to the canvas, as shown in the next image:

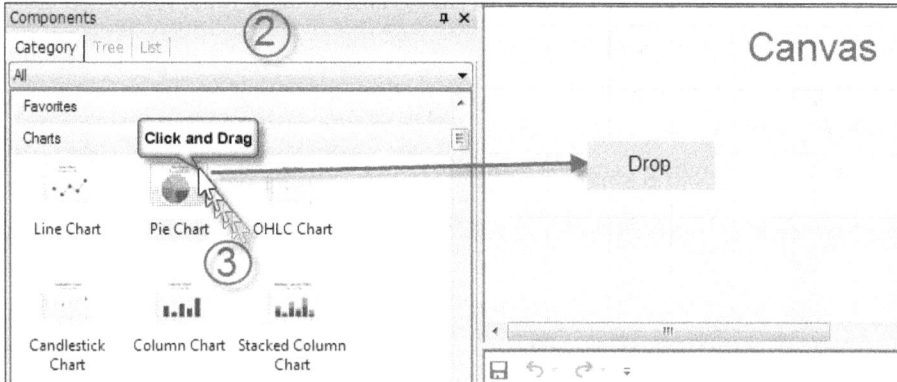

We can see the **Pie Chart** dashboard component on the canvas with the default settings, such as title and subtitle, as displayed in the following screenshot:

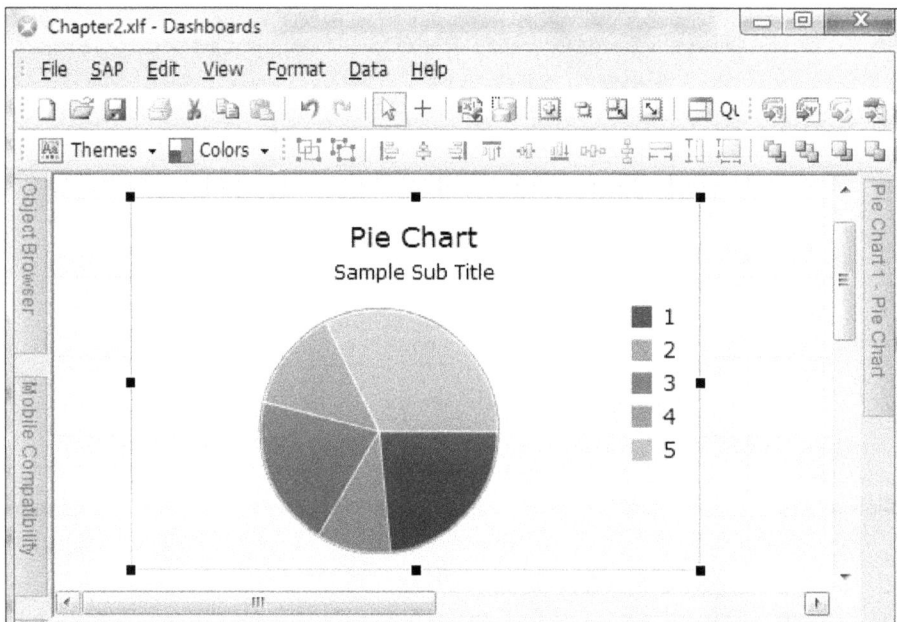

In the next section, we will learn how to link it with the data.

Linking the chart with data

Adding a chart to the canvas will add an empty dashboard component with the default settings. We need to link our chart with the data to display it on the chart. We need to perform the following steps to link it with the data:

1. Select the **Pie Chart**, or make sure that it is the active dashboard component.

2. Navigate to the **Properties** panel.

3. Navigate to data area in the **Values:** section, and click on the **select a range** icon.

4. Select the following range **Product!$D$4:$D$15**.

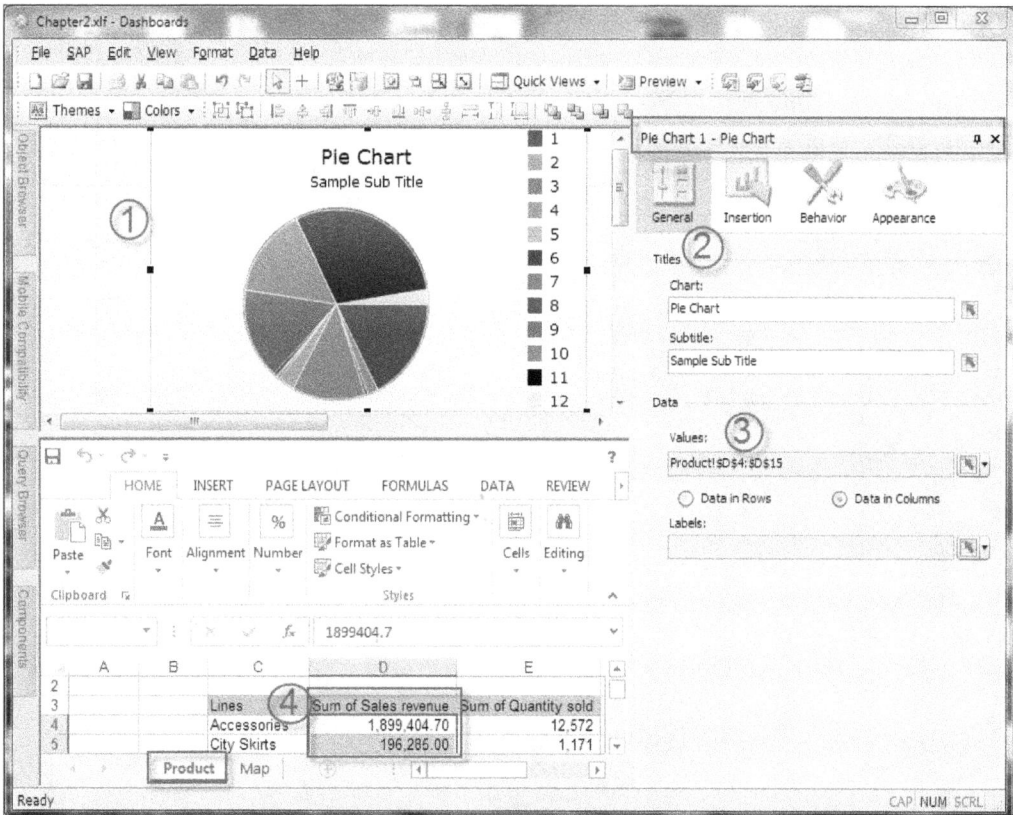

In the preceding image, note that the data is displayed on the pie chart, but because we didn't map the labels, they are displayed as 1, 2, 3, and so on. So, let's map the labels:

1. In the **Labels** field, select the following range **Product!$C$4:$C$15**.

2. Drag the chart to the middle of the canvas and note how the chart will snap to the grid. This will help us to control the layout of our dashboard's components.

3. Click on the **Preview** button to display the chart exactly as it will appear at runtime.

   The chart should look like the following:

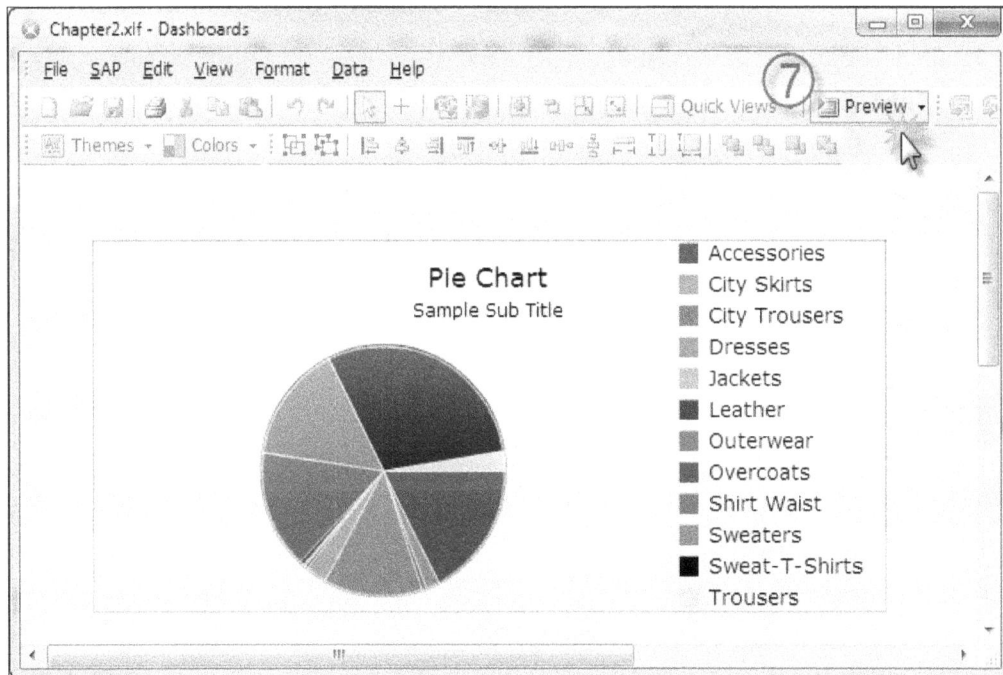

As we can see, a pie chart is the worst choice to display the sales by product line, as we have more than 12 product lines and the colors already mixed up. In the following section, we will learn how to improve this. We will find out together that bar or column chart is the best chart to display the sales by product information while introducing other chart types.

Configuring the main chart properties

Adding a chart component will use the default component settings. We can configure chart properties such as colors, text, fonts, behavior, and many other configurations to control the look and feel of our dashboard component. We will learn how to do many configurations, and how this will affect each dashboard components, through our book.

The next step after linking our chart with the data is to configure the main chart properties. Here, we will learn how to do things that are common among many chart types.

So, let's configure our pie chart:

1. Select our **Pie Chart** to make it active.

2. Then, go to **Properties** panel | **General** tab.

3. Type **Sales by Product Line** in the **Title** field.

4. Map **Subtitle** field to the Excel cell **Product!$D$3**.

    We can see the steps as displayed in the following screenshot:

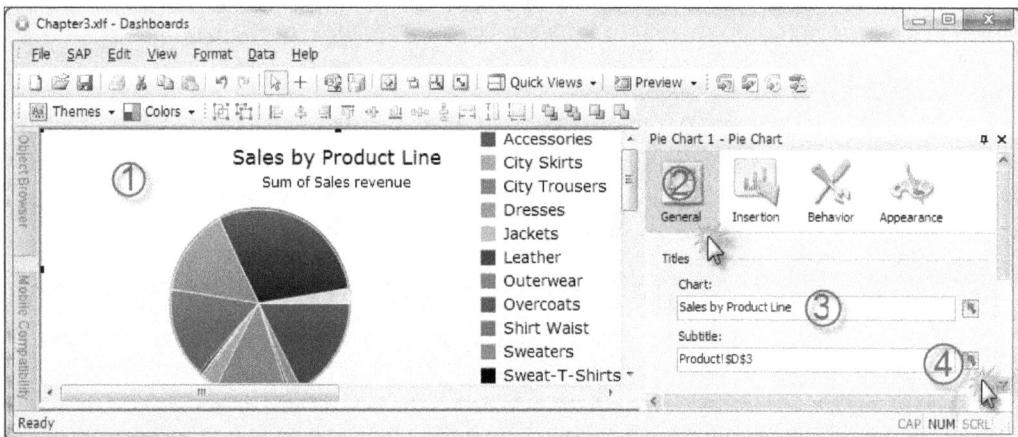

Note: Whenever you see the 🔃 icon, click on it and map the value of it to a cell in the Excel model. If the background of the property is white, then you can type or enter manual value as well. The property with gray background indicates that you can use the icon only to map it to a cell in Excel.

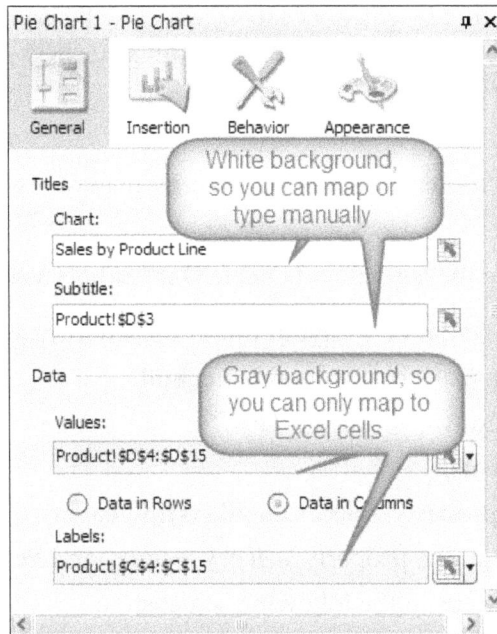

Now, let's perform the following steps to find out how to enable sorting by data or category labels:

1. Select the **Pie Chart** to make it active.
2. Then, go to **Properties** panel | **Behavior** | **Common** tab.
3. Tick **Enable Sorting**.
4. Select **By Data** and **Descending** order.

    You can see the steps in the following screenshot:

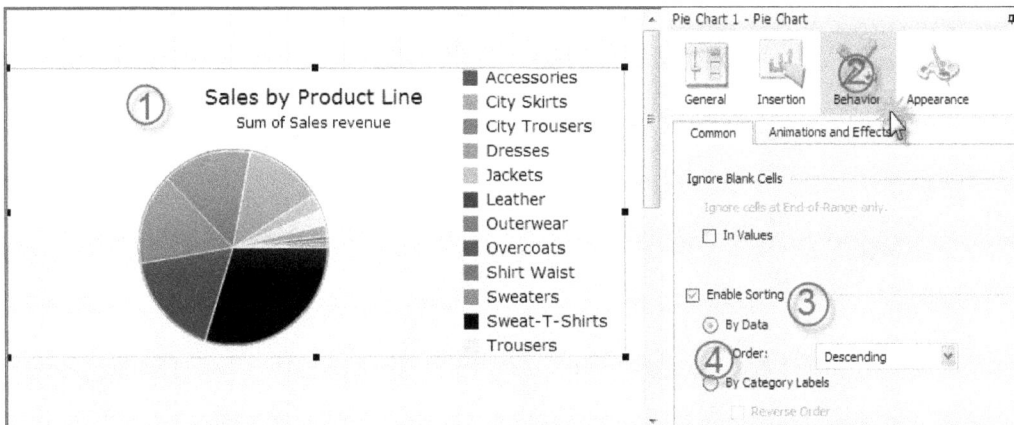

You can also enable sorting by category labels, which will sort the data based on the alphabetical order of the dimension values. You can also check "Reverse Order" to do the same but in descending order.

> The feature (enable sorting) is available in most of the chart types.

Now, let's try to remove the legend and enable **Data Labels** as follows:

1. Navigate to **Appearance | Layout** under **Pie Chart** properties.
2. Remove the tick mark beside **Enable Legend**.
3. Then, navigate to **Appearance | Text**.
4. Check **Data Labels**.
5. In the position property, select **Outside with Leader**.
6. In the **Label Contains** property, select **Category** and **Percentage**.

   We can see the steps in the following screenshot:

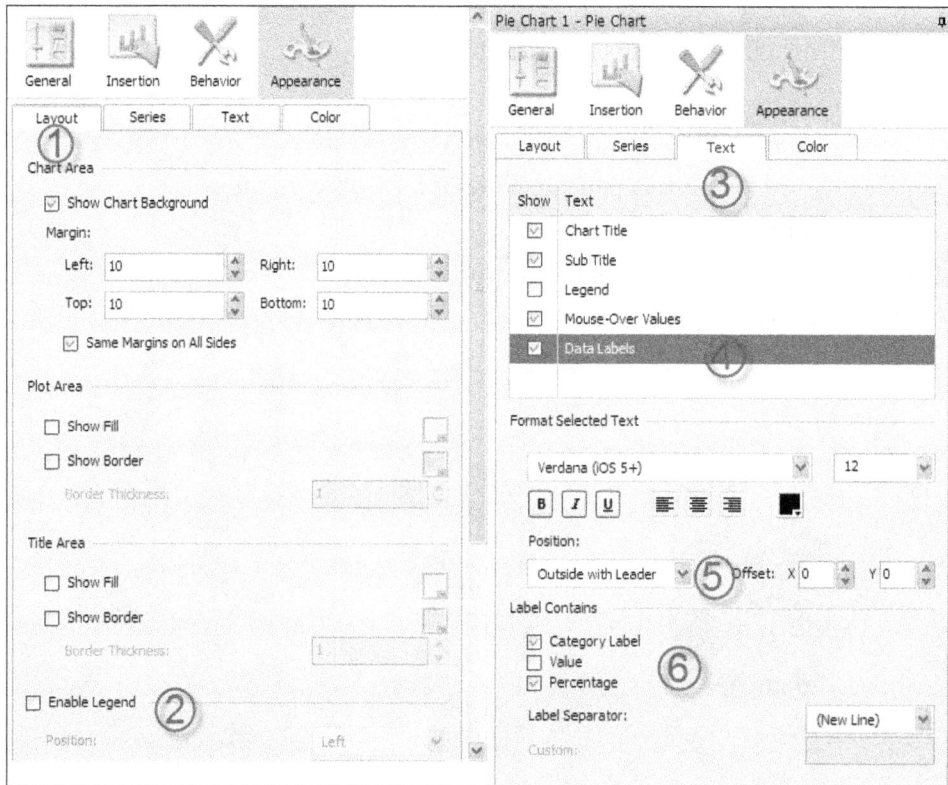

So, as we can see, there is no way to display the sales by product using a pie chart in a simple and readable way.

> If you have a case like this and still want to display the data using a pie chart, then you can display the top five dimension values based on their sales and group the remaining values under one category, "Others". This can be done from the presentation layer side (Universe) or from the query side, as we will discuss in *Chapter 9, Retrieving External Data Sources*.

We can see the previously mentioned hint applied in the following screenshot:

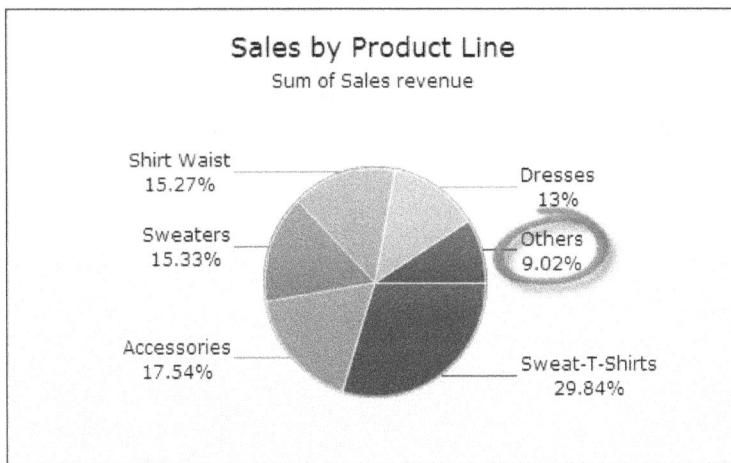

Introducing other chart types

Now, we should be more familiar with the process of creating a dashboard. In this section, we will go through the chart types that we have in SAP BO Dashboards, and we will focus on the column and bar charts as we will need them to create our eFashion dashboard project. We will cover the following dashboard components:

- Line, column, bar, and column line charts
- Bubble and scatter charts
- OHLC and Candlesticks charts
- Bullet charts
- Radar chart
- Tree map (heat map)

The column line chart is renamed in SAP BO Dashboard 4.1, and it was combined chart in the earlier releases.

Line, column, bar, and column line charts

Line chart can be used to show the relation between one dimension and one measure. This type of charts is perfect in a trend analysis when you want to display time trends, such as the sales by months. The main idea of this chart is to display a continuous line that reflects how our measure (sales in our example) changes across dimension values (months in our example).

> We can blindly select line charts when we want to display a time-based trend analysis.

We can empower a line chart by displaying more than one line (series). New series can be measure distributed on another dimension (such as the sales trend) by product, or another measure (such as target) that we want to compare our main measure with. We can see this in the following screenshot:

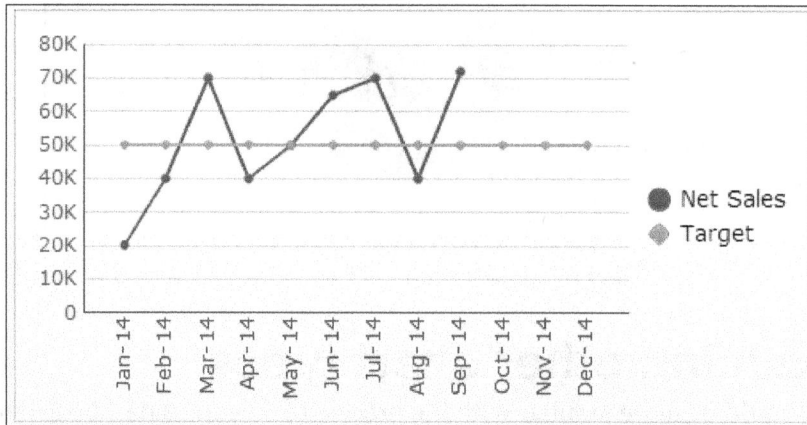

The column and bar chart are the same except the difference in the way they display the data. Bar charts are horizontal, and column charts are vertical. We can use it to compare multiple dimension values based on one metric, such as sales per brand, as we can see in the following screenshot:

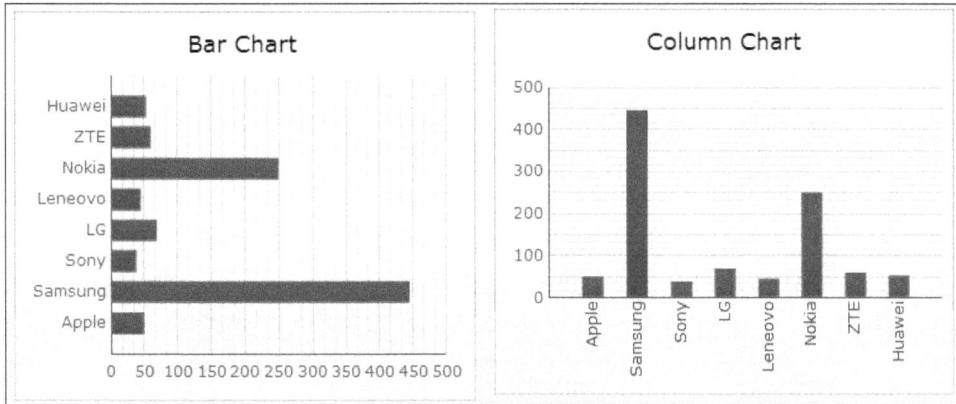

The column and bar chart can be used to show the relation between multiple series, so for example, we may have a column chart that gives the distribution of sales per product against region. In this case, we will create multiple series for region dimension, and we will use legend and color to differentiate between them.

There are two other versions of bar and column chart called stacked bar and stacked column chart. In this dashboard component, we display one stacked bar instead of side-by-side bars, as we can see in the following screenshot:

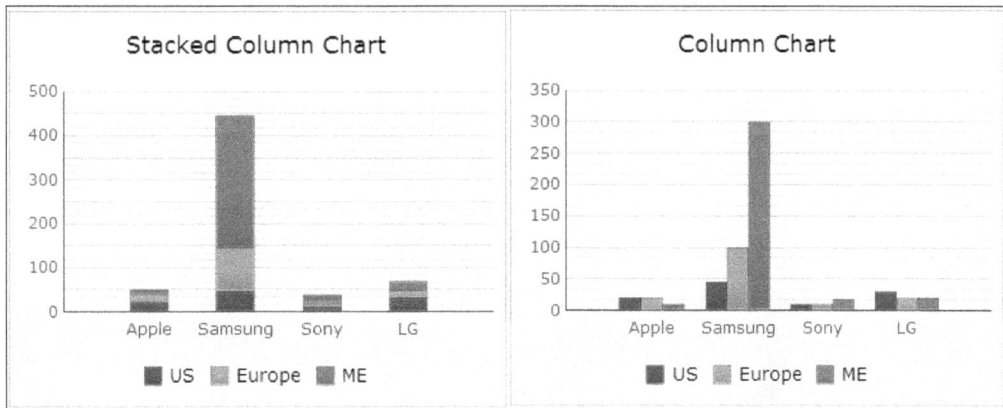

A column line chart is a combination of column and line charts. We can use a combined chart to show the relation between two measures such as sales and quantity, for example, with two different scale or axes. Indeed, we can't represent sales and quantity using the same scale, so we can't use the column or bar charts to do this.

We will create a combined chart as it is part of eFashion dashboard project:

1. Activate the **Components** panel.

2. Drag and drop a **Column Line Chart** component from the **Component** panel to the canvas.

3. Activate the **General** tab for the combination chart from the **Properties** panel.

4. Select **By Series** in the **General** tab under the **Data** section.

5. Click on the small (**+**) icon under series to create two series. Use the information in the following table to map the series information:

Series	Property	Value
Series1	Name	Product!$H$3
	Value	Product!$H$4:$H$11
	Plot Series On	Primary Axis
Series2	Name	Product!$I$3
	Value	Product!$I$4:$I$11
	Plot Series On	Secondary Axis
Category Labels(X)	Category Labels(X)	Product!$G$4:$G$11

We need to note the following:

- **Category Labels(X)** are shared between the chart series.

- We mapped some extra empty cells in our values and category labels. I did this on purpose to learn how to handle the missing chart values at runtime.

- Series1 will display the sales information on the primary axis, and series2 will display the quantity information on the secondary axis.

Let's continue with our chart:

1. In the **General** tab, map the following properties to the corresponding Excel model cells, as per the following table:

Property	Excel Cells
Titles | Chart	Titles!$B$4
Titles | Subtitle	Titles!$B$5
Titles | Category (X) Axis	Titles!$B$6
Titles | Value (Y) Axis	Titles!$B$7
Titles | Secondary Value (Y) Axis	Titles!$B$8

> The best practice is to keep titles and labels in a separate Excel sheet inside our model. This will keep our dashboard design more organized, easy to maintain, and can be understood the other developers.

We can see the discussed steps in the following screenshot:

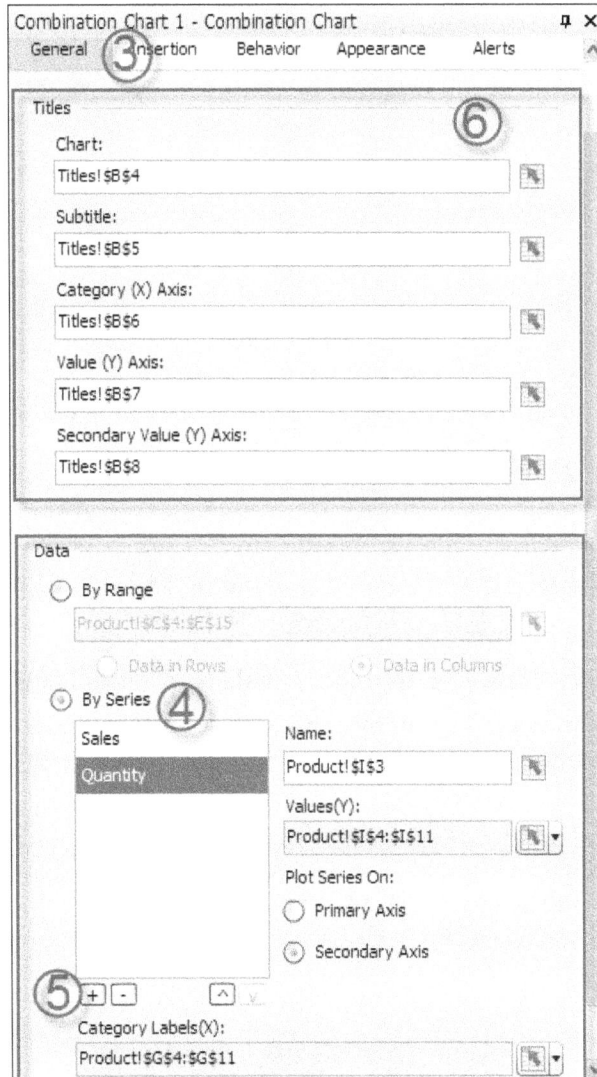

We can see the combination chart in the following screenshot:

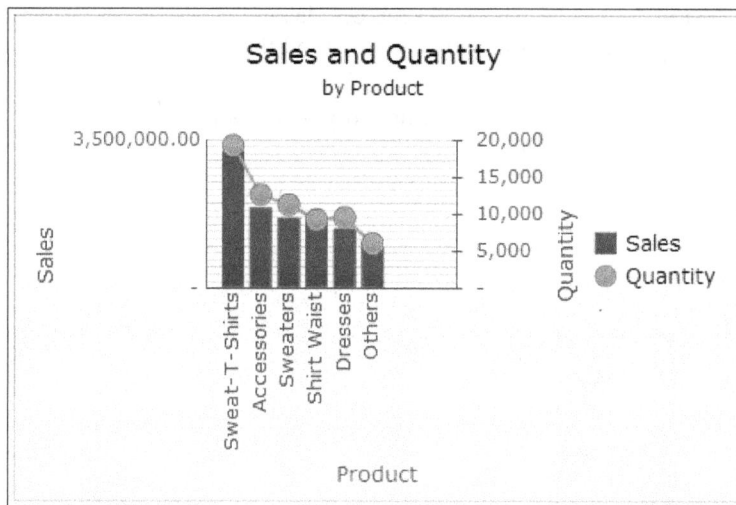

Now, let's change some properties to enhance the chart's look and feel:

1. Make sure that the combination chart is selected, and then navigate to the **Properties** panel.

2. Navigate to the **Behavior | Common** tab.

3. Under **Ignore Blank Cells**, select **In Series** and **In Values**.

4. Check the **Enable Rang Slider** option.

5. In the **Primary Scale** and **Secondary Scale** tabs, select **Fixed Label Size**.

6. In the **Appearance | Layout** tab, check **Enable Hide/Show Chart Series** at **Run-Time** option.

> You will be able to see the **Primary Scale** and **Secondary Scale** tabs only if you configured one of the series to be plotted on the secondary axis. If all series is plotted on the primary axis, then only one tab **Scale** will be there.

We can see the steps in the following screenshot:

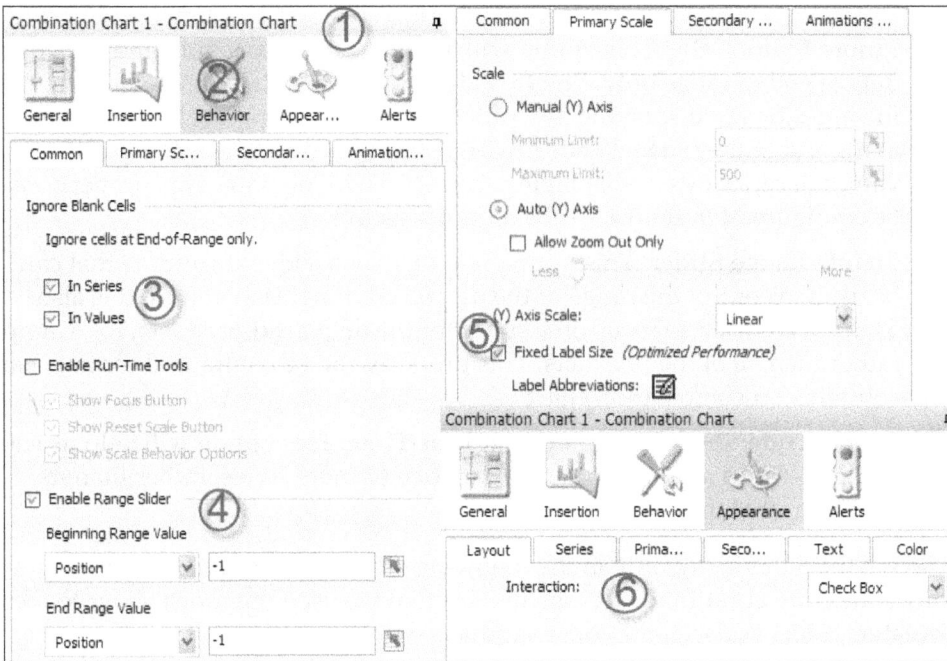

We can see the combined chart in the following screenshot:

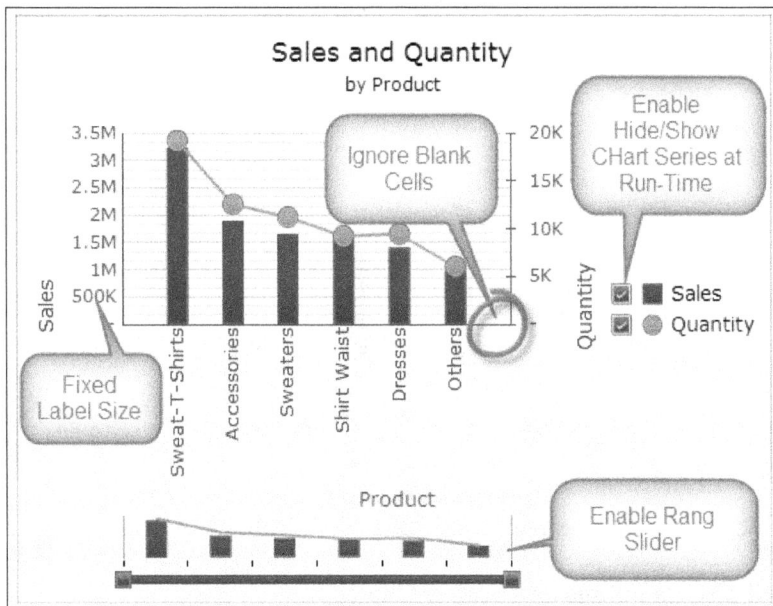

Finally, we need to discuss some of the features that we used to enhance our combined chart:

- **Ignore Blank Cells**: This option will allow the chart to handle the missing data at end of range only. The **In Values** option will handle the missing data in values by not displaying any product with no, or null, values if it comes at the end of the range. While the **In Series** option will handle the missing values in series by not displaying the series with no data. This property can be configured for almost all charts and selectors.

- **Enable Range Slider**: This option will display a slider at runtime that can be used to control the range of the displayed dimension values. It is also useful if we want to focus on a subset of the displayed products, for example, rather than all of the products. This property can be configured for line, bar, column, and combination chart.

- **Enable Hide/Show Chart Series at Run-Time**: This option will help us show and hide series at runtime to compare one or more series, rather than to compare all of them.

We can see the **Sales** series only in the following screenshot because we disabled the **Quantity** measure at runtime. We can also see that we used the range slider to focus on **Sweaters**, **Shirt Waists**, and **Dress** products only.

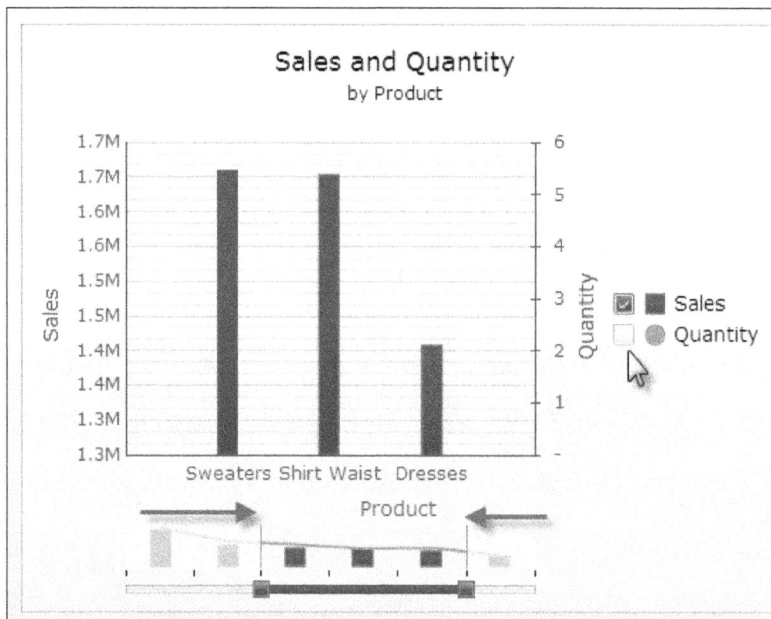

Next, we will discuss Bubble and Scatter Chart.

Bubble, scatter charts, and tree maps

Scatter chart can be used to show a relation between two variables (metrics) using dots. A bubble chart is exactly same as scatter chart, but it can be used to show the relationship between three variables. The relation between first two variable will also be presented by the coordinates of a dot on the chart, while the third variable will be presented by the dot size.

Tree map is a set of rectangles of different sizes which can also be used to show the relation between two variables, the same as scatter chart. The difference that the tree map will use the rectangle size and color intensity to show the relation instead of the scatter coordinates for the dots.

We can see how Bubble, Scatter, and Tree Map charts will look like in the following screenshot:

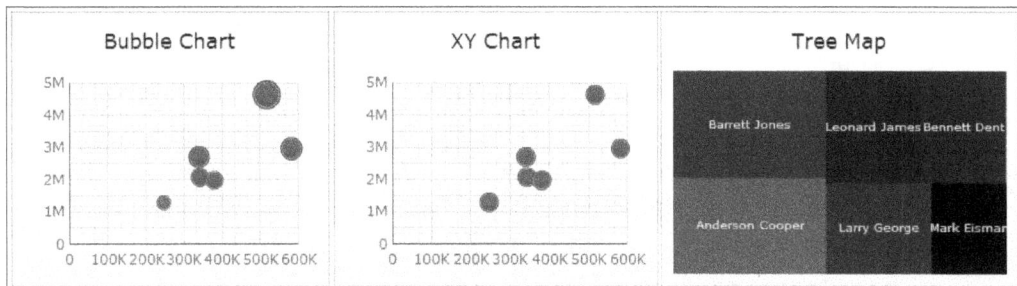

Now, we will build a bubble chart to show the manager's performance based on the revenue, discount, and margin:

1. Drag a bubble chart from the component panel and drop it on any empty space on the canvas (the **Dashboard** tab).

> Use the **Object Browser** panel to hide the combination chart and pie chart by clicking on the corresponding eye symbol if you don't have space.
>
> We can also use the **Lock** symbol to lock the marked object and prevent any changes till we release (un-tick) the lock again.

We can see the **Object Browser** panel in the following screenshot:

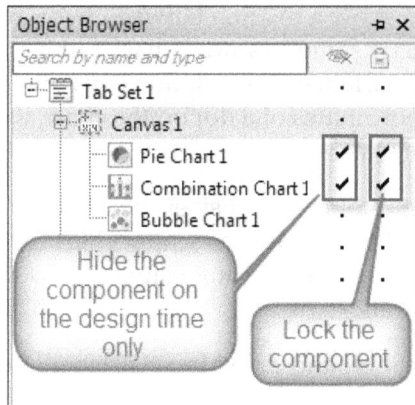

2. Navigate to **General** tab under the **Properties** panel and map the bubble chart titles to the corresponding Excel model cells under **Titles** sheet, as we can see in the following screenshot.

3. Create six series and start mapping the Name, Value(X), Value(Y), and size to the corresponding manager name, revenue, discount, and margin, as we can see in the following screenshot.

4. Adjust the scale from **Behaviour** tab by setting **Fixed Label Size**, as we did in the last combination chart.

We can see the steps in the following screenshot:

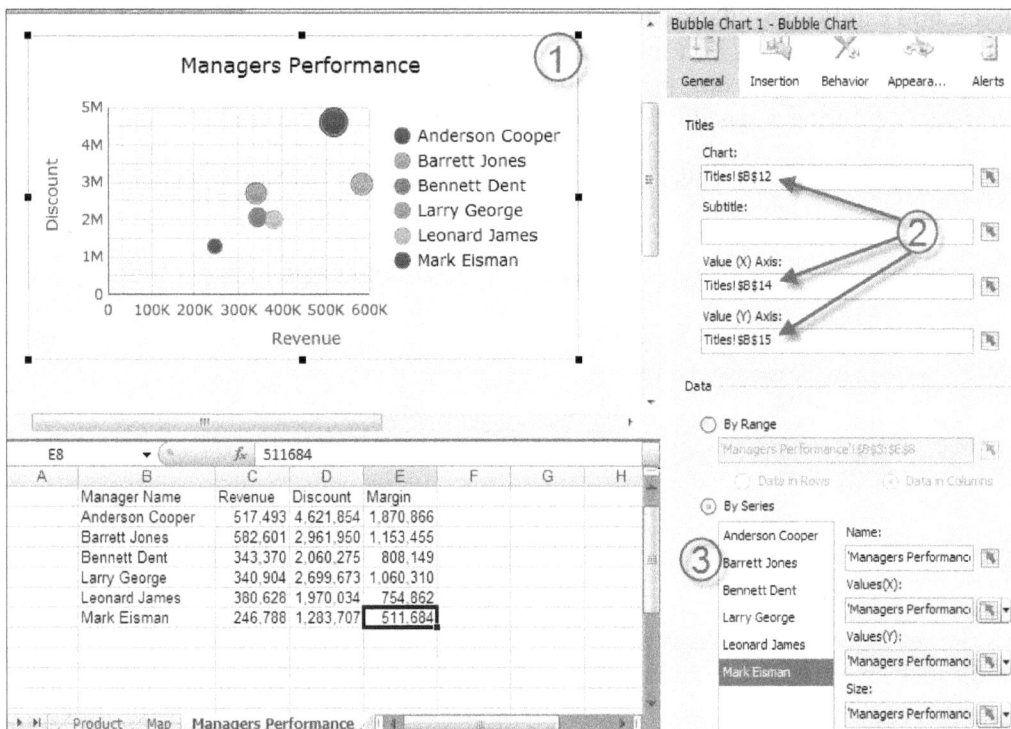

- ° **Exercise**: Try to enable **Data Labels** on the bubble chart in order to give it a meaning if we printed in a grayscale.
- ° **Exercise hint**: Use **Data Labels** under the **Appearance** tab.

OHLC and candlestick charts

OHLC and candlestick charts can be used to display stock price information over time. The stock price has four main values across the day; these are **open price, high price, low price, and closing price (OHLC)**. We can have a full picture of stock price performance during a specific day by displaying these four values.

We can see how to draw OHCL and candlestick charts for the mentioned stock price:

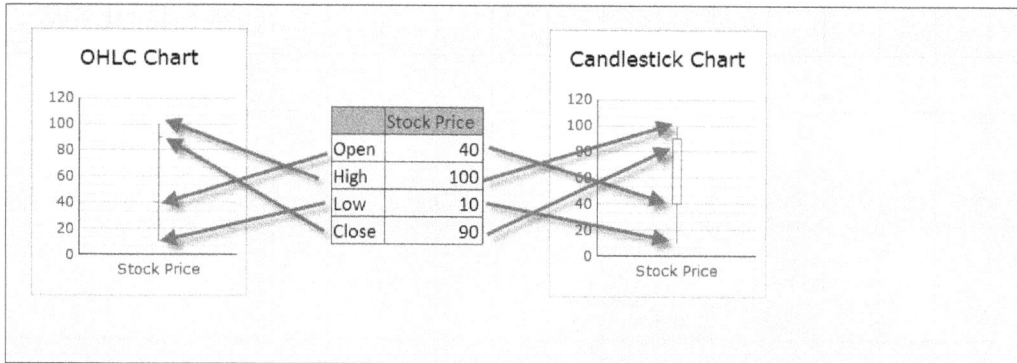

We can see same stock price information by date presented on OHLC and candlestick charts in the following screenshot:

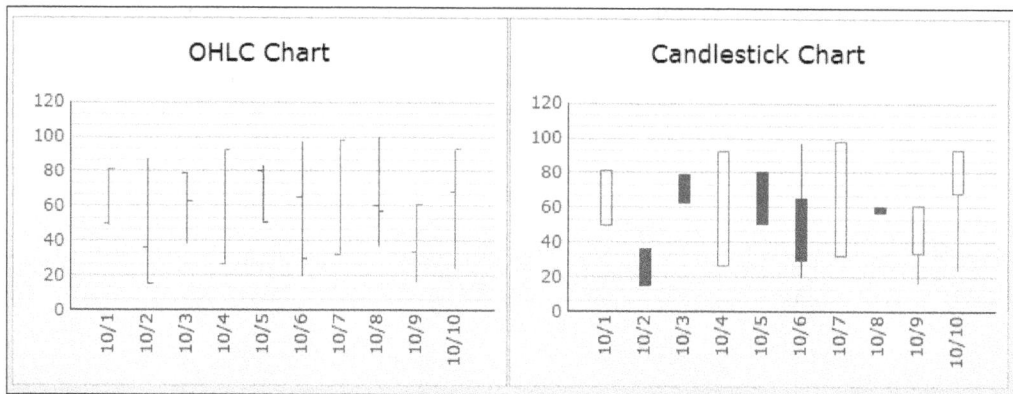

Exercise: Try to create an OHLC chart based on the stock excel sheet under **Example Code | Data | Excel | Stock.xls**

Bullet charts

The bullet chart is another version of the bar and column chart developed by Steven Few to replace dashboard' single value components, such as gauge and meters. The main problem with gauge and meters is that they consume large space and deliver small values from the information that we have. The bullet chart can display the following four metrics per bar:

- Actual (Performance)
- Target (Comparative)
- Lower scale
- Upper scale

We can see an example of a bullet chart in the following screenshot:

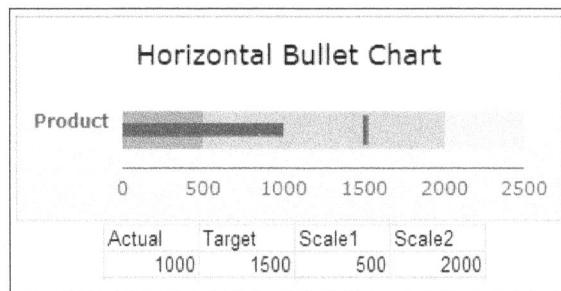

Radar charts

A radar chart can be used to represent different factors that can be used to measure something. For example, we may use the following factors: price, shipping time, average rating, and quality to measure a product. We have two types of radar charts:

- **Radar Chart**
- **Filled Radar Chart**

We can see a Radar Chart example in the following screenshot:

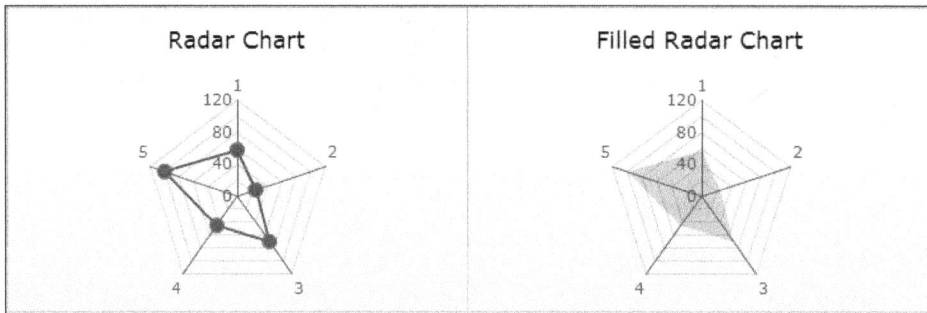

Adding a single-value component to our dashboard

The single value dashboard components can be used to display single metrics, such as growth percentage and total number of incidents. We will learn how to incorporate targets with single value components to create a KPI from the presented metric. We have many types of single value components that will do exactly the same but with a different visualization.

As a part of our eFashion dashboard project, we will add a gauge, value, and progress bar dashboard components. So, let's start with it.

Gauge and dial

The gauge and dial are exactly the same and can be used to display a metric value. The value can be indicated by a needle or marker. The only difference that I can see between gauge and dials is that gauge scale lies inside the circle, while the dial's scale lies outside the circle. Otherwise, they are exactly the same.

Let's follow the following steps to add a gauge to our dashboard:

1. Open the dashboard file and navigate to the **Dashboard** tab from the tab set.
2. Navigate to **Single Value** category under **Components** panel.
3. Drag a Gauge to the canvas.

4. Navigate to the **gauge** properties and map the following:

   ○ **Title: 'Single Values'!$B$1**

   ○ **Name: 'Single Values'!$A$2**

   ○ **Value: 'Single Values'!$B$2**

5. Make sure that indicator type is **Needle**.

6. Set the scale to **Auto | Value Based**.

   Please refer to the following image:

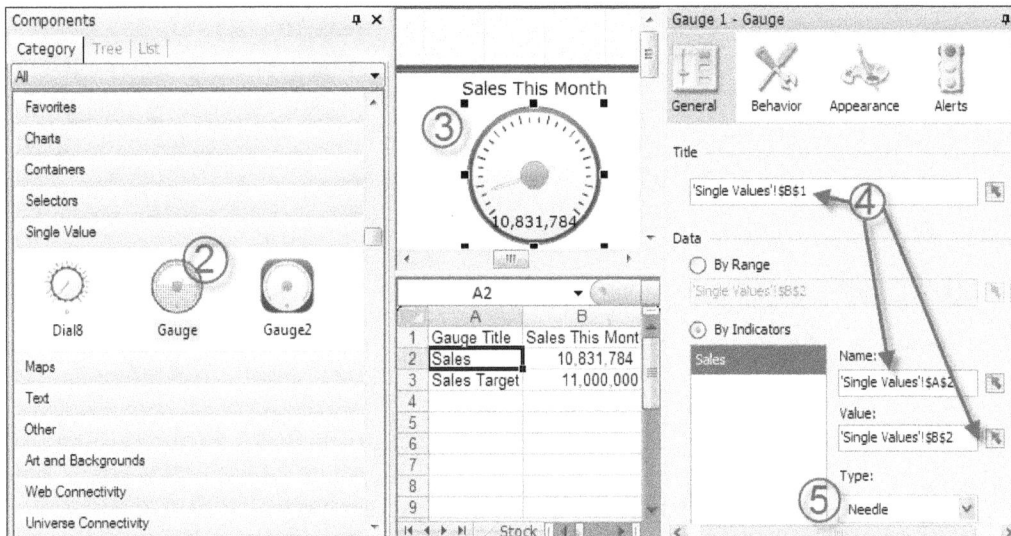

Now, let's try to enhance our gauge by performing the following steps:

1. Navigate to **Behavior | Common** tab.

2. Uncheck the **Enable Interaction** option.

3. Navigate to **Appearance | Layout** tab.

4. Select **Manual** under **Enable Ticks** area and set the major and minor number of ticks to **10** and **2**.

We can see the steps in the following screenshot:

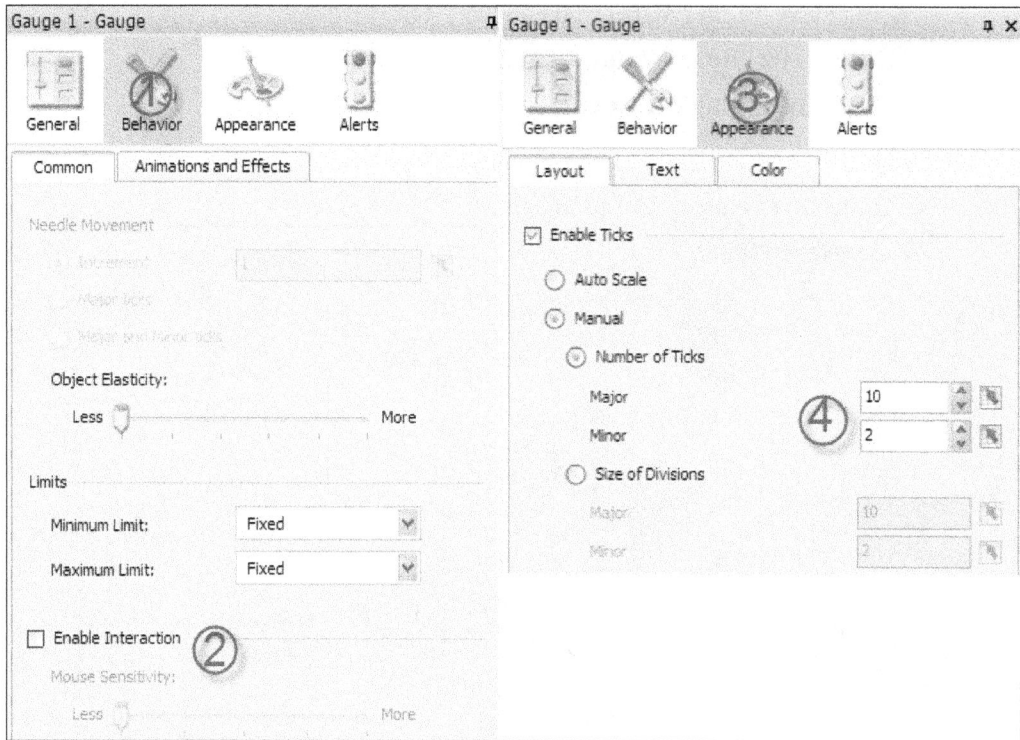

We can see the final gauge in the following screenshot:

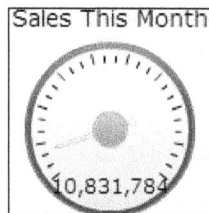

Before we move to the next single value dashboard component, let's discuss some of the new features introduced here.

- **Enable Interaction**: This option can be configured under **Gauge** properties **Behavior | Common** tab. If we enable this option, the gauge will act as an input as well. We can move the gauge needle, and the value will change accordingly at runtime only. This means that the new value will not be saved with the dashboard, and it will reset to the original value when we open the dashboard again. This feature can be used in "what if" scenarios. A "What If" scenario is a simulation for what may happen to a metric if we changed one of it's factors. For example reducing expenses (factor) and net profit (metric).

> We can control the needle movement increment from **Behavior | Common | Needle Movement** option if the **Enable Interaction** option is enabled. We can also control the mouse sensitivity, which will determine how fast the metric value will be changed based on the mouse move.

- **Enable Play Button**: This option can be configured under **Gauge** properties **Behavior | Common** tab. This option will automatically increment the gauge metric by the configured increment size. A small play button will be displayed in the center of the gauge, and it will show all the possible metric values in the predefined **Play Time (seconds)**.

> We can use **Auto Play** and **Auto Rewind** options to continuously play the gauge.

We can see this option in the following screenshot:

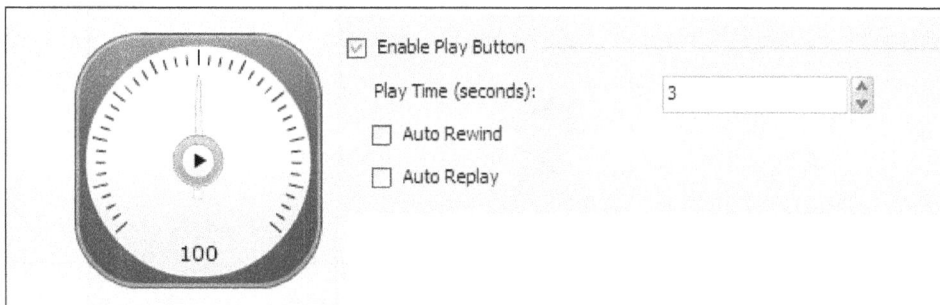

Next, we will discuss progress bars.

Progress bar and sliders

Progress bars and sliders can be used to show the progress of a metric; we can use it, for example, to display **year to date (YTD)** figures, **month to date (MTD)** figures, and so on. We can use both of them as an input as well, and we have the same interaction and play features that we have already explained. Sliders are most suitable for interaction, while progress bars are more suitable for data display. We have many different types of progress bar and sliders that vary between horizontal and vertical scales.

We can see a progress bar and slider in the following screenshot:

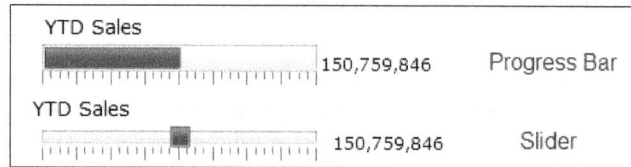

Exercise: Create a progress bar and map it to the corresponding data in the Excel single value sheet. The steps are exactly the same as what we did in the **Gauge** component.

> A dual slider is a special type of slider that can control two values at the same time.

Value and spinner

This is yet another two types of single value components that can simply display a value in a box. The main difference between the spinner and value is that you can control the metric value in the spinner by two small up and down arrows, while you can use the mouse to control the metric in the value component.

We can see the **Value** and **Spinner** dashboard components in the following screenshot:

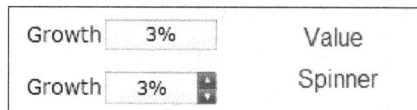

Exercise: Create the **Value** dashboard components and map it to the corresponding data in the Excel single value sheet.

Value and spinner components are not supported in Mobile desktop, and we can use **Label** component to replace them.

Play

The play dashboard component is nothing but a slider with play buttons. We can use it exactly in the same way as all the other single value components. The main difference is that this component is more suitable for play and interaction scenarios. We can see a play component in the following screenshot:

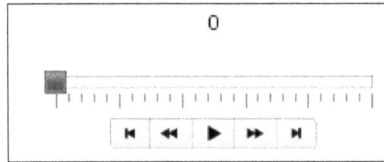

Exercise: Arrange dashboard components by dragging and dropping them to the right location, as displayed in the following screenshot:

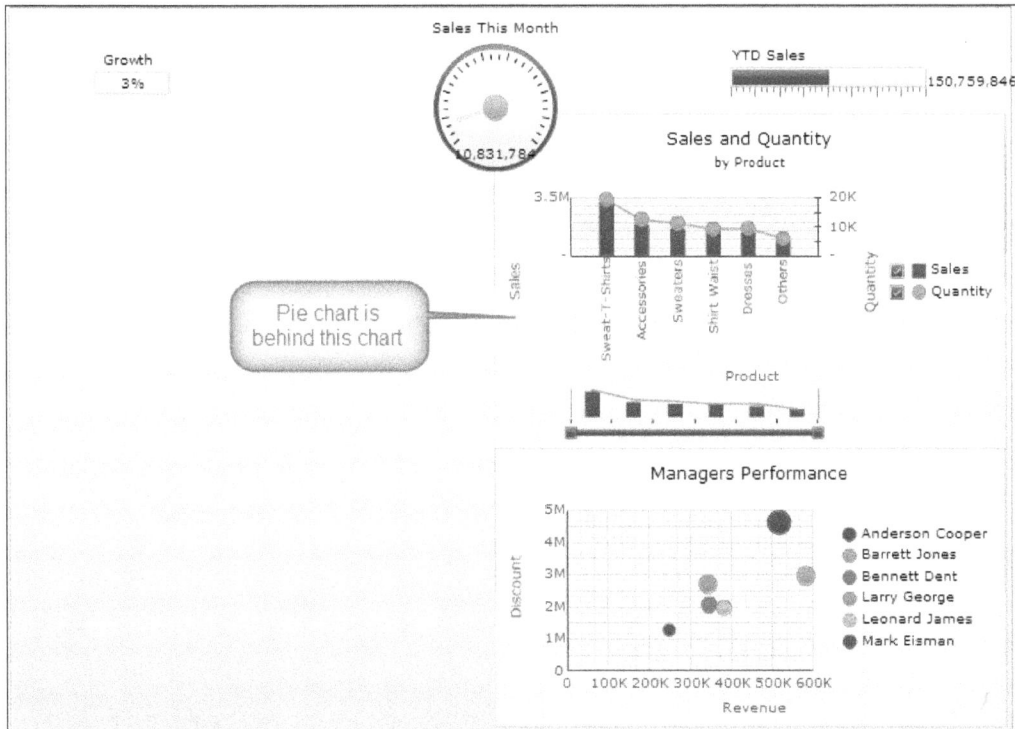

Summary

We started the chapter with various control preferences for the dashboard. We worked extensively on the canvas—adding charts and sizing it. Then, we moved to charts, learning common properties, such as handling the missing data and enabling a range slider. We concluded the chapter with the single value components in addition to dashboard, such as gauge and progress bars.

In the next chapter, we will continue with the eFashion project, adding predefined maps and other advance dashboard components, such as trend and calendar. We will also work with Google maps' add-on installation and embedding it in our dashboard.

4
Using Maps and Other Components

We have many dashboard components that we can use inside our dashboard. In the previous chapter, we discussed how to add charts and single-value components to our dashboard. In this chapter, we will learn how to add maps and other dashboard components.

In this chapter, we will discuss the following topics:

- Using SAP BO Dashboards built-in maps
- Configuring and using the CMap plugin
- Using other dashboard components, such as trend, icon, and calendar
- Configuring and using the dash print plugin
- Configuring and using the micro chart plugin

Maps

Maps are efficient when we want to represent data related to geographical dimensions, especially when we use indications and alerts to highlight the presented information. We can get more value from the data presented on a map than data presented on a chart or in a table. For example, you can easily find that your company's major sales are done in the MENA region using a map to represent sales information, while you may take a while to find out the same fact using the same sales information presented using a chart or table. This is because maps contain more geographical information than just the location. Another example is as follows: you can easily find a relation between the coastal states of the US. and, let's say, low average temperatures across the year. So, maps are prefect for locations and geographical dimensions, and as a best practice, it is recommended to use maps in such cases.

There are many prebuilt, or out-of-the-box, maps in SAP BO Dashboards that can be used directly by linking data, adding alerts, and using the drill feature. We can also use a third-party add-in to integrate and use Google maps inside our SAP BO Dashboards. You can refer to *Appendix*, *Built-in maps* available.

You will learn how to use a map to drill down to another dimensional level in the hierarchy. You will also learn how to configure the **Alert** and **Insert** properties for your maps in *Chapter 5*, *Interactive Analysis with Dashboards*.

Besides this, we will discuss other dashboard components, such as the calendar, trend icon, history components and many more.

Using maps

Maps are a very important subject, and so we need to pay special attention here. In this section, we will discuss these topics:

- Using built-in maps
- Using the CMap plugin

Adding built-in map dashboard components

In this section, you will learn how to add a US-based map to the eFashion sales data by state. Then, we will link this map with data already prepared from the Excel model.

Before we start, however, we need to open the latest .xlf dashboard file that we completed in the previous chapter. If you didn't complete the steps provided in the previous chapters to create the eFashion dashboard, or if you just want to practice with the map part, then you may open the Chapter3.xlf dashboard from the Dashboard (Ready) folder, which is available under the example code folder. We can see that folder in the following screen:

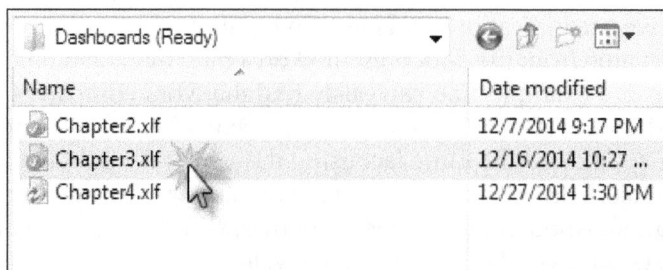

Now, let's add the US maps together:

1. Navigate to the **Maps** section under the **Components** panel.
2. Drag the **USA (continental)** map and drop it onto the canvas.

   We can see these steps in the following screenshot:

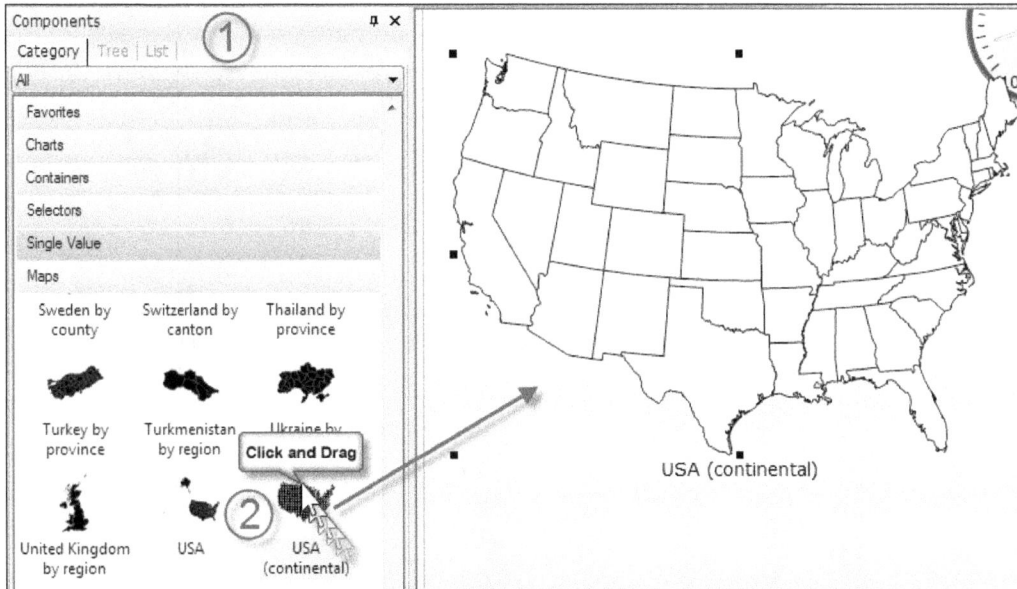

Now, let's link our USA map with our data about eFashion sales by state:

3. Select the **Map** sheet from the Excel model.
4. Make sure that the USA map is selected, and then navigate to the **General** tab under the **Properties** panel.
5. Edit **Region Keys** by clicking on this edit icon: ✏️.
6. Change the Washington region key to DC.
7. Link the **Display Data** field with the **Map!$B$4:$C$11** data range.

We can see these steps here:

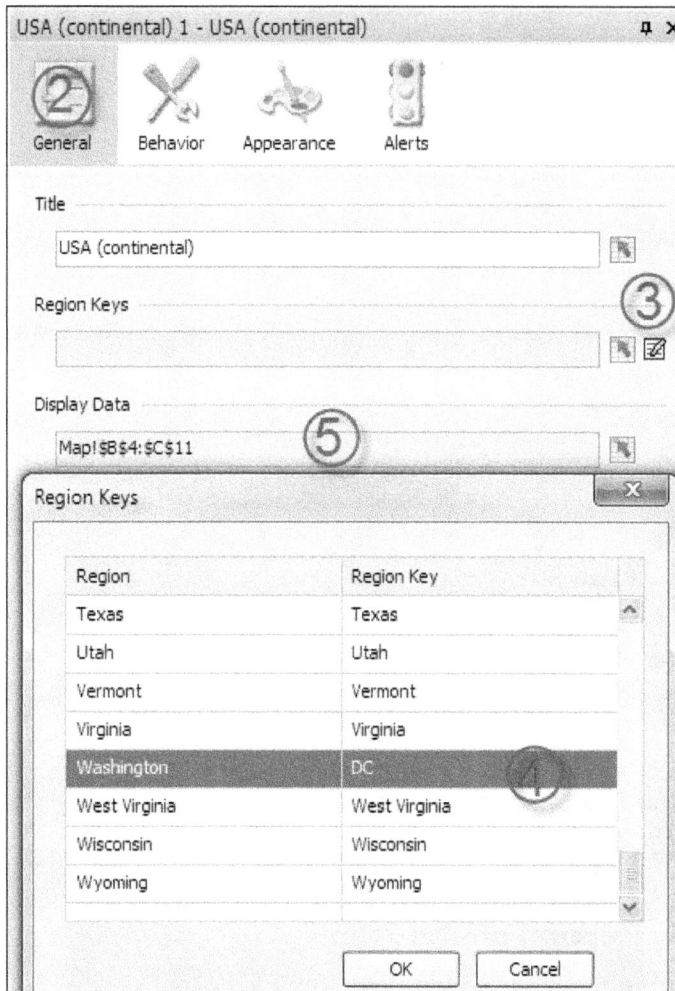

8. Click on the **Preview** button to see the map after linking it with the data. You can see it in the following screenshot:

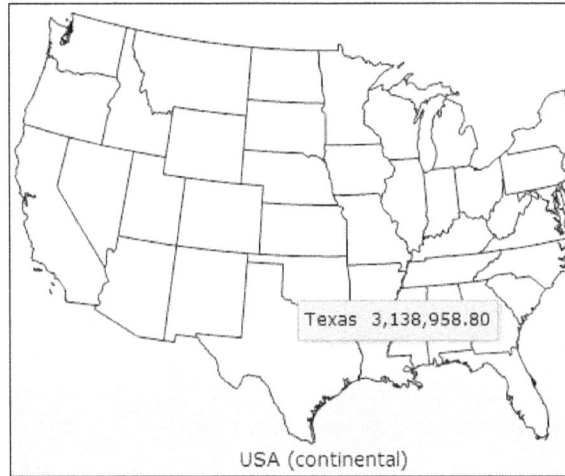

Before moving on to the next section, let's discuss some important terms related to maps:

- **Region keys**: Each map has a predefined set of regions. Each region has a name and a key. The map region's name can't be changed because it points to a location in the map, while the region keys are dynamic and can be adjusted as per our data. In our example, we changed the key for the Washington state from Washington to DC to match our data. We didn't need to make any other change because our data keys were matching with the right map region keys.

> The map region keys are case-sensitive and should exactly match your data region keys in order to be displayed correctly.

We can map the region keys to a range in your Excel model, but we need to make sure that our region keys' order and count matches the right order of region names and count, otherwise we will get a wrong mapping. We also need to note that the map of USA contains all the states, whereas we are displaying only eight states in our eFashion sales information.

Installing, configuring, and using the CMap plugin

CMap is a plugin provided by Centigon (http://cmapsanalytics.com/) to integrate Google maps with SAP BO Dashboards. The first thing we need to discuss is how to download and install this plugin. Then, you will learn how to create the same map of USA based on our eFashion sales information, but using the CMap plugin this time:

1. Go to http://cmapsanalytics.com/.

2. Navigate to **Products | CMaps Analytics | SAP Dashbords**.

3. Click on the **Download** button to download the trial version of the CMap plugin.

4. Fill in the form. Within a few seconds, you will receive an e-mail with the download link and your trial serial number.

   The page at http://cmapsanalytics.com/ is shown in this screenshot:

Now, we need to use **Add-On Manager** to install the CMap plugin:

1. Navigate to **File | Manage Add-Ons**.

2. Click on the **Install** button.

3. Navigate to the downloaded file, CMapsPluginMobile_4.2.0.xlx.

4. The program will ask you to save and exit, so do it.

You can see these steps in the following screenshot:

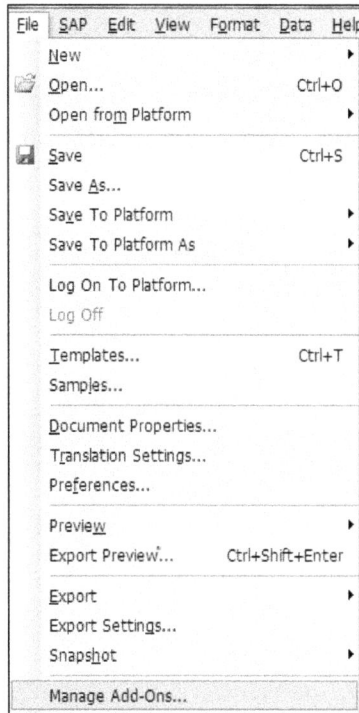

File	SAP	Edit	View	Format	Data	Help

New		▶
Open...		Ctrl+O
Open from Platform		▶
Save		Ctrl+S
Save As...		
Save To Platform		▶
Save To Platform As		▶
Log On To Platform...		
Log Off		
Templates...		Ctrl+T
Samples...		
Document Properties...		
Translation Settings...		
Preferences...		
Preview		▶
Export Preview...		Ctrl+Shift+Enter
Export		▶
Export Settings...		
Snapshot		▶
Manage Add-Ons...		

We can see the Add-On Manager in the following screenshot:

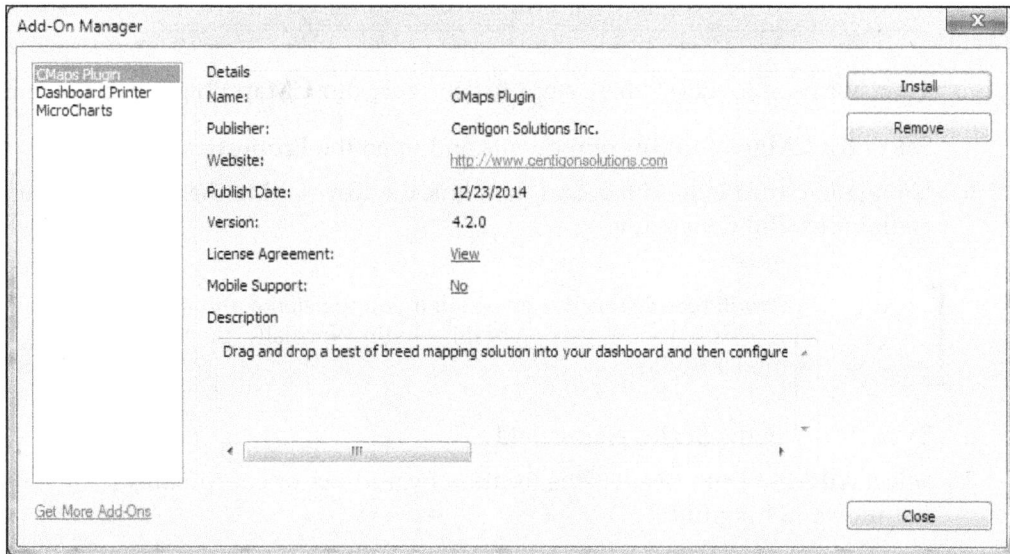

Add-On Manager

CMaps Plugin
Dashboard Printer
MicroCharts

Details

Name:	CMaps Plugin
Publisher:	Centigon Solutions Inc.
Website:	http://www.centigonsolutions.com
Publish Date:	12/23/2014
Version:	4.2.0
License Agreement:	View
Mobile Support:	No

Description

Drag and drop a best of breed mapping solution into your dashboard and then configure

Install

Remove

Get More Add-Ons

Close

Now, let's use the CMap plugin to create the same map that we created using built-in dashboard components:

1. Open the **Components** panel.

2. Then, navigate to the **Maps** category.

3. Drag the **CMaps Plugin** components and drop them onto the canvases.

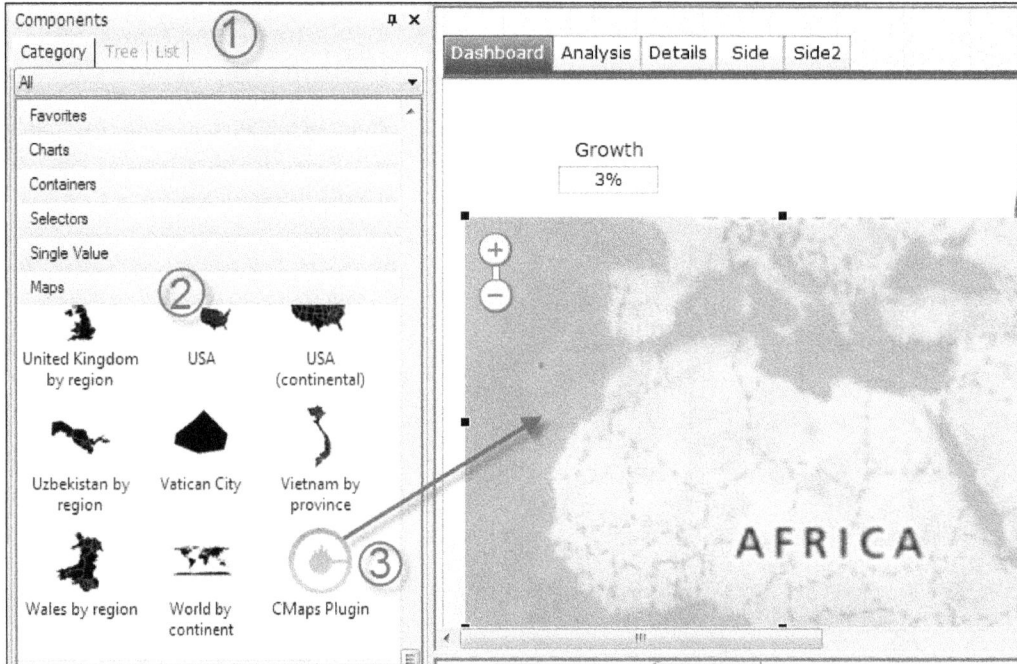

Then, we need to follow these steps to configure our **CMap Plugin** component:

4. Select the **CMaps Plugin** components and open the **Properties** panel.

5. Navigate to the **General** tab, and then link the **Key** field to the Excel cell that contains a valid CMap key.

> You will receive this key by e-mail if you registered and have downloaded a trial version of this plugin. Normally, the trial period is 14 days.

6. Type sales in the **Series Name** field.

7. Select **Address Data** to enter the location by address or coordinates (latitude and longitude).

8. Select the **Map!$B$4:$B$11** range in the **Address/Lag, Lng Range** field.

9. Select the following **Map!$B$4:$B$11** range in the **Labels** field and **Map!$C$4:$C$11** in the **Values** field.

You can see these steps here:

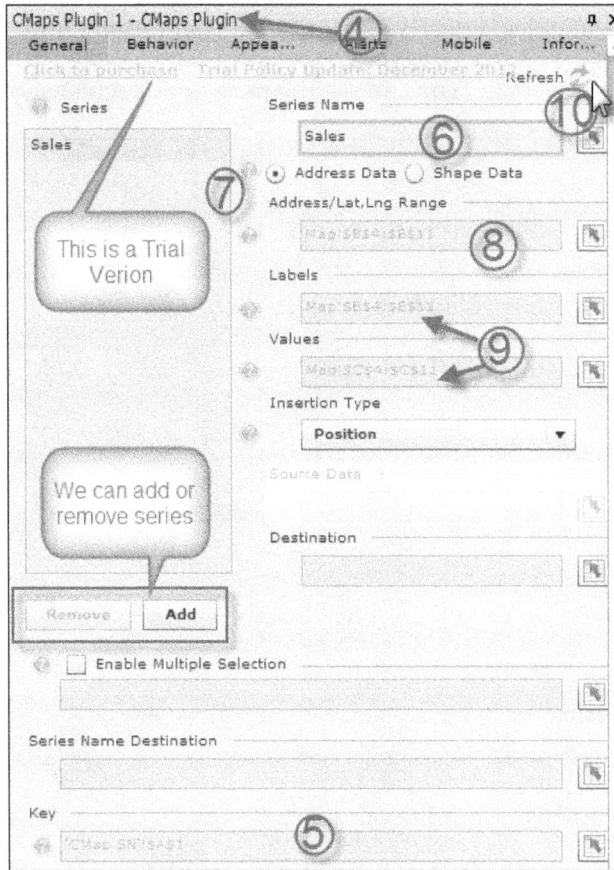

Before we conclude this part, let's discuss some important concepts:

- **Address data/shape data**: There are two modes that we can use to represent our data using the CMaps plugin. The first mode is **Address Data**, which can deal with address-related information in various formats such as zip code, city, state, or coordinates. Coordinates can be defined as a latitude and longitude separated by a comma (,). We can use the **Shape Data** mode to display polygons and lines that can be used to specify areas on the map. We may have a shape file that divides the map of USA into, for example, five main regions (central, eastern, western, northern, and southern).

> For more information about these two options, refer to the **Tutorial** tab under http://centigonknowledge.com/, or click on the question mark icon beside address data. You can also check for any restriction on address recognition for the location that you want on their site.

- **Labels** and **values**: These fields will be used to display the associated label and value with each address or coordinate. Each location will be presented as a point on the map. You can see the map in this screenshot:

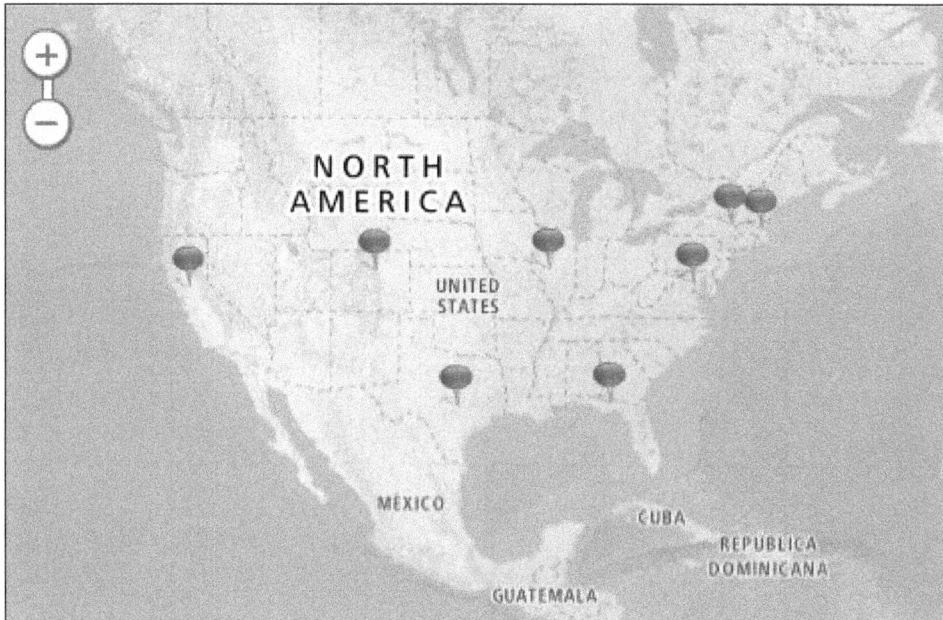

Now, let's add a shape data series to our map:

1. Select the CMap component and navigate to the **General** tab under **Properties** panel.

2. Create a new Shape series by clicking on the **Add** button under **Series**.

3. Select the **Shape Data** mode and click on **Shape Data** Options.

4. From the **Shape Options** window, select **Shape File URL**.

5. Select the following Excel range (list of states): **Map!$B$4:$B$11** in Shape **File Order Keys** under the **Data to Shape Linking & Visibility** section.

6. Select this Excel range: **Map!$C$4:$C$11** in **Data Order Keys** under the **Data to Shape Linking & Visibility** section. Click on **OK**.

7. Map the **Single Shape File URL** field to **Map!$B$1**, which contains the URL for the USA shape file ( ).

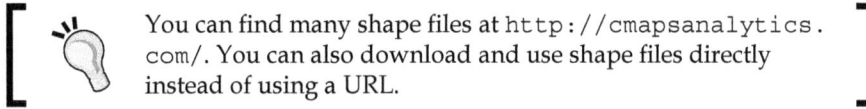

> You can find many shape files at `http://cmapsanalytics.com/`. You can also download and use shape files directly instead of using a URL.

8. Map **Labels** and **Values** field to the **Map!$B$4:$B$11** and **Map!$C$4:$C$11** ranges.

9. Click on the **Refresh** button.

You can find the steps illustrated in the following screenshot:

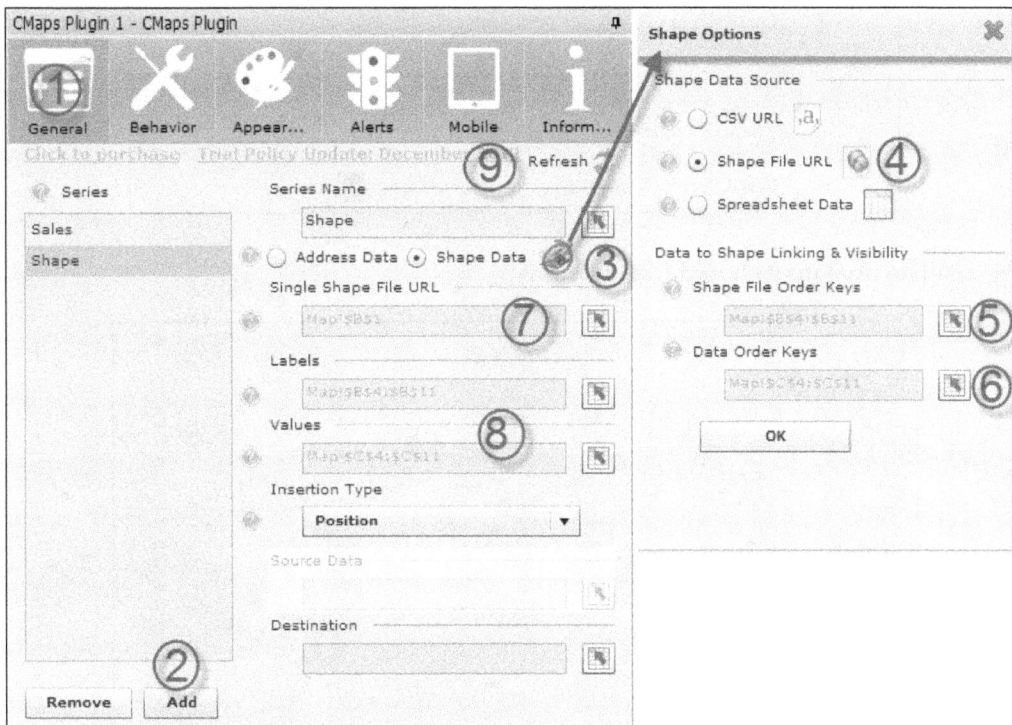

To enhance the map's visibility, we may need to adjust the **Transparency** setting for the shape series:

1. Navigate to the **Appearance** tab under the **CMap Component** properties.

2. Go to the **Icon** section and select the **Shape** series.

3. Set the **Transparency** setting to **75**.

You can see these steps marked in this screenshot:

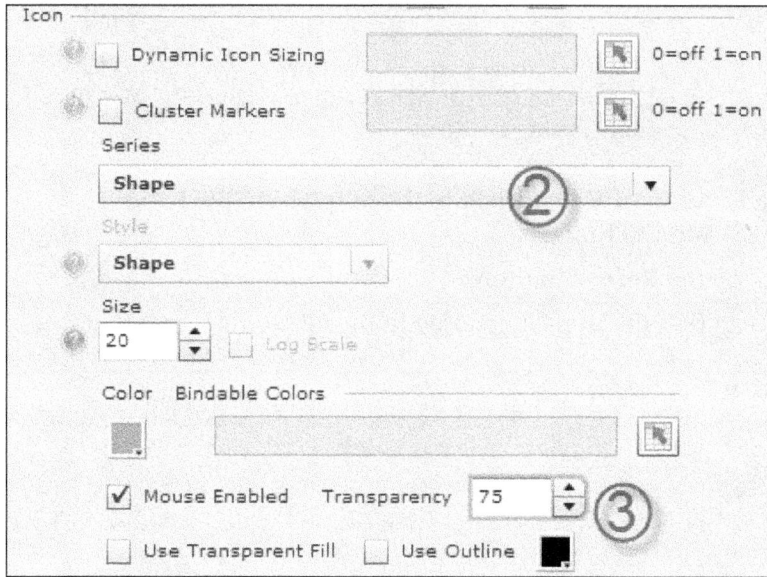

The final map should look like this:

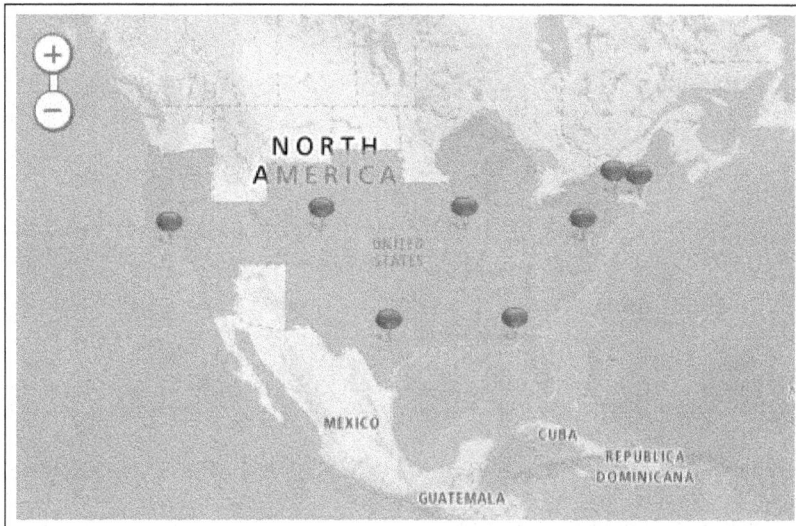

You will learn how to configure map alerts and how to use the insertion feature for maps in the following chapters. All that we need to focus on here is how to add and configure map components—either built-in maps or CMap plugin components.

Using other SAP BO Dashboard components

There are many other components that can't be categorized as charts, selectors, maps, or containers. These dashboard components are grouped under the **Others** category, and, as we will see, there is no relation among them. You will learn how to use other dashboard components in this section, such as:

- Calendar
- The trend icon
- The trend analyzer
- The print, reset, and local scenario buttons
- The history and source data components.

As mentioned before, dashboard components are divided into categories under the **Components** panel to make it easy to navigate and select the required dashboard component. We have the following main categories:

- **Charts**
- **Selectors**
- **Single Value**
- **Maps**
- **Other**

You can see the main component categories in the following screenshot:

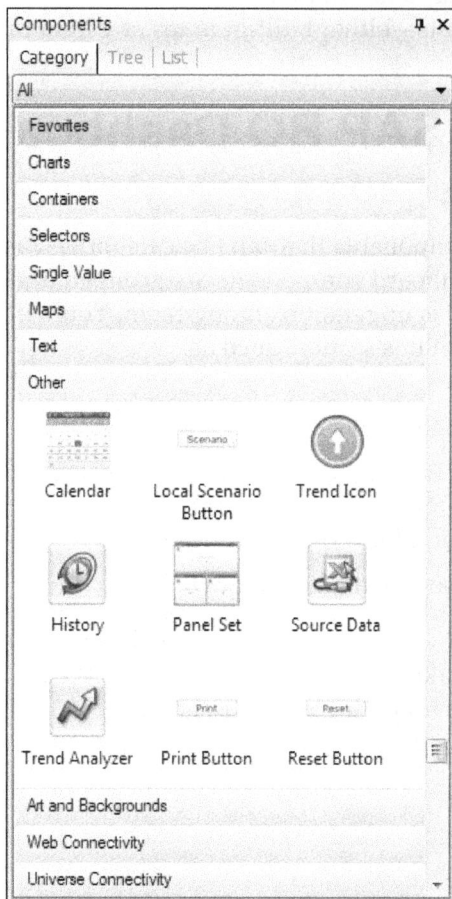

All the functions that cannot be performed under the existing/mentioned categories are stated under the **Other** dashboard components. Before we start discussing the various dashboard components under the **Other** category, we need to organize our dashboard.

As a best practice, we should give a unique name to each dashboard component in the **Object Browser** panel. We also need to hide and lock the completed and finalized components. As of now, we have a pie chart behind the combination chart and a built-in map of USA behind the CMap dashboard component.

To do this, let's follow these steps:

1. Navigate to **Object Browser**.
2. Rename the dashboard components as displayed in the following table:

Old component name	New component name
Pie Chart 1	**Sales by Product**
Combination Chart 1	**Sales and Quantity by Product**
Bubble Chart 1	**Managers Performance**
Gauge 1	**Sales Current Month**
Horizontal Progress Bar 1	**YTD Sales**
Value 1	**Value 1**
USA (continental) 1	**Sales by State**
CMaps Plugin 2	**Sales by State CMaps**

You will see **Object Browser** like this after the modifications:

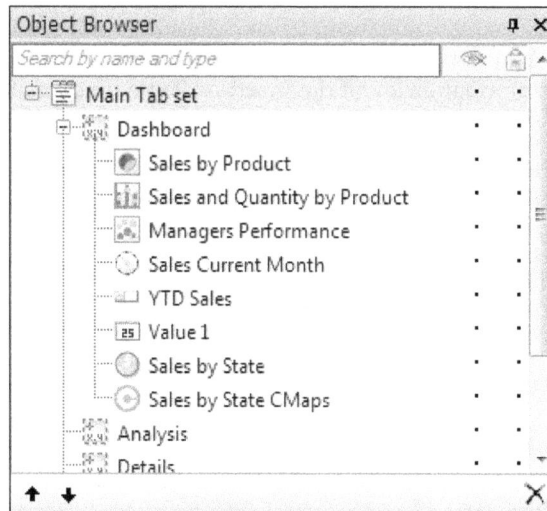

Now, let's start exploring the other dashboard components.

Using a calendar dashboard component

Calendar components are perfect for date input as they provide a calendar interface for selecting a specific date. They also provide easy navigation between months and years. The only disadvantage of this component is its large size. Therefore, we should use the dynamic visibility option to hide and show it as per requirements.

A **Calendar** component can be used to specify only one date. If we have a date range (a start date and an end date), then we may use two calendar components to define the period.

As we don't have any calendar component in our eFashion dashboard prototype, we will create a side example for the **Calendar** component:

1. Activate the **Side2** tab and drag a **Calendar** component into the canvas.

2. Navigate to the **General** tab under the **Properties** panel.

3. Enter **Snapshot Date** in the **Title** field.

4. Change **Insertion Type** to **Date**.

> You can click on ⏣ , the information icon, to get more information about the **Insertion Type** functionality.

5. Link Destination to the following Excel cell **'Side Examples'!$B$2**, **Month Destination** to **'Side Examples'!$C$2**, and **Year Destination** to **'Side Examples'!$D$2**.

   You can see these steps here:

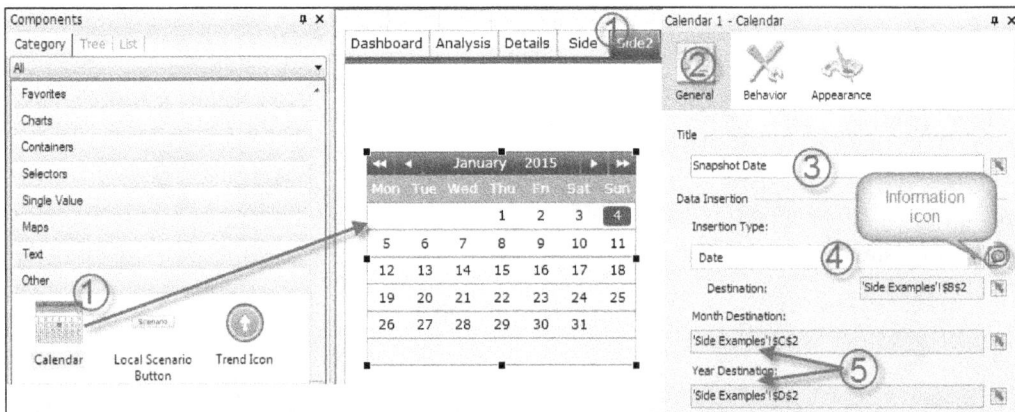

You can see the information box for **Insertion Type** in the following screenshot:

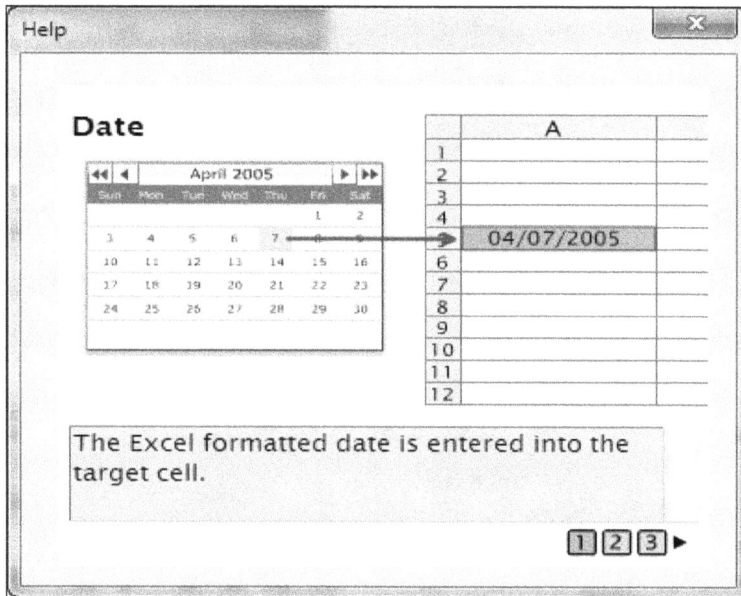

Now, let's adjust the behavior properties of our calendar component:

1. Navigate to the **Behavior** tab.
2. Select Use Custom Date as **Default Date**.
3. Link Day to **'Side Examples'!$B$3**, Month to **'Side Examples'!$C$3**, and Year to **'Side Examples'!$D$3**.
4. Tick the box beside **Enable Calendar Limits**.

You can see these steps in this screenshot:

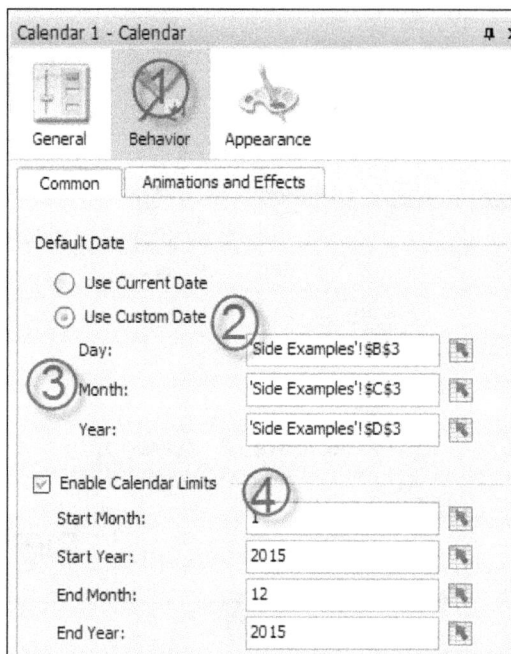

5. Now, add three text labels and map them to the **'Side Examples'!$B$3**, **'Side Examples'!$C$3**, and **'Side Examples'!$D$3** calendar destination Excel cells. Then, click on **Preview** to see a calendar like this:

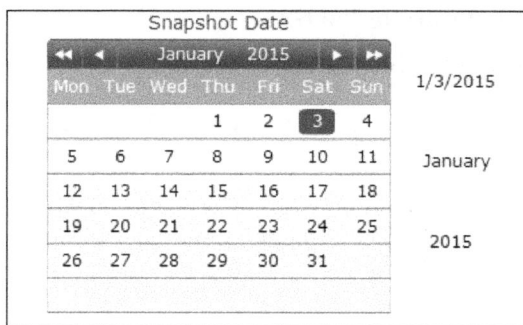

Before we end this section, let's discuss some calendar functionalities that we've used in our example:

- **Date/day insertion type**: We can choose to insert the entire calendar date or only the day portion of the date. For example, if we select *7-jan-2015*, the date insertion will be *7-Jan-2015*, while the day insertion will be only *7*.

- **Calendar default date**: This can be the current date, and it can be customized to a specific date. Normally, in a data warehouse implementation, the most recent snapshot date is the previous day's data because batch jobs and ETL jobs run overnight. We use the *Today()-1* Excel function to get the previous day's date and to set it as the default calendar date.

- **Enable calendar limits**: This can be used to limit the date navigation to a specific period. In our example, we limited the navigation to the current year.

> We can use the **Show Formula** option in Excel to display the formula entered in Excel cells.

You can see how **Show Formula** works in the following screenshot:

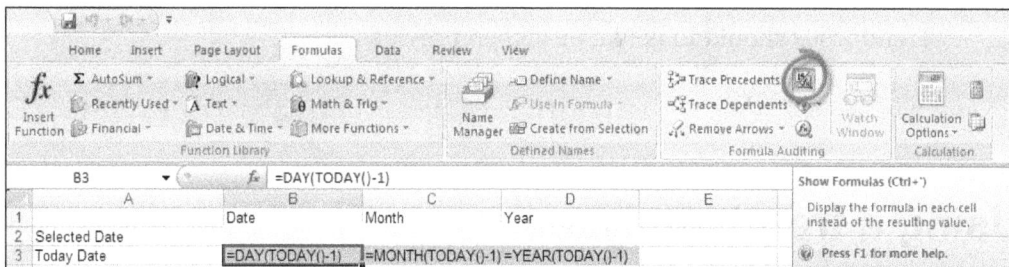

It is worth mentioning that the calendar is one of the selector components that we will discuss in detail in the next chapter.

Using the trend icon

The trend icon is one of my favorite dashboard components. It will display a blue up arrow if the linked value is positive, a yellow neutral sign if the value is zero, and a red down arrow if the value is negative. Let's try to create one:

1. Drag three **Trend Icon** dashboard components into the **Side2** tab set canvas.

2. Link the data field for the first trend icon to **'Side Examples'!$B$6**, the second to **'Side Examples'!$B$7**, and the last to **'Side Examples'!$B$8**.

We can customize only the Trend Icon's colors.

You can see one of the **Trend Icon** properties in this screenshot:

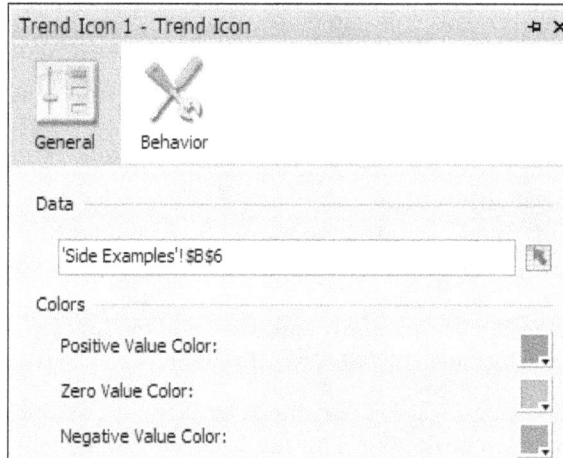

Trend icons should look like this when previewed:

Using a trend analyzer

A trend analyzer can help us show a trend of a data series, as well as forecasted trends based on historical data. The forecasted data is generated by many standard forecasting algorithms. These can be defined in the **Type** field in the trend analyzer component.

To test it, let's build the following side example, as we don't need a trend analyzer to build our eFashion dashboard:

1. Create a combination chart based and map the first data series (primary axes) to the sales information under the **Side Examples Excel** sheet.

2. Drag and drop the **Trend Analyzer** dashboard component onto the canvas.

3. Navigate to the **General** tab under the **Trend Analyzer** properties panel.

4. Link the **Data** field to **'Side Examples'!$B$12:$E$12**.

5. Select **linear** in the **Trend/Regression Type**.

6. Enter the **'Side Examples'!$B$13:$F$13** range in the **AnalyzedDataDestination** field.

7. Make sure that **NumberofForecastedPeriod** is set to **1**.

8. Select the combination chart again and create new series called **trend**.

9. Map the trend series values to **'Side Examples'!$B$13:$F$13**.

10. Make sure that the trend series is set as secondary axes.

Some of these steps are shown in this screenshot:

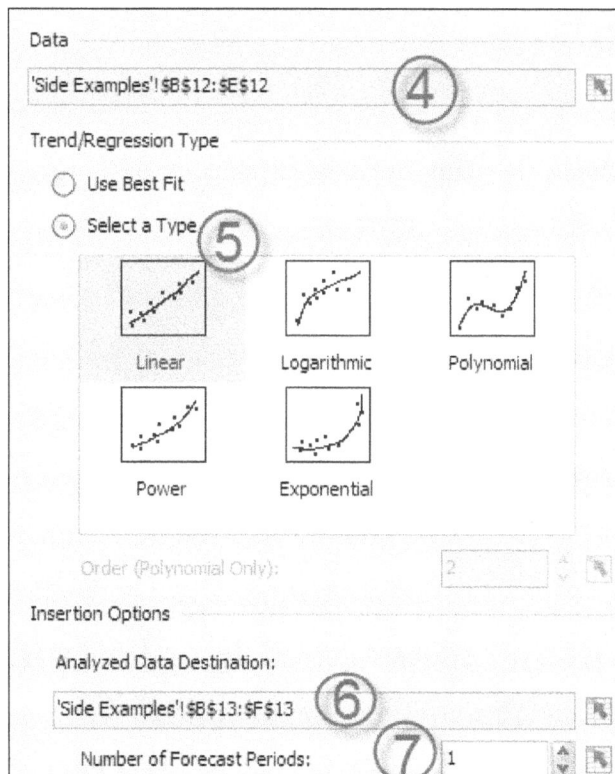

You can see the combination chart series in the following screenshot:

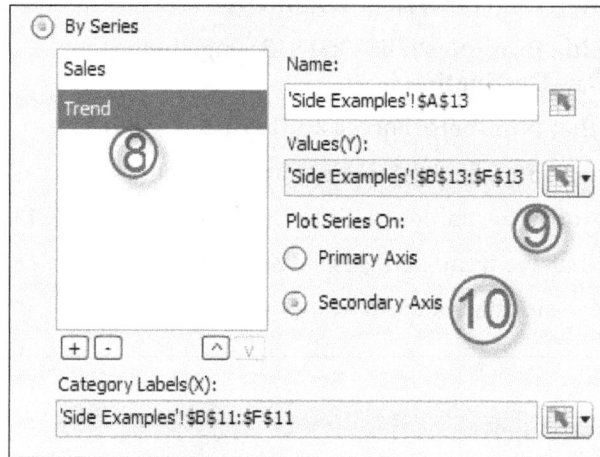

The line column chart output is shown here:

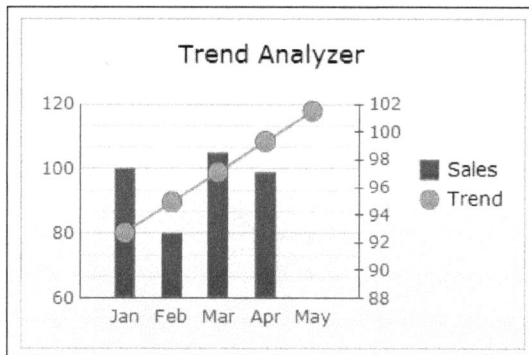

Using the print, reset, and local scenario buttons

The **Print** button can be used to print your dashboard. It is really a basic **Print** button, and there is not much to talk about here, but if you want a better alternative, you can go with the third-party add-on print button developed by Data Savvy.

> You can find more information about dashboard printed developed by Data Savvy on `http://datasavvytools.com/products/sap-tools/dashboard-printer`.

The **Reset** button will simply reset everything to the default initial state as if you have closed the dashboard and opened it again.

The local scenario button can be used for the **Save**, **Load**, **Delete**, and **Set Default** scenarios. For example, we can use a slider to implement a what-if scenario, and to save and load it, we can use this **Scenario** button. You can see the available **Scenario** button options in the following screenshot.

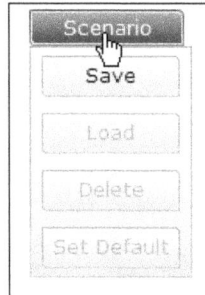

Using the history and source data dashboard components

The history component can be used to track data history. The component will store the previous values of a single value, and so, you can track the trend of that value. To set up a history component, you need to define a data cell, which will contains the dynamic changing metric, and a data destination range, which will contain the historical records of the data cell. We can set up the history component to capture a data cell value in time intervals or when data is changed.

The source data component can be used to select a value, row, or column from the source range to insert it into a target cell, based on an index cell. So, for example, if we have a source data range of four cells, then we can select one cell from that range to insert in a target cell based on the current index value.

> There is no specific use case for the source data component.

Let's use a side example to explain these two components, as we don't need to use **History** or **Source Data** components in our eFashion dashboard project:

1. Drag one of each of the following dashboard components into the **side2** tab under the current tab set:
   ◦ History
   ◦ Source Data
   ◦ Line chart
   ◦ Spinner

   The canvas should look like what is shown in this screenshot:

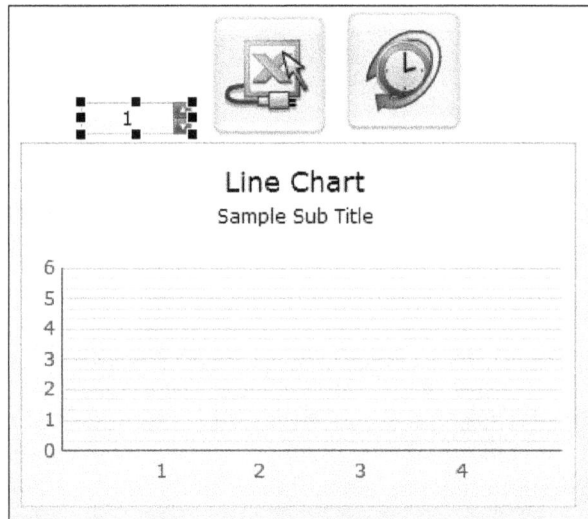

2. Select the **Source Data** component and navigate to the **General** tab under the **Properties** panel.

3. Make sure that **Insertion Type** is set to **Value**.

4. Link the **Source Data** field to the **'Side Examples'!$B$17:$E$17** Excel range, and the **Destination** field to the **'Side Examples'!$B$18** Excel cell.

5. Navigate to the **Behavior** tab and link the **Selected Item Index** field to **'Side Examples'!$B$19**.

You can see the **Source Data** component's configuration steps in the following screenshot:

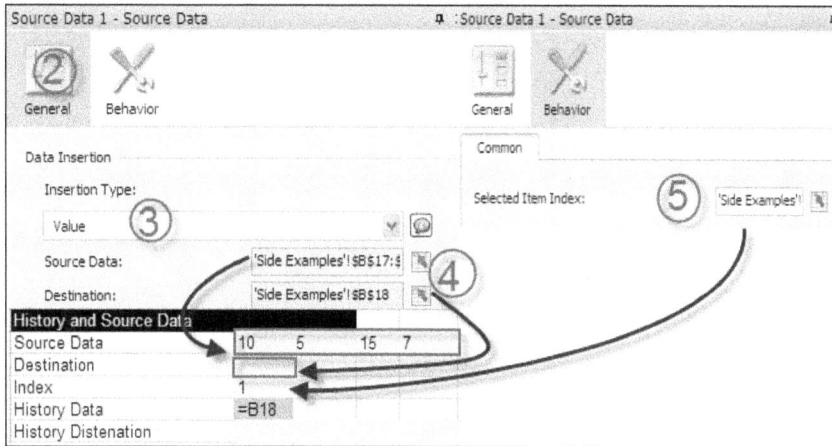

Now, let's configure the **History** component:

6. Select the **History** component and navigate to the **General** tab under the Properties panel.

7. Link the **Data** field to the **'Side Examples'!$B$20** Excel cell.

8. Then link the **Data Destination** field to the **'Side Examples'!$B$21:$E$21** Excel range.

9. Make sure that the **When Value Changed** option is selected.

The steps for configuring the **History** component are displayed in this screenshot:

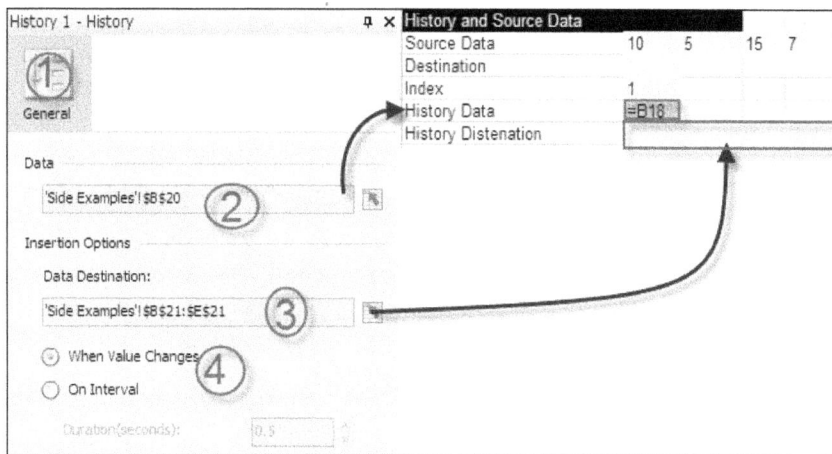

10. Finally, we need to configure our chart to display the **'Side Examples'!$B$21:$E$21** history destination range, and the spinner to change the **Source Data** index value **'Side Examples'!$B$19**. The final result should look like this:

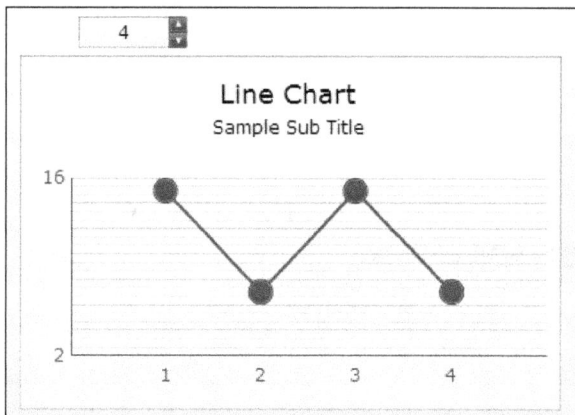

Before concluding this section, let's discuss the main features of the Source Data component:

- **Insertion Type**: We can use one of the three insertion types in the Source Data component. These are value, row, and column. We will discuss insertion types in detail in *Chapter 6, Advanced Interactive Analysis with Dashboards*. You can use the information icon, as described earlier, to learn how to use the Source Data component, as shown in this screenshot:

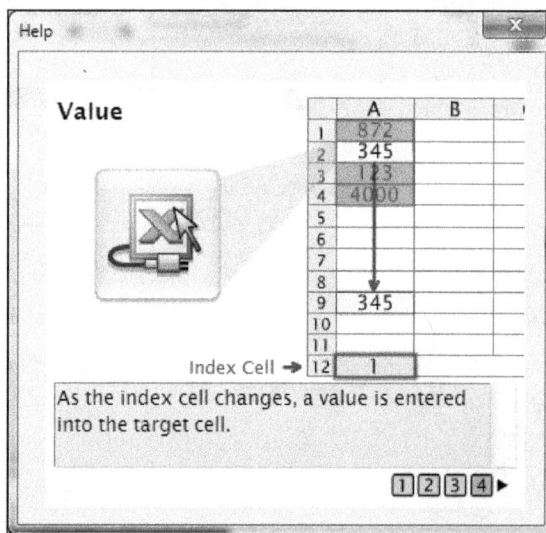

- **Selected Index Item**: This cell can be used to decide which cell, row, or column will be inserted into the source data destination.

We also need to discuss how the **History** component is used in this example. The line chart data is linked to the destination of the **History** component. This will allow us to see how the **History** data will change when we change the spinner value. The spinner value will control the index field for the source data. So, the first data to be entered in the history data field is **10** because the default spinner value is 1. When we change the spinner value to **2**, it will change the source data index to **2**, so it will insert the second value into the source data, which is 5. This will change the value of the history data, and so the history component will detect the change. This is because we set the insertion of historical data to **When Data Changed**. This will insert a new value into the historical destination range, will plot another point on the line chart, and so on.

Now that we've completed this section, we will talk about some important third-party plugins.

Using other third-party plugins

In this section, we will discuss the following third-party plugins:

- Dash printer
- Micro chart

Using a dash printer

Dash printer is a plugin developed by Data Savvy. It enables the end user to print their dashboard. This plugin will help you select an area to print, annotate, and then share flexibly, as you can see in the following screenshot:

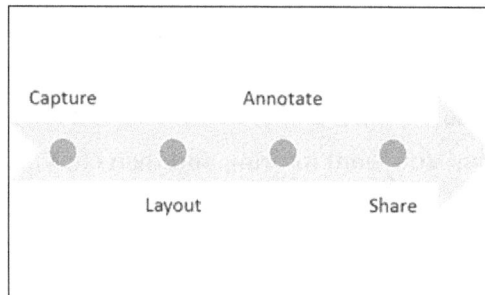

You can register and download it from the **Products** section at `http://datasavvytools.com/`. After you've downloaded the plugin, you can install it in exactly the same way we installed the CMap plugin.

Let's create a side example to learn how to use this plugin. Make sure that you've installed the plugin before you continue reading:

1. Navigate to the **Data Savvy Tools** category under the **Component** panel.
2. Then, we drag and drop **Dashboard Printer** onto our **Side2** tab canvas under the **Current** tab set.

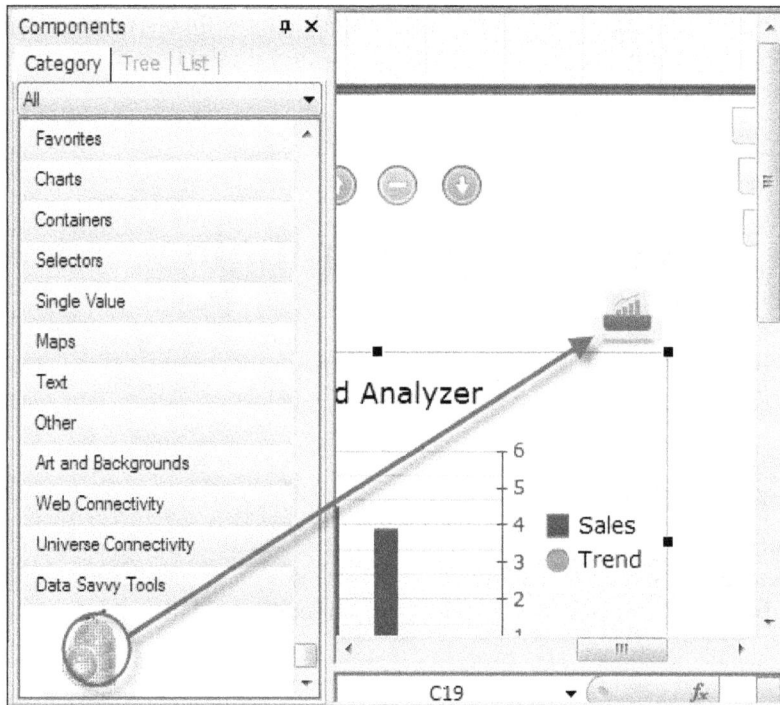

3. Click on the **Preview** button and then on the **Print** icon.
4. Select the area that you want to print, and then click on **Preview** (this is the printer preview).

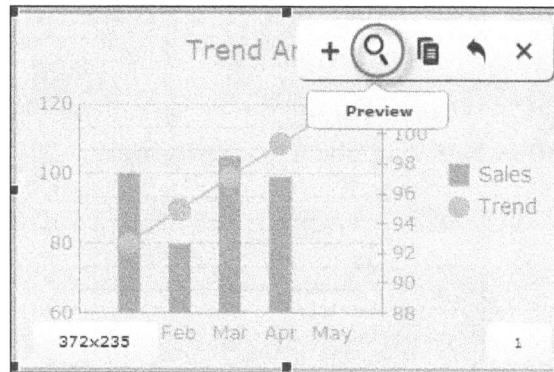

5. Check how the selected area will look after printing. You're also able to annotate on it.

Besides printing, you can also share it.

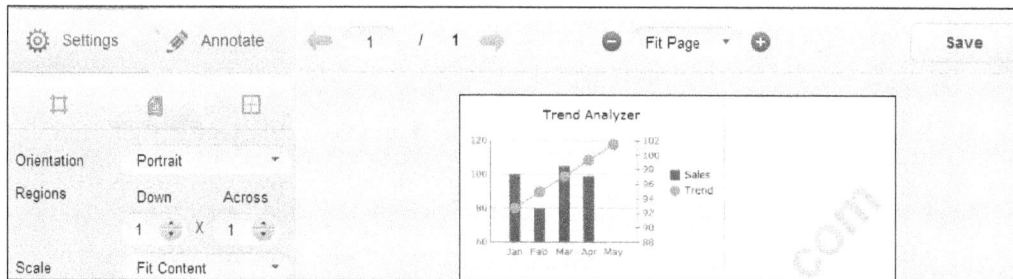

Using Micro charts

Micro charts is a plugin developed by Inovista (http://www.inovista.com/) to help dashboard developers create Micro charts. This is one of many plugins provided by Inovista, but we'll take this one as an example here.

> There are many other dashboard plugins provided by Inovista, such as SVG components, organization chart, and text and shape suites.
>
> Micro charts can be used to display charts in a small area.

We can download a trial version of the Micro chart plugin from the Inovista site and install it using the add-on manager just as we did before:

1. Navigate to the **Inovista Micro Charts** category under the **Component** panel.

2. Drag a **MicroBarChart** component into the canvas.

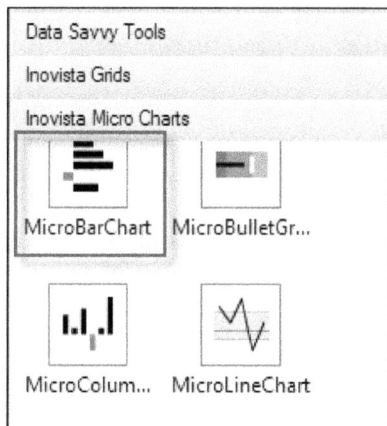

3. Select the **MicroBarChart** component and navigate to the **General** tab under the **Properties** panel.

4. Link the **Value** field to the **'Side Examples'!$B$24:$E$24** Excel range.

5. Make sure that the color selected for **Negative Line** is red and the checkbox is selected.

You can see some of the preceding steps marked here:

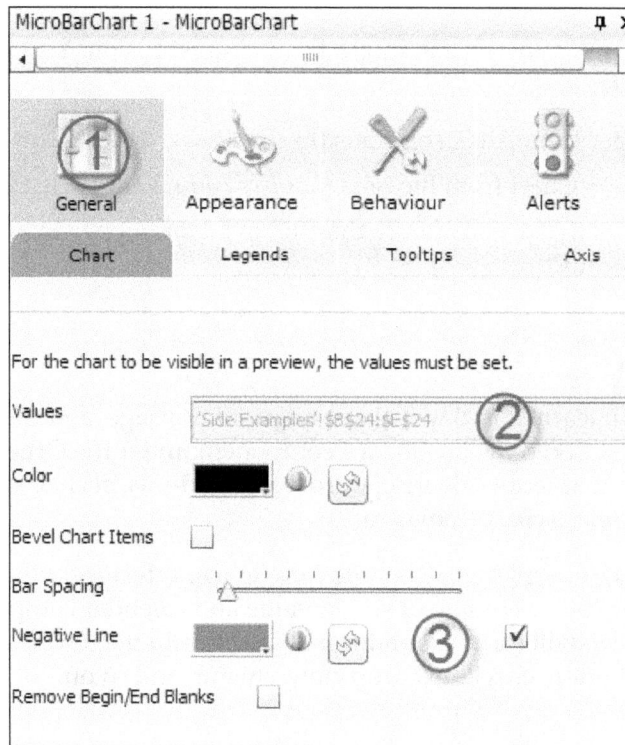

You can see the Micro chart in the following screenshot:

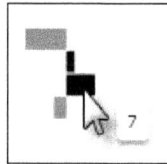

Now, it's time to save your dashboard in your development folder, enabling you to use it for exercises that we will cover in the upcoming chapters.

There are a number of add-ons that might be of interest to you. You can explore them at the following sites:

- RangeFinder from Altek solutions (`http://www.alteksolutions.com/`)
- Organization Chart from Inovista (`http://www.inovista.com/`)
- There are many add-ons (more than 40) available from visualbi (`http://visualbi.com/`)

Summary

In this chapter, you learned in detail about maps, their usage, and the CMap plugin. Then, we explored the dashboard component under the **Other** category. We concluded the chapter by covering third-party add-ons, such as dash printer (Data Savvy) and micro chart (Inovista).

In the next chapter, we will dive deep into **how to use selectors**, which was highlighted during the discussion of single-value and calendar components earlier. However, we will focus on traditional selectors in the next chapter, such as the radio button, checkbox, drop-down menu, and so on.

5
Interactive Analysis with Dashboards

Dashboards are used to display information, so as to help the end user analyze data in a simpler way. We have already discussed how to use charts, single-value components, maps, and other components in the last four chapters. In this chapter, you will learn how to use selectors to help dashboard end users interact with the dashboard.

Users will be able to select a value, which will subsequently trigger an action. For example, with triggers, users can change chart data, or hide or show a dashboard component by choosing the relevant selectors.

As selectors impact dashboards directly, mastering manipulation of selectors is very important for us. We will cover it in detail here, dedicating a complete chapter to it. Our approach will be to revisit traditional selectors, such as radio buttons and checkboxes, which we are already familiar with. Then, we will take a detailed look at all the new selectors, such as the fish eye and the sliding picture menu. We will also take a look at available insertion types and their usage.

However, there are only a few selectors that allow users to select multiple values. You have already learned how to use a single-value component to interact with dashboard end users, such as spinners and sliders. You have also learned how to use the calendar component to take an input value from users in *Chapter 4*, *Using Maps and Other Dashboard Components*. Selectors are another type of dashboard component. They allow end users to interact with our dashboards, but in a more advanced way, as we will see later.

In this chapter, we will be:

- Using traditional selectors, such as radio buttons and comboboxes
- Displaying data in a tabular layout
- Using advanced selectors, such as a sliding picture and fisheye menus
- Using other selectors, such as icons and filter

Using traditional selectors

We all know what traditional selectors are, and we are also familiar with their usage. In this section, we will discuss the following selectors:

- Radio button
- Combobox (drop-down menu)
- Checkbox
- Lists

Using radio buttons

A radio button allows you to choose only a single value. In this section, you will learn how to toggle between the USA built-in map, and the USA CMap that we created in the previous chapter. In the next chapter (*Chapter 6, Advanced Interactive Analysis with Dashboards*), you will learn how to use and link the dynamic visibility feature for both the maps with the selected value (output of the selector).

> Radio buttons are better with small numbers of labels, while a combobox is better when we have a large number of labels.

First, we need to open the latest dashboard file that we saved—Chapter4.xlf, in the Development folder. Alternatively, you can open it from the Dashboards (Ready) folder if you didn't execute or finish the practices of *Chapter 4, Using Maps and Other Components*. You can find both the folders under the example Code folder, as displayed in this screenshot:

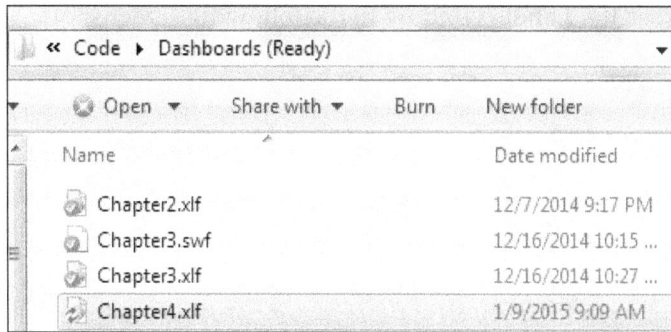

Save the file as Chapter5.xlf, and follow these steps to add the radio button:

1. Select the **Dashboard** tab under the **Tab** set.
2. Navigate to the **Selectors** category under the **Components** panel.
3. Drag and drop the **Radio Button** component onto the canvas.

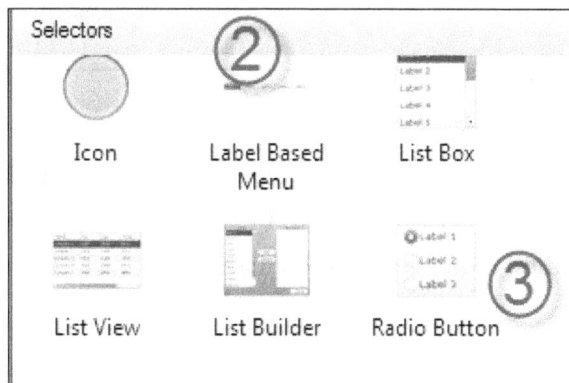

4. Navigate to the **General** tab under the **Properties** panel.
5. Link the **Labels** field to the **Selectors!$B$2:$B$3** Excel range.

> You can use , the edit label icon, to open the **Labels** window and enter labels manually.

You can see the **Labels** window in the following screenshot:

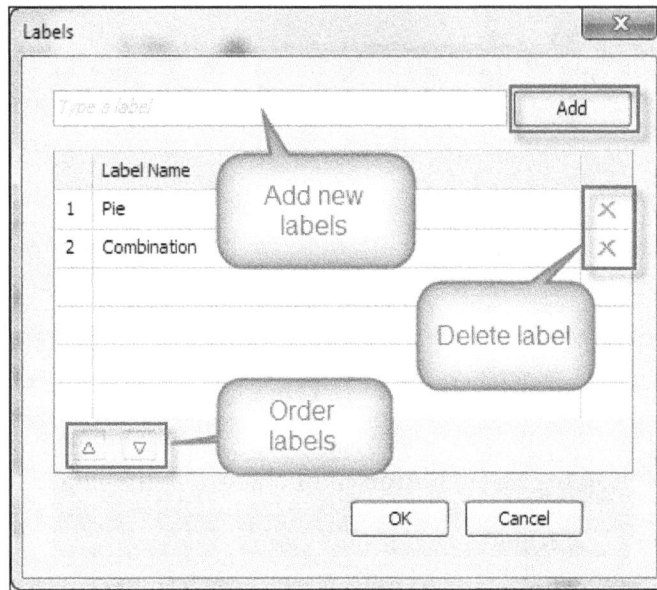

6. Select **Label** in **Insertion Type**.
7. Link the Destination field to the **Selectors!$B$4** Excel cell.
8. Select **Interaction Only** option from **Insert On:** property.
9. Select **Horizontal** in the **Orientation** area.

You can see these steps in this screenshot:

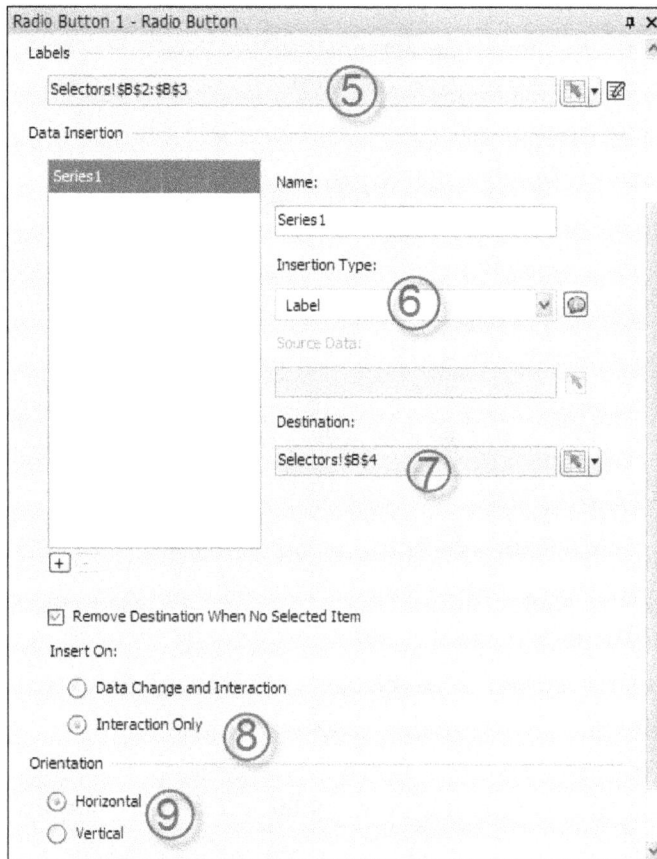

The radio button should look like this:

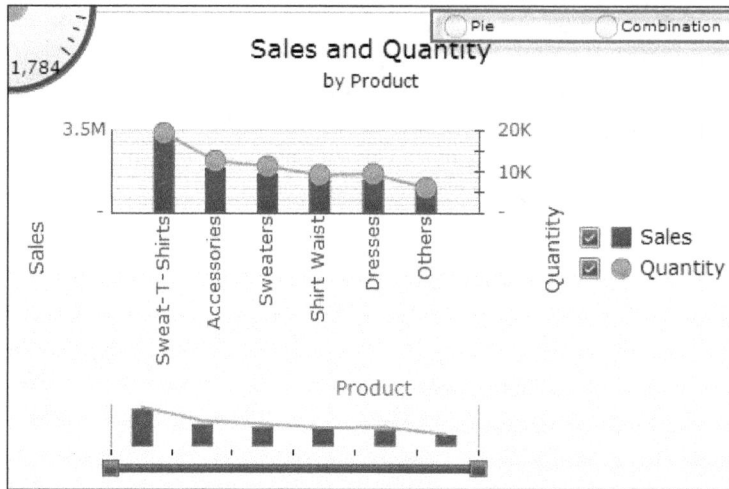

Now, let's apply some enhancements to our radio button:

1. Make sure that **Radio Button** is selected, and navigate to the **Behavior** tab under the **Properties** panel.

2. Make sure that **Type:** for the selected item is **Label** and **Item** is **Label1**.

3. Navigate to the **Layout** tab under **Appearance**, and uncheck the **Enable Background** option.

4. Set **Marker Size** to **14** and the horizontal and vertical margins to **2** and **4** respectively.

You can see these steps in the following screenshot:

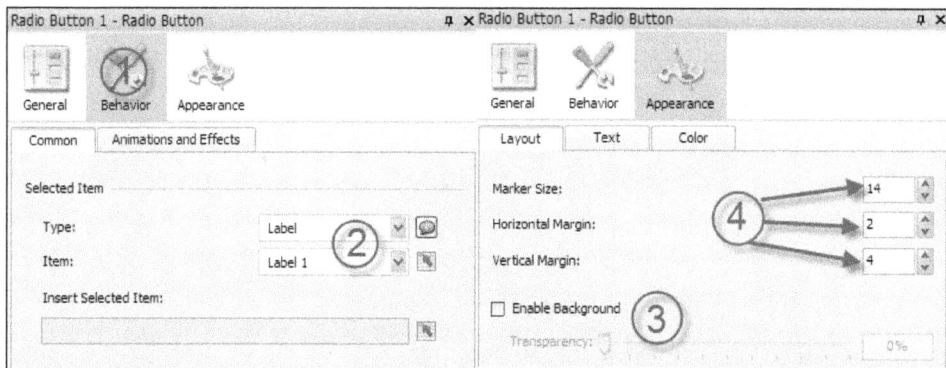

The radio button, after this enhancement, looks like what is shown in this screenshot:

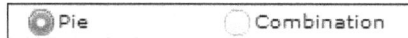

In the next chapter, we will link the dynamic visibility feature of the pie and combination charts with the radio button destination cell, so that we can detect whether we choose to display a pie or combination chart.

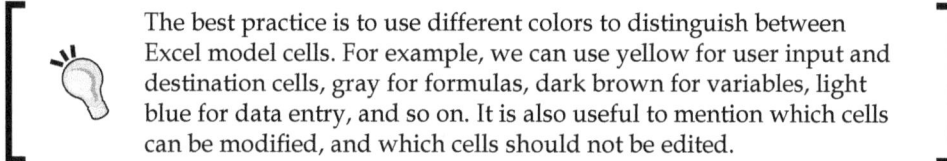

> The best practice is to use different colors to distinguish between Excel model cells. For example, we can use yellow for user input and destination cells, gray for formulas, dark brown for variables, light blue for data entry, and so on. It is also useful to mention which cells can be modified, and which cells should not be edited.

You can see the Excel color legend and the radio button's Excel range in the following screenshot:

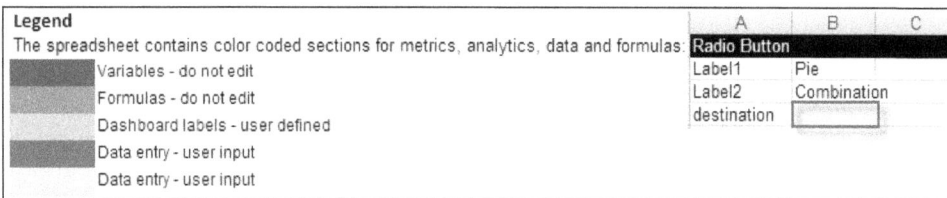

Before completing this section, let's discuss some of the radio button's features that we used in the previous example.

Orientation

In the orientation, we can select **Horizontal** to display the radio button labels horizontally (side by side), or vertically (on top of each other).

Insert On

We can configure the selector to trigger the predefined insertion based on **Data Change and Interaction** or **Interaction Only**. The **Interaction Only** option will trigger the defined insertion if the end user selects a new selector value. The **Data Change and Interaction** option will trigger the defined insertion if the bound selector data changes or a new selector value is selected by the user. "Data change" means that if we link the radio button labels to a specific Excel range and the value of the label changes, the insertion will be triggered when the **Data Change and Interaction** option is selected, even if the user didn't change the current selector value.

Insertion types

Insertion types is a complex topic, and it will require some time to master. So, we will use different insertion types with the selectors that we will be describing in the remaining sections in this chapter. We can also use the information icon to get help on how to use insertion types. We have many insertion types, as follows:

- **Position**: This will insert the position of the selected label in the destination cell. For example, if we select the first label, it will insert *1*.

  We can see the information window for position insertion in the following screenshot:

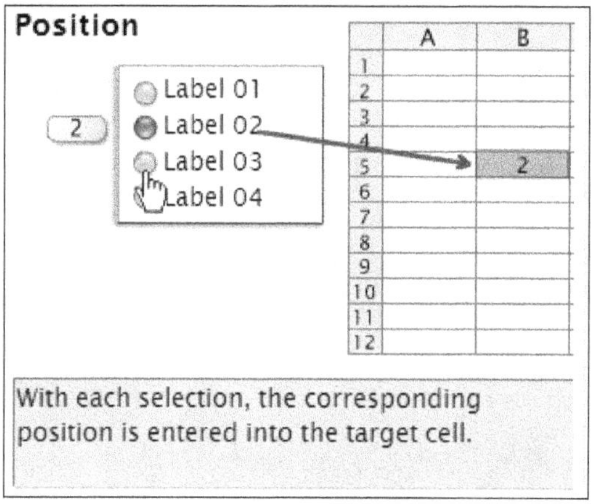

- **Label**: This will insert the label of the selected one in the destination cell. In our example, if we select **Pie** from the radio button, it will insert the label pie in the destination cell.

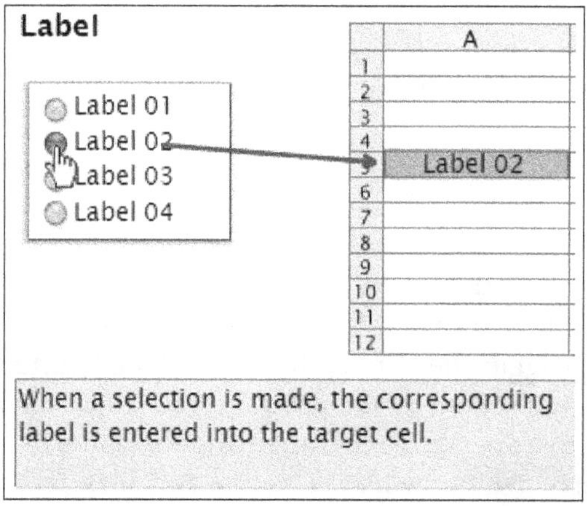

- **Value**: We don't need to specify source data for the position and label data insertions. Here, we will define a source range of Excel cells that match the number of selector labels. For example, if we have a selector with two labels, we should define a source for two cells. The value insertion will insert the first value in the range into the destination cell if the first label is selected, insert the second value if the second label is selected, and so on.

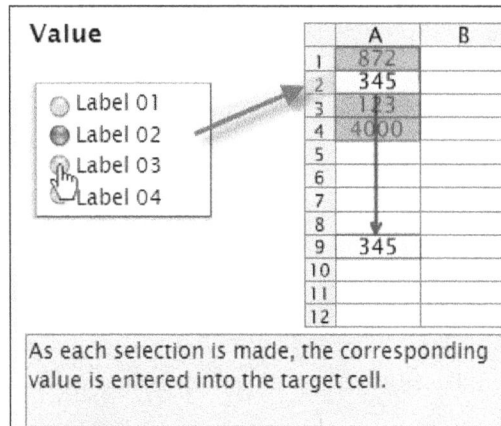

- **Row**: This insertion type is the same as the value type, but instead of defining a source range of Excel cells, we will define a source of Excel rows. The same rule applied to values also applies to row insertion, and so the number of source rows should match the number of the selector's labels. Another rule that we need to consider here is which destination for this insertion type should be a row. In this case, instead of a single cell, the number of cells in this row should match the number of cells in the source range rows.

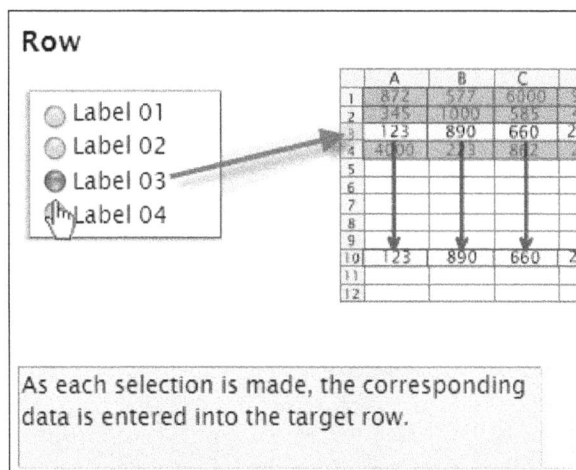

- **Column**: This is the same as row insertion, but instead of inserting rows we will insert columns in this type.

- **Status List**: In this insertion type, we define a destination range with the same size labels. For example, if we have four labels, then we should define a destination range with four cells. This insertion type will insert 1 in the corresponding cell for the selected label, and zeros in the other cells. For example, if we select the second label, (0, 1, 0, 0) will be inserted in the destination range.

As each selection is made, a "1" is inserted into the corresponding cell.

- **Filtered Rows**: This is a new insertion type that was not available in the earlier releases from SAP BO Dashboards. We can use this insertion type to filter rows in the source range based on the selected label, and insert them into the destination range.

As each selection is made, the item's filtered data is entered into the target rows.

Insertion types is a complex topic, and it will require some you will need time to master. So, we will use different insertion types with the selectors that we will be describing in the remaining sections in this chapter. We can also use the information icon to get help on how to use insertion types.

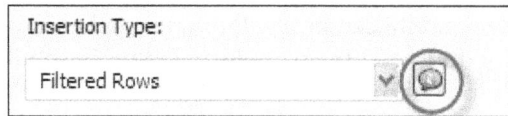

Selected item

This feature is common among almost all selectors. We can use it to set the default selected label. This feature is also very useful for creating a dynamic selector, by controlling the selector-chosen label dynamically at runtime, without any need for user interaction. For example, suppose we have two tabs that contain two different selector components that will execute the same action, and we want our change in the first tab to carry forward if we moved to the second tab, and so on. This can be done by linking both selectors to the same selected item. We can set the selected item type to the following:

- **Label**: This will use the label to dynamically set the current selected item.

- **Position**: This will use the position number to set the current selected label, based on its position.

- **Dynamic**: This is used to set the current selected label, based on the inserted label or position. You can use the information icon, which is circled in the following screenshot, for more details:

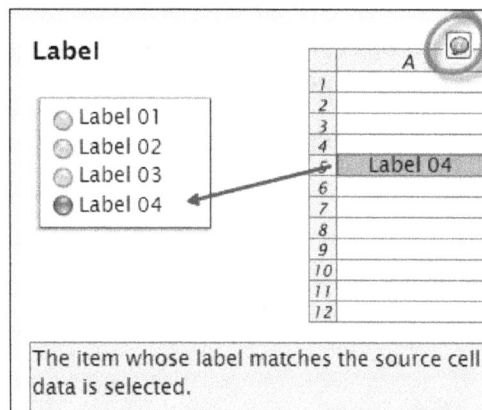

Finally, we want to differentiate between series insertion in the **General** tab, and **Insert Selected Item** in the **Behavior** tab. We can create multiple insertion series in the **General** tab, such as label, position, value, row, column, and so on. S series will trigger if the value of the selector is changed. Some of them don't need source data such as label and position, and others need source data such as value, row and column. The defined source data can be a cell or a range based on the insertion type. You may now ask, "Why do I need **Insert Selected Item** in the **Behavior** tab if I can do almost all insertion types from the series in the **General** tab?" The answer is that **Insert Selected Item** can be used to control the current selected value dynamically at runtime, because it is linked to the default and current selected labels in the selector.

Using comboboxes and list boxes

Comboboxes are also known as drop-down menus. The combobox is another traditional selector that can be used to save space, especially if you have a huge list of values to select from. This is because it will display the list of values only when the end user wants to select a value.

[The best scenario to use combobox components is when you have more than four labels to select from.]

As part of our eFashion dashboard project, we need to create three comboboxes in the **Analysis** tab, set to select the date period. So, let's do it:

1. Select the **Analysis** tab from the tab set.
2. Navigate to the **Selectors** category under the **Component** panel. Then drag and drop three **Combo Box** dashboard components onto the canvas.
3. Select the first **Combo Box** component from the canvas to display its properties in the **Properties** panel.

   You can see the preceding steps in this screenshot:

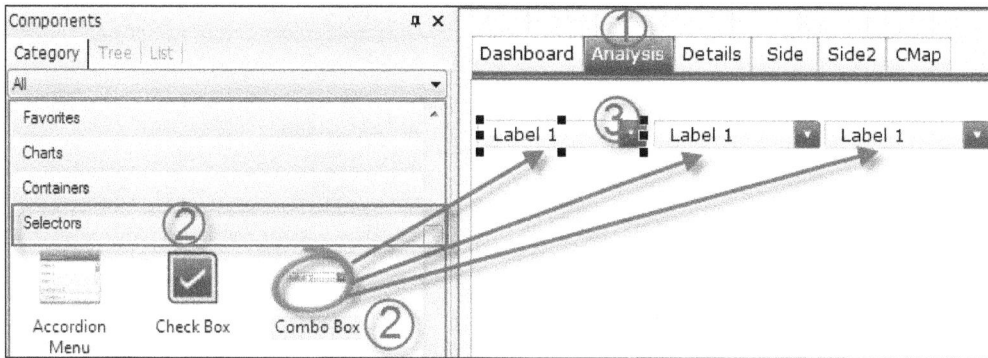

The first combobox selectors will be used to select years, the second for quarters, and the third for months. We will configure the year selector together and I will leave the other two selectors for you to configure. So now, let's configure the properties of the year selector.

4. Select the **General** tab under the **Properties** panel for the year combobox.
5. Link the **Title** field with the **Selectors!$A$7** Excel cell.
6. Link **Labels** to the **Selectors!$A$8:$A$12** Excel range.
7. Navigate to the **Behavior** tab.
8. Select **Label** in **Selected Item Type** and **Label1** in the **Item** field.

You can see some of these steps in this screenshot:

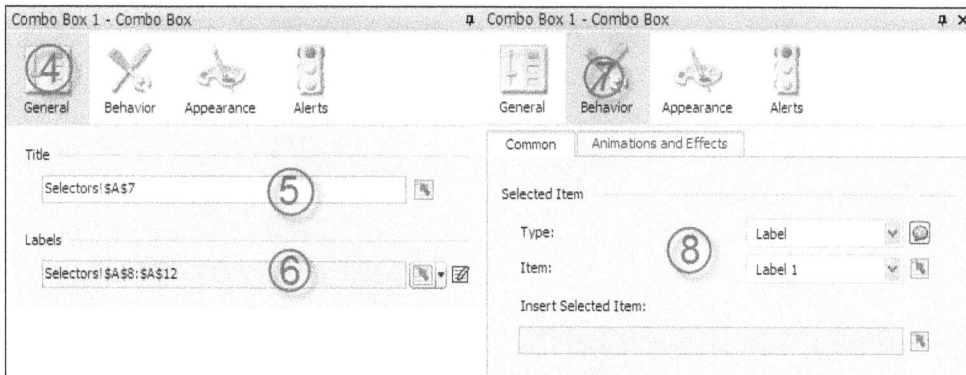

Let's do these two assignments:

- **Assignment 1**: Adjust the properties for the quarter and month selectors.
- **Assignment 2**: Create another combobox selector in the **Dashboard** tab, based on the product list that we have.

The final selectors should look like what is shown in the following screenshot:

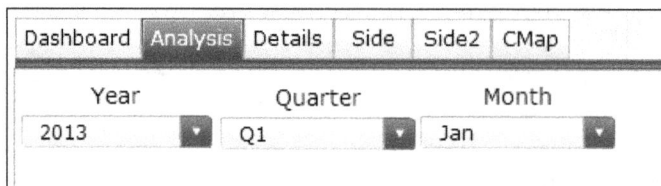

Dashboard	Analysis	Details	Side	Side2	CMap

Year	Quarter	Month
2013 ▾	Q1 ▾	Jan ▾

As we can see, the properties of the combobox are almost the same as the properties of the radio button. The only difference here is that we can use the **Alert** feature in the combobox, which is not available in the radio button.

A list box is the same as a combobox; the only difference is that a combobox allocates very little space, because it only shows the list if we click on the down arrow. In a list box, a specific number of labels will be displayed, and we can use the scroll bar to see the remaining labels.

> As best practice, we should use *a combobox* whenever possible, because it is a space-efficient component.

You can see a comparison between a combobox and a list box in this screenshot:

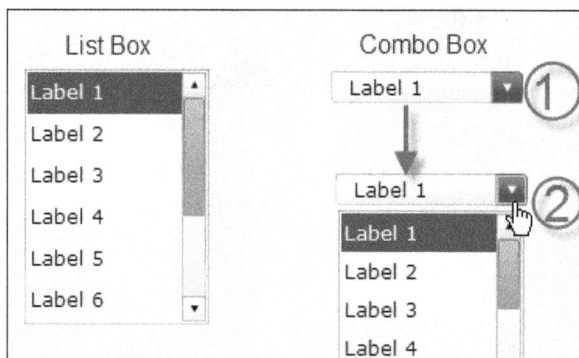

Using checkboxes

A checkbox is another traditional selector, that can be used to indicate whether the end user has ticked the corresponding box or not. Each checkbox will have two main values (checked and unchecked), and we will be able to insert the current status into a destination cell. This will allow us to take an input from the user at runtime, and then perform the corresponding action (or actions).

> A checkbox can only simulate two values for each box – checked and unchecked.

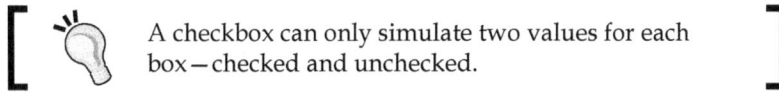

Because we don't need to create a checkbox in our eFashion dashboard, we will use a side example for this. Open an empty dashboard file, or create another tab set, and follow the steps:

1. Navigate to the **Selectors** category under the **Components** panel.
2. Drag and drop three checkboxes into the canvas.
3. Select the first checkbox to display its properties in the **Properties** panel.

You can see these steps in the following screenshot:

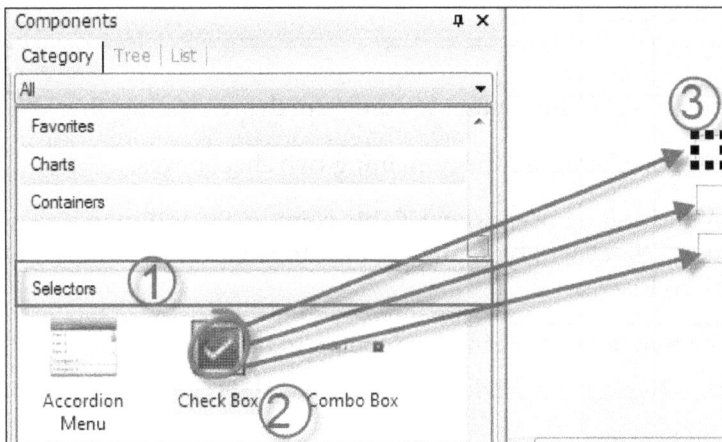

Now, let's configure the first checkbox.

4. Navigate to the **General** tab under the **Properties** panel.
5. Enter **E-Mail** in the **Title** field.
6. Leave the source data as default (0 means unchecked and 1 means checked).
7. Map the destination cell to **Sheet1!$D$2**.
8. Navigate to the **Behavior** tab.
9. Make sure that **Selected Item** is **Unchecked** and the **Click Label to Change Selection** option is ticked.

You can see these steps here:

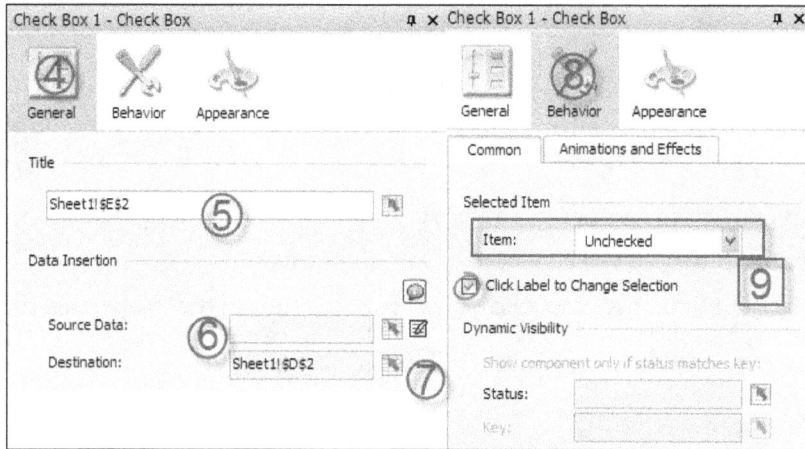

We can do the following assignment to configure the remaining checkboxes:

- Assignment: Configure the remaining two checkboxes.

Finally, we need to add a **Spreadsheet Table** component and map it to our Excel model to see how values will be changed at runtime based on selecting and deselecting of checkboxes.

1. Add the **Spreadsheet Table** component to the canvas.
2. Link the **Display Data** field with the **Sheet1!$D$1:$E$4** range.
3. Click on **Preview**.

   The final output should look like what you can see in the following screenshot:

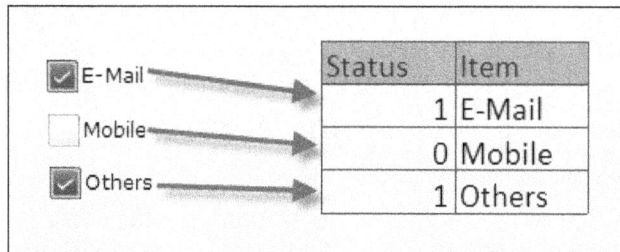

Before winding up this section, let's discuss the new features that we've introduced with the checkbox component:

- **Data insertion**: In a checkbox, we can define a source range of data that contains only two cells. The first cell value will be inserted into the destination if the box is unchecked (default), and the other value will be inserted if the box is checked. There is no other insertion type available with checkboxes.

You can see the information help wizard for checkbox data insertion in this screenshot:

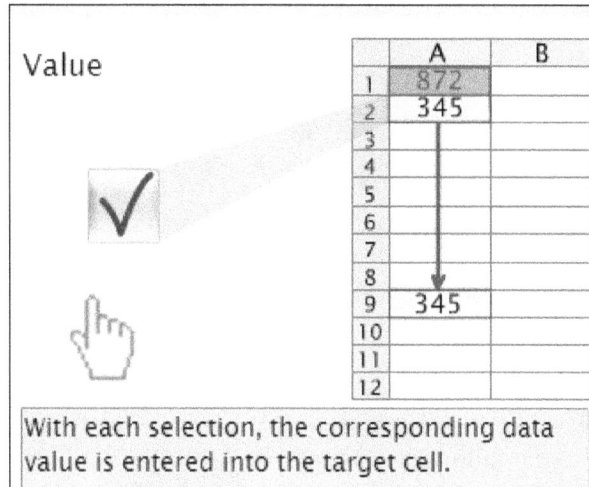

- **Click label to change selection**: This option will allow us to change the checkbox selection by clicking on the checkbox label as well. In our case, if we click on the **E-Mail** label, for example, it will toggle the checkbox state as well. If this option is not selected, you have to click on the checkbox itself to change its state.

List builder

All the selectors that we've discussed so far are used to select only one value. In this section, we will discuss the list builder, which can be used to select multiple values. The idea of the list builder is that we will have all possible values that we can select from in the source listban, and then we can use the **Add** and **Remove** buttons to populate our destination list. Once we are done, we can click on the **Update** button to trigger the list builder insertion.

> The disadvantage of **List Builder** is that it is a very huge component and will take up a lot of canvas space.

You can see the **List Builder** component here:

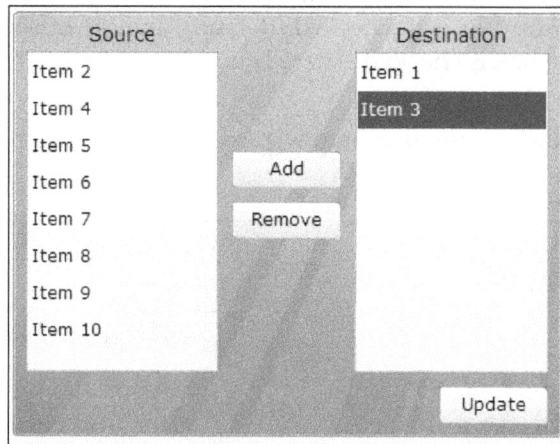

There is nothing new to discuss here, as we've already discussed all the features presented here, while explaining in the previous selectors. One thing to note is that we can control the buttons and panel names from the **General** tab. We can use only these insertion types: label, value, row, and column. We can use the information icon to get help about the selected insertion type. You can see the information box for the label insertion type in the following screenshot:

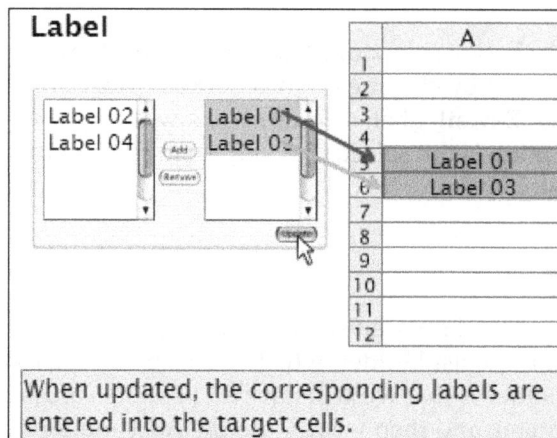

Displaying tabular data

We have five dashboard components that can be used to display tabular data. We can use those components to display data in a tabular format, and also use them as selectors. This is why they are shown under the **Selectors** category.

We have the following tabular selectors:

- List view
- Score card
- Hierarchical table
- Spreadsheet table
- Grid

We will discuss each one in more detail in the following sections.

List view

List view is one of the selectors that you can use to display tabular data. This component is useful if you want to display a normal table, but its main disadvantage is that you can use **Alerts** to highlight good and bad records. The list view component can also be used to display tabular data in mobile dashboards, as it is one of the mobile-supported components.

We have already discussed all the options and configurations available for the list view component in the previous selectors. So here, we will just display the component and its **Properties** panel.

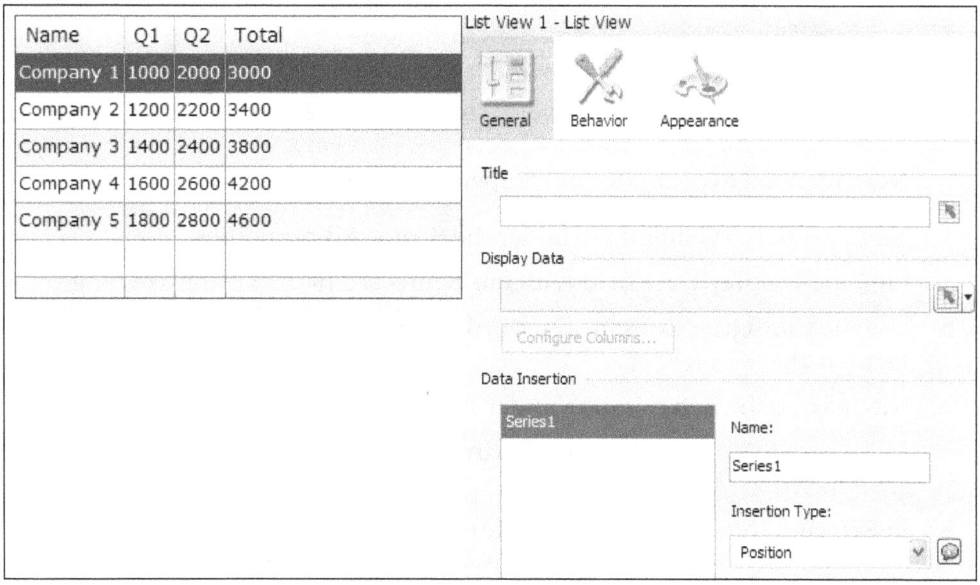

Scorecard

A scorecard is a list view with powerful alerting capabilities. You can alert records by color, icon, or both. One of the main advantages of a scorecard is that it is supported by mobile dashboards.

We need to execute the following steps to create a scorecard in our eFashion dashboard project:

1. Select the **Dashboard** tab from the tab set container.

2. Navigate to the **Selectors** category under the **Components** panel.

3. Drag and drop one **Scorecard** component into the canvas.

   You can see these steps in the following screenshot:

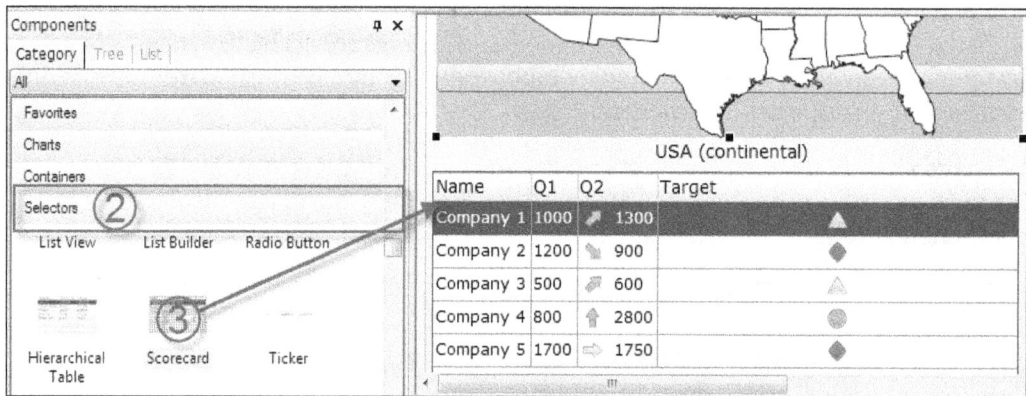

Now we need to configure the properties for the scorecard.

4. Navigate to the **General** tab under the **Scorecard** properties.

5. Link the **Display Data** field with the **'Scorecard'!$C$3:$E$9** Excel range.

6. Use the **Configure Column...** wizard to adjust the column sizes. Set all of them to `150 pixels`.

7. Navigate to the **Behavior** tab under **Properties**.

8. Make sure that **Allow Column Sorting** and **Enable Case-Insensitive Sorting** are enabled.

9. In **Selected Item**, make sure that **Rows are Selectable** is enabled.

You can see these steps here:

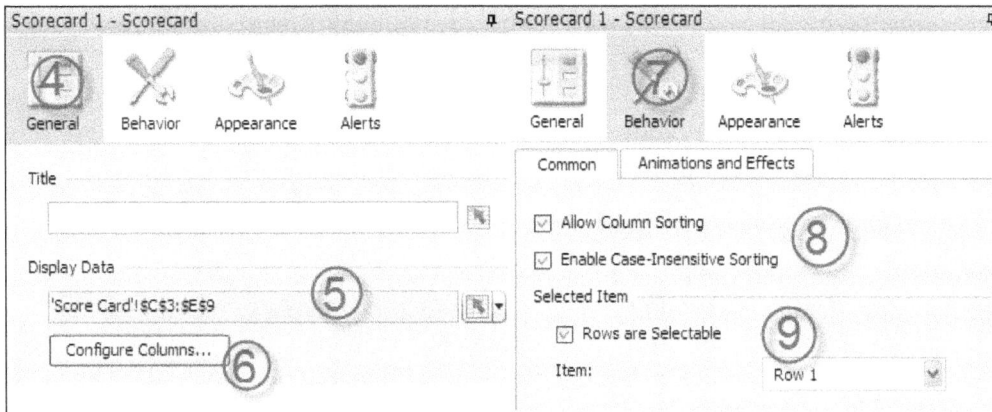

You can see the **Configure Columns...** wizard in the following screenshot:

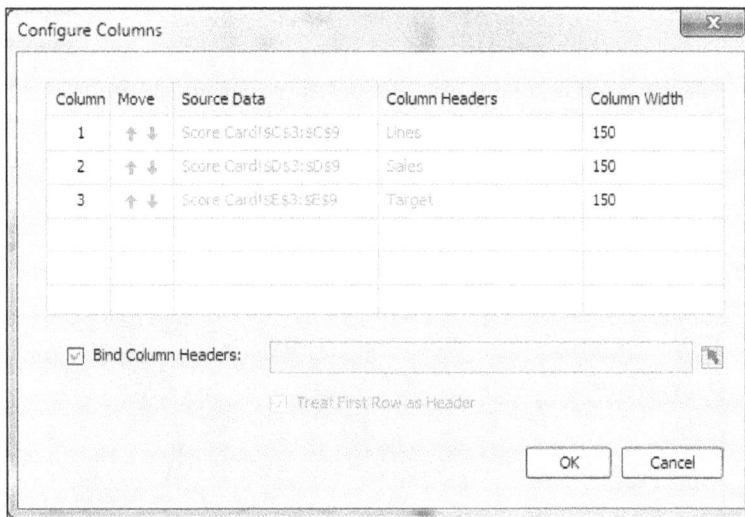

We will see how to configure the alerting feature for this score card in the next chapter. Before winding up this section, let's highlight the new features and options that were introduced here:

- **Allow column sorting**: This feature will allow the end user to interact with the score card at runtime, by sorting the data based on a selected column. You can simply click on one column to sort data in ascending order based on that column, click again to sort it in descending order, and so on.

- **Enable case-insensitive sorting**: This option will enable case-insensitive sorting. So, `Accessories` and `accessories` will come together, instead of displaying all words that start with a capital letter first and then displaying all words that start with small letters.

- **Rows are selectable**: This option can be used to make our score card a selector. If this is not selected, the score card will be used only to display data.

The hierarchical table

This component is another type of list view that shows hierarchical data. Hierarchical tables display data as nodes that can be expanded and collapsed. We can use the alert feature in this component. This component can't display data stored in the Excel model directly, and we need to build a query to retrieve the required data. Then we can bind it to this component. You will learn how to create Universe queries in *Chapter 9*, *Retrieving External Data Sources*. We also need to make sure that we've already defined the hierarchies (navigation paths) in the Universes in order to be able to make use of this component.

> You can find more information on *how to configure navigation paths* in my previous book, *Creating Universes with SAP BusinessObjects*.

You can see this component in the following screenshot:

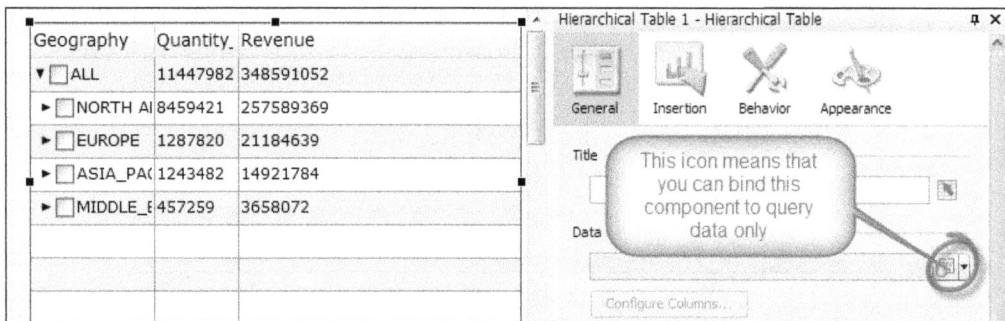

The spreadsheet table

This component is the same as the scorecard, but with limited functionality. You can use it as a selector and use the alert feature. However, you can't sort records (for example), and you have limited control over display features, such as which grid line to show. Also, this is component is not compatible with mobile dashboards.

You can see the spreadsheet table component in this screenshot:

A1	B1
# 210	CA
# 45	FL
# 88	NY
# 105	MD

Grid

Grids can be used to display tabular data. You still can use the alert features and control the display of data, but the only thing to note here is that this is not a selector, and it is not compatible with mobile dashboards. You will find this component under the **Other** category in the **Components** panel. You can see the grid component in the following screenshot:

1	2	3	4	5
2	4	6	8	10
3	6	9	12	15

In the next section, we will start talking about advanced selectors.

Using advanced menus

We have four main advanced menu dashboard selectors that we can use inside our dashboard. We have already introduced **Accordion Menu** in the first chapter, in the accordion menu sample. Here, we will discuss the features and options for those menus in more detail:

- Label-based menu
- Sliding-picture menu
- Fisheye menu
- Accordion menu

Let's discuss each of these in more detail.

Label-based menu

Label-based menu will display labels horizontally or vertically. It is very similar to the drop-down menu, and can be configured to display the menu name only, in order to save space. It will expand when you click on it. The other option is to display all labels – as we mentioned – horizontally or vertically.

We've already created a combobox to present the quarters in the analysis tab, as to be seen in the tab set container tab. We will try to simulate the same, using a label-based menu:

1. Select the **Analysis** tab from the tab set container.

2. Navigate to **Label Based Menu** under the **Selectors** category in the **Components** panel.

3. Drag and drop a **Label Based Menu** component onto the canvas.

   You can see these steps marked here:

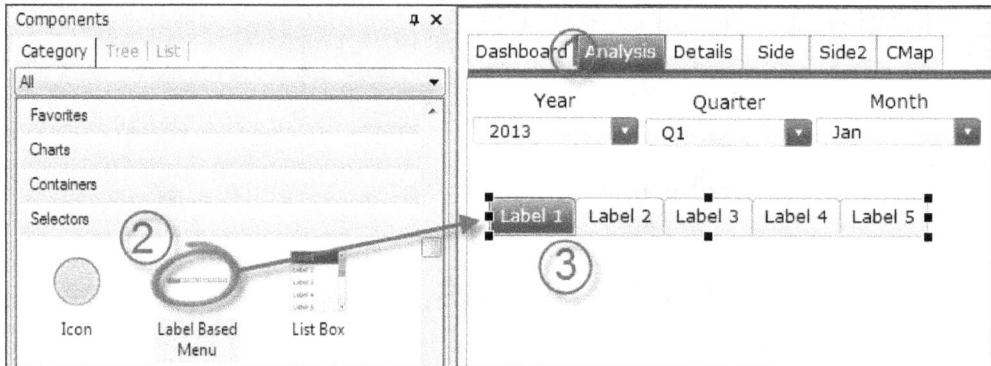

   Now let's follow the steps to configure the properties for **Label Based Menu**.

4. Select the **General** tab from the **Properties** panel.

5. Link the **Title** field with the **Selectors!$B$7** cell.

6. Link **Labels** field with the **Selectors!$B$8:$B$11** Excel range.

7. Select **Horizontal** in the **Orientation** area.

   You can see the general properties of the label based menu in the following screenshot:

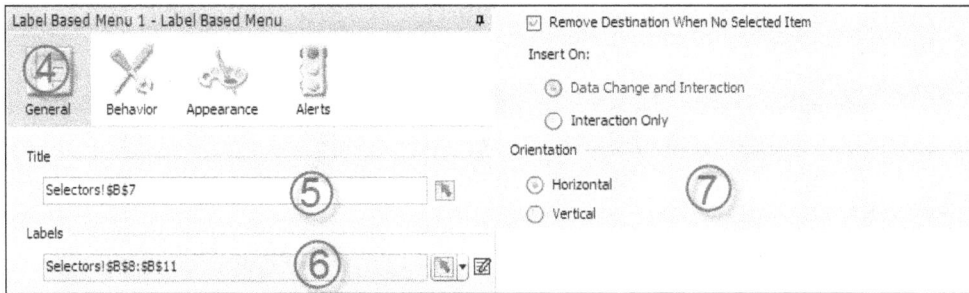

Now let's move on to the **Behavior** tab and follow these steps.

8. Navigate to the **Behavior** tab.

9. In the **Insertion Options** properties, uncheck the **Always Expanded** option.

10. Make sure that the **Expand On** property is set to **Mouse Click**, the **Expand Direction** property is set to **Right**, and **Open Animation** is checked.

11. Make sure that **Selected Item Type** is **Label** and select **Label1** in the **Item** property.

12. Save and preview.

You can see these steps in this screenshot:

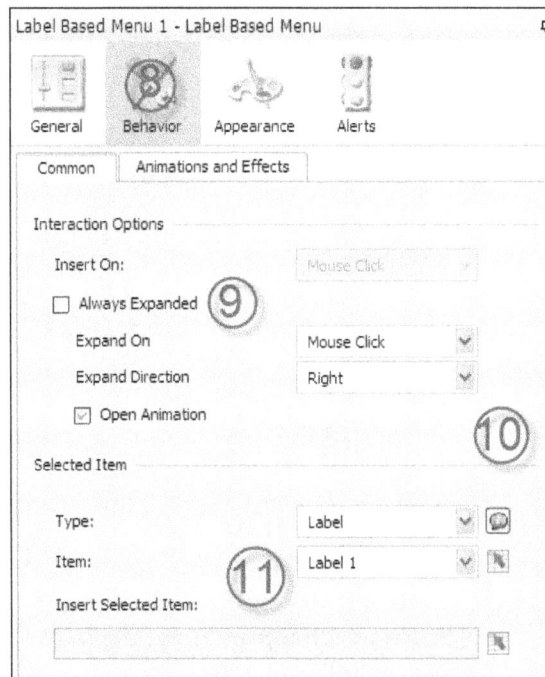

Before we move on to the next section, let's discuss the new properties introduced here:

- **Orientation**: We've already introduced the orientation feature with the radio button component. You just need to see the following screenshot to be able to distinguish between horizontal and vertical orientation:

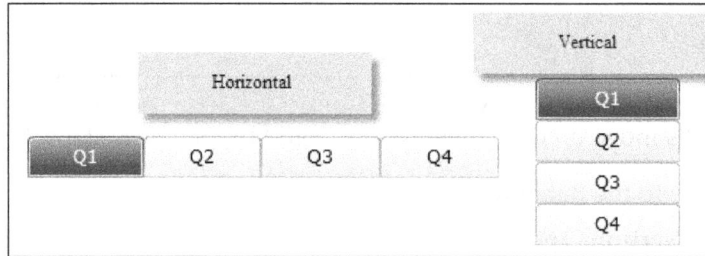

- **Always Expanded**: The label-based menu will be expanded by default if this option is checked. On the other hand, it will be collapsed if it is unchecked. The menu will expand based on the **Expand On** property. We can set this property to expand the label-based menu when triggered by a mouse click or a mouseover action. We can also set the expand direction. You can see the difference in this screenshot:

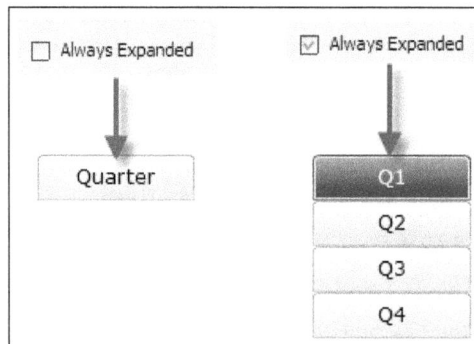

We delete the created label-based menu before saving, as we don't want a label-based menu in our eFashion dashboard project.

Sliding picture fisheye menus

Sliding picture menus and fisheye menus are almost identical. Only the animation effects are different. The size of the picture shown in a sliding-picture menu is fixed, and we can slide between pictures which represent labels. In the fisheye menu, it will generate an animation style that is similar to MAC OS.

You have to assign sliding-picture or fisheye menus to a range of labels. Then you will need to use the **Import Thumbnail** window to import a corresponding image for each label.

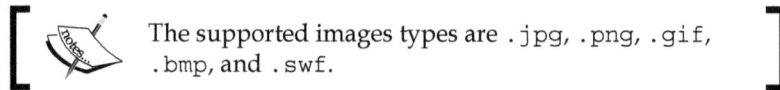

> The supported images types are .jpg, .png, .gif, .bmp, and .swf.

You can see the thumbnail window in the following screenshot:

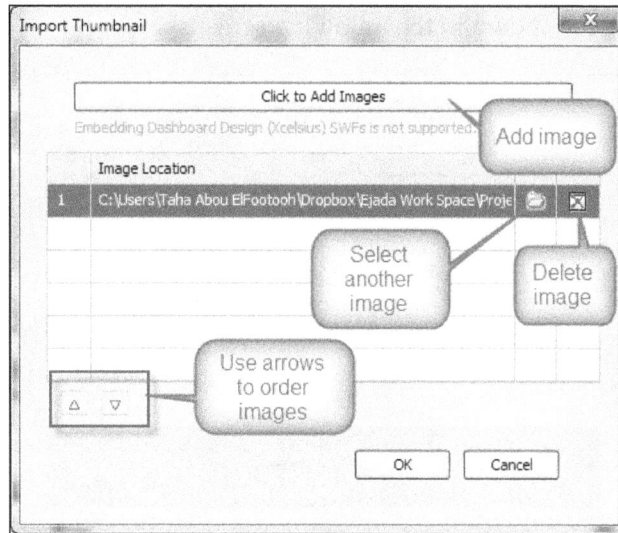

Sliding-picture and fisheye menus work exactly like the other selectors that we've already described. You can see an example of a sliding-picture menu and a fisheye menu in this screenshot:

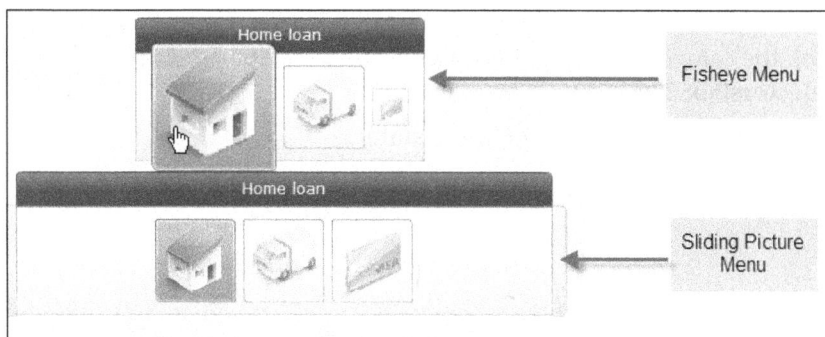

Accordion Menu

The **Accordion Menu** tab has already been introduced in *Chapter 1, Getting Started with SAP BO Dashboards*. Here, we will try to build a similar menu, because our design requires it. We need to create it in the **Analysis** tab in our eFashion dashboard project:

1. Select the **Analysis** tab from the tab set container.
2. Navigate to the **Selectors** category under the **Components** panel.
3. Drag and drop **Accordion Menu** onto the canvas.

   These steps are shown in the following screenshot:

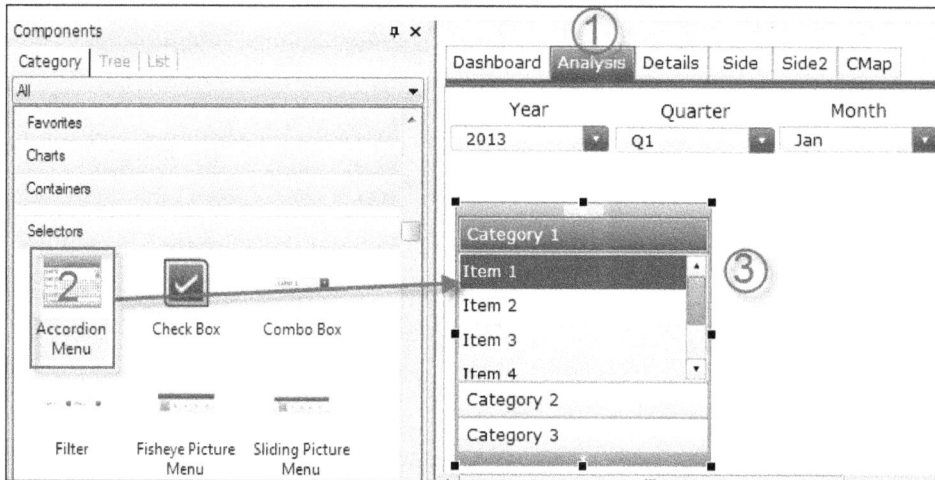

   Now let's configure the properties for **Accordion Menu**.

4. Select the **General** tab, under the **Properties** panel.
5. Create a new category by clicking on the **+** sign.
6. Link the category name to **Selectors!$A$22** and the labels to **Selectors!$B$22:$B$23**.
7. Repeat the same for the remaining states.

   You can see these steps in the following screenshot.

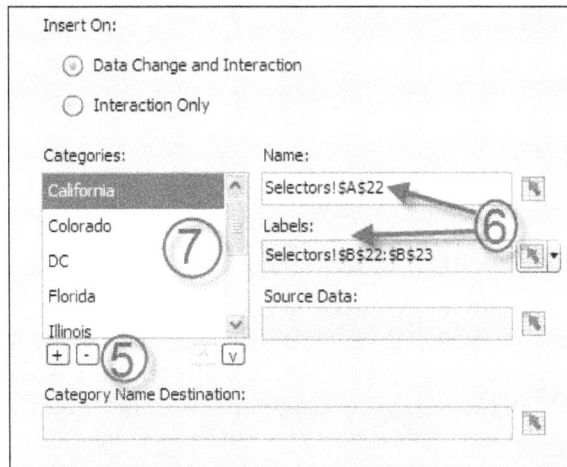

The final output is shown here:

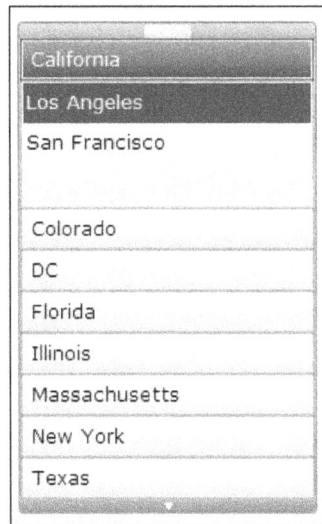

We will configure the insertion and destination properties in the next chapter.

Using other selectors

We've almost covered all the available selectors. The remaining ones are similar to the previous selectors. Therefore, we'll just describe each one, and discuss any new features if they are applicable.

We will discuss the following selectors:

- Icon
- Filters
- Push and toggle buttons

Using the icon

The icon dashboard component is exactly the same as the checkbox component. It can be used to toggle between two source values (checked and unchecked). The advantage of using the icon component here is that you can use the **Alert** feature to give a color indication, based on the assigned value and target. A green icon indicates good performance, while a red icon requires more attention. The title will be displayed when the user hovers over the icon component at runtime.

> We can use a transparent icon with a title and no value on the top information image to act like a tool tip.

We can see an example here:

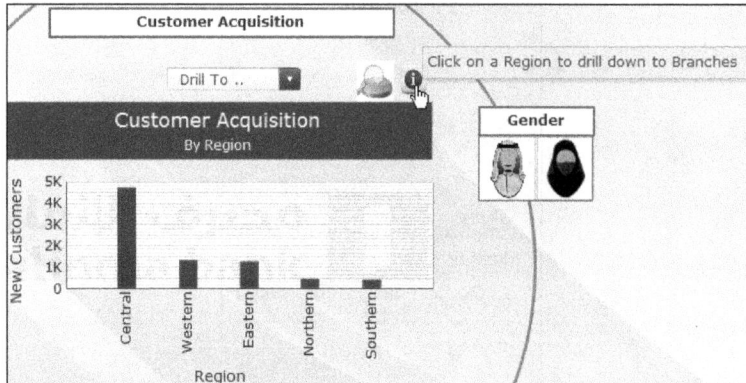

An example of the icon component is shown in the following screenshot:

Using Filter

Filter is one of the most useful components that we have seen so far. It can be used to select from multiple-level hierarchies. It has one advantage over the accordion menu: it can be configured to use up to 10 levels, while the accordion menu can manipulate only two levels. We will create a side example to simulate the state-city selection that we've already implemented using the accordion menu:

1. Create a new dashboard file.

2. Navigate to the **Selectors** category under the **Components** panel.

3. Drag and drop the **Filter** component onto the canvas.

You can see these steps in this screenshot:

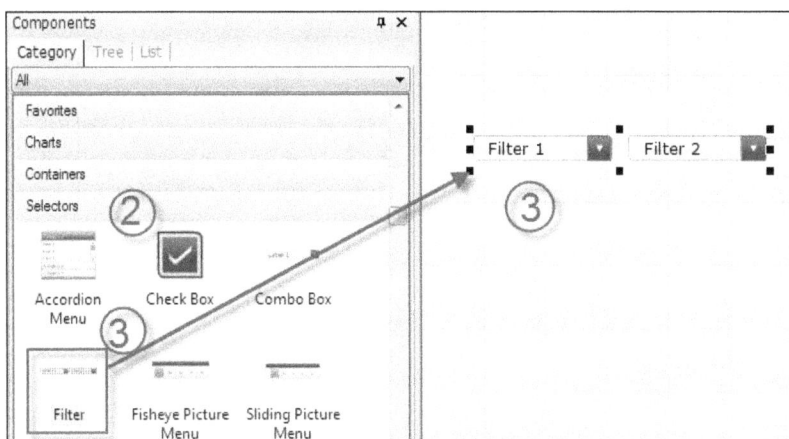

Input the data into Excel, as shown in the following screenshot:

	A	B
2	State	City
3	California	Los Angeles
4	California	San Francisco
5	Colorado	Colorado Springs
6	DC	Washington
7	Florida	Miami
8	Illinois	Chicago
9	Massachusetts	Boston
10	New York	New York
11	Texas	Austin
12	Texas	Dallas
13	Texas	Houston

Now let's configure the filter properties.

4. Navigate to the **General** tab under the **Properties** panel.
5. Link the **Titles** field to the **Sheet1!$A$2:$B$2** Excel range.
6. Then link **Source Data** to the **Sheet1!$A$3:$B$13** Excel range.
7. Next, link **Destination** to the **Sheet1!$D$2:$E$2** Excel range.
8. Make sure that **Number of Filters** under **Display Options** is set to **2**.
9. Click on **Preview** to test the filter.

You can see these steps in this screenshot:

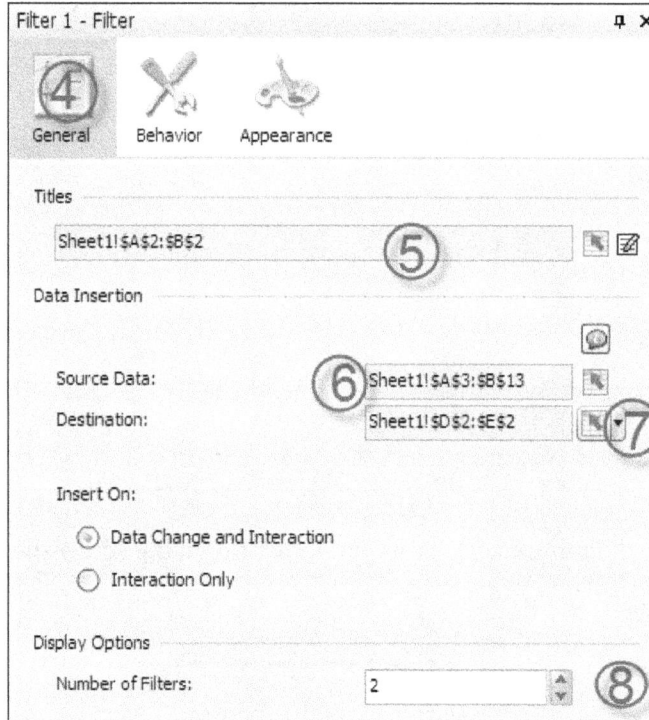

The filter is shown here:

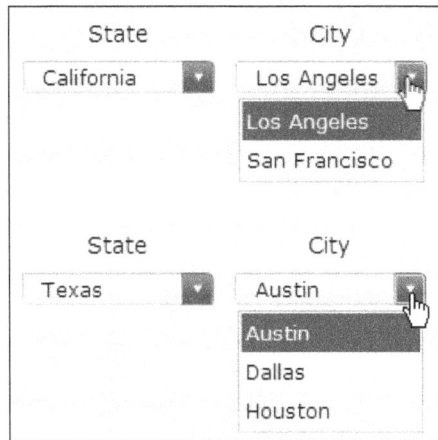

Using push and toggle buttons

A push button is used to insert its source data into a destination target whenever clicked on, while a toggle button acts like both a checkbox and icon selectors. It toggles between two states (on and off). We will use these buttons in *Chapter 7, Styling Up*, with images to create nice-looking buttons.

Using third-party selectors

You may notice that we don't have many selectors that can help the user select multiple values. We only introduced the list builder, but this selector is inefficient due to its large size. InfoSol provides a solution for this, by providing the following plugin selectors:

* Multi-selector combobox
* Multi-selector list box
* Multi-selector dynamic grid
* Drop-down menu
* Hierarchy tree

[For more information on these, you can visit the InfoSol web site, at http://www.infosol.com/.]

Summary

In this chapter, we discussed how to use traditional selectors, such as radio buttons and checkboxes, to receive input from dashboard users, and then trigger an action or a set of actions, based on the selected value. These actions are called insertions. We can use many types of insertions, such as label, value, row, and column, which allow us to easily interact with our dashboard. We also introduced modern selectors, such as fisheye and sliding picture menus.

One section was dedicated to discussing how to display tabular data in our dashboard using the list view, score card, spreadsheet table, and grid. Then we discussed selector types, such as icons and filters.

Selectors have many common features, such as series insertion, default selected label, and so on. We introduced many new selector-related properties, such as orientation. Finally, we introduced some third-party plugins provided by InfoSol. These plugins allow multiple selections.

In the next chapter, we will see how to use the output of selectors, which is the data inserted in the destination cells. Also, you will learn how to use a selector's destination cells to dynamically look up data, or use it as an input for a Universe query to retrieve filtered data.

Then, we will talk about one of the most important features available in SAP BO Dashboard, which is called **Alerts**. This feature can help us highlight good or bad performance, based on indicated colors. So, just take a small break and then we'll move on.

6
Advanced Interactive Analysis with Dashboards

In the previous chapter, we saw how to create **Selectors**, and described how they can be used to make our dashboard interactive. This means that the end user can select a specific value from the selector's available values, and based on the selected value label, some actions can happen. In this chapter, we will discuss how **Selectors** can be configured with specific actions.

Since you have learned about insertion types, such as column, row, and label, in this chapter, we will move on to see how the same selector can have multiple different insertion series with different types. Also, you will learn about the dynamic visibility feature, based on inserted values, with which we can show and hide other dashboard components.

We will take a look at various drill-down options for our interactive dashboard design, and work on the **Alert** options to track KPIs. We will close the chapter with a discussion on how to link a dashboard to a report, using the OpenDocument function and URL button.

To summarize, our focus here will be on these topics:

- Using the dynamic visibility feature
- Grouping components
- Using containers, such as the canvas container and panel container
- Using alerts
- Using the drill-down feature (**Insertion**)
- Linking a dashboard to a Webi or Crystal report

Using the dynamic visibility feature

Dynamic visibility is used to show and hide a specific component at runtime, based on specific predefined conditions. It's available for most dashboard components.

Before we start explaining how to use the **Dynamic Visibility** feature, let's prepare the dashboard file using the following steps, which we are going to use during this chapter:

1. Navigate to the `Code` sample folder on your PC.

2. Open the **Chapter5** dashboard under the `Dashboard (Ready)` folder.

3. Save it in the same location as **Dashboard6** in your `Development` folder.

    You can see these steps in the following screenshot:

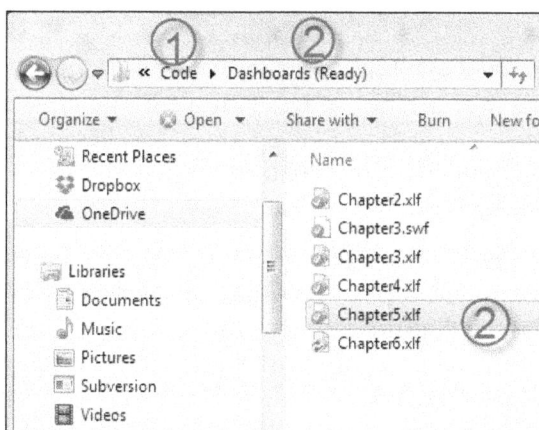

In the following section, we will see how to use the radio button that we created in the previous chapter to toggle between the pie and combination charts in the **Dashboard** tab:

1. Select the **Dashboard** tab from the tab set.

2. Open the **Object Browser** panel and select the **Sales by Product** pie chart.

    You can see these steps here:

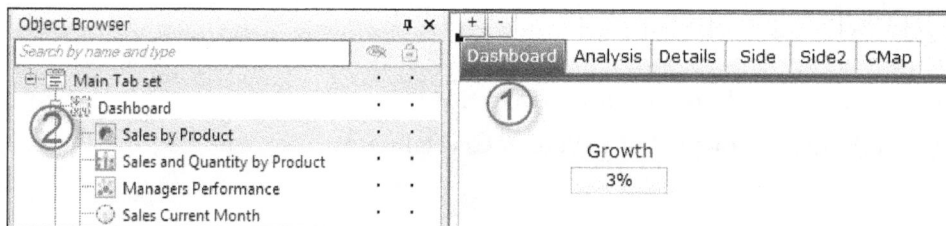

Now we need to perform the following steps to configure the dynamic visibility feature for the **Sales by Product** pie chart:

3. Navigate to the **Behavior** tab under the **Pie Chart** properties.
4. Select the **Common** tab under the **Behavior** tab.
5. Map the **Status** field to the **Selectors!$B$4** Excel cell.
6. Then map the **Key** field to the **Selectors!$B$2** Excel cell.

You can see the preceding steps in this screenshot:

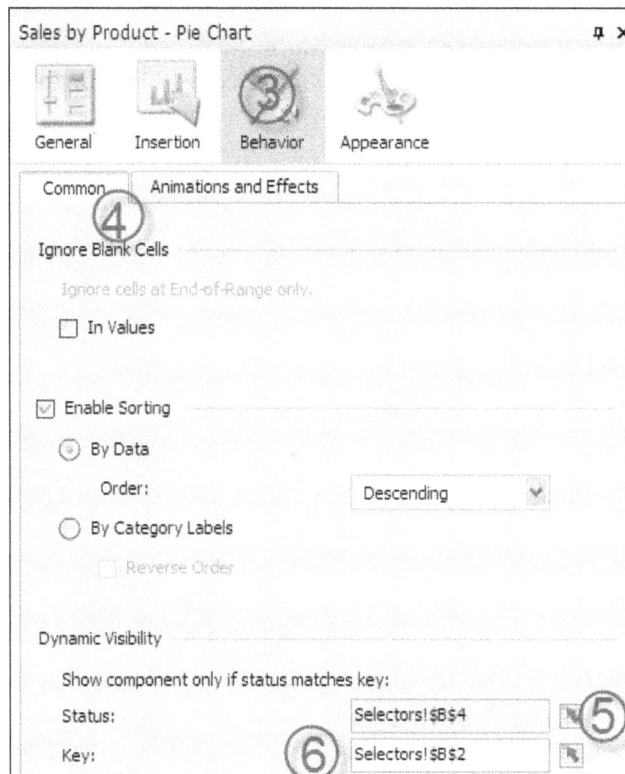

Here's an assignment: we need to do the same steps and to configure the **Dynamic Visibility** feature for the **Sales and Quantity by Product** combination chart. It will be exactly the same, but we will change the key value to **Selectors!$B$3**.

You can see the **Dynamic Visibility** property for the combination chart in the following screenshot:

Now we need to preview our dashboard and test our radio button to check whether they work fine or not. Click on the **Preview** button and try to toggle between the **Pie** and **Combination** labels from the radio button selector. Then make sure that the pie chart is displayed while selecting **Pie** from the radio button, and the combination chart is displayed if the **Combination** label is selected from the radio button. You can see the display for both the labels here:

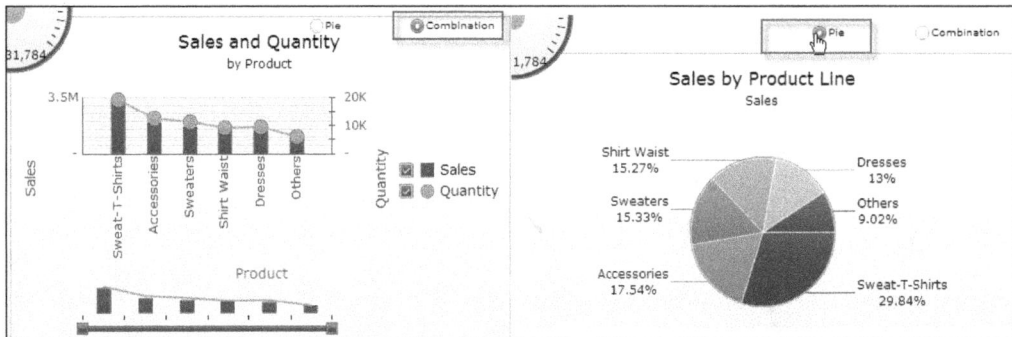

Before we conclude this section, we need to discuss the following topics:

- **Dynamic Visibility**: This feature compares the value in the **Status** field to the value in the **Key** field. If the values match, then the dashboard component will be visible, and if they don't match, the dashboard component will not be visible. Normally, the **Status** field is a dynamically changing value that will be based on a destination for one of the selectors. In this example, the **Status** field is the insertion destination Excel cell for the radio button, and so this cell will change at runtime based on the radio button selected. The **Key** field is normally a status value that is waiting to match in order to display the dashboard component. In our example, the **Key** value is mapped to a static Excel cell that contains **Pie**, because this is the value that we need in the Status value as well in order to show the **Pie** chart component.

You can see the **Dynamic Visibility** property of the **Sales by Product** pie chart in the following screenshot:

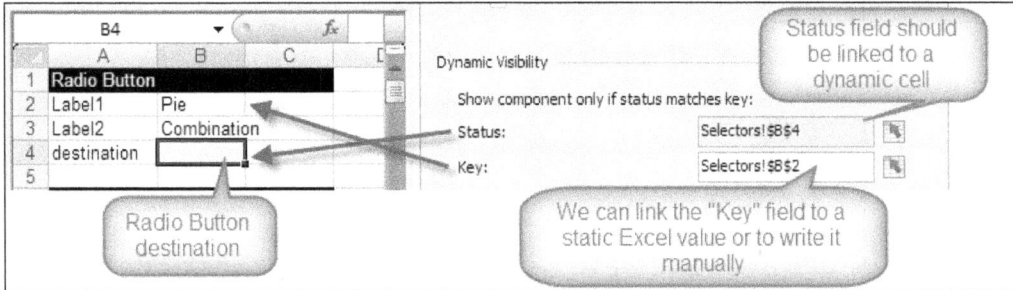

- **Object Browser**: You might have noticed that the **Sales by Product** pie chart and the **Sales and Quantity by Product** combination chart are stacked on top of each other. We need to control their visibility from the Object **Browser** panel, by giving a meaningful name to the dashboard object, and control the order of the displayed objects by moving the dashboard components up and down, which means from visible to invisible. The top dashboard components will be in the background, while the bottom dashboard components will be at the front. To try this, lets perform an example.

We can see that the maps that we created in *Chapter 4, Using Maps and Other Components*, are on top of the **Sales This Month** gauge. To fix this, just move this dashboard component until it is on top of the other two maps, as you can see in this screenshot:

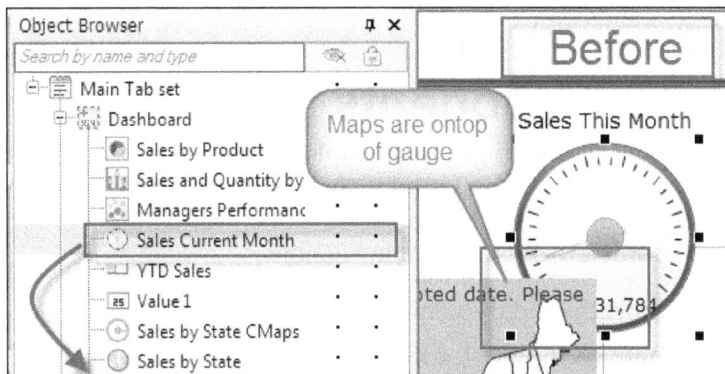

We can see the Gauge on top of the map after moving to forward

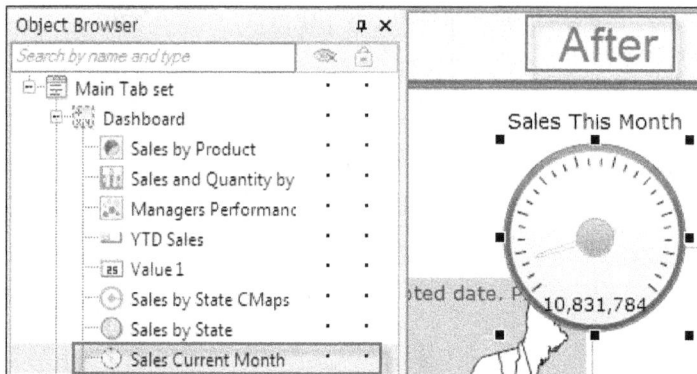

We can also use the following shortcut toolbar icons and shortcut keys:

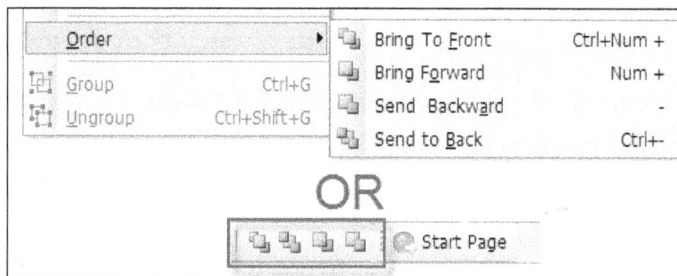

Here is an assignment: can you create a toggle button to toggle between the **US Map** dashboard component and the USA CMAP that we created in *Chapter 4, Using Maps and Other Components*. Note that we will need this button in the next chapter.

Grouping components

Grouping components is used to group multiple dashboard components to make it easier to move and control them. Usually, the grouped components are already configured, and all of their properties are already set. We can use a group of components to perform any of the following actions:

- Move them together on the canvas

- Control dynamic visibility for the entire group, instead of configuring it for each dashboard component inside the group

- Group dashboard components in an object browser and lock, show, and hide the entire group, instead of doing this for each dashboard component member

Now let's see how to use this feature:

1. Navigate to **Object Browser**.
2. Hold down *Ctrl* and select the following items:
   ° The **Sales by Product** pie chart
   ° The **Sales and Quantity by Product** combination chart
   ° **Radio Button 1**
3. Right-click and select **Group** from the menu that opens.

   You can see these steps marked here:

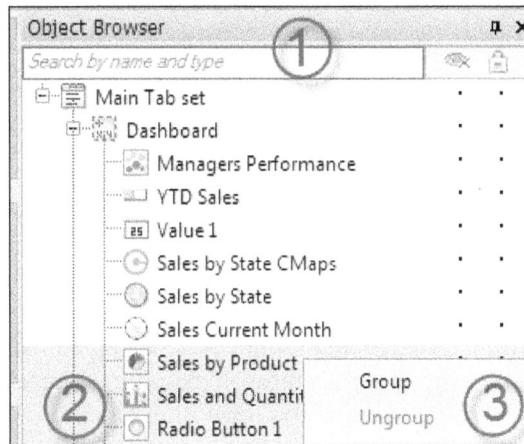

The created group is shown in the **Object Browser** panel like this:

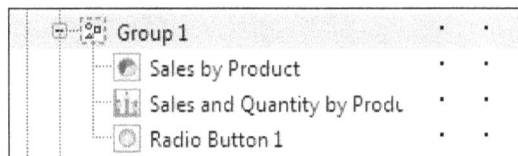

You can see the properties of the created group in the following screenshot:

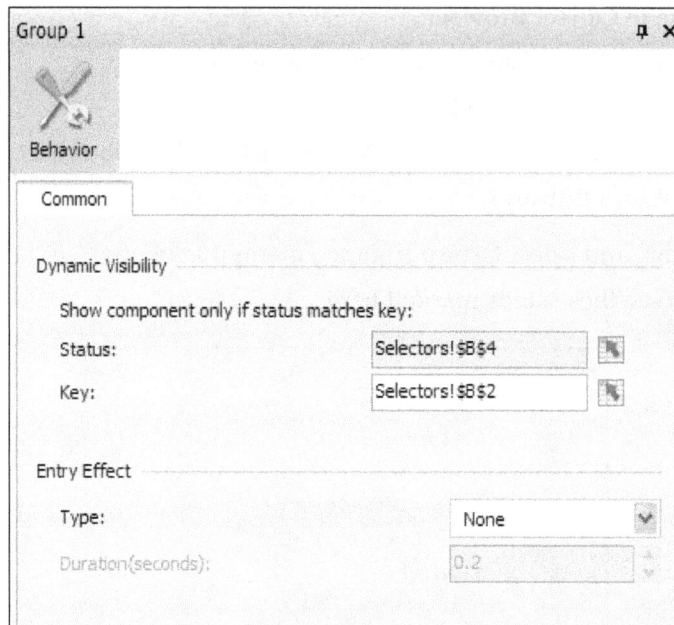

We can use the **Ungroup** feature to dismantle, or break a group of dashboard components, and return to the original status. Normally, we use **Ungroup** if we want to change the properties of one of the components inside the group.

> We can use *Ctrl + G* to group the selected components and *Ctrl + Shift + G* to ungroup them.

Using Containers

Like the group function, containers are also used to group dashboard components together. The major difference between these two is in the freedom of movement of components inside the group. The grouping functionality is more of a design time, and containers are runtime. We have two types of containers that we will be discussing in this section:

- **Panel Container**
- **Canvas Container**
- **Tab Set**

We can find the containers under the **Container** category in the **Components** panel, as shown in the following screenshot:

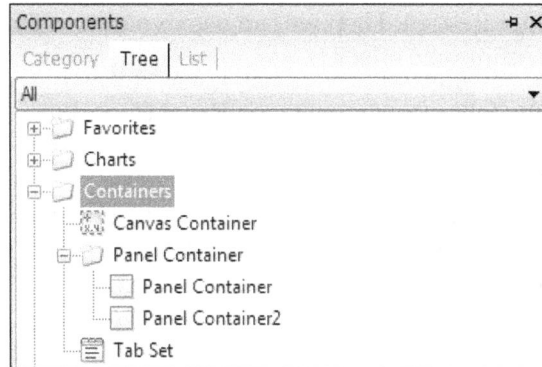

Using Panel Container

The **Panel Container** component can be used to hold multiple dashboard components. It contains a header and a frame, as you can see in this screenshot:

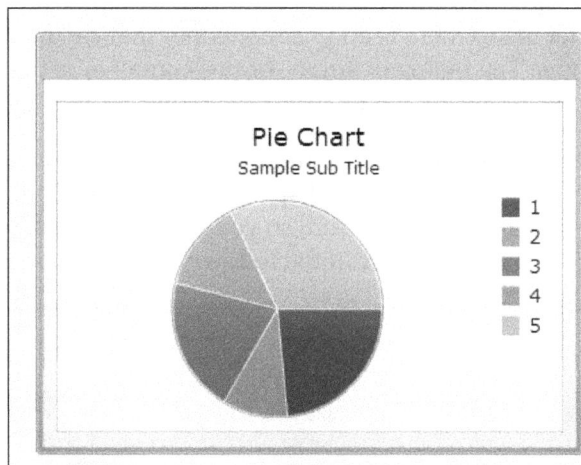

Panel containers can be used in any of the following situations:

- If you want another level of information to be displayed when the dashboard user executes a specific action; for example, to click on a product to display the product analysis panel containers that contain product-related KPIs.
- If you don't have space in your canvas and you want scroll capability in your dashboard.

- If you want to create a zoom screen or simulate (maximize and minimize) a window. This can be done by getting two panel containers: the first one with small-sized objects, and the second one with large objects (the same objects but larger in size). Then we can use dynamic visibility to simulate the maximize/minimize effect.

We need to consider the following when using Panel **Container**:

- It is not supported by mobile dashboards.

- It is a not recommended dashboard object, as it consumes a lot of resources and produces a dashboard with bad performance. Check out the following link for a complete article on this.

> As per http://everythingxcelsius.com/, Panel Container is mentioned as one of the three dashboard components to avoid, due to its instability and high CPU usage. They also mention that it will cause a major increase in dashboard files.

Using Canvas Container

The **Canvas Container** component is another container that can be used to hold other dashboard components. The main advantage of this container is that it is very flexible, as you can easily move objects in and out, or copy, move, and/or delete them.

You can also scroll inside the **Canvas Container** component to see a large number of components inside the same predefined space. The Canvas Container component also comes with a transparent background, so you can add a background if you wish. You can see a Canvas Container in the following screenshot:

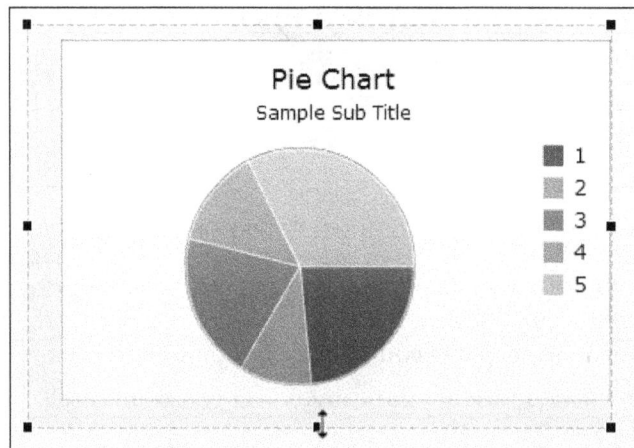

There is nothing new to discuss in the properties of **Canvas Container**, but we have the following hints.

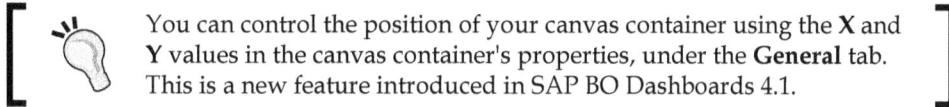

> You can control the position of your canvas container using the **X** and **Y** values in the canvas container's properties, under the **General** tab. This is a new feature introduced in SAP BO Dashboards 4.1.

You can see the position property in this screenshot:

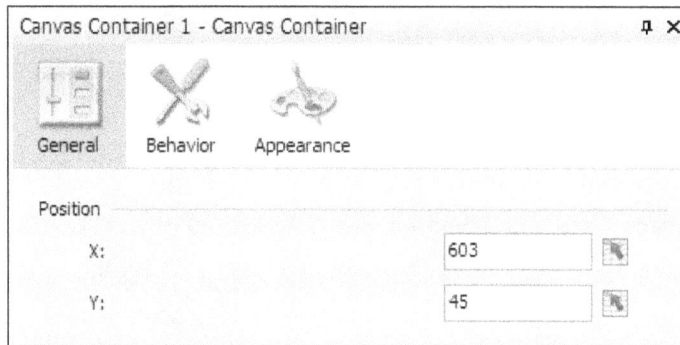

We will use the canvas container to implement a zoom screen (maximized) for a scorecard:

1. Open the **Components** panel and navigate to the **Containers** category.
2. Drag a **Canvas Container** option into the **Dashboard** tab set.

    You can see these steps in the following screenshot:

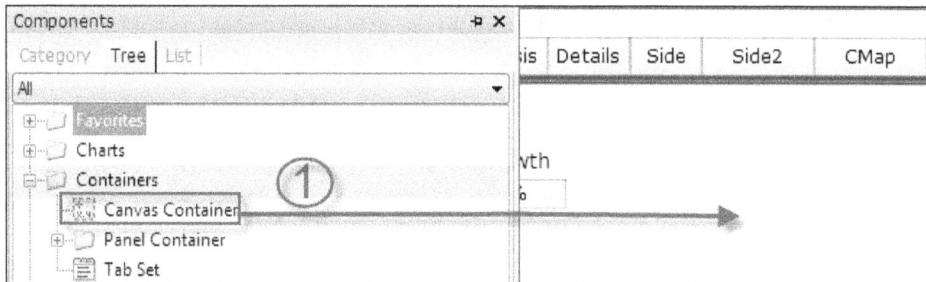

3. Adjust the **Canvas Container** size.
4. Drag **Scorecard** into Canvas **Container**.
5. Link the new scorecard to the same data that we used with the old one.

6. Drag one push buttons into Canvas **Container**.

You can see these steps marked here:

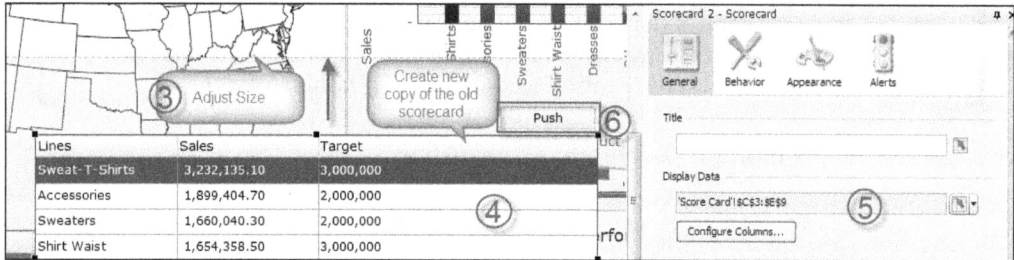

Select the **Push** button, and make the following configuration:

7. Type **Close** in the **Label** field.

8. Link **Source Data** to the **'Score Card'!$H$3** Excel cell.

9. Link Destination **Data** to the **'Score Card'!$I$1** Excel cell.

You can see the preceding steps in the following screenshot:

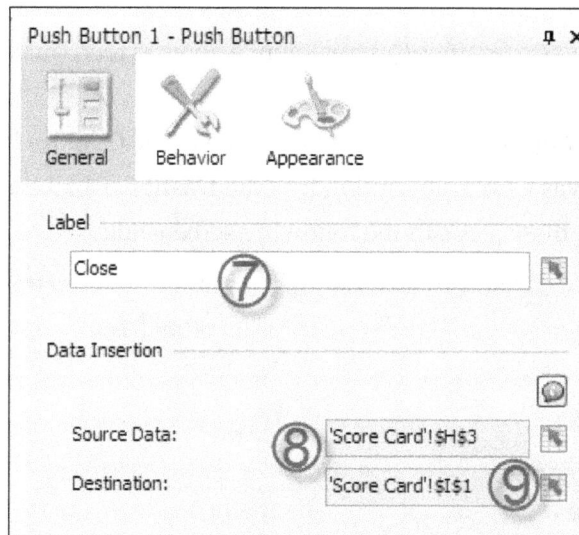

Then we need to link the Canvas Container dynamic visibility field with the destination cell for the close button:

10. Select **Canvas Container** and navigate to the **Properties** panel.

11. Navigate to the **Behavior** tab.

12. Set **Status** under **Dynamic Visibility** to **'Score Card'!$I$1**.

13. Link the **Key** field under **Dynamic Visibility** with **'Score Card'!$H$2**.

These steps are shown here:

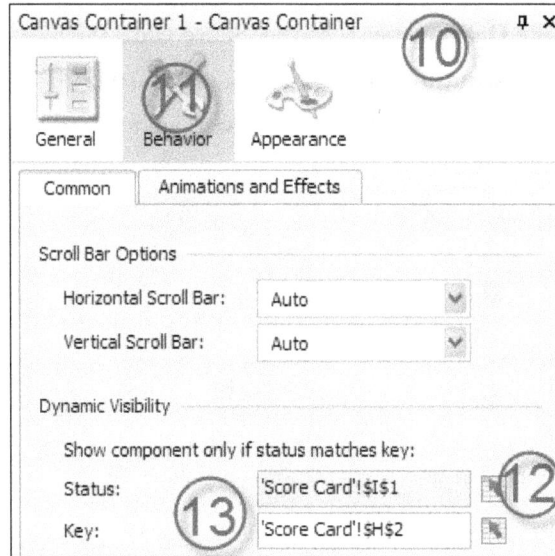

Now go to the **Object Browser** panel, and hide **Canvas Container** at design time to be able to create the **Open** button.

You can see how to do this in the following screenshot:

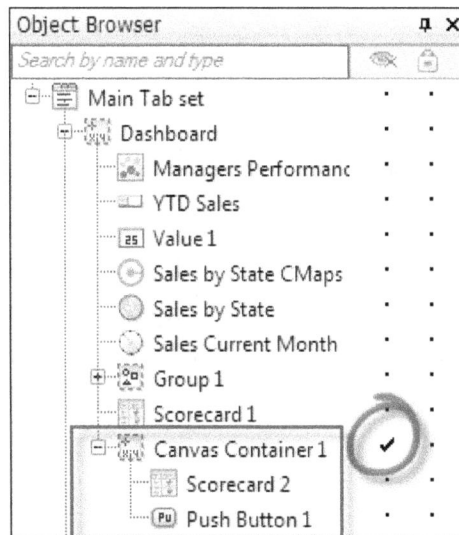

Now drag another push button and put it on top of the original score card. Then follow these steps:

14. Select **Push Button** and navigate to the **Properties** panel.

15. Type Open in the **Label** field.

16. Link the **Source Data** property to the **'Score Card'!$H$2** Excel cell.

17. Then link the **Destination** field to the **'Score Card'!$I$1** Excel cell.

You can see the preceding steps in this screenshot:

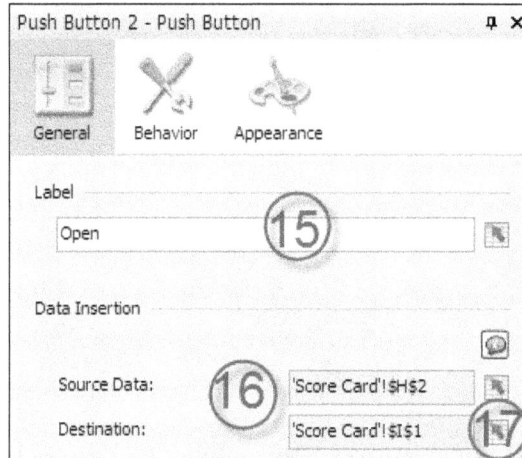

Now let's preview our dashboard. It should be the same as what you can see in the following screenshot:

Lines	Sales	Target
Sweat-T-Shirts	3,232,135.10	3,000,000
Accessories	1,899,404.70	2,000,000
Sweaters	1,660,040.30	2,000,000
Shirt Waist	1,654,358.50	3,000,000
Dresses	1,408,594.90	1,000,000
Others	977,250.90	1,000,000

Before we wind up this section, let's try to understand and recap together what we've done.

The canvas's dynamic visibility property will hide or show the whole canvas container, with all the objects inside it. In this example, we created a new canvas container to hold a maximized version of the old score card, and we used two buttons to control the dynamic visibility of this canvas. One button will open it (show), and the other button will close it (hide).

> Another difference between grouping and containers is that grouping is a feature, while containers are dashboard components.

Using a Tab Set

We have used and configured a tab set in our eFashion dashboard project, and we saw how useful this component is. We can add many tabs and they will act such as containers, with different names. Each tab can act like a separate view that contains its own dashboard components, and, as we've already seen, we have three main views in our eFashion dashboard:

- **Dashboard**
- **Analysis**
- **Details**

You should use a tab set in the following cases:

- If you have different views or perspectives that you want to present in the same dashboard
- If the canvas size is too small to hold all your KPIs and you want to categorize and group related KPIs under some tabs

> The tab set is supported by mobile dashboards as well.

We can see a tab set component in which **Tab 1** is active in the following screenshot:

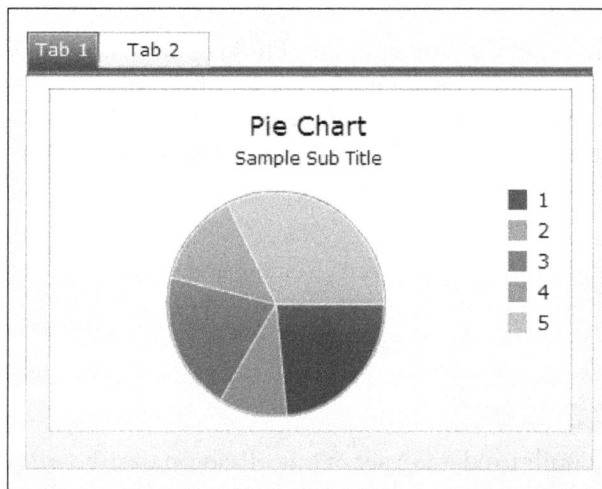

Using Alerts

The **Alerts** feature is a very important feature that we will be using in our dashboard. The **Alert** feature allows us to add an indication, a single-value component, a map or even a selector to our chart. As we mentioned in the preface, using only measures, numbers, or metrics is not enough to give a clear idea about performance. We also mentioned that a KPI is a combination of a metric and the target value for that metric. The comparison between a metric and its target will add the required indication, and so we can judge whether we are performing well or badly based on the comparison results.

In this section, you will learn how to configure the **Alert** features for different components types, such as Charts, Single-value components, Maps, and Selectors using different configurations.

Using Alerts with Charts

We have an **Alerting** tab in almost all charts. In this section, we will see how to configure alerting for the **Sales and Quantity by Product** combination chart:

1. Open the object browser and expand the **Group1** group.
2. Select the **Sales and Quantity by Product** combination chart.

We didn't select the combination chart from the canvas directly because it is part of a group, and trying to select it will lead to selecting the whole group. You can see these steps in the following screenshot:

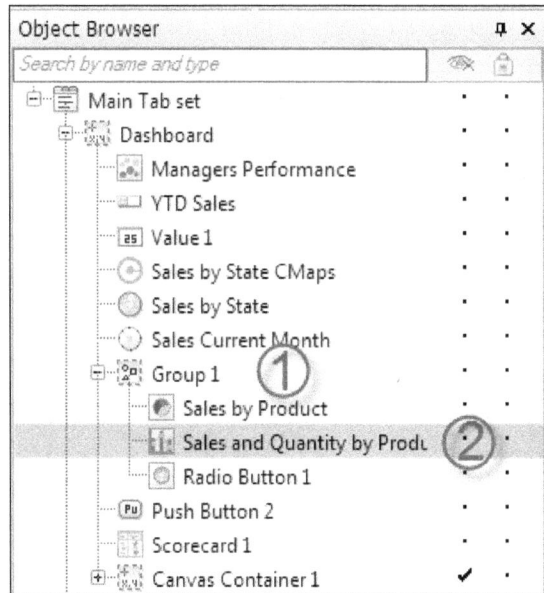

Now go to the **Properties** panel and perform the following steps:

3. Navigate to the **Alerts** tab.

4. Select the Sales series from the **Series** panel.

5. Tick the Enable **Alerts** checkbox.

6. Select the **As Percentage of Target** option, and link the **Target** field to the **Product!$J$4:$J$9** Excel range.

7. Add the **100%** value to the already existing alerts thresholds.

8. Select **70%** and change it to **90%**. Then select **30%** and change it to **75%**. The steps so far are shown here:

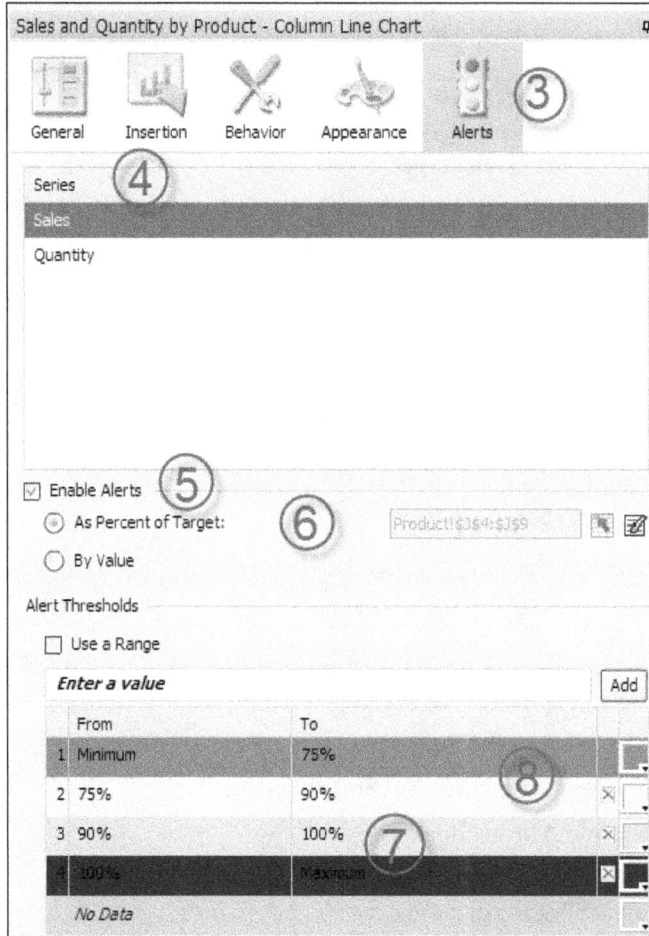

9. Uncheck the **Enable Auto Colors** box, and change the next color to 100% and **Maximum** to blue.

10. Select **High values are good** under **Color Order**.

You can see these steps marked in the following screenshot:

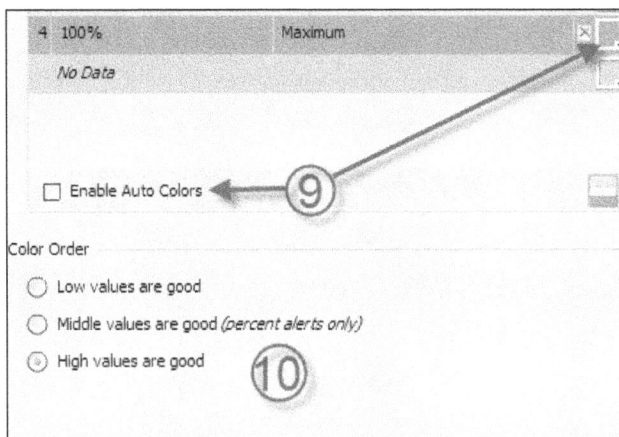

Now click on **Preview** to see the combination chart, which looks like this:

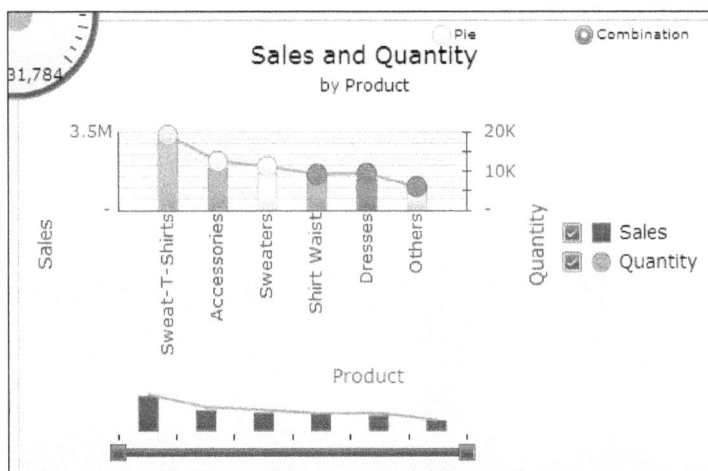

Now let's configure the **Alerts** property for the **Quantity** series:

1. Select the **Quantity** series from the **Series** area under **Sales and Quantity by Product**, under the **Alerts** tab.

2. Tick the **Enable Alerts** option and select **By Value**.

3. Then tick the **Use Range** option under **Alert Thresholds**, and link it to the **Product!$K$4:$K$6** Excel range.

4. Make sure that the **High Values are Good** option is selected.

You can see these steps in the following screenshot:

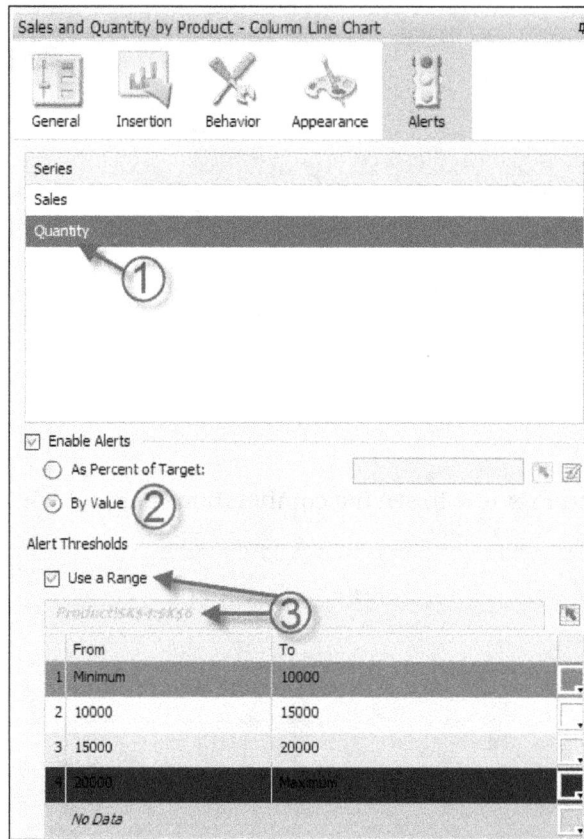

The final combination chart should look like this:

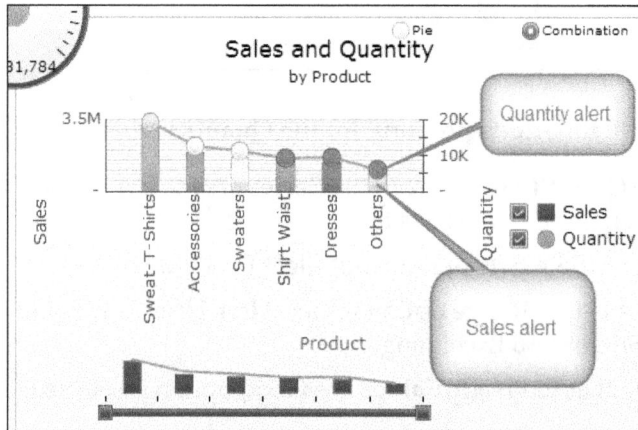

Before concluding this section, let's discuss the new features introduced here:

- **Enable Alerts**: This option will enable or disable the **Alert** property for the selected dashboard component. We can set the alert to be any of these:
    - **As Percentage of Target**: This should be used if we have a target for our metric, and we want to configure the indication to be a percentage of the predefined target. Let's say that we have a target of **100** and a metric of **90** as the value. The percentage will be 90/100 in this case, which equal to 90 percent. Then we need to check which threshold 90 percent will map at. If we are using the default **High values are good** threshold settings, then our 90 percent value will be in the 70 percent and Maximum bucket, which corresponds to a green color, as shown in the following screenshot.
    - **By Value**: We can also configure the alert to be based on a specific value. In this case, we directly compare the actual metric value against the threshold value, and there is no target involved.

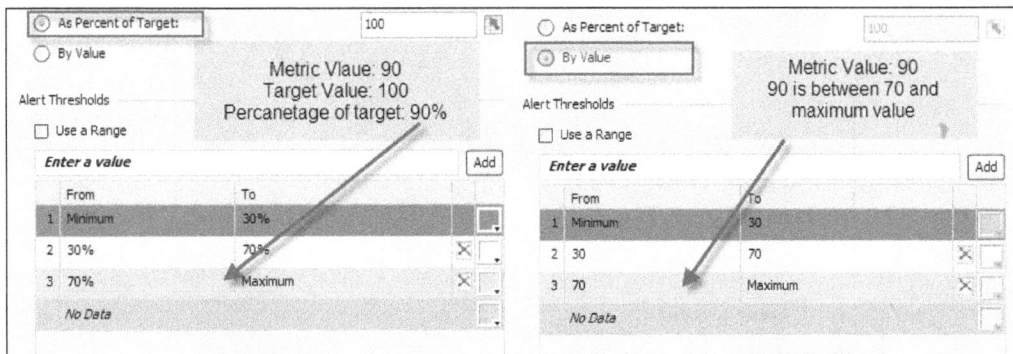

- **Alert Thresholds**: This option will define our coloring mechanism. We can enter our threshold directly in the threshold area or map it to an Excel range. We can also set the following operations:
    - **Use range**: Link Alerts Thresholds to the Excel sheet range instead of entering them manually, which we did in the **Quantity** series alert example.
    - **Add value**: By default, there are three threshold colors (red, yellow, and green) with default thresholds as follows: Minimum to 30% (red), 30% to 70% (yellow), and 70% to Maximum (green). This is good in the case of high values. We can add new threshold values and define a color for them. For example, we can add 50% to add a new threshold value, as shown in the following screenshot.

- ○ **Remove value**: We can click on the **X** button beside a threshold to remove this value.

- ○ **No Data**: By default, the **No Data** metrics will displayed as gray to indicate that the comparison against the Alerts value is not a value. We can change this color as per our requirement.

- ○ **Enable auto colors**: We will not be able to select threshold colors if this option is enabled, as the threshold color will be automatically picked up used. We can disable this option if we want to select threshold colors ourselves.

You can see **Alert Thresholds** in the following screenshot:

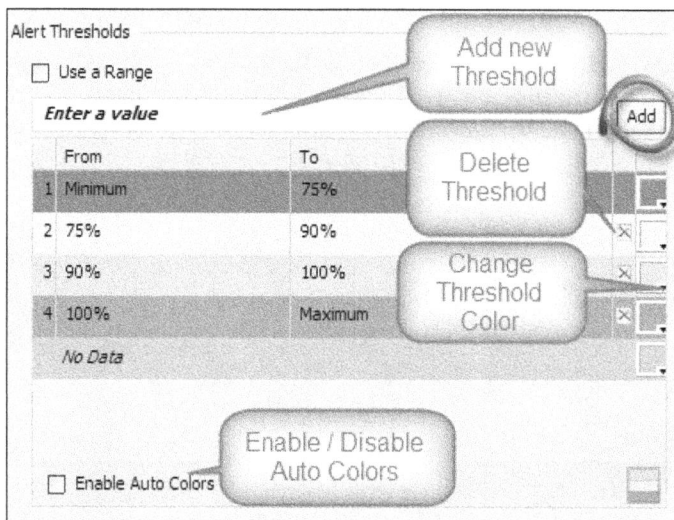

- • **Color Order**: For this, we have the following options:

  - ○ **High values are good**: In this case, some KPIs are increasing by their nature, such as customer satisfaction. This means that high values of customer satisfaction are good in this case.

  - ○ **Low values are good**: In this case, KPIs are decreasing by their nature, such as customer complaints. So, low values are good, and our target is to maintain a low value for such a KPI.

- ° **Middle values are good (percent alerts only):** Finally, there are some KPIs that are balanced by their nature, for example, temperature. We want to keep their values somewhere in the middle—neither very hot, nor very cold. In this case, we should select the Middle values are good option.

Color Order

○ Low values are good

○ Middle values are good *(percent alerts only)*

◉ High values are good

Using Alerts with the single-value component

Alerts can also be used with a single-value dashboard component. The only difference here is that we have only one metric value. We have already discussed most of the settings for alerts, but we will introduce a new feature here. It is available with single-value components only.

Let's follow these steps to enable an alert for the **Sales Current Month** gauge:

1. Select the **Sales Current Month** gauge, and navigate to its property panel.
2. Navigate to the **Alerts** tab.
3. Check the **Enable Alerts** option, and select **As Percentage of Target**.
4. Set the target value to 15000000.
5. Uncheck **Enable Auto Colors**, and change the font color of the red threshold from black to white.
6. Check **Alert**, **Marker**, and **Value** in the **Alert Location** property.

You can see steps 5 and 6 in the following screenshot:

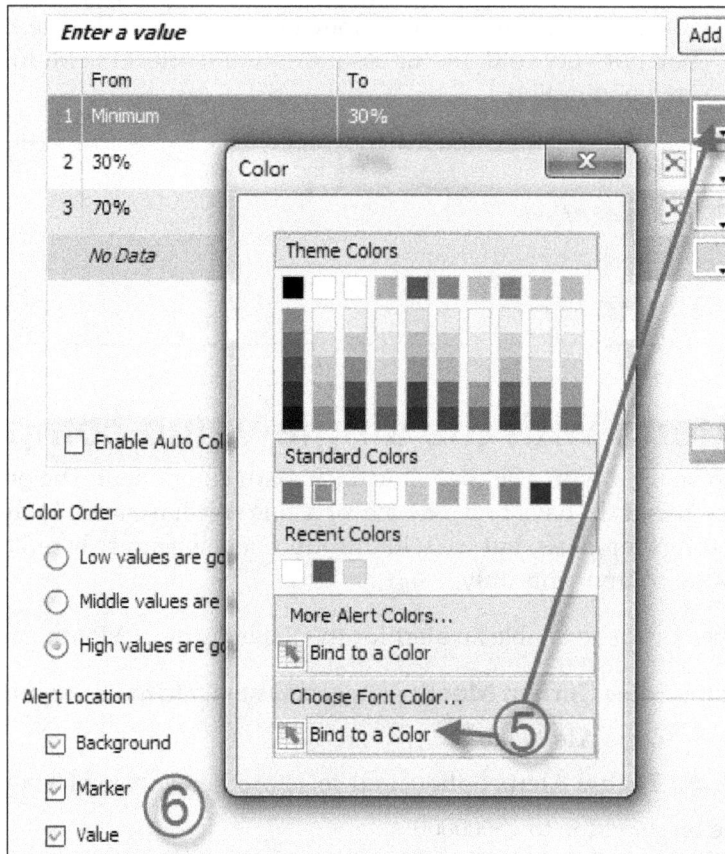

You can also follow these steps to add another indicator for the target:

1. Navigate to the **General** tab.
2. Add a new indicator.
3. Type **Target** in the **Name** field and 15000000 in the Value field.
4. Select **Outside Marker** in the **Type** field.

These steps are shown here:

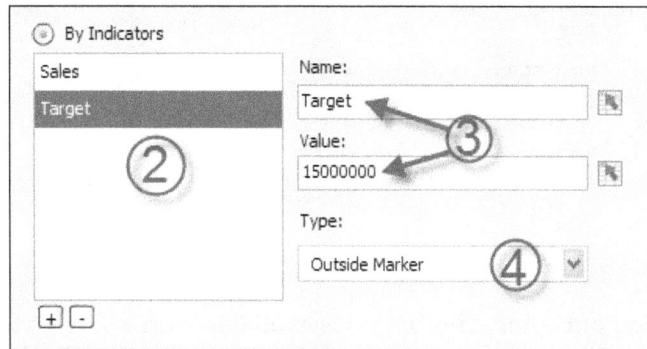

The single-value component, after configuring the alert property, looks like what is shown in the following screenshot:

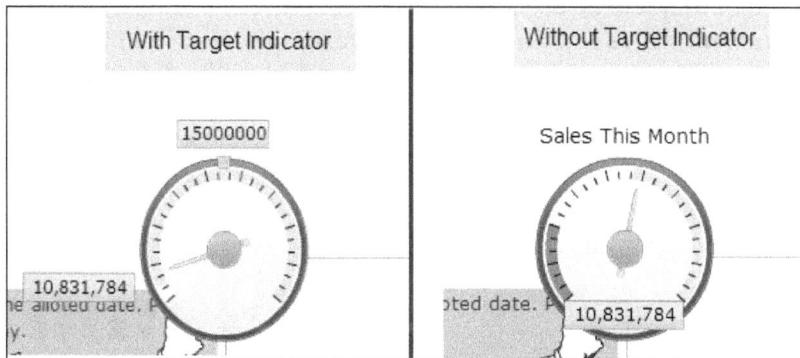

Before winding up this section, we will discuss the new features introduced here:

- **Alert Location**: This option is available only in single-value dashboard components, and can be used to define the alert's location. We have the following possible alert locations:
    - ° **Background**
    - ° **Marker**
    - ° **Value**

You can see what each of them corresponds to in this screenshot:

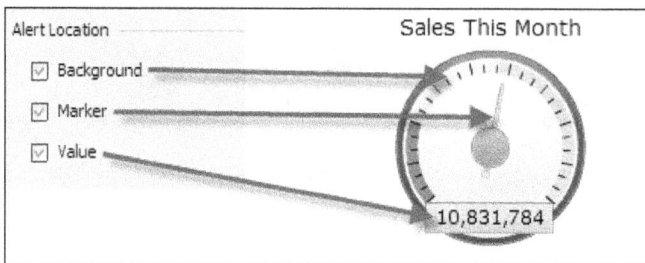

- **Threshold Font color**: This option is available with a single-value component. This is because we can configure the alert to be displayed with the value as well. Sometimes, the value will be not readable if we have a black font for the value and a dark threshold color. To overcome this, we can change (configure) both the threshold color, as well as the font color that will be used with this threshold. For example, we've used a white font with a red threshold in this example. Note that the green and yellow thresholds will use the black font, which is the default, because we didn't change it.

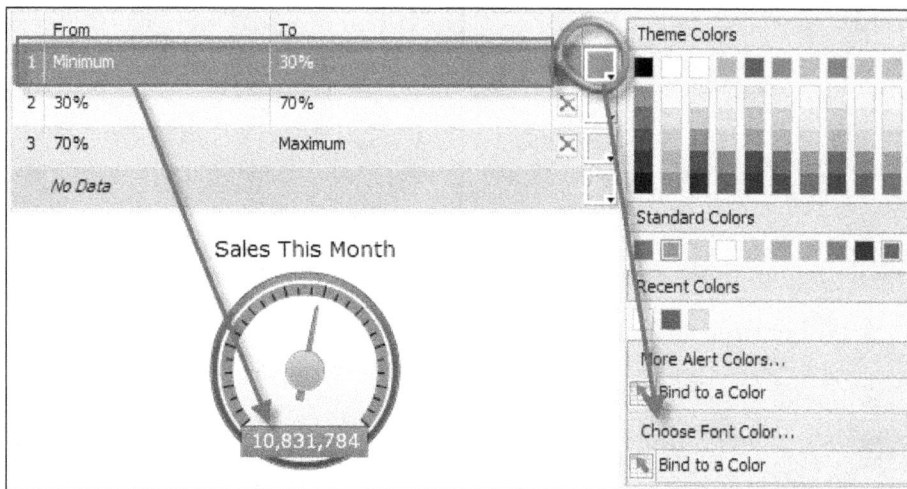

- **Multiple Indicators**: We can display multiple indicators on the gauge. Each indicator needs this configuration: name, value, and type. We have the following indicator types:
  - ° **Needle**
  - ° **Outside Marker**
  - ° **Inside Marker**

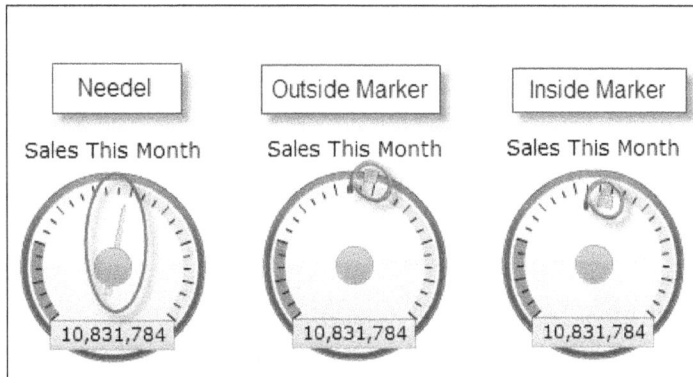

Using Alerts with maps

The **Alerts** feature can be used with maps as well. The indication will color the map area, based on the corresponding metric and target, or based on the metric value. Here, we will see how to configure the alert feature for the USA map that we already have in our eFashion dashboard project, but to explain something new to you, we will use the alert property and color intensity to indicate the sales size. We will use blue scales to do this:

1. Select the **Sales by States** map and navigate to the **Properties** panel.
2. Navigate to the **Alerts** tab.
3. Check **Enable Alerts** and select **By Value**.
4. Check **Use a Range** in the **Alert Threshold** property, and link the values to the **Map!$F$4:$F$6** Excel range.
5. Uncheck **Enable Auto Colors** and configure the colors of the threshold to be dark blue for the 5,000,000$ sales, blue for sales from 3,000,000$ to 5,000,000$, and light blue for the last threshold.

You can see these steps in the following screenshot:

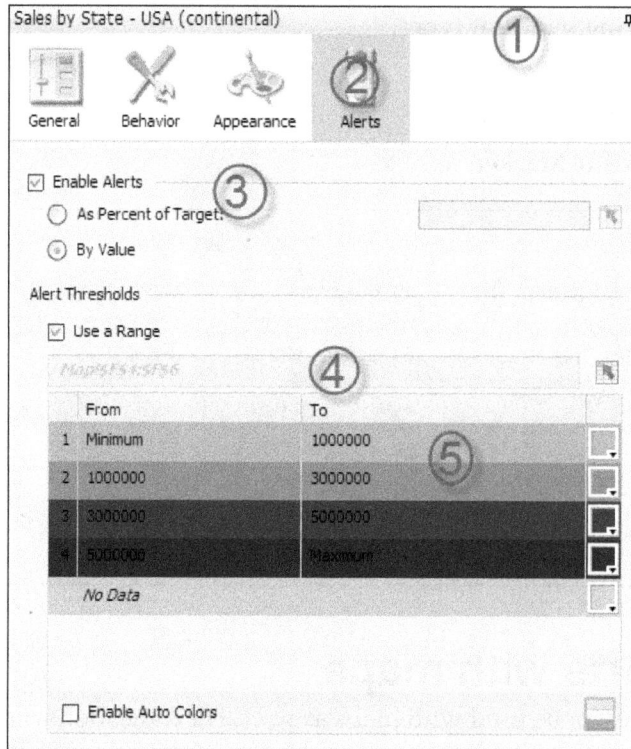

The map is shown in this screenshot:

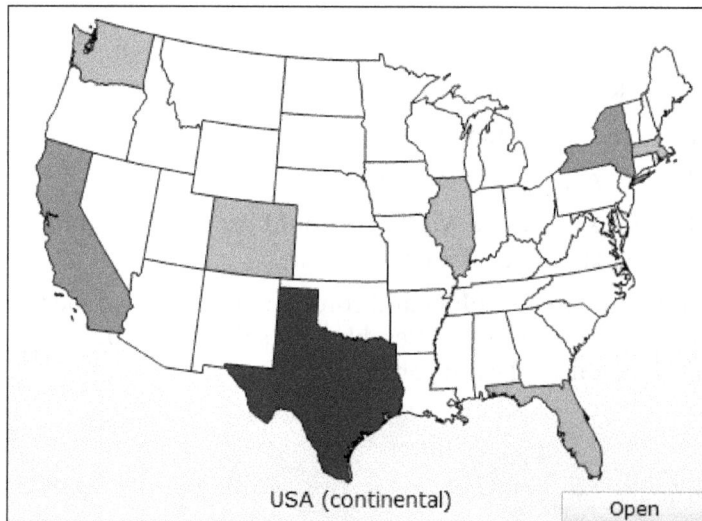

It is best practice to add a color legend to the map. In this case, we will see how to do it together:

1. Drag a **Spreadsheet Table** component into the canvas and place it in the bottom-left corner of the map.

2. Link the **Spreadsheet Table** data to the **Map!$E$3:$F$6** range.

3. Navigate to the **Appearance** tab and remove **Gridlines**.

Note that the **Spreadsheet Table** component takes the colors that we've defined in the Excel sheet, and uses the same format that we have applied in the Excel model. This component is very good for displaying Excel-like data.

You can see these configurations in the following screenshot:

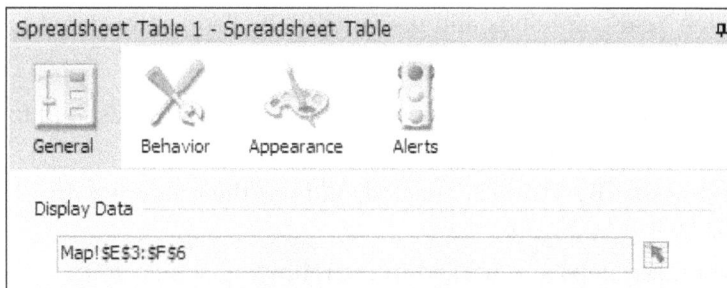

The final map component is shown in this screenshot:

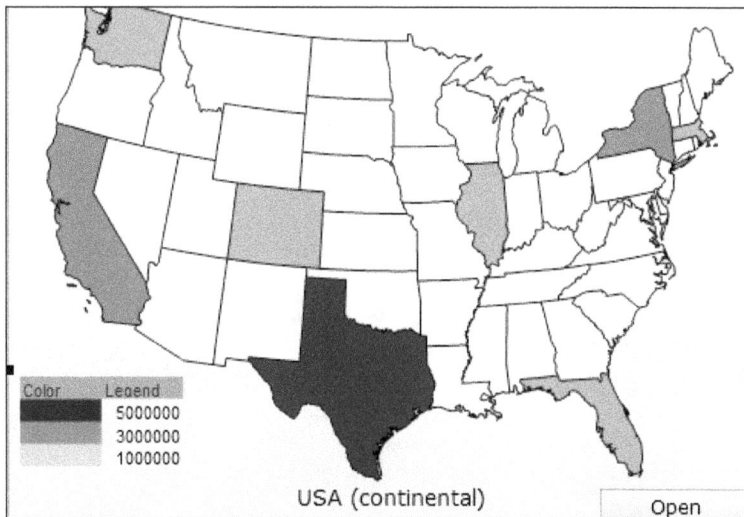

Using Alerts with Selectors

Alerts can also be used with selectors to give an indication of the displayed labels. This can help the dashboard's end user make a selection for a specific product if, for example, it is highlighted in red. You will now learn how to configure alerts for the following selectors:

- Combo Box
- Scorecard

Using Alerts with the Combo Box selector

Let's follow these steps to configure the alerts for the **Year** combobox under the **Analysis** tab set:

1. Select the **Analysis** tab from the tab set container.

2. Select the **Year** combobox and navigate to the **Properties** panel.

3. Then navigate to the **Alerts** tab.

4. Check the **Enable Alerts** option and link the **Alert Values** field to the **Selectors!$F$8:$F$12** Excel range.

5. Make sure that **By Value** is selected, and use the following threshold values: 10,000,000 to 15,000,000.

   Some of these steps are marked in the following screenshot:

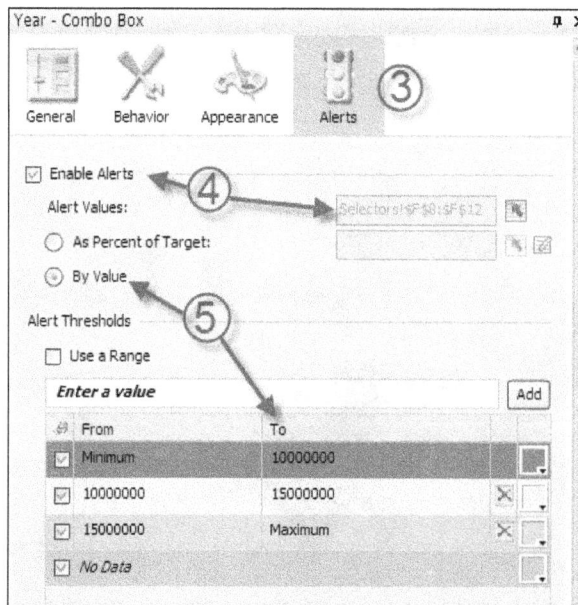

The **Year Combo Box**, after configuring the **Alerts** property, looks like what is shown in this screenshot:

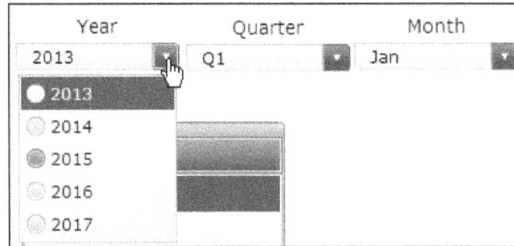

Before ending this section, we will discuss the following newly introduced features:

- **Alert Values**: We used the metric's value in the previous alert example to indicate the KPI, but here we have a combobox selector that contains only years as labels. In the selectors, we need to define a list of values that will be associated with each selector label. These metric values will be used in comparison with the target or the threshold values to map each label to its performance bucket. In this example, we have "sales by year" data, and so we build our selector alerts based on this information. We need to note that we don't have data for 2016 and 2017, and this is why they are displayed in gray.

Using Alerts with the Scorecard selector

A scorecard is another type of selector that we will use in this section to configure the alerts property. You will learn how to configure alerts' colors and shapes for any scorecard column, so let's do it together:

1. Select the **Dashboard** tab from the main tab set container.
2. Select the **Products Scorecard** dashboard component, and navigate to the **Alerts** tab under the **Properties** panel.
3. Select the **Lines** column in the **Enable Alerts** area.
4. Link **Alerts Values** to the **'Score Card'!$D$4:$D$9** Excel range.
5. Select **As Percentage of Target** and link the target to the **'Score Card'!$E$4:$E$9** Excel range.
6. Make sure that high values are good in the colors order.
7. Uncheck **Enable Auto Colors** and use these thresholds: 70% and 90%.

8. Edit the indicator icons for each threshold buckets to be same as what is shown the following screenshot.

You can see most of the preceding steps marked here:

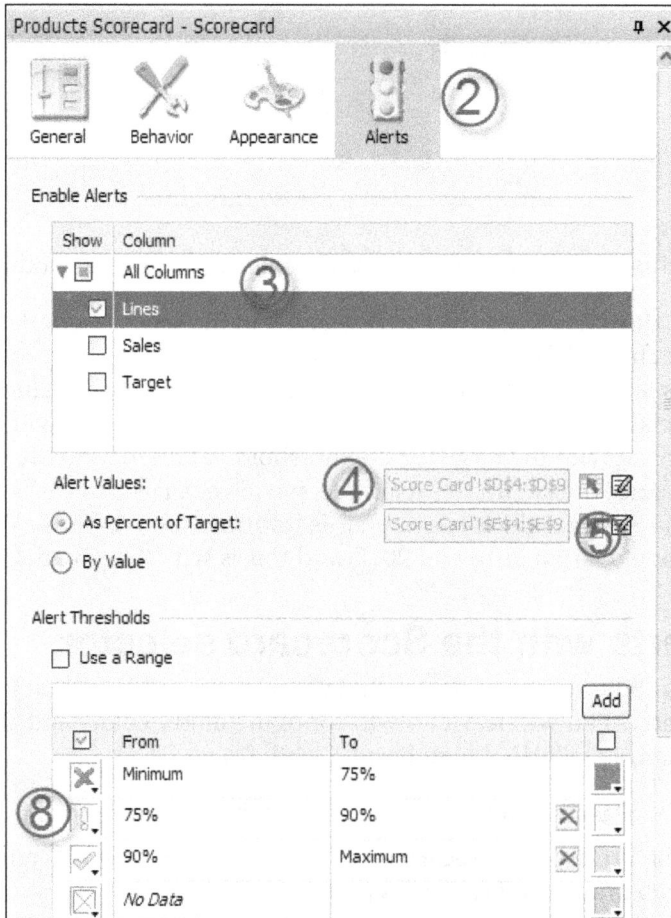

You can see the scorecard with alerts in the following screenshot:

Lines	Sales	Target
✔ Sweat-T-Shirts	3,232,135.10	3,000,000
Accessories	1,899,404.70	2,000,000
♀ Sweaters	1,660,040.30	2,000,000
✘ Shirt Waist	1,654,358.50	3,000,000
Dresses	1,408,594.90	1,000,000
Others	977,250.90	1,000,000

Before winding up this section, let's discuss the newly introduced features:

- **Icon**: We've used colors as indicators in all the previous examples of alerts. Scorecard is a special dashboard component that mainly focuses on scoring items by highlighting them. We can use colors as well as icons. To change the threshold icon, just click on the icon button and select a proper one.

> We can use colors, icons, or both as indicators in **Scorecard**.

You can see what the icon window looks like in this screenshot:

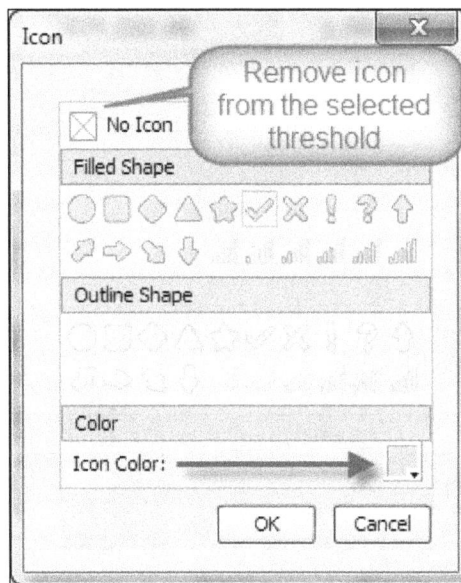

You can see how to use colors as indicators, besides icons, in the following screenshot:

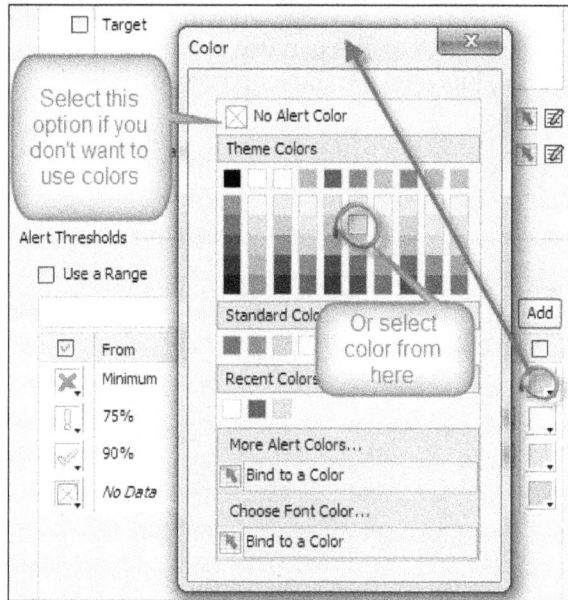

Here's an assignment: configure the color indicator for the rest of the thresholds. The final output should be like this:

Lines	Sales	Target
✔ Sweat-T-Shirts	3,232,135.10	3,000,000
Accessories	1,899,404.70	2,000,000
Sweaters	1,660,040.30	2,000,000
✖ Shirt Waist	1,654,358.50	3,000,000
Dresses	1,408,594.90	1,000,000
Others	977,250.90	1,000,000

Using the drill-down (Insertion) feature

This feature was known as drill-down in earlier releases, but now it is known as **Insertion**. The main idea of this feature is that you can interact with the chart, and treat it like a selector. So, for example, if you click on any part of a pie chart that shows the sales by product, you can insert the selected product in a specific cell, and then filter the data in another chart to display only the information for that product. This was also known as the master-detail concept in other tools.

Here, we will configure the insertion feature for the **Sales and Quantity by Product** combination chart:

1. Select the **Sales and Quantity by Product** dashboard component, and navigate to the **Properties** panel.
2. Select the **Insertion** tab.
3. Check the **Enable Data Insertion** option.
4. Link **Series Name Destination** to the **Product!$H$17** Excel cell.
5. Select **Column** in **Insertion Type**.
6. Select **Sales** from the **Series** area. Link **Source Data** to the **Product!$H$19:$M$27** Excel range, and **Destination** to the **Product!$P$19:$P$27** Excel range.
7. Select **Mouse Click** for **Insert On** under **Interaction Options**.
8. Select **Sales** from **Series**, and select the number for **Item** under **Default Selection** as 1.

You can see these steps marked in this screenshot:

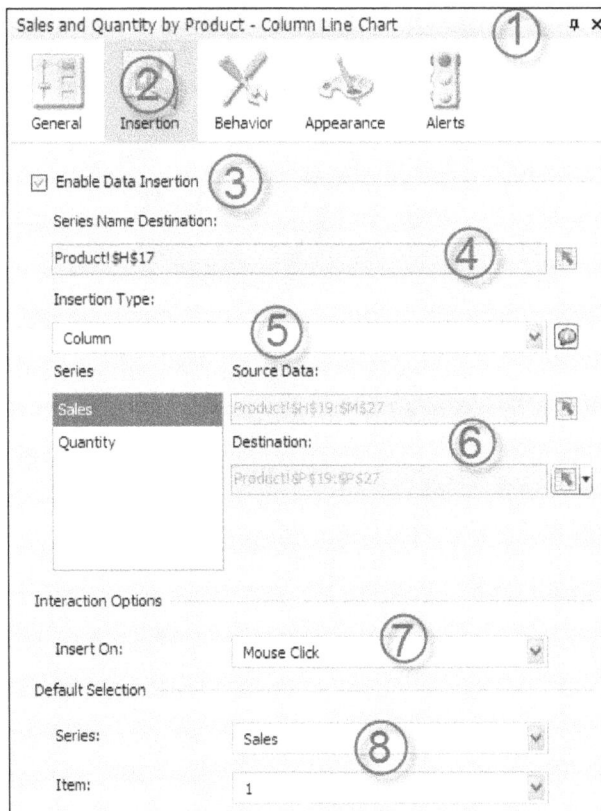

Now we will insert a new map dashboard component to display the data inserted into the destination range. This data will display sales for the selected product distributed by region:

1. Drag and drop a new USA map, resize it, and then put it under the combination chart legend.

2. Navigate to the **General** tab and link **Display Data** to the **Product!$O$20:$P$27** Excel range.

3. Navigate to the **Alerts** tab and enable alerts.

4. Use the following threshold values: 300,000 and 700,000.

   You will see the final output like this:

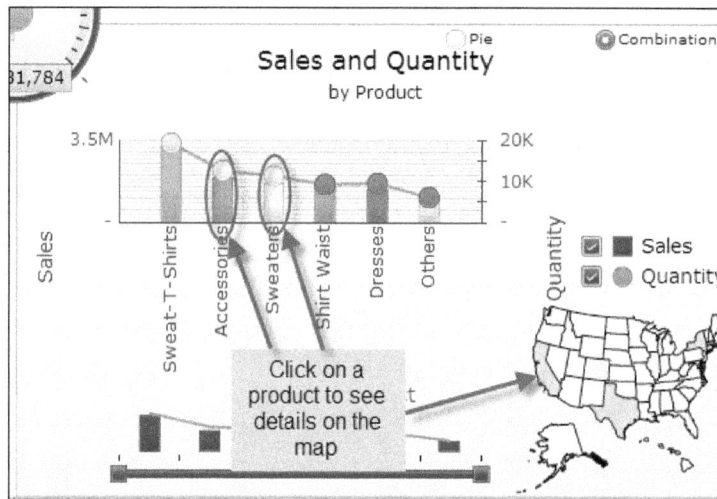

Here is another assignment: create another insertion based on the **Quantity** series in the **Combination** chart. Create another USA map to display the quantity of the selected product across all states. Configure dynamic visibility for the sales and quantity USA maps to show and hide, based on the selected series.

As we saw, insertion will make our chart act like a selector, and we will have many common properties, such as default selected values and the insertion type that we have already introduced with selectors.

Linking a dashboard to a Webi or Crystal report document

This feature can be used to link your dashboard to a detailed Webi or Crystal report. This is very useful, because you can't display a large amount of detailed information in your dashboard. Moreover, this this is not what dashboards are meant to be used for. We can use the OpenDocument function to specify the report that we will open, and to pass the required parameters to the report prompts.

We can use the URL button dashboard component and a link to the required report, along with prompt values.

> You can read a complete guide on how to configure and use the OpenDocument function at https://help.sap.com/businessobject/product_guides/boexir4/en/xi4_opendocument_en.pdf.

Summary

In this chapter, you learned how to create interactive dashboards, and we introduced many advanced features of dashboards. You learned how to use the dynamic visibility feature to show and hide components at runtime, based on a specific condition. Then we introduced containers and discussed the main differences between panel, canvas, and tab set containers.

We also highlighted the main difference between the container and grouping features. Furthermore, we discussed what alerts are, and how to use them with charts, single-value components, maps, and selectors. Finally, we introduced the insertion feature and saw how to link a dashboard with a Webi or crystal report.

In the next chapter, we will teach you how to style up our dashboard by adding images and logos, and using art components, such as lines, circles, and squares. We will also learn about themes, color binding, and many other styling options that will give a strong, professional look and feel to our dashboard.

7
Styling Up

We have almost completed the development phase of our eFashion dashboard project. In this chapter, we will see how to apply our corporate design guidelines and style to our dashboard using relevant colors and themes. You will learn how to create a coherent dashboard in terms of size and shape, with a better understanding of various controlling elements.

You will also learn how to use art and background components and add logos, images, and icons to enhance the look and feel of your dashboard.

In this chapter, the main focus will be on:

- Using text and label dashboard components
- Dealing with colors using color schemes, themes, and color binding
- Using art and background dashboard components
- Formatting and controlling the layout of dashboard components

Using text dashboard components

Any dashboarding application tool or utility should provide a way to incorporate text and labels into the dashboard. We have a **Text** category under the **Components** panel, which contains the following:

- **Input Text Area**
- **Label**
- **Input Text**

You can see these components here:

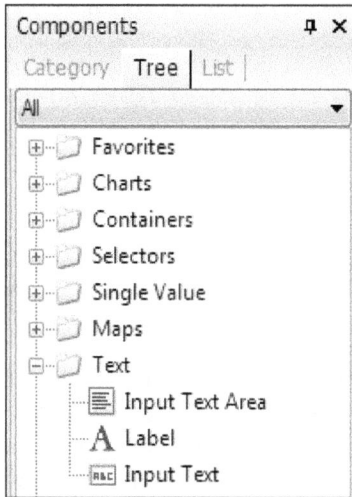

Before practicing this, let's prepare the dashboard file for this chapter:

1. Navigate to the Code sample folder from your PC.
2. Open the **Chapter6** dashboard under the **Dashboard (Ready)** folder.
3. Save it in the same location as **Dashboard7** in your **Development** folder.

   You can see these steps in the following screenshot:

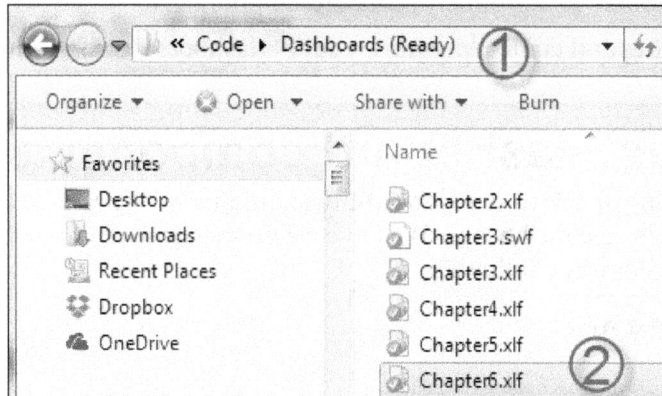

Now let's talk about text dashboard components.

Using Input Text Area

Input text can be used to enter a long string, such as a description paragraph, or directions on how to use the dashboard. This dashboard component can be used as an input or output. The **Input Text Area** option can be found under the **Text** category in the **Components** panel. We can use it to display and enter long clarification text. You can see **Input Text Area** in this screenshot:

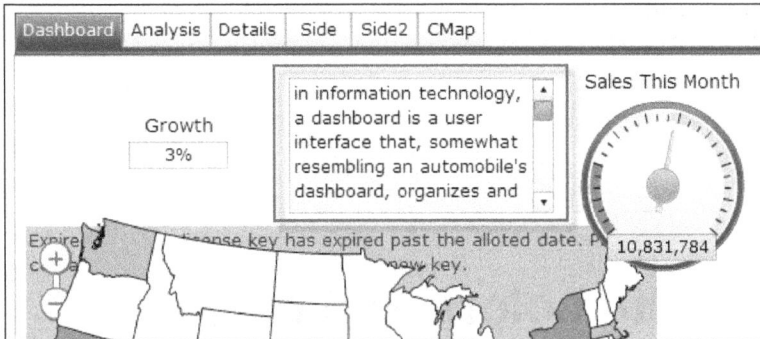

Using labels

Labels are used to display data only, and can't be used as an input. They are ideal for the dashboard title and help information.

> We can use labels to debug destination values, and to see what is inserted during runtime based on our selection.
>
> We can use labels that are mobile-compatible components instead of the **Value** and **Spinner** components, which are not supported in mobile phones.

Using Input Text

The **Input Text** component is ideal for a small, one-line text input, and it can be used to enter, for example, passwords and user names.

We can see the **Input Text** component in the following screenshot:

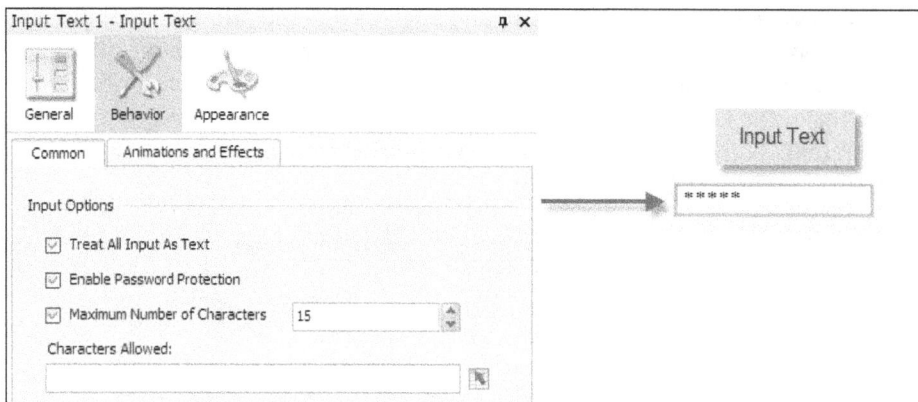

Dealing with colors and themes

In this section, you will learn how to deal with colors, and control the appearance of dashboard components. We will start with how we can change the colors of a selected component in the first place. Then we will see how to bind it to predefined color codes in the Excel model. After that, you will learn how to change the entire color scheme by selecting one of the predefined color schemes, or by creating your own customized color scheme. Finally, we will talk about themes, and how we can use them along with the color theme.

Using the Appearance tab

We can find any property related to appearance, such as layout, color, and text. We can find this tab under almost every dashboard component's properties, which can be accessed from the **Properties** panel. Here, we will try to configure the appearance properties of the **Sales and Quantity by Product** combined chart:

1. Select the **Sales and Quantity by Product** combination chart and navigate to the **Properties** panel.
2. Select **Layout** under the **Appearance** tab.
3. Make sure that **Show Chart Background** is selected.
4. Check **Show Fill** in **Title Area**.
5. Select **Blue Lighter 40%** in the **Fill** color.
6. Check **Show Border** and select **Gray Lighter 35%** in the border color.
7. Leave **Border Thickness** as **1**.

You can see the preceding steps in this screenshot:

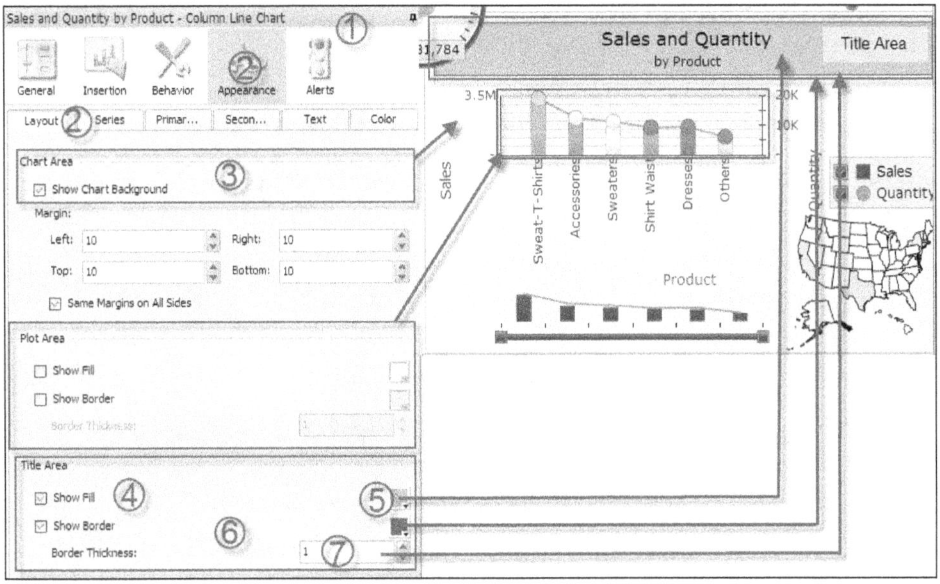

Now let's configure the remaining layout appearance properties:

1. Make sure that **Enable Legend** is checked.
2. Then make sure that **Position** is set to **Right**.
3. Check **Show Fill** and **Show Border**, and pick up your favorite colors.
4. Check the **Enable Hide/Show Chart Series at Run- Time** option.

You can see these steps in the following screenshot:

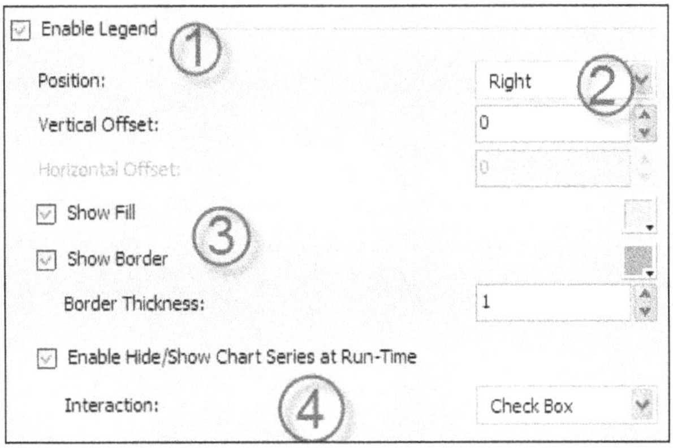

Now let's discuss the newly introduced features before we end this section:

- **Show Chart Background**: We can use this property to show a background in our chart, or to make it more transparent
- **Enable Legend**: We can use this property to show the legend and configure all properties related to it, such as position, fill, and border

Now let's move on to the next tab under **Appearance**, which is **Series**. In this tab, we can control series colors and shapes. We can also control the marker size for line series.

The **Series** tab is shown here:

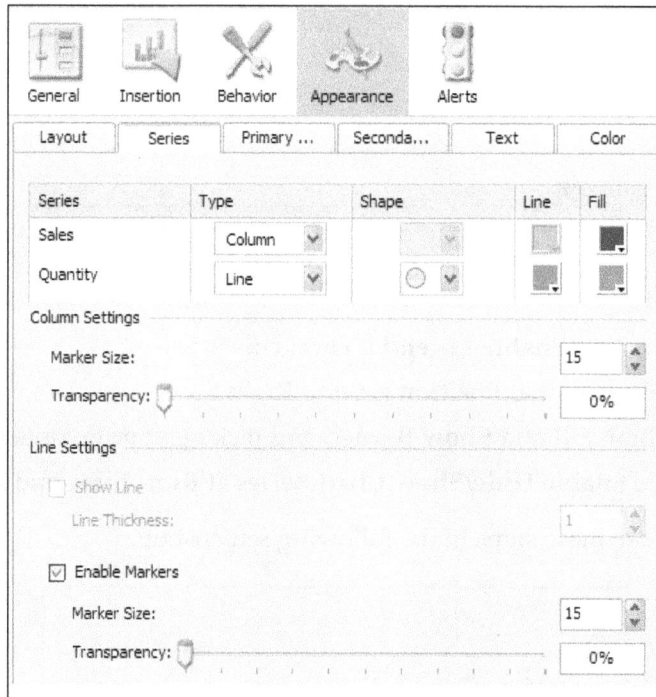

We will be able to see the **Primary Axes** and **Secondary Axes** tabs in the selected chart, which supports displaying data on dual axes. We can use these tabs to control the following options:

- Vertical axis
- Horizontal axis
- Horizontal grid lines

You can see the **Primary Axes** and **Secondary Axes** tabs in the following screenshot:

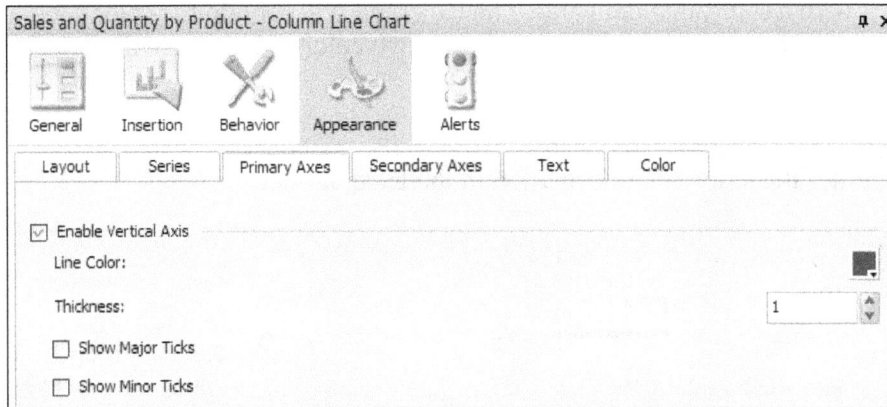

We can use the **Text** tab to control the text properties, such as font type, color, size, effect (bold, italic, and underline), alignment, and format. You can see the **Text** tab in this screenshot:

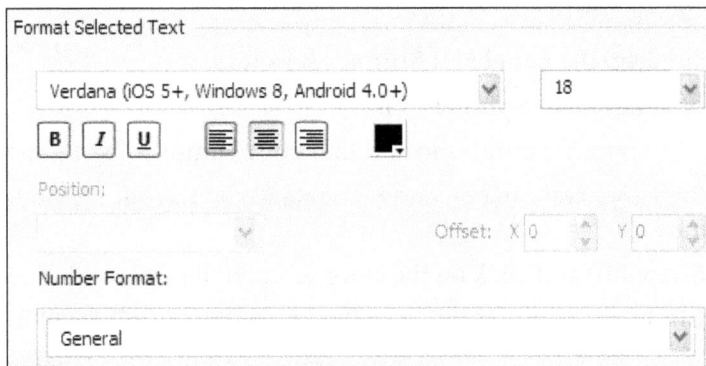

Finally, there is the **Color** tab. In this tab, we can configure anything related to the color of the selected component.

Color binding

The color binding feature can be used to link a color to an Excel cell, instead of setting it with a static, manual value. The Excel cell will contain the color code in hexadecimal format, or the color name for known colors. Here, we will perform a simple side exercise to learn this:

1. Open a new dashboard file.

2. Enter the following information in the Excel model:

	A	B	C	D	E	F	G
2		Value				Red	#cc0000
3		0				Yellow	#fff600
4						Green	#00ff00
5	Background color	#fff600				White	#FFFFFF
6	Font color	#000000				Black	#000000

3. Use the following Excel formulas for the background and font colors:

    ○   Background: `=IF(B3<0,G2,IF(B3>0,G4,G3))`

    ○   Font: `=IF(B3<0,G5,G6)`

4. Drag and drop the **Label** and **Spinner** selectors.

5. Link both **Label** and **Spinner** to **B3**.

6. Adjust the spinner's minimum and maximum limits to be 10 and 10.

7. Select the **Label** component, and navigate to the **Layout** tab under **Appearance**.

8. Select **Show Fill** and click on the color to open the **Color** window.

9. Select **Bind to a color** and link it to the **Sheet1!$B$5 (#FFF600)** Excel cell.

10. Navigate to the **Text** tab under **Appearance** and bind the label font color to the **Sheet1!$B$6 (#000000)** Excel cell.

You can see the color window in this screenshot:

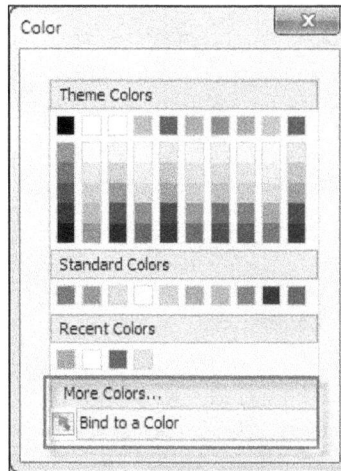

Note that the color property will be changed to the following icon to indicate that this color is bound to an Excel cell:

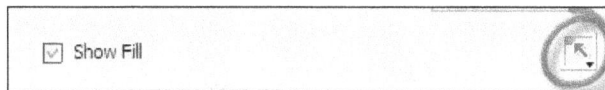

Using the color scheme

The color scheme is a pallet that contains all the colors used for dashboard components. There are many built-in color schemes, although we can also create our custom color scheme. We can select a color scheme from the color scheme drop-down menu, displayed as follows:

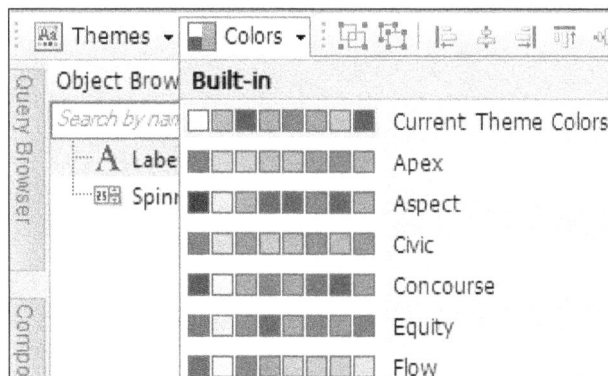

Selecting a color scheme will apply it to an existing dashboard component, if this option is checked.

> As best practice, we need to define our color scheme before we start developing a dashboard.

We can see these two options in this screenshot:

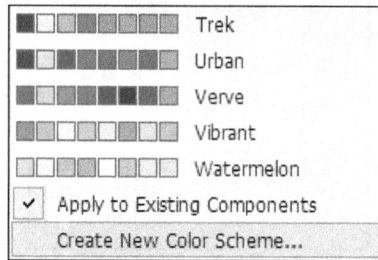

■□■■■■■	Trek
■□■■■■■	Urban
■□■■■■■	Verve
■■□□□■□	Vibrant
□□■■□□□	Watermelon
✓	Apply to Existing Components
	Create New Color Scheme...

Now let's create our own color scheme:

1. Click on the **Colors** drop-down menu from the tool bar to expand the default available color schemes.

2. Navigate to **Create New Color Scheme...**.

3. Type eFashion Color Scheme in the **Name** field.

4. Click on **Advanced Settings** to expand the advanced settings.

5. Set the colors for the properties under each tab. This enables you to set custom colors for every component that will be shown.

> We can't use the color binding option here. We have to select the color manually from the color pallet, or enter the corresponding color code for each property group.

You can see the **Create New Color Scheme** window in the following screenshot:

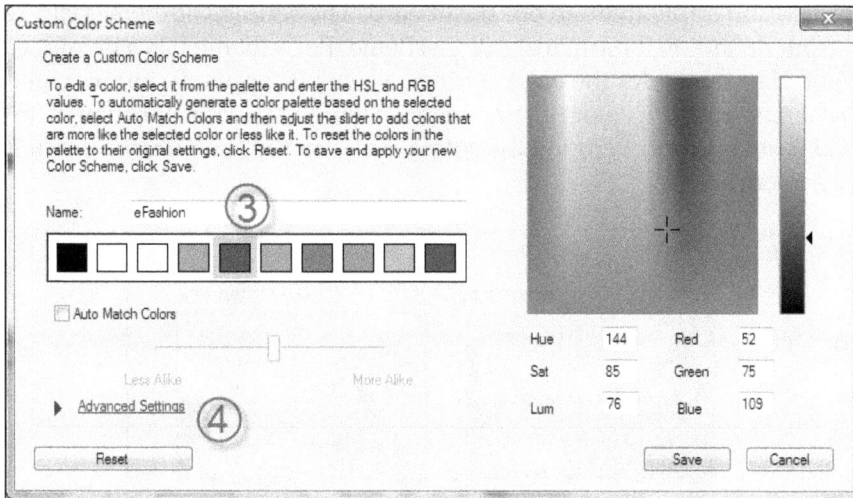

The color scheme's advanced settings are shown in this screenshot:

In this section, you learned how to change colors. You will learn how to change the appearance and themes in the next section.

> We can use **Auto Match Colors** to generate the remaining pallet colors automatically, based on the manually entered colors. We can use the **More Alike** and **Less Alike** options to control the likeness of the generated colors.

Using Themes

The **Themes** sets the look and feel of the dashboard. We can choose themes from the theme list, and apply them to our dashboard. The settings of themes can be changed from default to a particular color scheme. Each theme has a default color scheme (and thus overrules the color settings we've just applied), but we can change it (color scheme) from the color scheme menu. Therefore, a rule of thumb is to select the desired theme before changing the colors. You can see the **Themes** menu in the following screenshot:

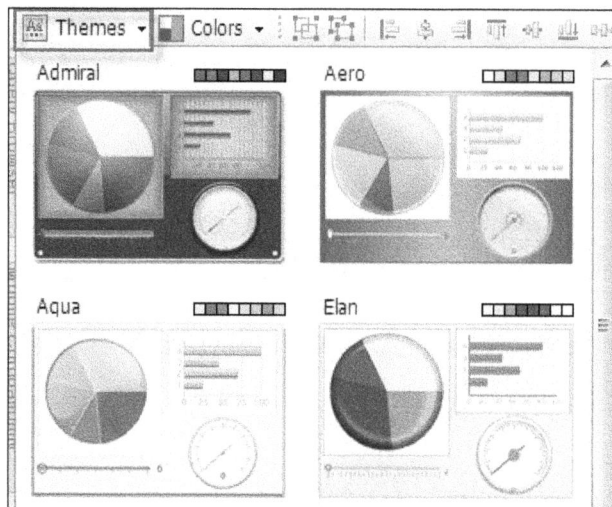

You can see an example of how Themes will affect the appearance of components in this screenshot:

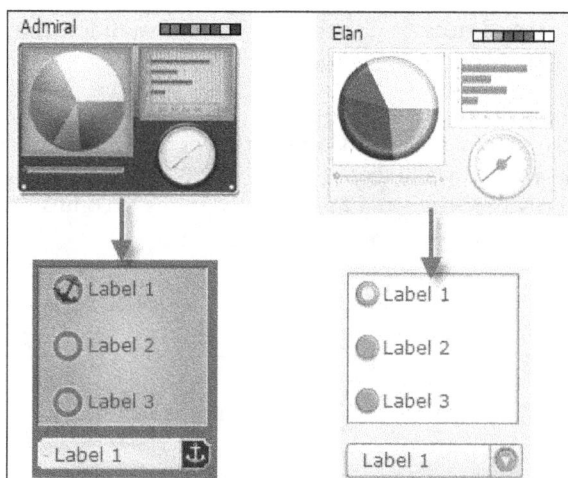

Note this hint: the **Nova** theme is the only supported theme for mobile dashboards.

Using art and background components

Art and background components can be used to give a stylish look to our dashboard. We can access these components from the **Art and Backgrounds** category under the **Components** panel, as shown in the following screenshot:

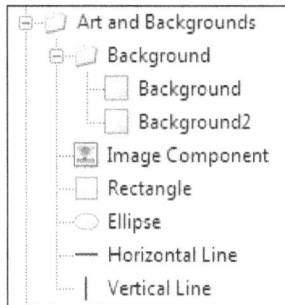

Using basic art components

The following is the first of two examples showing you how to use the **Art and Background** components to add a style to your dashboard components:

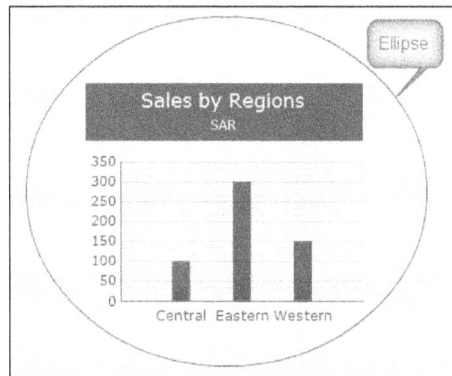

Here is the second example:

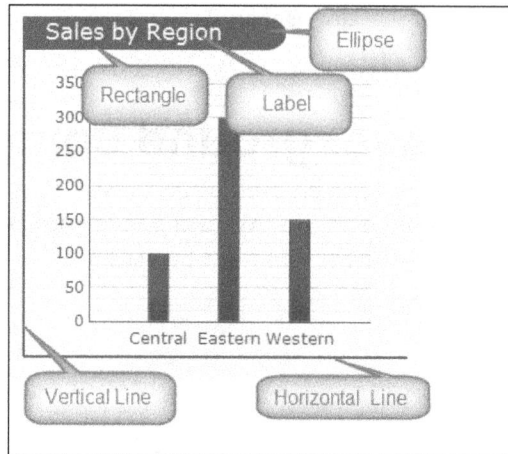

Using the image component

Images are an important element for supporting the look and feel of our dashboards. Adding logos, some related icons, and stylish buttons can make a big difference. In this section, you will learn how to add a logo and an icon:

1. Open the **Components** panel, and navigate to the **Art and Background** section. Then drag and drop an **Image Component** option onto your eFashion dashboard canvas.

2. Select the **Image Component** tab and open its properties in the **Properties** panel.

3. Navigate to the **General** tab and select **Resize Image to Component**.

4. Click on **Import** under an select the `zoom_in.png` icon from the following path: `Code Sample folder/ Design`.

You can find these steps marked in the following screenshot:

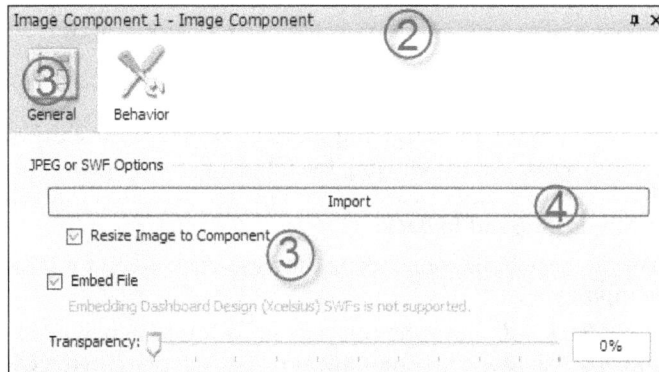

5. Select **Image Component** and the **Open** pushbutton together, by pressing *Ctrl* and clicking.

6. Click on **Make Same Size** and **Align Top**. Then click on **Align Right** from the **Format Tool bar**.

> Format operations, such as alignment and size adjustment, will be based on the first selected components. For example, if you have selected the icon first and then the push button, the alignment will be relative to the icon, because it was selected first.

You can see the previous steps in this screenshot:

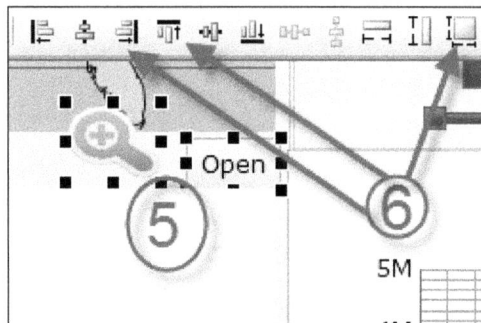

7. Reorder the components, so that the icon will be behind the push button. We can do this from the **Object Browser** panel.

8. Select **Push Button** to open its properties. Clear **open** from the **Label** field, and then navigate to the **Appearance** tab.

9. Set **Transparency** to 100 percent under the **Layout** subtab.

> We can also use the following shortcut keys to control the order of components, instead of using the **Object Browser** panel: - for **Send Back**, + for **Bring Forward**, *Ctrl* + Plus for **Bring to Front**, and *Ctrl* + Minus for **Send to Back**.
>
> We can also do the same using the right-click menu for the selected component.
>
> **Send Back** will move the component back one step, while **Send to Back** will move the component to the first place in the **Object Browser** panel for the current layer.

You can see the right-click menu for one of the components in the following screenshot:

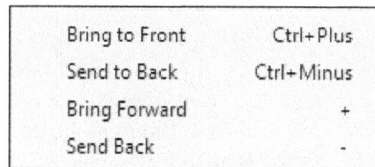

The steps we just performed are shown in this screenshot:

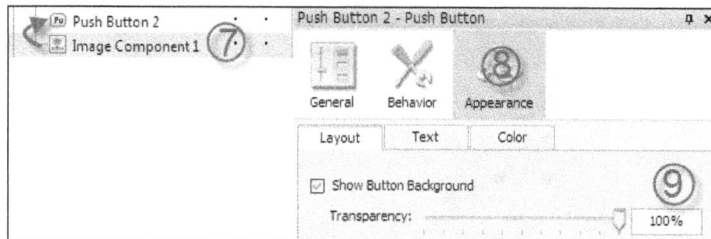

You can see the final shape of the icon in the following screenshot:

Lines	Sales	Target
✓ Sweat-T-Shirts	3,232,135.10	3,000,000
Accessories	1,899,404.70	2,000,000
Sweaters	1,660,040.30	2,000,000
✗ Shirt Waist	1,654,358.50	3,000,000
Dresses	1,408,594.90	1,000,000
Others	977,250.90	1,000,000

Now we should be able to do the following two assignments:

- **Assignment 1**: Do the same with the **Close** button in the pop-up canvas container. You can use the close icon from the `Design` folder under the `Code` example folder.

- **Assignment 2**: Do the same with the **Toggle** button used to switch between CMap and the built-in map. Use the switch icon from the `Design` folder for this purpose.

Before we conclude this section, let's discuss the newly introduced features:

- **Image component**: This component can be used to import one of the following media formats: `.jpg`, `.gif`, `.png`, `.bmp`, and `.swf`.

- **Resize image to component**: This option will automatically resize the imported image size, to match the current component size. If this option is not selected, the component will be resized as per the original image size.

Formatting the dashboard components

We can use formatting options to control the position, size, and alignment of our dashboard components. This will help us adjust the dashboard layout to deliver the right look and feel to the end user. We need to remember that a dashboard is totally dependent on delivering information using a simple and good look and feel.

We can perform the following activities to format our dashboard components:

- Aligning components
- Adjusting component size
- Spacing components
- Ordering components
- Grouping and ungrouping components

We've already used many formatting features while we were progressing through this book, and we will keep using them. You can see the formatting toolbar in this screenshot:

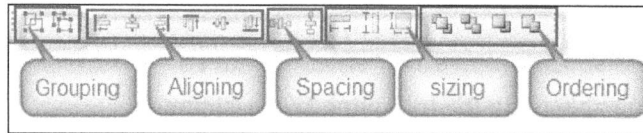

Summary

In this chapter, we saw how to enhance and customize the look and feel of our dashboard to make it more stylish, and more related to our organization's theme. Adding labels and titles is the first step that we need, in order to style our dashboard. Then we need to customize colors using the **Appearance** tab, color scheme, color binding, and themes, in order to apply our corporate design guidelines and style. After that, we saw how to use art and background components to add a professional and art-like touch on our dashboard, using images and other art components. Finally, you learned about formatting a dashboard's components by aligning, grouping, spacing, and sizing them using the format toolbar.

In the next chapter, we will see how to export, publish, and import our dashboards, as this is the final step in the dashboard creation process. From then on, you will learn how to share the final dashboard output with the dashboard's users.

8
Exporting, Publishing, and Importing Dashboards

We have almost completed the development phase of our eFashion dashboard project. In this chapter, you will learn how to share our dashboards with other users, and how to save our dashboard `xlf` file in the SAP BusinessObjects repository so other developers can access it. There are two ways to share our dashboard with business users. The first is to export our dashboard to a Flash, PowerPoint, PDF, and so on. These files can be e-mailed, or sent to the business user. This method is only applicable for prototypes and you will not be able to retrieve data from your database because your dashboard is not yet published in the BusinessObjects repository. This is why we need the second method, which is publishing to enable the end user to use and dynamically refresh dashboard data.

In this chapter, you will learn:

- Exporting dashboard file
- Publishing dashboard
- Importing dashboards

Exporting the dashboards file

The exporting dashboards process will generate a `SWF` flash file or HTML5 file and save it in the selected export format. We can export our dashboard in one of the following formats:

- **Flash (SWF)...**
- **AIR...**
- **HTML...**

- **PDF...**
- **PowerPoint Slide...**
- **Outlook...**
- **Word...**

> Previewing a dashboard will export a temporary Flash or HTML5 file based on the preview method (for desktops or for mobiles) that will be used for preview purposes, then it will be ignored after closing the preview mode. So previewing generation is just a temporary export.

We can access the **Export** menu submenu from the file menu, as you can see in the following screenshot:

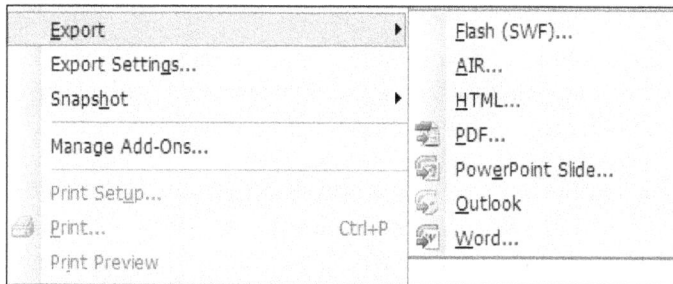

Export	▶	Flash (SWF)...
Export Settings...		AIR...
Snapshot	▶	HTML...
Manage Add-Ons...		PDF...
		PowerPoint Slide...
Print Setup...		Outlook
Print...	Ctrl+P	Word...
Print Preview		

Let's execute the following steps to export our dashboard to a PDF file:

1. Open our last version of the eFashion dashboard project.
2. Navigate to **File | Export | PDF...**
3. Type eFashion-PDF in the file name.

We can open the generated PDF and see a blank PDF file that contains only one page, which displays the **Flash** component generated from our dashboard.

> Exporting a dashboard will always generate a Flash file and, based on the export type, it will embed the generated flash component in an empty document from the selected export type. The dashboard will always fit on one page.

You can see the PDF file in the following screenshot:

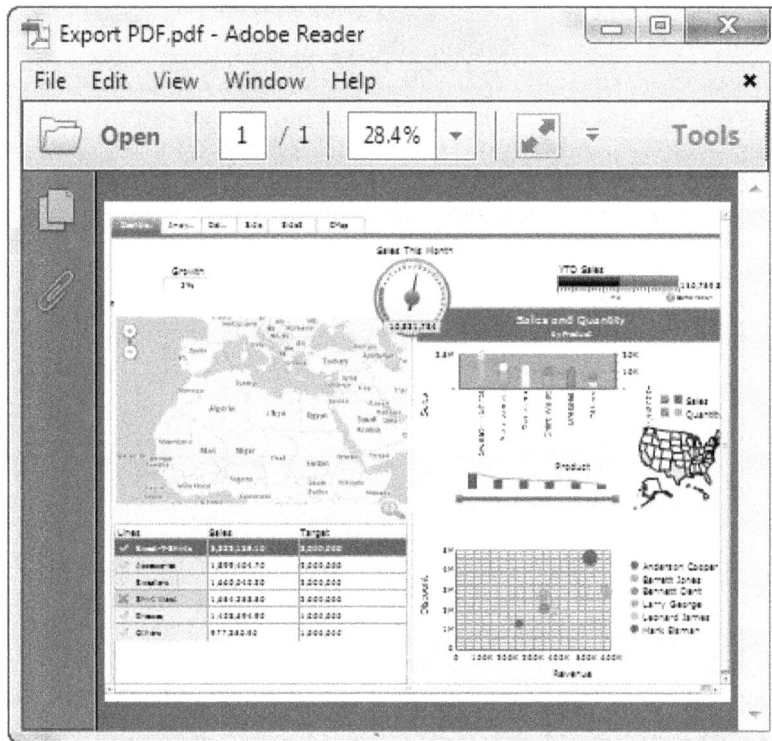

To export a dashboard, we will use the current data stored in the Excel model. We can change the **Export Settings** to replace the current Excel data. We can replace the current data with data stored in another external MS Excel file. To do this, let's follow these steps:

1. Navigate to **File | Export Settings ...**

2. Select **Use Current Excel Data** or **Use Another Excel File:**.

   You can see the **Export Settings** window in the following screenshot:

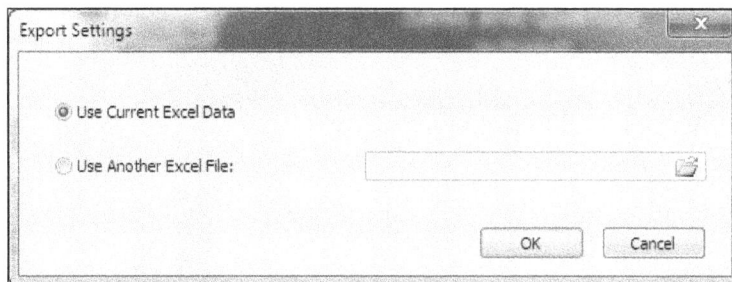

Before we leave this section, let's discuss some important aspects:

- **Data Import and Export**: The dashboard export that we discussed here is totally different from the data export that we talked about in *Chapter 1, Getting Started with SAP BO Dashboards* and *Chapter 2, Understanding the Dashboard Creation Process*. In the **Data** menu, we can import and export our Excel data model into and out of our dashboard file. In this section, we are talking about exporting the file dashboard output and sharing it with others. You can see the **Data** menu in the following screenshot, which navigates to **Data | Import** and **Data | Export**:

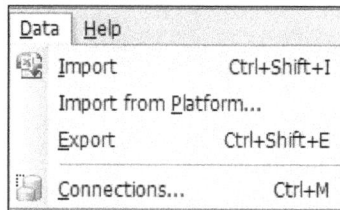

- **Exporting to AIR**: We can also export our dashboard to the Adobe AIR format, which can be consumed by any device or operating system as a widget. Widgets are lightweight BI components that reside on the device's front screen (desktop on PCs or home screen on mobile devices). We need to have the following prerequisites before publishing to the AIR format:

  - Download and install Adobe Flash Builder from the Adobe site (http://www.adobe.com/products/flash-builder.html). We need a Flex 3.0 (or higher) SDK, which is already included in Flash Builder. This SDK will act as a plugin that will help SAP BO Dashbords to deal with the AIR format.

  - Download and install Adobe AIR (https://get.adobe.com/air/). As per Adobe's site (http://www.adobe.com/):

    The Adobe AIR runtime enables developers to package the same code into native applications and games for Windows and Mac OS desktops as well as iOS and Android devices, reaching over a billion desktop systems and mobile app stores for over 500 million devices.

  - We still need to download and install Adobe Flex SDK 4.0 in order to be able to export in this format.

```
┌─────────────────────────────────────────────────────────────────┐
│  Adobe Flex 4 SDK Not Found                               [ X ]   │
├─────────────────────────────────────────────────────────────────┤
│                                                                   │
│   Could not find Adobe Flex SDK 4. To resolve this issue, do the  │
│   following:                                                      │
│                                                                   │
│     1. Download the Adobe Flex SDK 4.0.        Download Here      │
│                                                                   │
│     2. Choose the root folder location of the Adobe Flex 4 SDK.   │
│                                                                   │
│       C:\Program Files\Adobe\Adobe Flash Builder 4\sdks\4.0.0     │
│                                                                   │
│                              ┌──────────┐    ┌──────────┐         │
│                              │    OK    │    │  Cancel  │         │
│                              └──────────┘    └──────────┘         │
└─────────────────────────────────────────────────────────────────┘
```

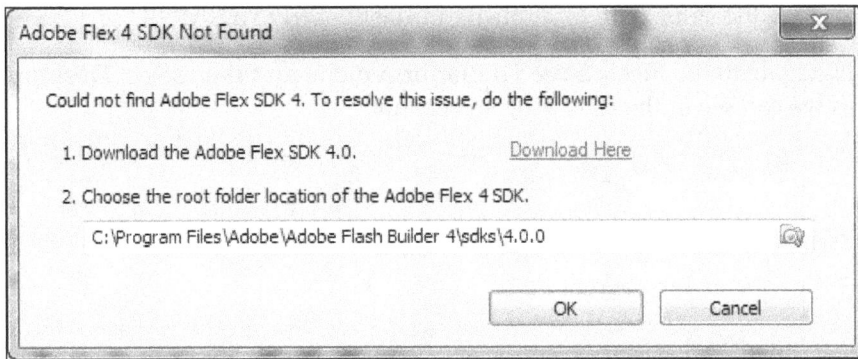

- **Allow block content warning**: We will get a warning message when we open the exported dashboard file. This happens because the export will embed a flash object in the target exported file. We need to accept the security warning and allow the block content (our flash dashboard object). We will get this warning in MS formats such as Word, PowerPoint, Outlook, and so on.

- **Data connections and secured https servers**: The exported dashboard file will still work and connect to external data if you have a data connection defined and used inside your dashboard, such as Live Office or Direct Query for example, and your BO server is not secure. The same connection will not work if you have a secure (HTTPS) server, and only the published dashboard will work.

Publishing dashboards

Publishing a dashboard means exporting it to a SAP BO server. We can publish a dashboard using the **Save To Platform** and **Save To Platform As** sub-menus located under the **File** menu, as illustrated in the following screenshot. Publishing a dashboard will generate a dashboard object, which contains:

- The exported dashboard's format (desktop, mobile, or both)

- The .XLF file, which can be imported by another developer who can continue working on it

You can follow the steps here to publish our dashboard to a SAP BO server:

1. Navigate to the **File | Save To Platform** menu and then select **Desktop Only** as we can see in the following screenshot.

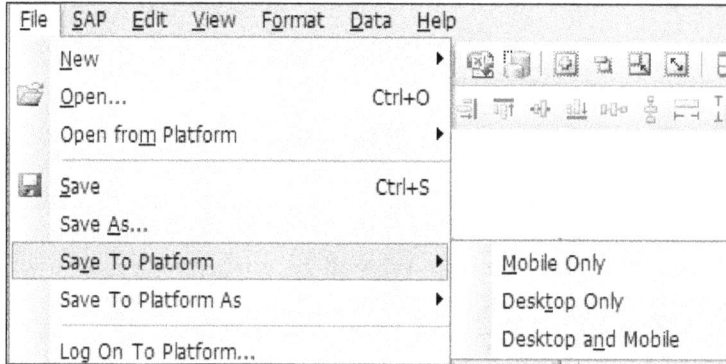

2. Enter `System` and `credential` information within the **Log On to BusinessObject Enterprise** window.

3. Select the `eFashion` folder and click **Save**.

   We can see the steps in the following screenshot:

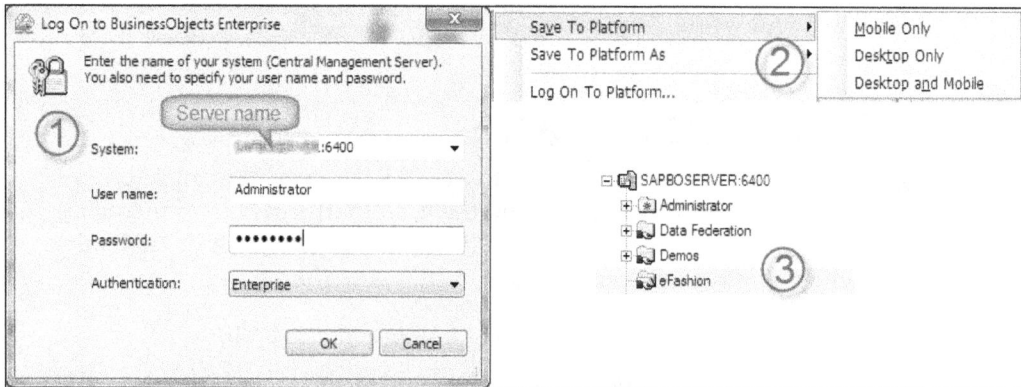

To access this dashboard from the SAP BO server, you need to follow these steps:

1. Enter the BI launch pad URL in your browser.

2. Log in using a valid user name and password.

3. Navigate to the `eFashion` folder.

4. Open the `Chapter8.xlf` file by double-clicking on it.

You can see the steps in the following screenshot:

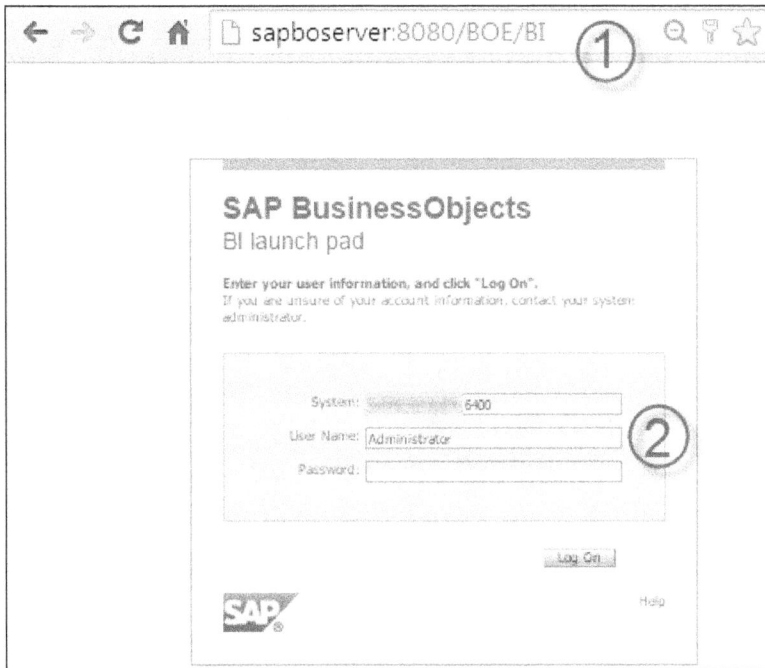

Steps 3 and 4 are shown in the following screenshot:

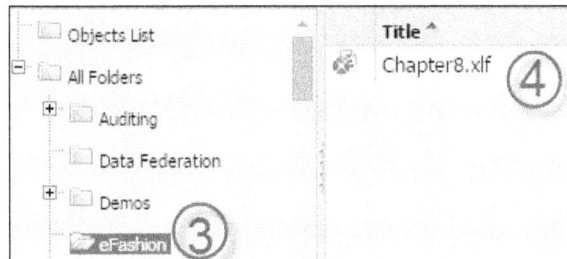

You can see the dashboard as it will open in the browser, in the following screenshot:

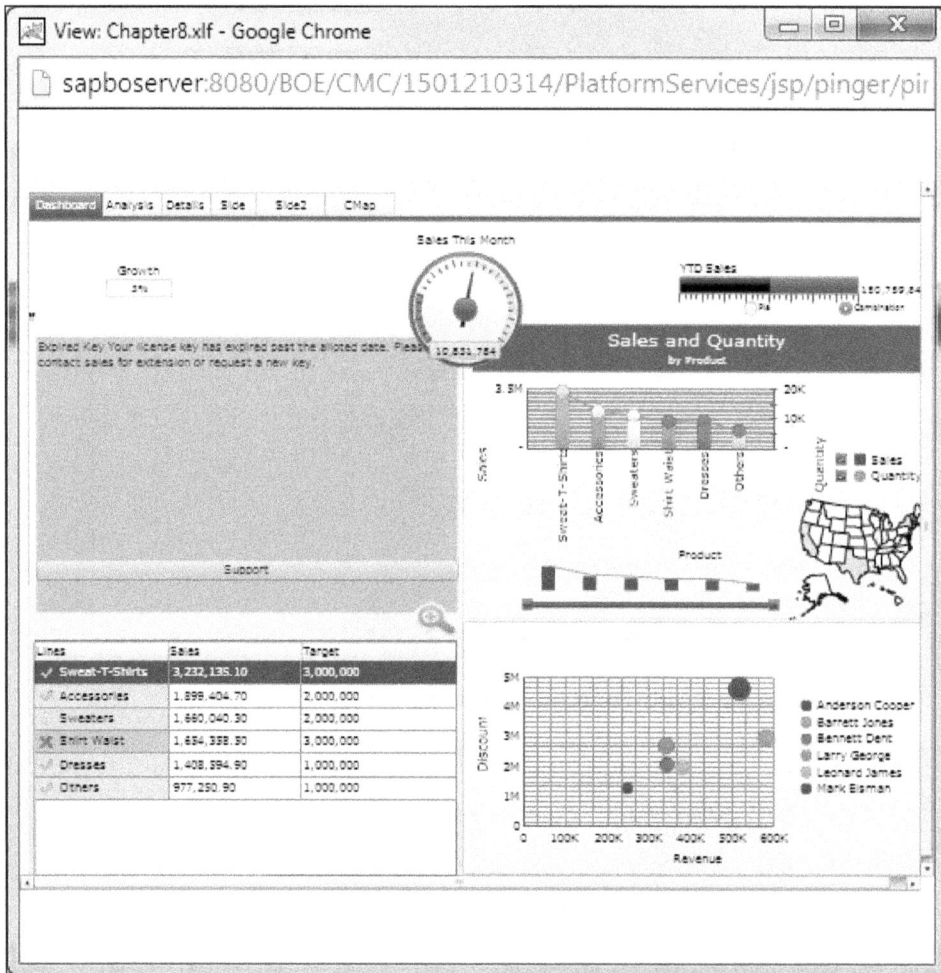

Before we leave this section, let's discuss the newly introduced terms here:

- **Save To Platform**: We can save our dashboard as **Mobile Only**, **Desktop Only** , and **Desktop and Mobile**. Based on our selection, the dashboard will be made available to the targeted users. For example, if we save it as **Mobile Only** , then our dashboard will be accessible only through mobile devices.

- **Dashboard Object to Replace Flash Object**: The dashboard file was published as a Flash file in the previous SAP BO releases such as XI 3.1 and backward. You can also save your dashboard as an `.xlf` file on the SAP BO server, but in a different file, and it will not be part of the publishing process. On the other hand, we can publish our dashboard to the SAP BO server as a dashboard object, which will contain both the `consumable` file (desktop and mobile) as well as the XLF file. We can use the option **Dashboard Object to Replace Flash Objcet** to migrate old dashboard formats.

Importing dashboards

After publishing our dashboard, we can import it again to continue working on it or to make modifications. We will need to publish it again after applying the changes in order to see them.

You can use the following steps to import our dashboard:

1. Navigate to **File | Open from Platform** and select **Dashboards Objects**.
2. Log in to our SAP BO system.
3. Navigate to the `eFashion` folder and select the `Chapter8.xlf` file.
4. The dashboard `.xlf` will open in SAP BO Dashboards.

   You can see step 1 in the following screenshot. The remaining steps are same as the publishing step.

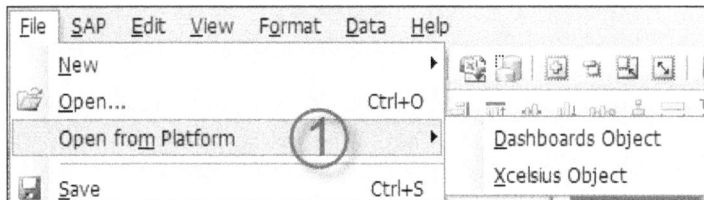

Summary

In this chapter, you learned how to export our dashboard project into another format that can be shared offline, such as PDF, SharePoint, and SWF file. The exporting option is only valid for prototype sharing and once you've linked your dashboard to the data, you'll need to publish it to make it accessible for the targeted users. You also learned how to publish our dashboard into the SAP BO repository in desktop, mobile, and desktop and mobile formats. Finally, you learned how to import our dashboard file from the SAP BO repository to be able to open the `Dashboard Object` file and make the required modifications or changes.

In the next chapter, you will learn how to connect our dashboard with external data sources, such as web services, direct query, and Live Office. We've used static data in all our examples so far, but this is not what happens in real-life projects. We need to connect our dashboard to a data source, and we should be able to refresh our data at run time without the need to reimport data. You will learn how to create a query to retrieve data based on a specific Universe, and how to link the resulting data with our dashboard components. You will also learn many other methodss to accomplish this, such as how to connect to web service or Live Office report.

9
Retrieving External Data Sources

So far, we have worked with static data that was stored in an Excel data model of our dashboard. In real-life scenarios, we need to link our dashboard with an external data source, such as a database or web service.

In the earlier releases of SAP BO Dashboards (XI 3.1 and older), we used to connect our dashboard to dynamic data using methods such as Live Office, web services, XML data, and XML maps. But these methods were complex and difficult to use and couldn't fulfill the end user's needs. We have a new method introduced in the release of version 4.0, which is called **Direct Query**. Using this method, we can build a direct query on a top of universe and send the parameters in an easy way. We can also directly connect the dashboard components to the query output. In this chapter, we will discuss the old methods as well as the new one.

> Direct query is the most stable and recommended data connectivity method.

Each data connection method has its own pros and cons. Our primary goal is to explain each method, and then we will highlight the best use cases for each method and when we should use or avoid a method.

In this chapter, we will learn how to:

- Use direct query as a data source
- Use web services as a data source
- Use Live Office as a data source
- Use XML data and XML maps

Using direct query

Direct query is a new feature introduced in the SAP BusinessObjects Business Intelligence platform 4.0. This feature can be used to create a query based on a Universe and then use the query output in our dashboard. We can link it directly with a dashboard component, so we don't need Excel as an intermediate layer. We can also load it into Excel, and from there, we can deal with it in the same way as we did in the previous chapters. In this section, you will first learn how to create a query, and then you will learn how to link it with your dashboard components and current Excel model.

> Direct query can use only the .UNX Universe, which was developed by the SAP BO Information Design Tool. You can refer to my first book, *Creating Universes with SAP BusinessObjects*, for more information about creating Universes.

Before we start using direct query, let's prepare the dashboard file for this chapter:

1. Navigate to the Code sample folder from your PC.

2. Open the Chapter8.xlf file dashboard in the Dashboard (Ready) folder.

3. Save it in the same location as **Dashboard9** in your Development folder.

   You can see these steps here:

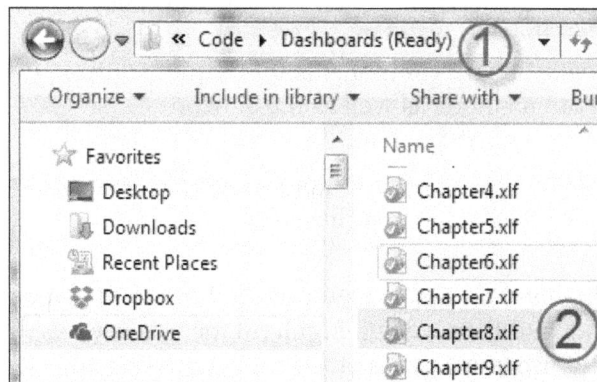

   There are five steps that we need to follow in order to add the query wizard.

4. **Select a Data Source**.

5. **Select a Universe** or **BEx Query**.

6. **Build Query**.

7. **Preview Query Results**.

8. **Usage Options**.

You can see these steps in the following screenshot:

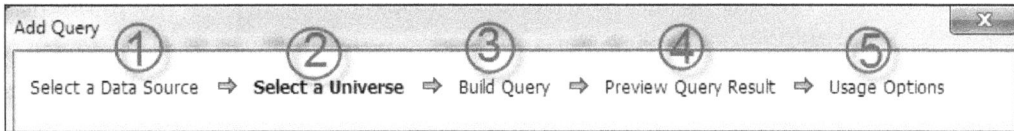

In this section, we will cover in detail each step for adding a query. So let's start:

1. Navigate to the **Query Browser** panel.

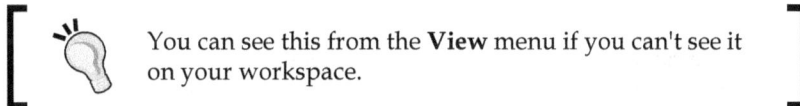

> You can see this from the **View** menu if you can't see it on your workspace.

2. Click on the **Add Query** button.

You can see steps 1 and 2 in this screenshot:

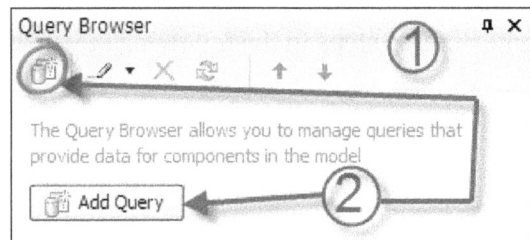

3. If you don't have an active session, it will ask you to log in to your system by entering your system information and credentials.

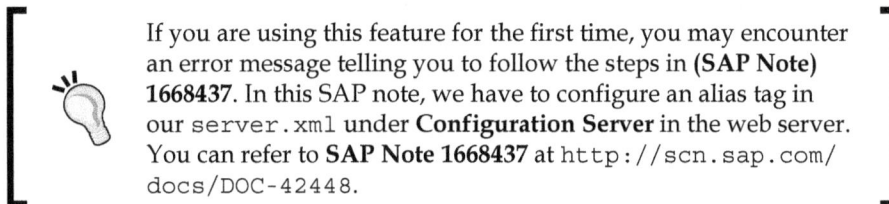

> If you are using this feature for the first time, you may encounter an error message telling you to follow the steps in **(SAP Note) 1668437**. In this SAP note, we have to configure an alias tag in our `server.xml` under **Configuration Server** in the web server. You can refer to **SAP Note 1668437** at `http://scn.sap.com/docs/DOC-42448`.

The error message looks like this:

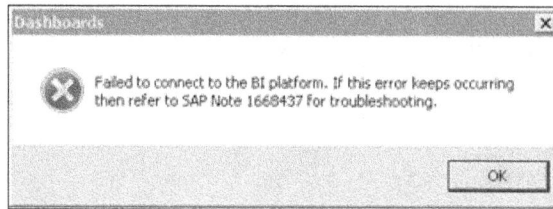

4. Select **Universe** as the data source, and then click on **Next**.

5. Select the **eFashion** Universe. If you don't see this Universe in the list, then you need to convert it from the old version (.UNV) to the new one (.UNX) using the information design tool.

> We can't create a query on top of Universe using a connection to the access database such as the case of eFashion. I managed to convert it into an Oracle database by running the script downloaded from http://www.forumtopics.com/busobj/ viewtopic.php?t=22133 on the Oracle database and changing the Universe connection.

You can see some of these steps in the following screenshots:

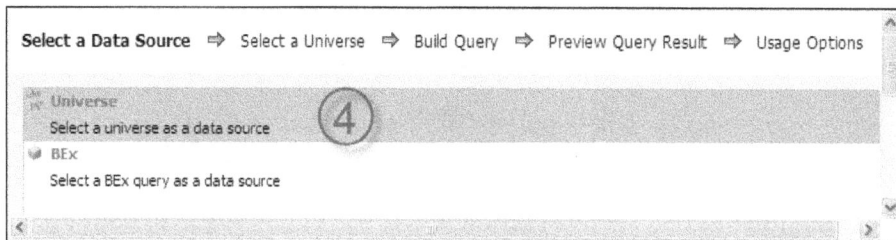

We can find the eFashion Universe in the follwoing screenshot:

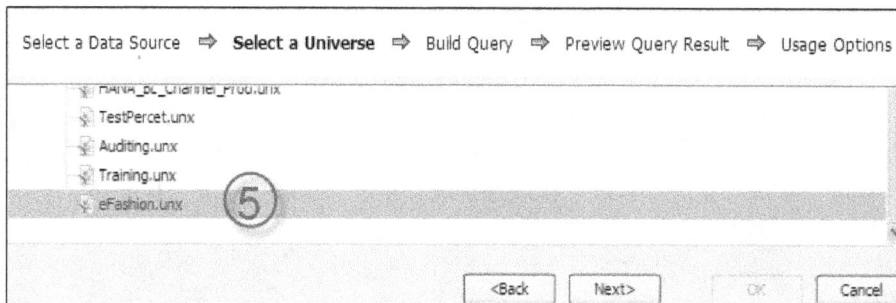

6. Add the **State** dimension (**Store | State**) and the **Sales revenue** measure (**Measures | Sales revenue**) to the **Results Objects** panel.

7. Next, add the **Year** dimension (**Time Period | Year**) to the **Filters** panel and make sure that the operator is **EqualTo**. Then, configure it to be prompted by selecting **Prompt** from the right operand list. After that, click on **Next**.

These steps are shown in this screenshot:

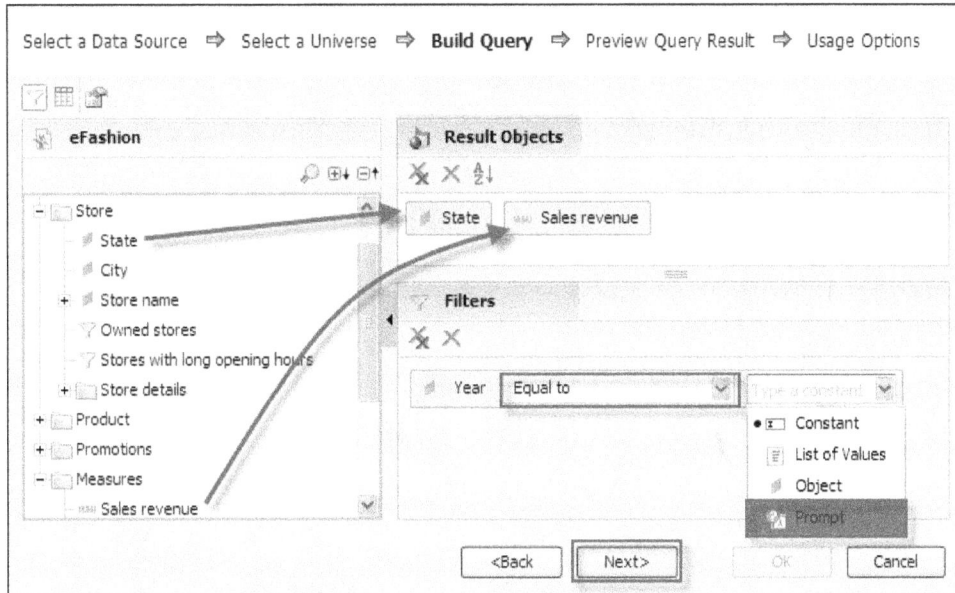

8. Preview the query results and click on **Next**.

You can see the preview panel in the following screenshot:

9. Enter **Sales by State** in the **Query Name** field.

10. In **Refresh Options**, check the **Refresh Before Components are Loaded** option.

11. In the **Refresh Trigger** area, link **Trigger Cell** to the **Map!$C$2** Excel cell.

12. Select the **When Value Changes** option.

13. Check the **Enable Load Cursor** and **Disable Mouse Input on Load** options under the **Loading Status** area. Then, click on **Ok**.

You can see these steps here:

The query will be displayed in the **Query Browser** windows, as shown in the following screenshot:

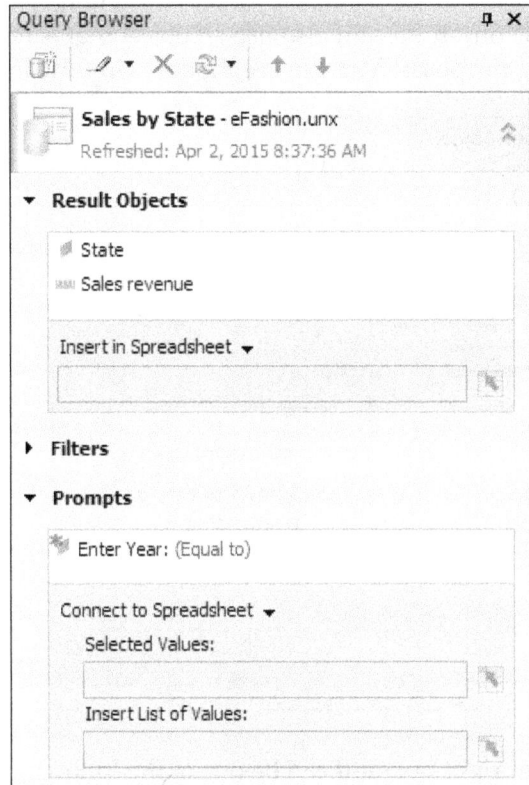

Before we conclude this section, let's discuss the newly introduced features and options:

- **Data Sources**: We can select one of the following data sources to use to build our query:
  - ○ **Universe**: The .UNX Universe format is the only supported Universe format. You can't build a direct query using the old .UNV Universe format.
  - ○ **Business Explorer (BEx)**: BEx queries can be developed by the BEx query designer, which is available as part of SAP NetWeaver 7.0 and later versions.

- **Build Query**: While building a query, you can also use the following features:
    - ° **Sort**: You can sort the data retrieved from your query based on an object used in the result set panel. This will help us show data in a specific order. We can also use an object that is not displayed for sorting purposes. You can see the sort window in this screenshot:

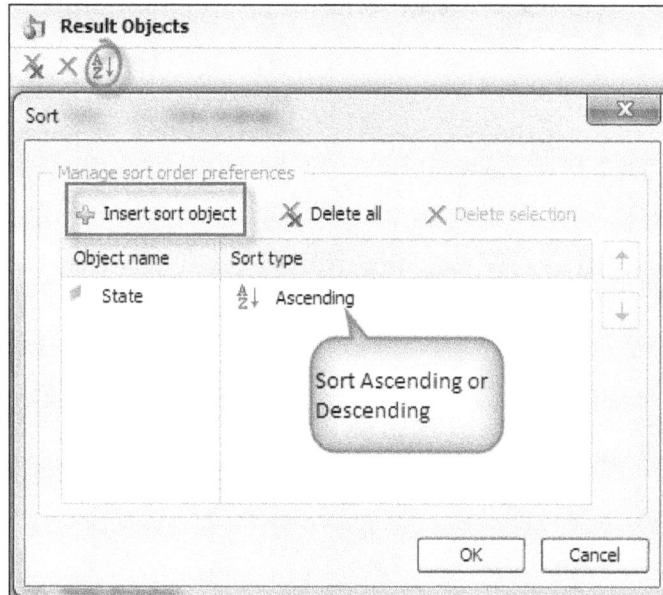

- The query filter right operand can be one of the following:
    - ° **Constant**: You can type a value here. It will be static and will be used to set the value for the object used in the filter, for example, *Year = 2004*.
    - ° **List of value**: This is the same as **Constant**, but instead of typing a value, this option will display a list of all possible values to select from.
    - ° **Prompt**: This can be used to create a dynamic filter by prompting the user to enter the required filter value, or it can be mapped to an Excel cell and dynamically pass different filter values based on the cell value. The prompt value can be mandatory or optional. Mandatory prompts should be passed to the query every time it is triggered, while an optional one will be passed only if it contains value. It will be ignored if there is no value passed to this prompt.

- **Refresh Before Components are Loaded**: This refresh option will run the query in the initial phase before the dashboard components are loaded. You can tick this option if you have a default value and want to initially run the query and display the values corresponding to the default value after loading the dashboard.

- **Refresh Every**: You can set your query to refresh after every specific time interval, for example, 5 seconds. You need to define the value and time metric (seconds, minutes, and so on).

- **Trigger Cell**: We can use a specific cell to trigger our query to run. We have two types of triggers here:

    ○ **When Value Changes**: This option will trigger the query to run every time the trigger cell value changes.

    ○ **When Value Becomes**: This option will trigger the query to run when the trigger cell value equals the specified value. For example, if the trigger cell is **Year** and we set the **When Value Becomes** to **2004**, then the query will run only when the value equals **2004**.

- **Loading Message**, **Ideal Message**, and **Insert On**: We can use these options to set a dynamically loading and ideal message. Then, we can map the current message, based on the current query status (running or ideal), to a specific cell in the Excel model to display it later on using a label or any other text component.

- **Enable Load Cursor**: This option will change the cursor shape to "loading" (an hourglass) while our query is running. The cursor shape will return to the normal state (an arrow) in the query's ideal state.

- **Disable Mouse Input on Load**: This option will prevent any mouse interaction with any dashboard component while the query is in the loading state. You will be able to interact with the dashboard again after the query completes loading.

- **Hide Error Message Window**: By default, any error message will be displayed in a specific error window that will pop up when the error occurs. You can use this option to handle the error without interrupting the user or by displaying the error message in another window that you will design and use it instead of the default one.

The next step is to link the query output and prompt with the right Excel model cells.

Let's follow these steps to establish the link:

1. Navigate to the **Query Browser** window and open the **Sales by State** query.

2. Select **Results Objects**, and then select **State**. Next, click on **Insert in Spreadsheet**.

3. Click on the **Excel** icon and link the **State** data to the **Map!$B$4:$B$11** Excel range.

4. Select **Sales Revenue** and link it to the **Map!$C$4:$C$11** Excel range.

5. Navigate to **Prompts** and select **Enter Year:**. Then, link the selected value to the **Map!$C$2** Excel cell and **Insert List of Values** to the **Map!$A$2:$A$5** Excel range.

    You can see all of these steps in the following screenshot:

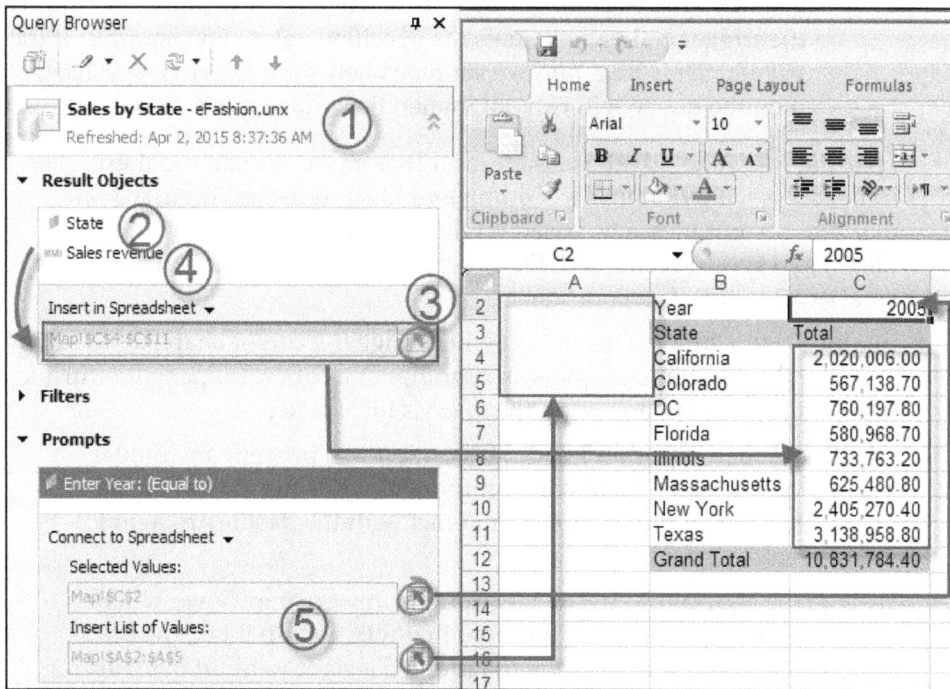

- **Assignment**: Create combobox selectors that display the **Map!$A$2:$A$5** labels, and the insert destination is the **Map!$C$2** cell.

We can preview our dashboard using **Preview** and check out how the map data will be changed based on the selected year. Each time we change the year value, our query trigger will run the query and the new values will be loaded to our map.

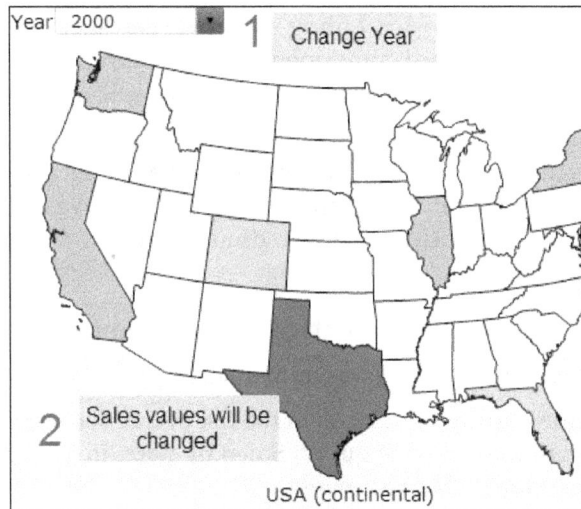

Before we conclude this section, let's discuss the options related to this feature:

- **Query Browser**: We can use the **Query Browser** panel to perform the following actions:
    - Add new query
    - Edit an existing query
    - Delete and existing query
    - Refresh an existing query

You can see the query browser options in this screenshot:

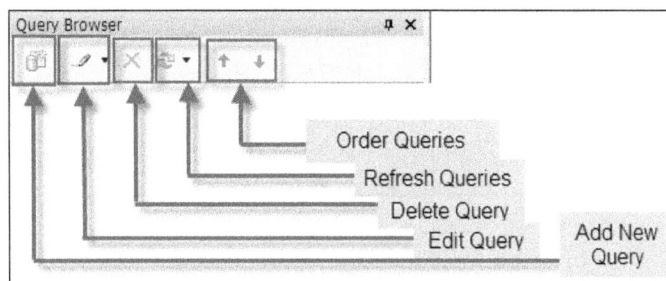

- **Refresh using buttons**: We can also use a use a **Query Refresh** button dashboard component under the **Universe Connection** category from **Components** panel to refresh a query or multiple queries. This option is very useful if you want the dashboard user to trigger the query run instead of building dynamic triggers based on the Excel cell value or setting a time to refresh the query. The good thing is that we can set a trigger for the **Query Refresh** button dashboard component based on an Excel cell. This is very useful if the same trigger cell has to trigger multiple queries.

- **Direct data binding**: We can directly bind our dashboard component with the query results. The dashboard component values or categories will be mapped to a result set in one of the created queries. We can link the values to measures and categories (labels) to dimensions. To do this, perform the following steps:

6. Click on the small arrow next to the Excel data mapping.

7. Select **Query Data** from the pop-up menu.

8. Next, select the required query from the list of queries that we've already created. We can see only one query, **Sales by Sate**, in this example because this is the only query that we created.

9. Select the required dimension or measure to bind this field with.

    You can see these steps in the following screenshot:

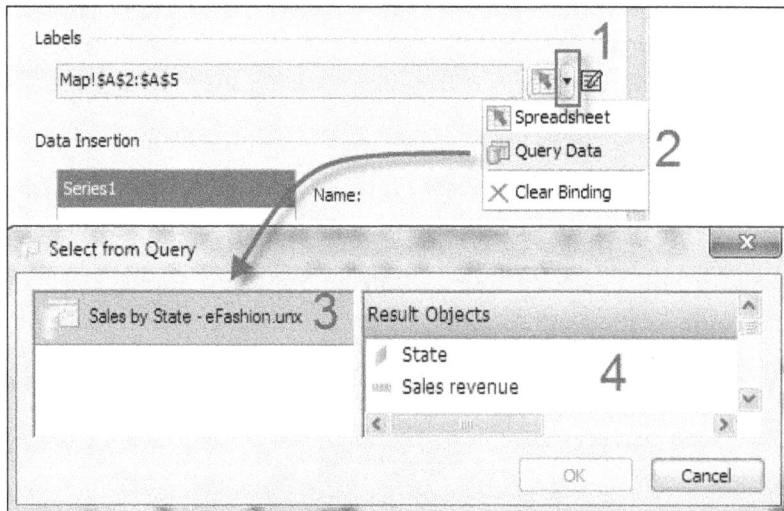

Using web services

We can also use web services to populate our dashboard with data. Web services are a common way of exchanging data between different systems. We can use one of the following web service to consume data retrieved from a web service:

- **Web service query**: This will be created by **Query As a Web Service Designer**. This tool can be used to create web services based on a Universe.

- **Web service connection**: This connection type can retrieve data from any standard web service.

Web service query

In this section, you will learn how to use **Web Service Query** to retrieve sales and quantity by product data, and use it in the **Sales and Quantity by Product** combo chart. But first, let's summarize the high-level steps required to accomplish this:

- Learn how to use the **Query As a Web Service Designer** tool to create a web service query based on the eFashion Universe

- Create the **Web Service Query** data connection in your dashboard to call this web service

- Configure the **Usage** options for this connection

Let's start by creating the Web service query:

1. Navigate to **Start | All Programs | SAP Business Intelligence | SAP BusinessObjects BI platform 4 Client Tools | Query As a Web Service Designer**.

   You can see this item in the following screenshot:

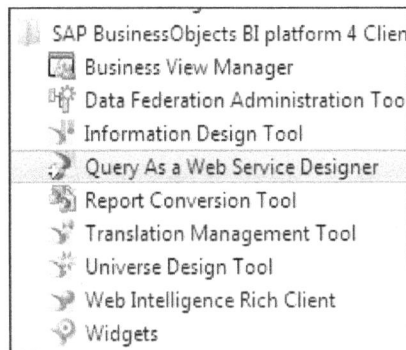

2. Add a new **Host**, if this is your first time to use query as web service designer, by entering the system information (server name) and your credentials (user name And pssword).

3. Navigate to **Query | New | Query....**

4. Enter **sales_quantity_by_product** in the **Web Service Name** field.

5. Enter **This web service will respond with sales and quantity by products. Universe: eFashion** in the description field.

1. Description	2. Select a universe	3. Query	4. Preview
Define the Web Services properties: Web Service name, service name in the WSDL, and the description.			

Web Service Name:

sales_quantity_by_product

Web Service Description:

This web service will respond with sales and qunatity by products.

Universe: eFashion

6. Select the **eFashion** Universe from the list of Universes.

> We can build a query as a web service on top of the .UNV Universe only. We can't use the .UNX Universe like the **Add Query** method. The Universe type is a key factor while deciding which method to use to populate your dashboard with data.

7. Build the query by adding the following BusinessObjects to the **Result Objects** panel:

   ○ **Lines**

   ○ **Sales revenue**

   ○ **Quantity sold**

> This build query step is exactly the same as the build query step in the direct query method, which we discussed earlier in this chapter.

8. Leave **Filter Objects** empty and click on **Next**.

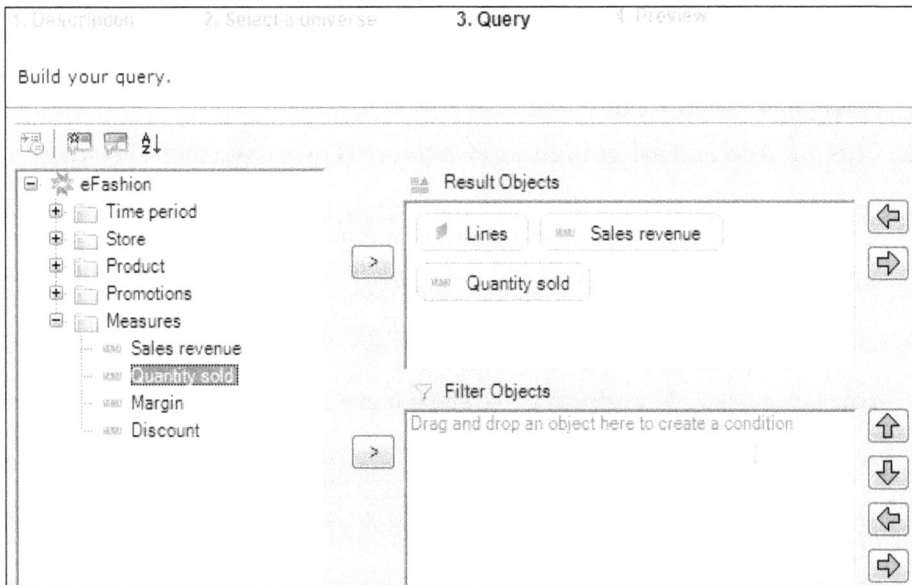

9. Preview the web service data and then click on **Publish**.

10. We copy the web service URL, as we will be using it inside our eFashion dashboard to call this web service.

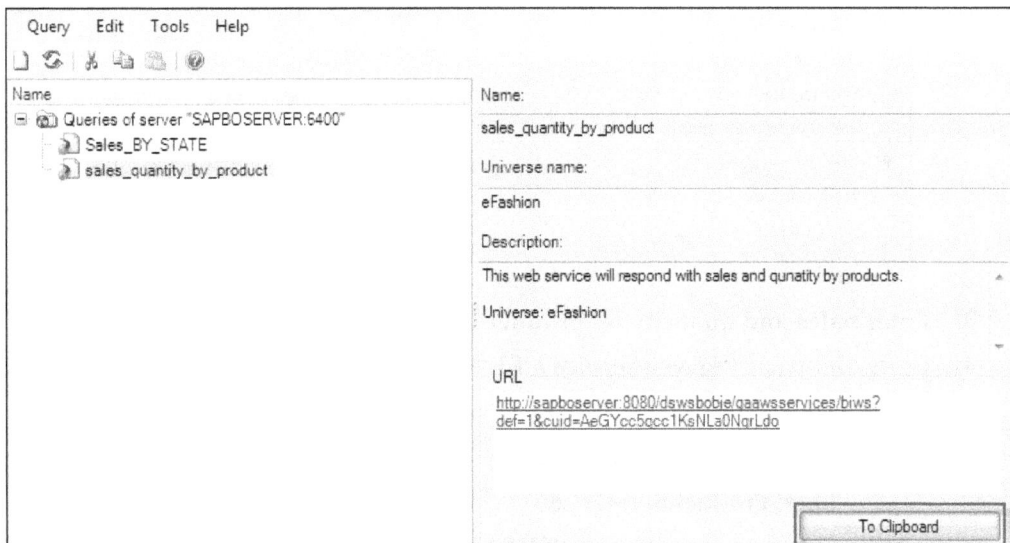

Now, let's open our dashboard file and follow these steps to add a new data connection based on the created web service query:

1. Navigate to **Data | Connection**, or press *Ctrl + M*.
2. Click on **Add** and select **Web service query (Query as a web service)***.

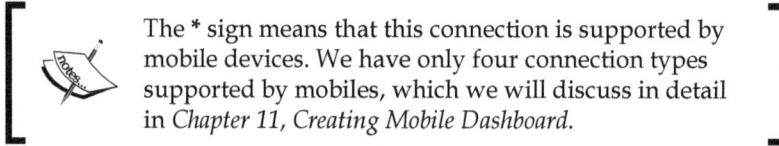

> The * sign means that this connection is supported by mobile devices. We have only four connection types supported by mobiles, which we will discuss in detail in *Chapter 11, Creating Mobile Dashboard*.

You can see how to perform these steps here:

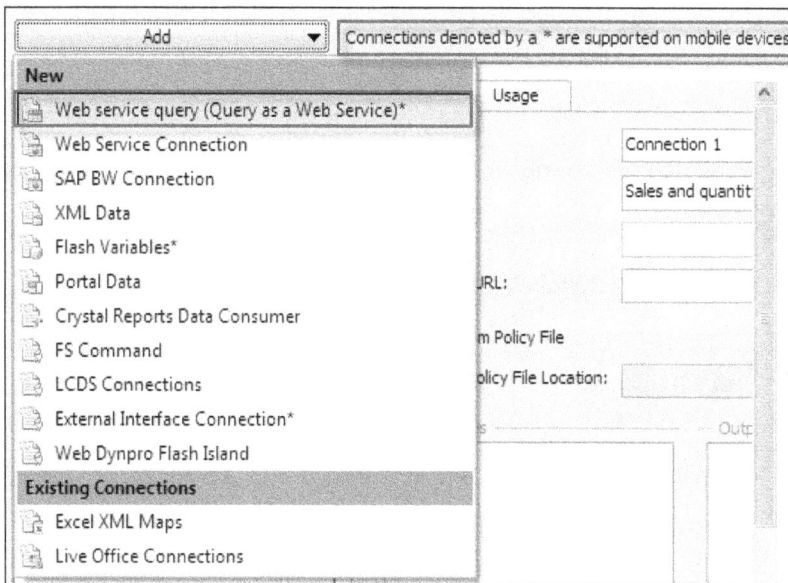

3. Enter **Sales and quantity by product** in the **Name:** field.
4. Copy and paste the web service URL in the **WSDL URL** field.
5. Click on **Import**.
6. Map the following business objects to the corresponding Excel ranges:
   - Line: **Product!$G$4:$G$9**
   - **Sales revenue: Product!$H$4:$H$9**
   - **Quantity sold: Product!$I$4:$I$9**

You can see these steps marked in the following screenshot:

Now, navigate to the **Usage** tab and configure the web service query connection to be refreshed before the dashboard components are loaded.

> The usage page is exactly the same as the query usage option, which we discussed earlier this chapter.

Preview the dashboard and make sure that the connection is running successfully.

> Don't forget to link the **Login** and **Password** fields under **Input Value** to the Excel cells that contains your login credentials.

Web service connection

We will use a public web service to retrieve information on the weather of a selected country or city. Let's follow these steps:

1. Select **USA Map** and configure a **Row** insertion by selecting the **Map!$B$4:$C$11** range in **Source Data** and **Map!$B$13:$C$13** in **Destination**.

2. Navigate to **Data | Connections...** and add a new **Web Service Connection**.

3. Enter **Weather** in the **Name** field.

4. Enter the http://www.webservicex.net/globalweather.asmx?WSDL URL in the **WSDL URL** field.

5. Select **GetWeather** in the **Method:** field.

6. Link **Input Values | CityName** to the **Map!$B$13** Excel range.

7. Link **Output Values | GetWeatherResults** to the **Map!$D$13** Excel cell.

8. Add a label component to the dashboard canvas and link it to **Map!$D$13**.

You can see these steps in this screenshot:

Configure the **Usage** option for this connection to trigger when the **Map!$B$13** Excel cell value changes. Then, preview the dashboard and test the connection.

Using Live Office

To understand how Live Office came into being and what it is in the first place, let's briefly go through the history of SAP BO Dashboards. As we mentioned in the preface, SAP BO Dashboard was formerly known as Xcelsius, and it was a standalone tool that was used to develop amazing dashboards using Flash's superb graphs and Excel's powerful calculation engine. Then, BusinessObjects bought this tool and added it to its portfolio. At that time, integrating this standalone tool with the then-current BO tools was a big challenge.

Live Office is a plugin that can be installed and plugged into MS Office so that you can query data and reports from BusinessObjects and use them in MS Word, Excel, PowerPoint, and so on. This plugin is very useful because many business users are comfortable with MS Office, and their main concern is how to retrieve and utilize data from BO. Here, an idea came which why we can't use Live office to integrate the SAP BO Dashboard tool with other SAP BO tools. At the end, SAP BO Dashboards contains two main modules (the Excel and Flash interfaces). Using the Live Office plugin, we can retrieve data by querying the Universe or retrieving a report (Webi or crystal) and storing it in an Excel data model inside our dashboard file. We can set a trigger for data refresh based on an Excel cell value that has changed or a specific time interval.

SAP AG bought BusinessObjects and started drawing up a new vision for its BI tools. One of the major new releases under SAP id Sap BI Platform 4.0 and 4.1, which contains many new features and enhancements.

We first need to download and install the Live Office plugin from the SAP Support Portal (`https://support.sap.com/home.html`).

> There was a separate license for Live Office in the previous releases (SAP BO XI 3.1 and earlier). It is available for use in SAP BO 4.x if you have a valid server license.
>
> We need to make sure that we are using Live Office with the same batch version of SAP BO server. For example, if we have SAP BO 4.1 SP5, then we need to download and install Live Office 4.1 SP5 only. Otherwise, we will not be able to connect to the server.

The first thing that we need to test after installing SAP BO Live Office is the connectivity with the server. We need to follow these steps to verify this:

1. Open any Excel file and navigate to the **Live Office** tab.

> You may need to enable Live Office after the installation if you still can't see the **Live Office** tab in Excel. To do this, you need to navigate to `C:\Program Files (x86)\SAP BusinessObjects\SAP BusinessObjects Enterprise XI 4.0\LiveOffice` and click on `enable_addin.exe`.

The following screenshot shows **enable_addin**:

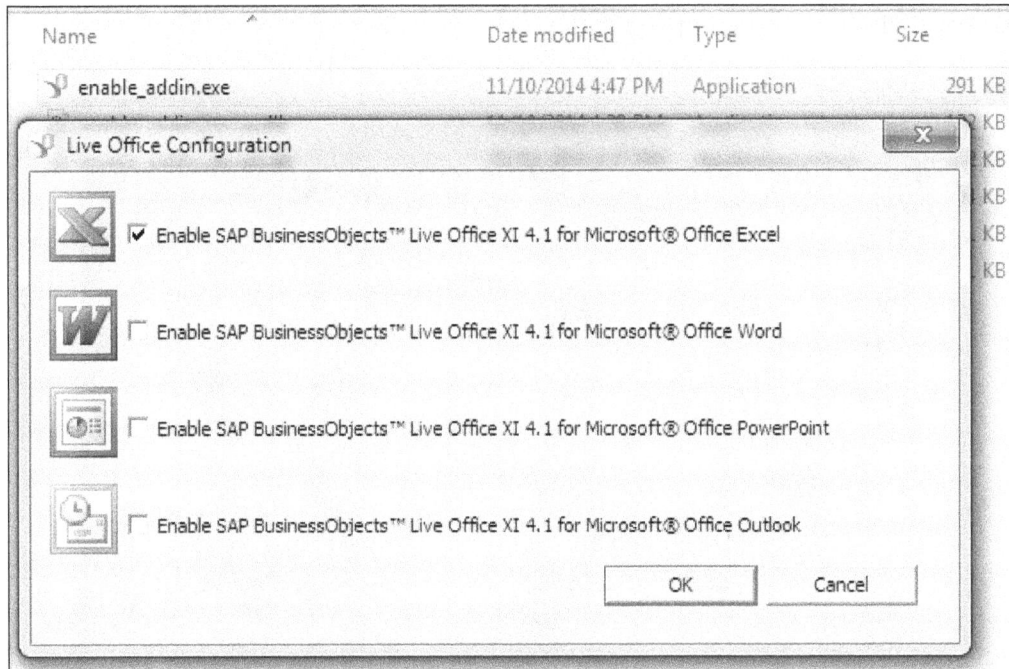

2. Navigate to **Application Options**.
3. Next, navigate to the **Enterprise** tab.
4. Enter **System**, **UserName**, and **Password**.
5. Click on the **LogOn** button.

If you've logged in successfully, then you can start using the Live Office add-on and start creating Live Office components. You can see the preceding steps in this screenshot:

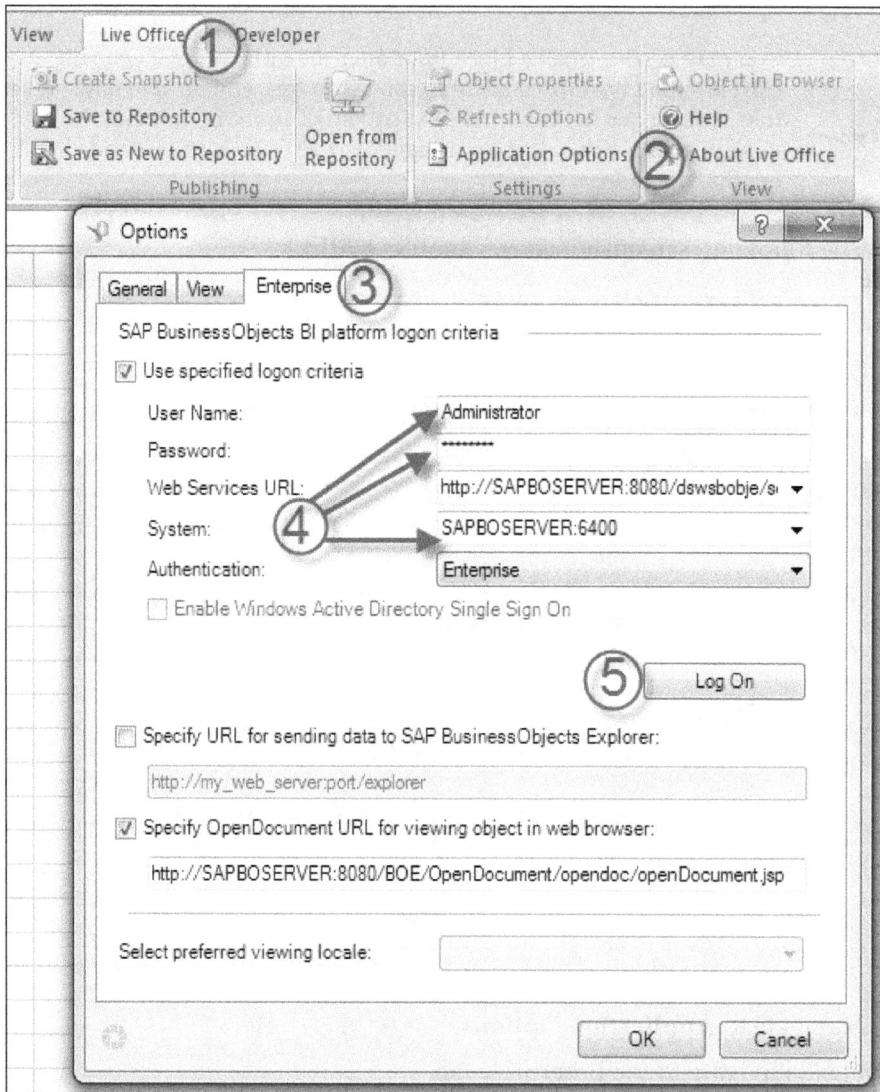

Note that you should use Live Office with the same version and same service patch number of the server. Otherwise, you will not be able to establish the connection with the server.

Now, let's summarize the main steps in the process of using Live Office as a data connection:

1. Connect Live Office to the SAP BO server.

2. Retrieve a report or build a query for an existing Universe.

3. Link your dashboard components to the retrieve Live Office data.

4. Configure the prompts and refreshing mechanism for the Live Office data connection.

5. Save the Excel data model on your platform.

> Step 5 is the most important step, and almost everyone who forgets to do it fails to establish a Live Office connection.

6. Export the Excel data model from your platform to ensure the link between your dashboard and the Excel file published on the SAP BO server.

7. Add the data connection and configure the refreshing mechanism.

8. Publish your dashboard.

> The prompt is a dynamic query parameter that requires user feedback (input) to include it in the generated query before sending it to the database. Normally, a popup will prompt the user to fill in the parameters value, but we can also map this prompt to a dynamic Excel cell, such as a selector destination for example.

We can create a Live Office connection based on any of the following:

- Crystal report
- Web Intelligence report
- Universe query

To complete this example, we need to create the following simple report:

Name of manager	Sales revenue	Discount	Margin
Anderson	$1,023,061	$199,111	$476,761
Barrett	$693,211	$195,644	$310,356
Bennett	$448,302	$104,654	$203,701
Larry	$561,123	$114,579	$253,464
Leonard	$427,245	$118,114	$189,064
Mark	$238,819	$78,751	$111,453
Michelle	$682,231	$104,172	$320,629
Queen	$529,079	$105,952	$247,881
Quinn	$737,914	$129,348	$348,750
Richards	$644,635	$103,377	$302,540
Steve	$1,704,211	$495,472	$774,893
Tuttle	$405,985	$75,336	$192,479

Report 1

Now, let's try to link our eFashion dashboard with this report:

1. Navigate to the **Live Office** tab.

2. Select the following **Sales by Manager** data range: **Managers Performance !$B$2:$E$8** under the **Managers Performance** sheet.

3. Select the **Web Intelligence** icon from the **Insert** ribbon.

4. Click on **Yes** when you are prompted by a message that warns you from overwriting the current Excel content.

   These steps are shown in the following screenshot:

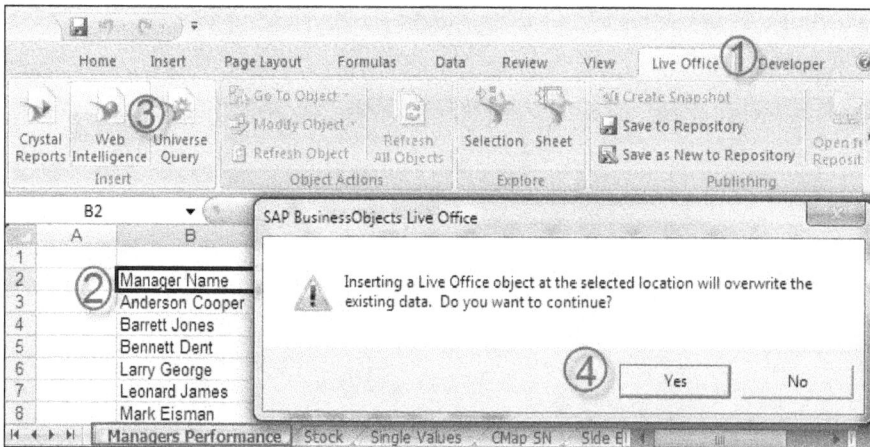

Then, we need to continue with the following steps.

5. From **Live Office Insert Wizard**, navigate to the location that you saved the report at. Then, select the created report and click on **Next**.

6. You can select any part of the report to use it. Here, we will select the managers' table. Then, click on **Next**.

   You can see the last step in the following screenshot:

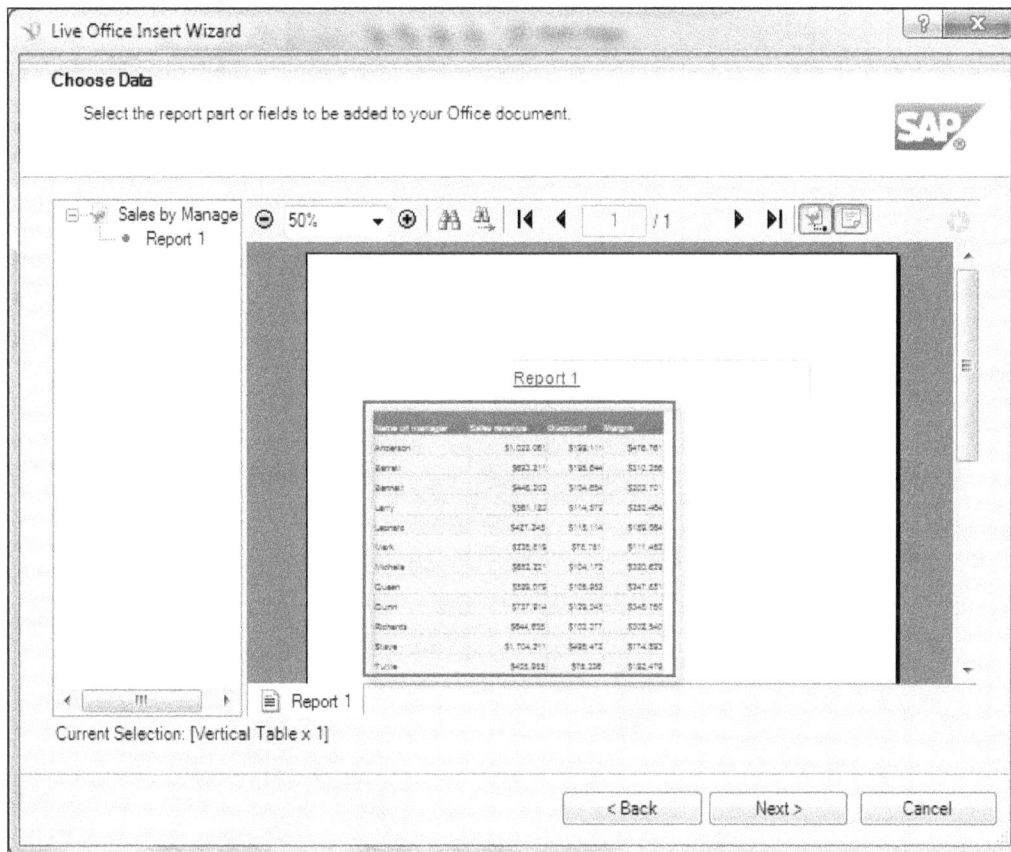

7. Enter **Sales by Managers** in **Live Office Object Name(s):** and click on **Finish**.

You can see that the new Live Office component has been added and overwrite the old static Excel sales by manager information. Notice also that Bubble chart data changes accordingly.

B	C	D	E
Name of manager	Sales revenue	Discount	Margin
Anderson	1,023,061	199,111	476,761
Barrett	693,211	195,644	310,356
Bennett	448,302	104,654	203,701

After that, we need to configure the **Refresh** trigger and link the prompt to the Excel cell:

1. Refresh the **Live Office** component by clicking on the **Refresh** icon. This step is mandatory in order to see the prompt wizard.

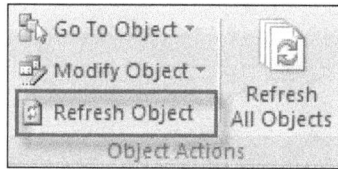

2. Click on **Prompt Setting...** under the **Modify Object** menu. This option will be disabled if you didn't refresh your Live Office object.

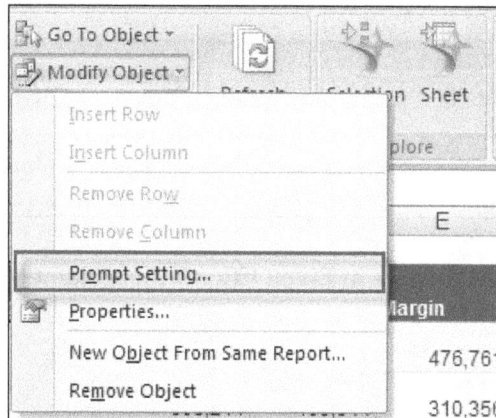

3. Select the **Enter Year: Prompt**, and then select the **Choose Excel Data Range** option. Next, link it to the **Map!$C$2** Excel cell. This cell contains the year selected from the year selector, and it will be passed to our Live Office component prompt.

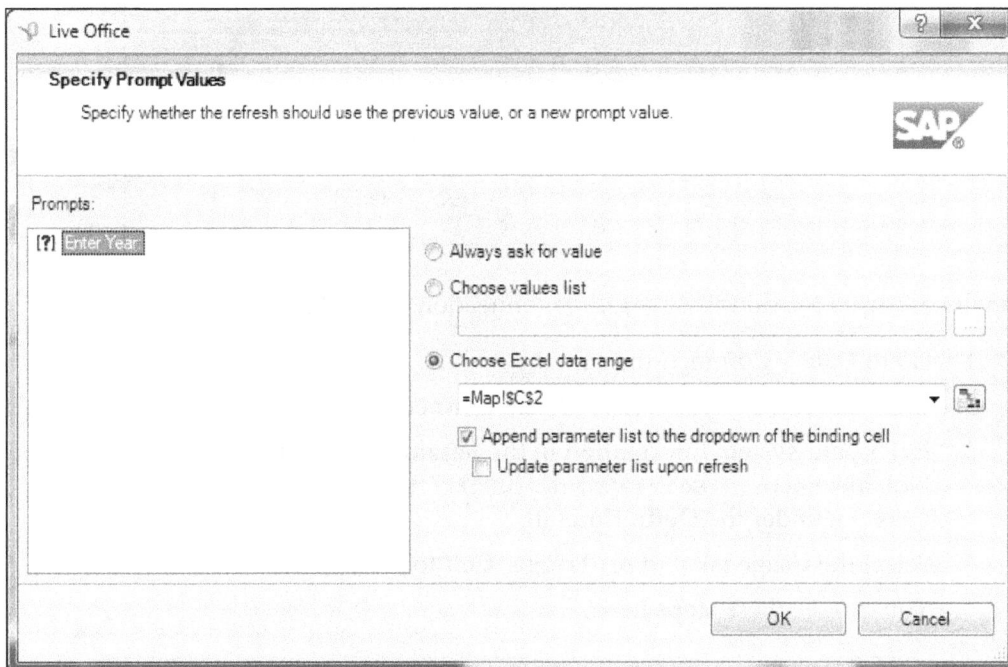

4. Notice that the year cell is now gray and it has a drop-down menu to select a year from. Select **2004** and make sure that the Live Office component refreshes automatically.

5. Click on **Save to Repository** under **Publishing** from the **Live Office** ribbon, and select a folder for which you have write permission.

6. Go to **Import from Platform | Data**, navigate to the same location, and import the file that you just published on the Live Office.

We can see these steps in the following screenshot:

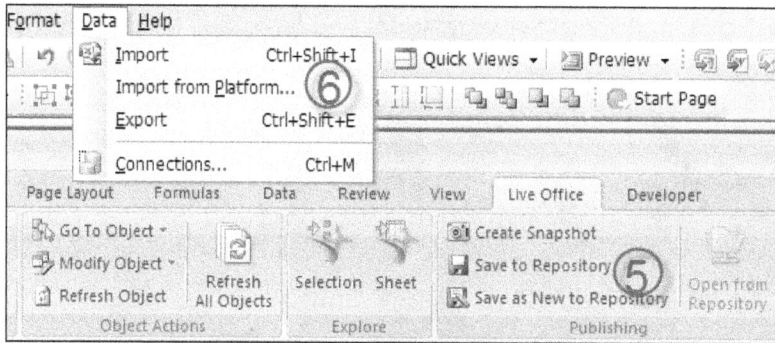

Finally, we need to add this Live Office connection to the data manager:

1. Go to **Data | Connections...**.

2. Click on **Add** and select **Live Office Connection**.

3. Enter your system information in the **Session URL** field. The URL should look like `http://<Server Name>:<Port Number>/dswsbobje/services/Session` under the **Definition** tab.

4. Select the **Usage** tab and set **Trigger Cell** to **Map!$C$2**.

   You can see these steps here:

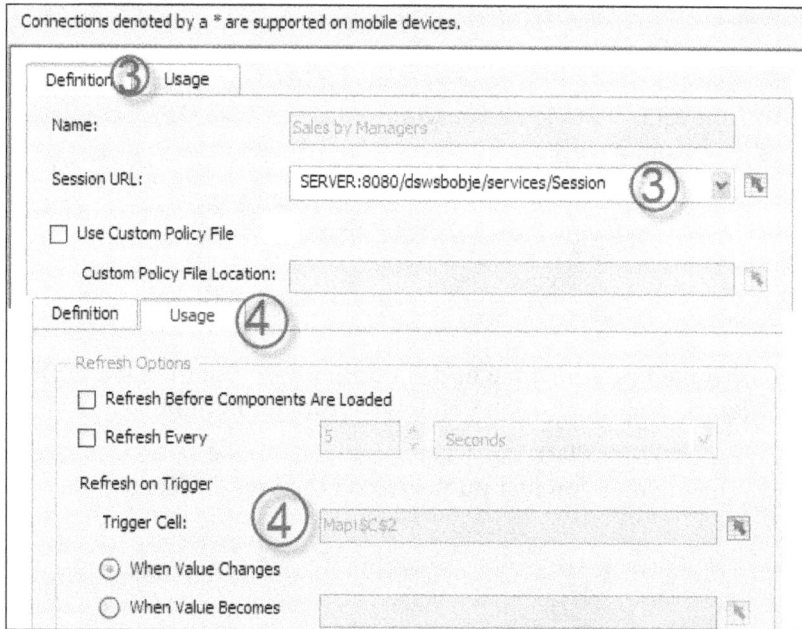

Now, let's preview our dashboard and check whether the newly established Live Office connection is working or not.

Before concluding this section, we need to list the pros and cons of using Live Office:

- Pros of using Live Office:
  - Using SAP BO reports capabilities to shape your data
  - The ability to use instances for reports with long response times
- Cons of using Live Office:
  - Slower
  - Complex
  - Unstable
  - Needs many deployment steps

Using XML data

We can use XML data to populate our dashboard with data. To do this, we first need to display the **Developer** tab in Excel. This is because we will call the XML URL from the **Excel Developer** tab.

Go to the **Excel** options and show the **Developer** tab, as marked in the following screenshot:

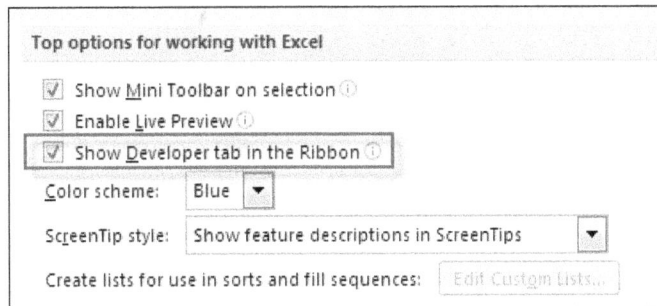

Now, let's follow the steps to establish an XML connection:

1. Open a new dashboard file, or you can open **XML Maps.XL** from the side examples folder under the example code.
2. Navigate to the Excel model and click on the **Developer** ribbon.
3. Click on **Source** and then on **XML Maps....**

4. Click on **Add...** and enter the following URL in the open field: `https://maps.googleapis.com/maps/api/timezone/xml?location=39.6034810,-119.6822510&timestamp=1331161200`. This is a link to a public XML service that will ask for a location and respond with the time zone of that location.

5. Click on **Ok**.

You can see these steps in this screenshot:

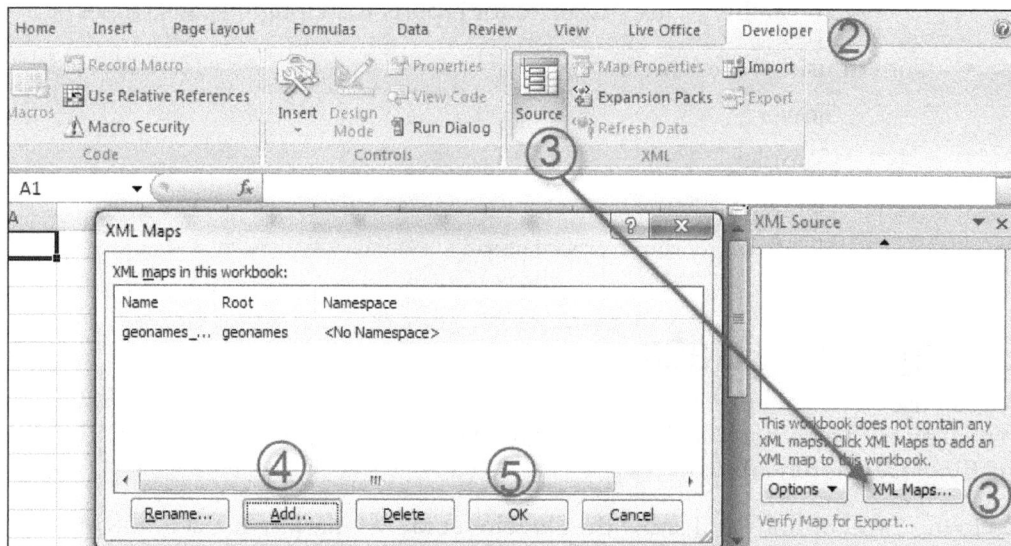

Now, we need to use the XML source in our Excel model. Then, we can bind this information with any dashboard component:

1. From the **XML Source** panel, drag and drop all the available XML tags onto any Excel cell.

2. Click on the **Refresh Data** icon.

These steps are shown in the following screenshot:

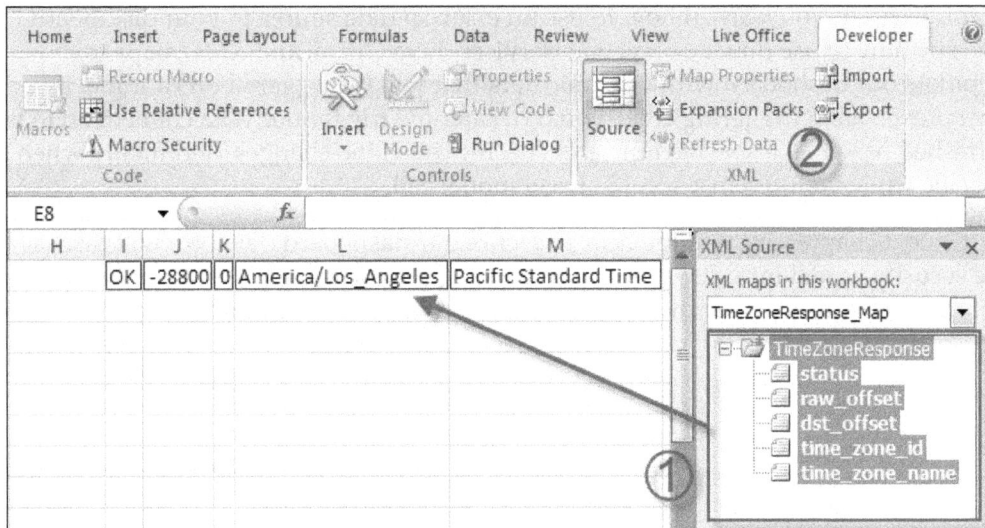

Now, we need to add this connection to our side example dashboard. Let's follow these steps:

1. Go to **Data | Connections...** to open **Data Manger**.

2. Click on **Add**, select **Excel XML Maps**, and then select **TimeZoneResponce_Map**, which we have already defined in the Excel model.

3. Click on the **Usage** tab and configure the refresh to occur every 5 seconds.

   You can see these steps here:

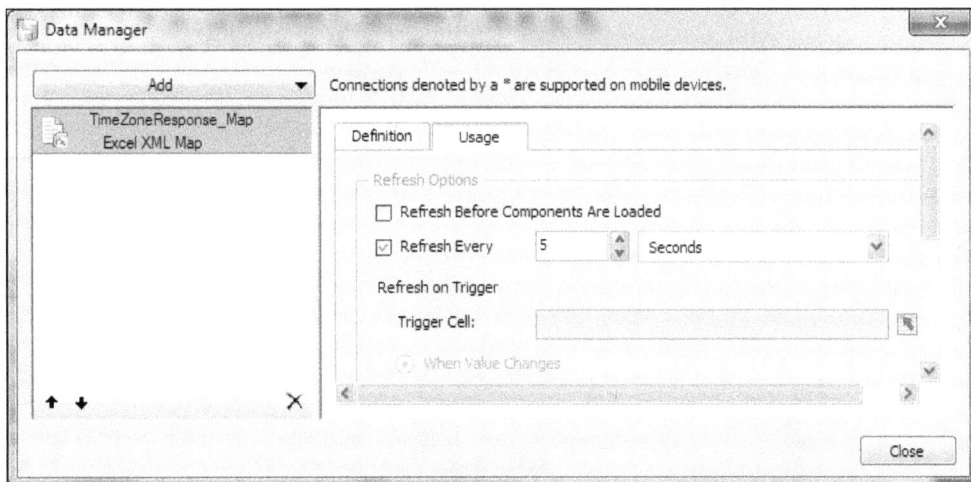

Summary

In this chapter, you learned how to use an external data source in your dashboard. We saw how to use direct query, web services, Live Office, and XML maps to populate our dashboard with dynamic data that will be triggered on runtime, based on a prespecified triggering condition. We can now trigger our data connection to be refreshed based on a specific time and specific cell value changes, and finally when a specific value is stored in a specific Excel model cell.

In the next chapter, we will see how to secure our dashboard data. We will discuss the security model introduced in the SAP BO BI platform, and then see how to use security methods such as row-level security and object-level security.

10
Managing Dashboard Security

Managing security is a mandatory requirement in any BI solution, and this is why it is handled very well in almost all available BI tools. In this chapter, we will discuss the security model in SAP BusinessObjects BI Platform 4.x, and then how to apply security levels on our dashboard by managing the user's access through **Central Management Console (CMC)**. You will learn also how to filter the data displayed in our dashboard, based on a predefined condition that will be applied to a user or a group. This is a very important feature because we can secure our data using the data security profiles defined inside SAP BusinessObjects Universe.

In this chapter, you will learn about:

- The security model in SAP BusinessObjects BI Platform 4.x
- Applying and using object level security from CMC
- Applying and using row level security from Universe

Understanding the SAP BusinessObjects security model

The security model in SAP BusinessObjects BI Platform 4.x can be classified into three main categories:

- Object level security
- Functional or application level security
- Data level security

We will briefly discuss each category as it is managed and handled outside SAP BO Dashboards, but we still need to know about the basics of security management. This book will offer further references on each category, if you want to go deeper into the subject. The idea of this chapter is to give you an overview about what can be done to secure your dashboard. We will also provide some examples on each topic. In this section, we will focus on some terms related to security that everyone should be aware of:

- **Authentication**: This is a general security term that refers to the process of verifying the user's identity. We have many authentication types in SAP BO such as:
  - ○ Enterprise
  - ○ LDAP
  - ○ Windows Active Directory
  - ○ SAP

> For a full list of the available authentication types in SAP BO, please refer to the administration guide (http://help.sap.com/bobip).

- **Authorization**: This is the process of verifying that the user has sufficient rights to perform the required action (such as view, edit, refresh, and so on.) For a specific object (such as report, dashboard, folder, and so on), we can define a user or group authorization from within CMC.

- **Single sign-on (SSO)**: SSO means that SAP BO can use the same operating system (O/S) user authentication, so that the user can access to SAP BO without having to enter their username and password again. This means that the user will be authenticated on one system and the same authentication will carry forward to other systems as well.

- **Access level**: Access level is a set of security rights that users frequently need, and is also known as security roles in many other systems. You can consider access level as a template of rights that can be assigned to multiple users or groups without the need to define the specific required rights every time. In SAP BO, we have two types of access level:
  - ○ Predefined
  - ○ Customized

We will talk about access levels in detail in this chapter.

- **Rights**: A right is a permitted action that can be performed on a specific object such as view or edit. We can grant rights to users or deny them. Only users with sufficient rights will be able to perform the required action. Some actions require more than one right to be assigned to the user in order to be authorized to perform this action.

- **Grant access**: Grant access gives user or groups permissions on specific rights.

- **Deny access**: Deny access revokes permissions from a user or group.

- **User Group**: A user group is a group of users who will share the same access levels. For example, any user under **Administrator** group will have administration privileges. Users can be part of different groups, for example, a user can be part of an administration group as well as being part of a developers group. The higher access level will override the lower one so, for example, if the administrators group has edit privileges and the developers group has view privileges only, then the common user between these two groups will have the higher access level, which is edit in our case. Users and groups can be managed through CMC.

> SAP BO offers two license schemes, **Named User** and **Concurrent Users**. You can refer to the SAP website for more information about the differences between these two schemes. You can find more information at the following URL as well: `http://scn.sap.com/thread/891007`.

- **Inheritance**: There are two inheritance mechanisms. The first one is the object level, and the second is the group level. Inheritance will allow the child object or subgroup to inherit (take the same permissions set) from the parent object or group.

Next, we will start discussing each category of the SAP BO security model.

Applying object level security

The main idea of applying object level security is to give access to the authorized users or groups to BI objects stored on in the BI repository. Normally, end users will access BI objects (or Documents) from the SAP BI Launch pad. We can apply object level security on any of the following:

- Folders
- Categories
- Web Intelligence reports

- Crystal reports
- Dashboards

> A category is a virtual logical folder that can contain BI documents from different physical folders, while folders are a physical location for BI documents on the server.

We can grant or deny access to user or a group of users. The best practice is to organize our folders based on the BI document's subject area. For example, in the banking industry we can store all reports and dashboards related to loans in one physical folder, while we can create multiple categories based on departments, such as one for the risk department and another for Finance. These categories will just have pointers to BI documents, while the original document is stored in the physical folder. This feature facilitates the security assignment because if we have a report that should be accessed by two departments, we can store it in a folder and assign department security on the category level.

> All information mentioned in this chapter applies on Webi reports, Crystal reports, and SAP BO dashboards.

Let's start by assigning security to our eFashion dashboard. But first we need to make sure that we can access the dashboard (this excises requires access to a SAP BO server. You should also have completed the dashboard publishing exercise as described in *Chapter 8, Exporting, Publishing, and Importing Dashboards*).

1. Open **SAP BI Launch Pad** and log in to the BO server using your credentials.
2. Click **Documents** and then select **Folders**.
3. Navigate to the eFashion folder that we used to publish our dashboard, then double-click on the eFashion dashboard.
4. You should be able to access and view the dashboard.

> The BI Launch Pad URL should be something like
> http://<Server name or IP address>:8080/BOE/BI.

We can see the steps in the following screenshot:

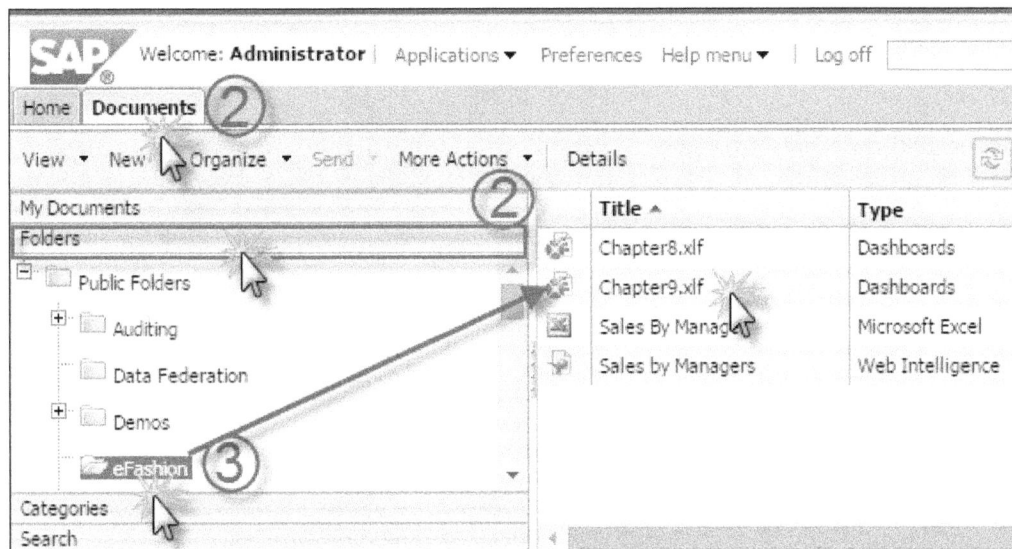

Now, let's create two users (User 1 and User 2) and grant access to the first user on the folder level and deny access to the second user on the folder level as well. Then we will log in with each user and notice how this will affect them.

1. Open CMC and log in using your credentials. Your user should have access rights in order to be able to log in, because this is the main administration screen in SAP BO BI Platform 4.x.

> The BI Launch Pad URL should be something like
> `http://<Server name or IP address>:8080/BOE/CMC`.

2. Select **Users and Groups** from the **Organize** panel.

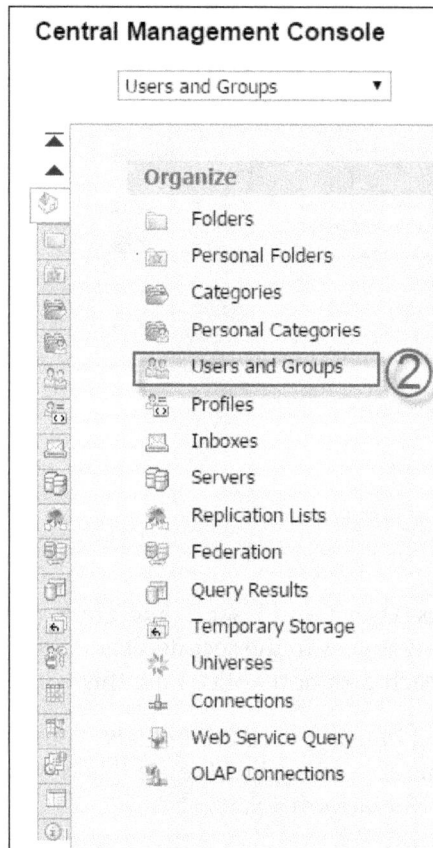

3. Click on the create new user icon:

4. Enter User1 in the **Account Name** field and file the rest of information.
5. Create User2 in the same way.

You can see the steps in the following screenshot:

Now let's assign a security level to those two users:

6. Open CMC, and navigate to **Folders** from **Organize tasks** under your home page.

7. Navigate to the eFashion folder and then select **User Security** from the right-click menu.

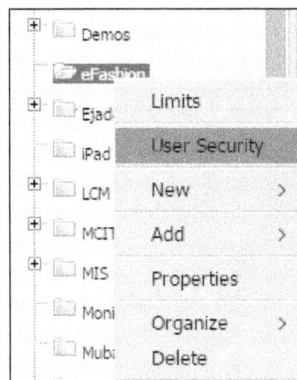

8. Click on **Add Principals**.

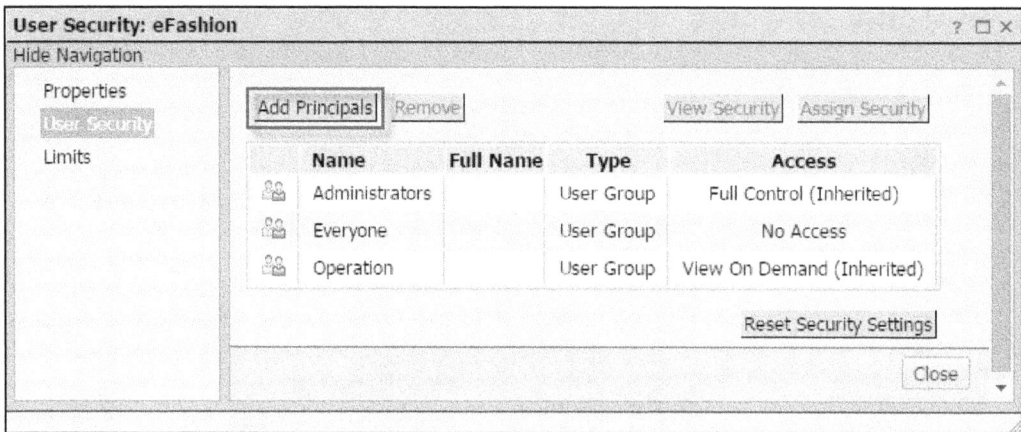

9. Add **User1** to the **Selected Users or Groups**. Then click on the **Add and Assign Security** button.

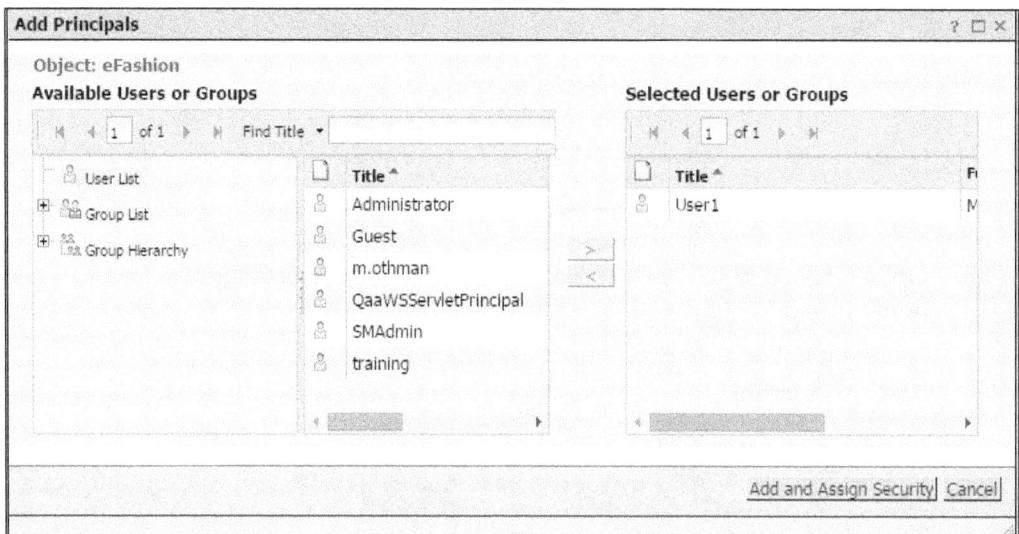

10. Add **View On Demand** to **Assigned Access Levels** for **User1** and click on **OK**

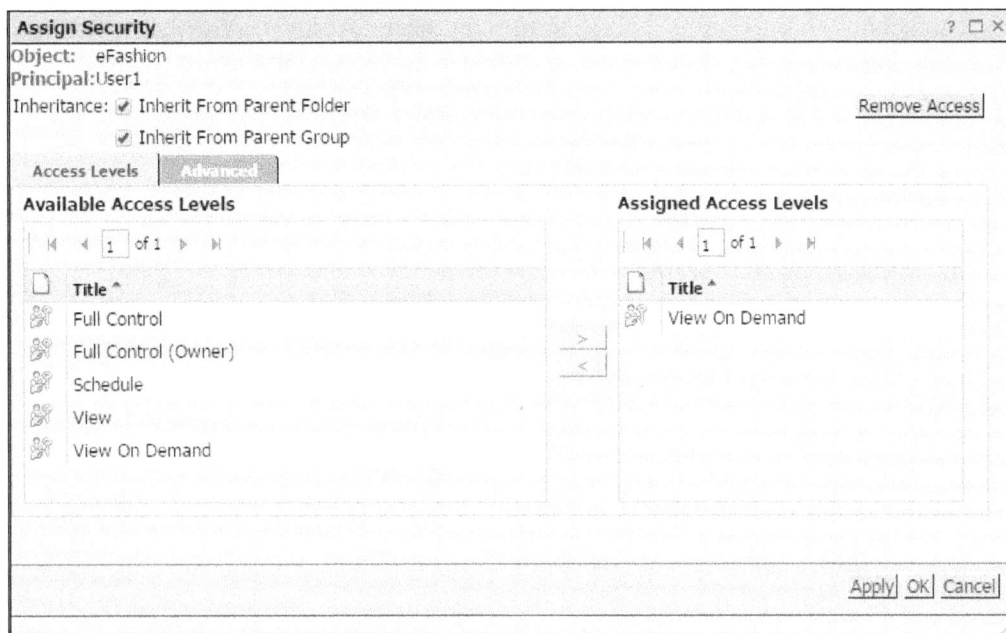

11. Log in to BI Launch Pad, make sure that you can access the eFashion folder, and run the eFashion dashboard.

> The best practice is to assign security access levels to groups, not users.
>
> We need to make sure that users have permission (**View On Demand**) to see Public folder, which is the root folder, in order to be able to see folders under it. We will not be able to see the eFashion folder if we have access permissions to it but not to the root folder.

12. Now we want to remove access from **User2** and prevent them from accessing the eFashion folder, by doing exactly the same as we did with **user1** but clicking on the **remove access** button on the access level screen (step 5). Try to log in with **user2** and make sure that you can't see the eFashion folder.

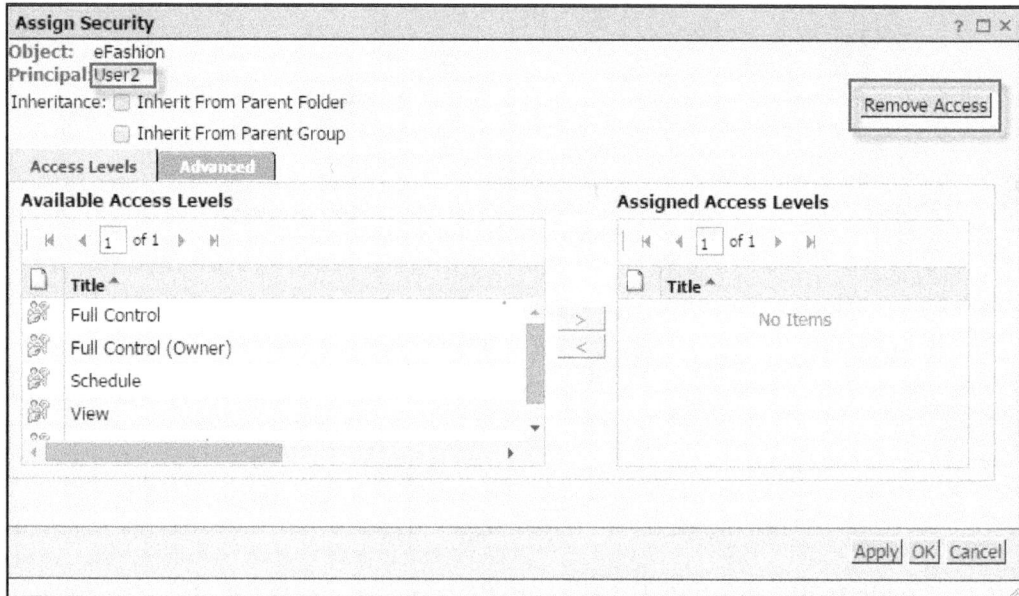

Assign Security		? □ ×

Object: eFashion
Principal:[User2]
Inheritance: ☐ Inherit From Parent Folder   [Remove Access]
        ☐ Inherit From Parent Group

Access Levels | Advanced

Available Access Levels   **Assigned Access Levels**

⏮ ◀ 1 of 1 ▶ ⏭   ⏮ ◀ 1 of 1 ▶ ⏭

☐ Title ▲   ☐ Title ▲

Full Control   [>]   No Items

Full Control (Owner)   [<]

Schedule

View

[Apply] [OK] [Cancel]

Before we leave this section, let's discuss some new topics introduced here:

- **Access levels**: There are six predefined access levels in SAP BO described as follows:
  - **Full Control**: The user will have full control over all object properties in that folder.
  - **Full Control (Owner)**: Users are granted full control over objects that they own.
  - **Schedule**: Users can schedule reports to run and have full access for the scheduled instances that they own. The scheduling feature is only applicable with reports (not dashboards), and can be used to schedule a report to run at a specific time with specific parameters. The output of the report scheduler is a report instance that contains an updated version of the report with the data refreshed by the scheduler.

- ◦ **View**: The user can view and edit objects in the assigned folder, but can't refresh them. They still can copy the report to their favorite folder and refresh it from there. Each user will have their own favorite folder (personal folder), and they will have full access to all objects inside it.

- ◦ **View On Demand**: The user can view, edit, and refresh documents inside that folder. This is the required access level to be assigned in order to be able to access dashboards. The user still needs to have **View On Demand** access level in the Universe and connection used in dashboards or reports inside that folder.

- ◦ **No Access**: This access level will set all permissions to **not specified**. This doesn't explicitly mean denying access, but it will take permissions from the parent groups (Inheritance).

- **Advanced rights**: We can access the advanced rights tab from the **Assign Security** window to grant or deny specific rights for the selected user or group. We can do one of the following actions:

  - ◦ **Grant**: Give rights access to this user

  - ◦ **Deny**: Deny rights access to this user

  - ◦ **No specify**: Don't specify rights access and inherit it from the parent group

  - ◦ **Apply on object**: Apply to selected object only

  - ◦ **Apply on sub-object**: Apply to sub-objects as well

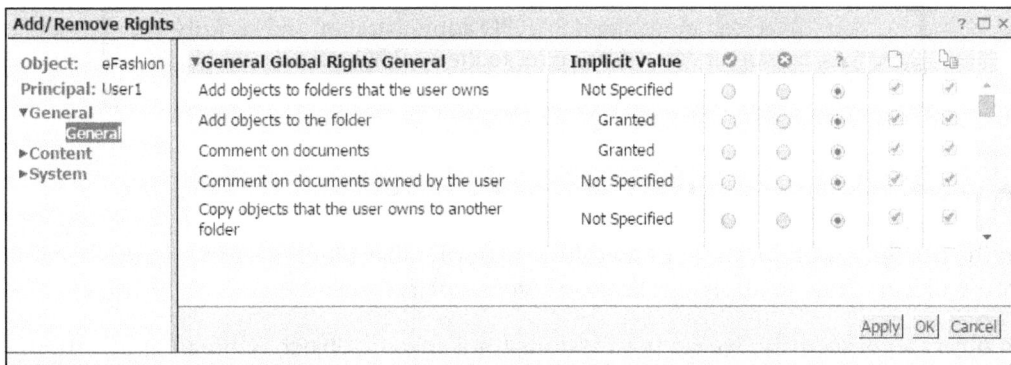

- **Inheritance**: Inheritance means taking the same assigned rights as the parent. We have two inheritance types:

  ○ **Inherit from parent folder**: This option will inherit the same user access granted in the parent folder level. So, for example, if the user has view on demand in the parent folder and has checked this option, they will have also view on demand access level in the current folder, even if they have a lower access level (such as view or no access for example).

  ○ **Inherit from parent group**: This option will inherit the same access level granted for the parent group and will override the current user's access level.

- **Custom access levels**: One of the most powerful features in SAP BO is that you can create customized access levels, aside from the predefined ones.

- **View security and Assign security**: In the security window, we can perform one of the following actions:

  ○ **Add principal**: Adds a new user or group to manage the security access for the selected object or folder

  ○ **View Security**: Checks the current access level and current rights status (granted or denied)

  ○ **Assign security**: Starts assigning access levels and rights for the selected users or groups in the selected object/folder

> To read more about SAP BO administration and security assignments, please refer to the SAP BO official user guide (http://help.sap.com/bobip).

Applying application level security

In the previous section, we discussed how to apply object level security. In this section, you will learn how to apply application level security.

In object level security, we set permissions for a specific object, while in application level security we define a set of actions and features that the user can use when accessing this application. We have many applications in SAP BO such as:

- CMC

- Universe designer

- Information design tool

- Web Intelligence
- BI Launch Pad
- Dashboards

Under each application, you will see a list of all the available actions and features. The user should have the proper access to application features, as well as the proper access to a specific object, in order to be able to utilize it. For example, we can give a user **View on Demand** access to a specific object, which enables them to edit that object, but still we can prevent them from using the drill functionality in any Web Intelligence report.

1. We can access **Applications** from CMC | **CMC Home** | **Manage** | **Applications**.

   You can see the **Applications** menu in the following screenshot:

   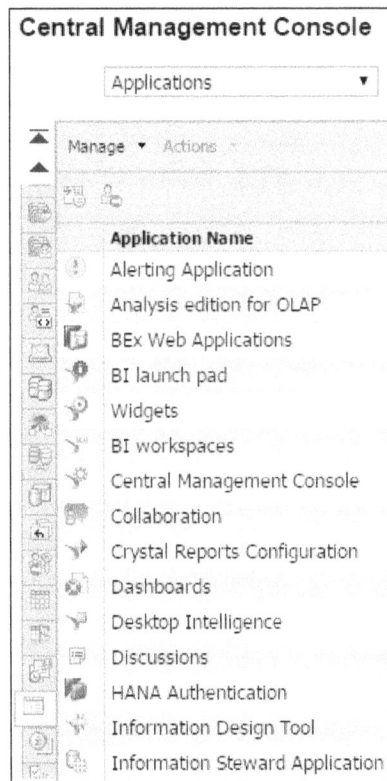

   Now let's check the available permissions under **Dashboards**.

2. Right-click on **Dashboards** and select **User Security** from the right-click menu:

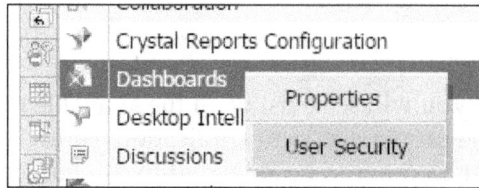

		Crystal Reports Configuration	
		Dashboards	Properties
		Desktop Intell	User Security
		Discussions	

3. Select the **Everyone** user group and then click on **Assign Security**.

4. Click the **Advanced** tab and then click **Add/Remove Rights**.

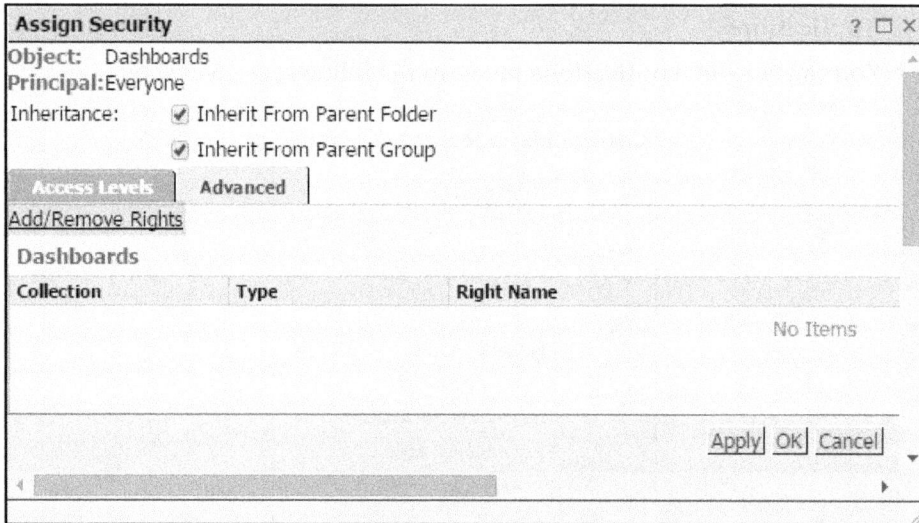

Assign Security   ? □ ×

Object: Dashboards
Principal:Everyone
Inheritance: ☑ Inherit From Parent Folder
                    ☑ Inherit From Parent Group

Access Levels	Advanced

Add/Remove Rights

Dashboards

Collection	Type	Right Name	
			No Items

Apply OK Cancel

The following window will open and you can specify the access level for each right:

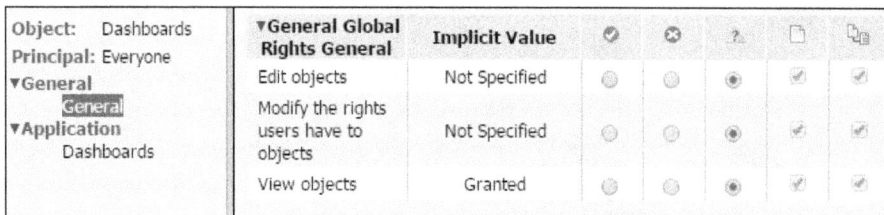

Object: Dashboards Principal: Everyone	▼General Global Rights General	Implicit Value	✓	✗	?	☐	☐
▼General	Edit objects	Not Specified	○	○	◉	☑	☑
General	Modify the rights users have to objects	Not Specified	○	○	◉	☑	☑
▼Application Dashboards	View objects	Granted	○	○	◉	☑	☑

As you can see, there are not many rights that we can assign for dashboards, as it is a separate application and the generated output file is Flash (SWF). On the other hand, let's for example, check the same window for Web Intelligence reports and find out that you can control each single feature and option available in reports. To do this, follow the steps mentioned in the Dashboards application, but select the Web Intelligence reports this time. You can see a set of Web Intelligence rights in the following screenshot:

Object:	▼Specific Rights for Web Intelligence		Implicit Value	◉	◎	?	▢	▣
Web Intelligence	Data - enable data tracking		Granted	○	○	◉	✓	✓
Principal: Everyone	Data - enable formatting of changed data		Granted	○	○	◉	✓	✓
▼General	Desktop Interface - enable local data providers		Granted	○	○	◉	✓	✓
General	Desktop interface - enable Web Intelligence Desktop		Granted	○	○	◉	✓	✓
▼Application	Desktop interface - export documents		Granted	○	○	◉	✓	✓
Web Intelligence	Desktop interface - import documents		Granted	○	○	◉	✓	✓
	Desktop interface - install from BI launch pad		Not Specified	○	○	◉	✓	✓
	▼General Rights for Web Intelligence	Override General Global	Implicit Value	◉	◎	?	▢	▣
	Edit this object	▢	Not Specified				✓	✓
	Log on to Web Intelligence	▢	Not Specified				✓	✓
	Modify the rights users have to this object	▢	Not Specified				✓	✓
	Securely modify rights users have to objects.	▢	Not Specified				✓	✓

Applying row level security

Row level security is a part of the security profiles, that can be created from **Information Design Tool (IDT)** or from managing restrictions under **Universe Design Tool (UDT)**. Both IDT and UDT have amazing capabilities in securing Universe access. We can use this feature to secure or restrict user access for any query, report, and dashboard or web service based on that Universe. Universe is the semantic layer that exists between the physical data source and the end business users.

> You can refer to *Creating Universes using SAP BusinessObjects, Taha M. Mahmoud, Packt Publishing* for more information about creating Universes.

Row level security can be used to restrict the assigned user to see a specific set of data. So for example, we want **User1** (who we already created in the previous section) to see the following states only (California, Colorado, and DC) and **User2** to see the following states only (Massachusetts, New York, and Texas). Both users will access the same dashboard but the row level security will be applied based on the current logged-in user and only allowed data will be retrieved and displayed.

You will learn how create row level security using the following tools:

- Information design tool
- Universe design tool

> By default, the eFashion Universe is a .UNV file, which is created by UDT and you can convert it to .UNX from the IDT tool if you want to use the new features offered in SAP BO BI 4.x, such as Direct Universe Queries in dashboards, which has already been explained in the previous chapter.

Creating a row level security data profile using IDT

In this section, we will create row level security to restrict **User1** and **User2**'s data access. We will use IDT to create two data security profiles and assign each of them to the corresponding user. You need to have the SAP BusinessObjects client tools installed on your local machine to complete the following example:

> I assume that you have basic knowledge of how to create and develop a Universe using IDT and UDT tools. For more information about this topic, you can refer to *Creating Universes with SAP BusinessObjects, Taha M. Mahmoud, Packt Publishing*.

1. Open IDT (**Windows | Start | SAP Business Intelligence | SAP BusinessObjects BI Platform 4 client tools | Information Design Tool**),
2. Create a new project and name it eFashion.
3. Right-click on the eFashion folder and select **Retrieve a published Universe from a repository**.
4. Click on the **Security Editor** icon.
5. Select the **eFashion** Universe from the list.

6. Click on the **Insert Data Security Profile** icon:

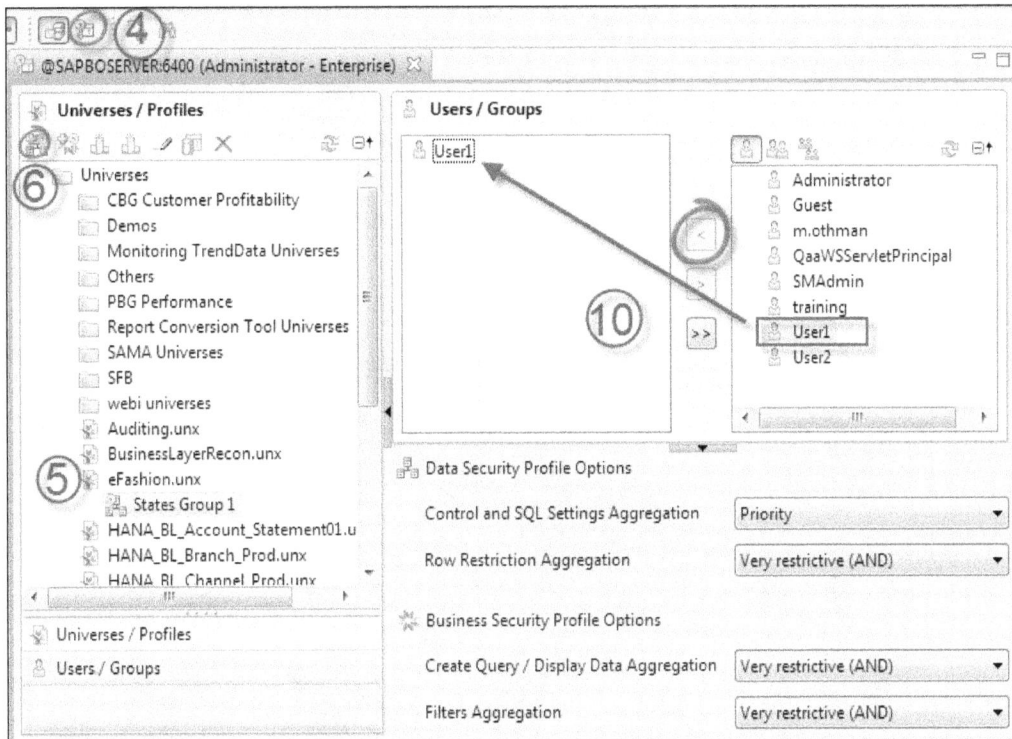

7. Enter `States Group 1` in **Data Security Profile Name**.

8. Navigate to the **Rows** tab and click on the **Insert** button.

9. Select the **OUTLET_LOOKUP** table and enter the following `OUTLET_LOOKUP.STATE in ('DC','California','Colorado')` in the **Where Clause** field. Then click on **Ok**.

10. Select **States Group 1** and add **User1** to the **Users/Groups** panel, to apply this security profile to that user.

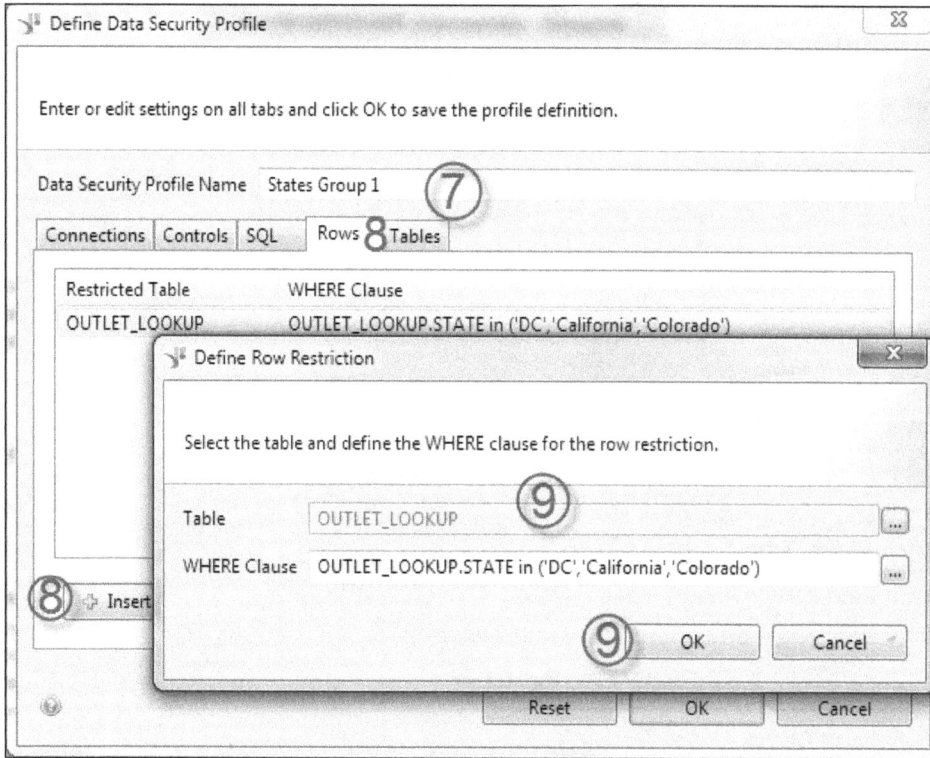

Now try to log in to the BI Launch pad by using **User1** and opening the dashboard. Note that you can only see the three restricted states.

- **Assignment**: Do the same and create **States Group 2** by filtering rows on (Massachusetts, New York, and Texas). Then assign this security profile to **User2**. After that, log in to the BI launch pad and open the **eFashion** dashboard. Notice that only the restricted three states are displayed.

Creating row level security access restrictions using UDT

Universes can also be created and developed by UDT. The main difference between UDT and IDT is that IDT is the new tool released in via SAP BO BI Platform 4, and so all new features introduced in this release require the Universe to be developed by this tool. We already discussed this in the previous chapter when we created the direct Universe query. UDT on the other hand is the old tool, which is also known as Universe Designer and is there for compatibility purposes. You can convert .UNV Universe, which was created by UDT to .UNX Universe, which was created by IDT in one single step from inside IDT. In this section, you will learn how to create restrictions that correspond to security profiles in IDT.

1. Open UDT (**Windows | Start | SAP Business Intelligence | SAP BusinessObjects BI Platform 4 Client Tools | Universe Design Tool**).

2. Log in the to BI system using your credentials.

3. Select **File | Import ....**

4. Select the **eFashion** Universe.

5. Navigate to **Tools | Manage security... | Manage Access Restrictions ....**

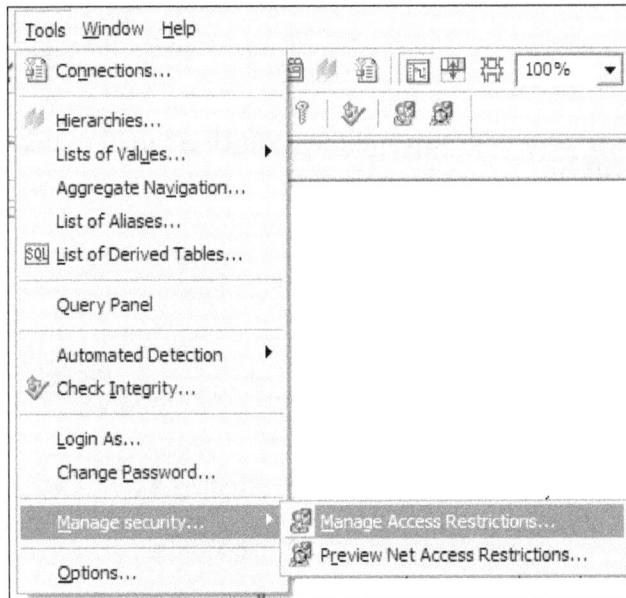

6. Click on the **New** button and enter `States Group 1` in the **Restriction Name** field.

7. Navigate to the **Rows** tab and click on **Add**.

8. Select **OUTLET_LOOKUP** table and enter `OUTLET_LOOKUP.STATE in ('DC','California','Colorado')` in the **Where Clause**. Then click on **Ok**.

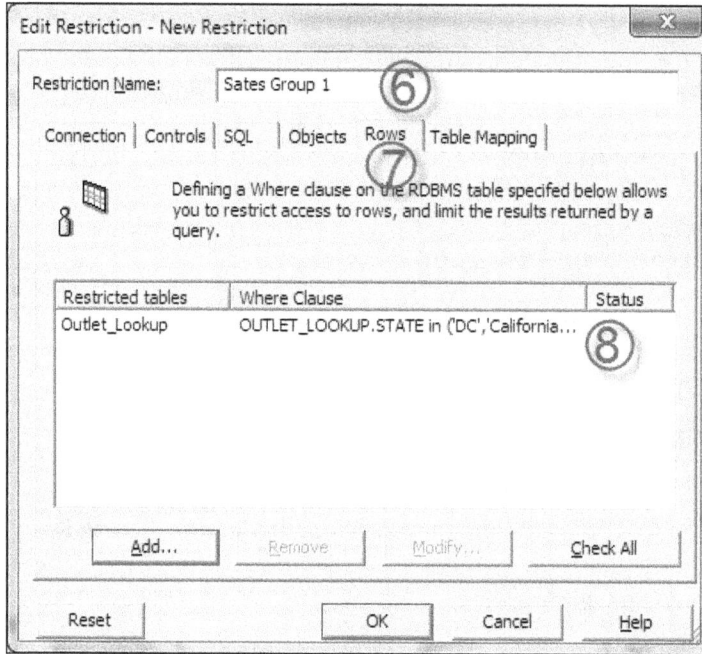

9. Click on **Add user or group** and then add **User1** to have this restriction applied to them.

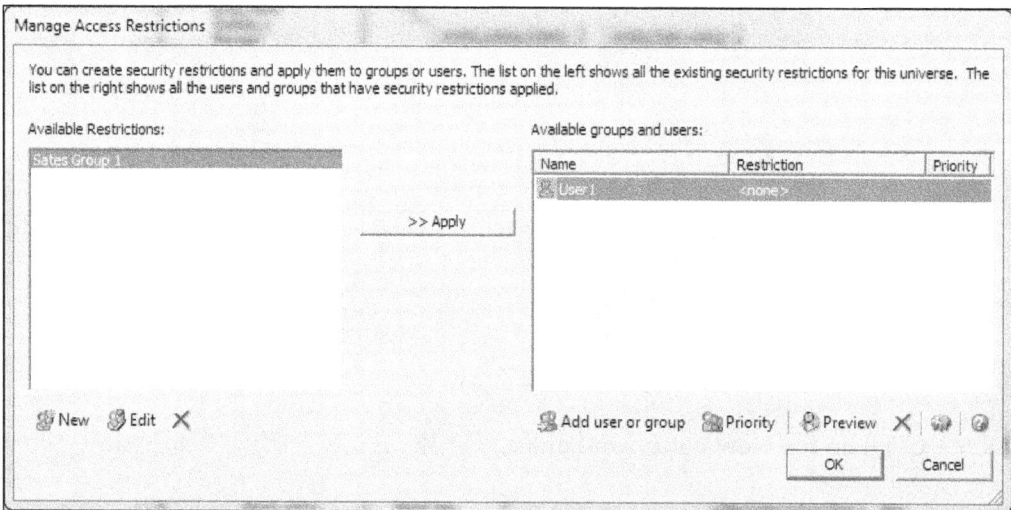

Now log in to BI Launch pad using **User1**, open the **eFashion** dashboard, and make sure this user can only see the restricted states. Please note that based on the connection method you used and the Universe that you access, the data will be filtered accordingly. This means that if we are using one direct query based on **eFashion.unx**, which was created by the IDT tool, and query as web service based on **efashion.unv**, which was created by UDT, only the security used in the corresponding Universe will be applied when data is retrieved by the data connection.

Assignment: Try to create **States Group 2** and assign it to **User2**, then try to check whether the restrictions created have been applied or not when displaying data in the eFashion dashboard.

Applying security best practices

In this section, we will discuss the best practices that you need to save your time and efforts while designing your security model:

- **Security matrix**: We may need to prepare a security matrix for your users before even starting the development of our dashboard. We need to identify the users and groups who will access our dashboard, and start defining security profiles and restrictions that need to be applied to our data to secure it. You may need more than one security matrix view, for example, one for the object level security, another one for the application level, and maybe a final one for the row or data level matrix. A security matrix might be something like what is displayed in the following screenshot:

User/Group	View	View on Demand	Schedule	Full Control	Full control (owner)
Administrators group				Yes	
User1		Yes			
User2	Yes				

- **Customized access level**: We can utilize this feature to create customized access levels that serve different users' needs. We should consider using predefined access levels whenever possible, but in many cases we will need to create customized access levels that grant and / or deny rights not included in the predefined one.

- **Row level security**: We need to create generic row level security profiles or restrictions that can be reused many times within users and groups. Following the example that we already discussed in this chapter, we may need to create a separate security profile for each state instead of grouping all of them in one profile. This will allow us to easily apply or revoke this profile on multiple users or groups. Specific row level security profiles will end up being applied on only one user or group because they are customized for this user only. Generally, we need to avoid a security profile per user or group and to think how to reuse profiles by making them more generic.

- **Inheritance**: This is a powerful and magical feature that can save you time and efforts if we use it wisely; on the other hand it can bring trouble if you didn't don't control it. Inheritance can end up giving access to unauthorized users to restricted objects if they have inherited permissions from the parent group of folder. So we need to take care.

Summary

In this chapter, you learned how to secure our dashboard as an object by applying the proper access levels to the corresponding users. You also learned how to control and assign dashboard application privileges. After that, you learned how to secure our data by applying row level security. Finally, we discussed the best practices that we need to consider while designing our security model for our dashboards.

In the next chapter, you will learn how to create mobile dashboards and how to identify mobile supported components. Also, you will learn some tricks and tips on how to overcome unsupported mobile components.

Creating Mobile Dashboards

11

In the last few decades, the usage of smart devices, such as mobile phones, tablets, and smart watches has increased dramatically. Now, the hardware of smart devices is powerful enough to handle all that we need it to. Indeed, we are now carrying smart devices with us all the time, that act like small, but powerful, computers. Here comes the idea of Mobile BI. We need to select the most important information for the BI end user to track on the go, using their smart devices.

> According to the **Industrial Design Center** (**IDC**: http://www.idc.com/), by 2017, 87 percent of all connected devices sold will be tablets and smartphones.

SAP BusinessObjects has different BI tools that handle different user requirements. They have the following BI reporting tools:

- **Web Intelligence (Webi) reports**: This tool can be used to help business users to execute their day-to-day reports. The main advantage of Webi reports is that you can schedule them to run and be sent directly to users by e-mail. This is a very powerful tool, because it is very similar to MS Excel, so business users can start using it directly, without a lot of effort and time.

- **Crystal reports**: This is one of the most famous report types. We call it a pixel-perfect report because we can control and adjust our report design, up to the pixel level. Normally, we use these reports to create the annual and quarterly reports used and published by an organization's end users.

- **Dashboards**: This is the tool that you are learning in this book. Dashboards are a powerful way to deliver information to the top management and executives.

- **Lumira**: This tool is a data discovery tool that can help data and business analysts explore data. It is very powerful and can connect to any source data. In minutes, you can come up with neat and wonderful dashboards and charts with this tool. The idea behind this tool is that you don't have initial requirements to implement, but you have data to explore instead.

- **Explorer**: This is another powerful data discovery tool, but its main focus is on analyzing data rather than presenting it. You can use it to explore the information you have.

- **Design studio**: This is a new dashboard tool. It was released at the end of 2013 for designing and implementing dashboards. It needs coding experience, as it is heavily dependent on JavaScript. Someone with technical skills should use this tool to produce dashboards, and then make them available to the end user. A lay user will not be able to create their own dashboards using this tool, at least at the current stage. SAP is focusing on upgrading this tool to be their main dashboard tool.

We can find a matrix that shows the supported content on each device, as follows:

BI document*	iPad*	iPhone*	Android tablet*	Android phone*
Webi	Yes	Yes	Yes	Yes
Crystal	Yes	Yes	No	No
Dashboards	Yes	No	Yes	No
Design studio	Yes	Yes	Yes	Yes
Explorer	Yes	Yes	No	No
Lumira	Yes	No	No	No

* This is as per Q4-2014.

> SAP BO Dashboard can be viewed only on tablets, and not cell phones (as per the current available release SAP BO BI platform 4.1 SP5).

In this chapter, we will focus on the following topics:

- Creating dashboards for mobile devices
- Developing mobile dashboards
- Publishing mobile dashboards
- Accessing mobile dashboards

Creating dashboards for smart devices

Mobility is one of the main enterprise goals for all market leaders. Mobility is a term that refers to providing company services for the customer through smart devices (including mobile devices). So, having a mobile application is one of the factors of an organization's success. Facebook, Google, Twitter, and many other enterprises across the globe are competing with each other to reach people everywhere. You don't need to use a computer to buy something from Amazon.com. All that you need now is to install the Amazon application on your device and buy anything, at anytime. The fact that we are carrying our smart devices all the time, and using them regularly, makes them a golden place for reaching people. Business Intelligence also found that smart devices are perfect for delivering BI content to the end users, and to achieve the concept of giving the right information to the right person at the right time.

We can use SAP BO dashboards to create one of the following dashboard types:

- Desktop
- Mobile
- Desktop and mobile

As we mentioned in *Chapter 2, Understanding the Dashboard Creation Process*, the first step that we need to consider before starting our dashboard design is deciding the target audience and devices. If we are targeting desktop users only, we don't need to worry about the compatibility of dashboard components, as all components are compatible with desktops; whereas, we need to take care if we are targeting mobile users. We need to avoid unsupported components and find alternatives and workarounds, as we will discuss in this chapter.

Here, we must mention one big difference between desktop and mobile dashboards, which is the technology used in each. The technology used in desktop dashboards is Macromedia Flash, while the technology used in mobile dashboards is HTML5. This is the main reason that all the desktop dashboard components that we discussed throughout this book are not supported in the mobile version. You will learn how to find unsupported components and how to avoid them in the first place, if you are targeting mobile users.

The second thing that we need to be aware of is the hardware limitation on mobile devices in comparison with powerful desktop and client tools. We need to consider using lightweight dashboard components and presenting the most important and critical information, which the end user really wants to track and monitor on the go. These types of KPIs need immediate action and can't wait until the user returns to their office.

Here are the main steps for creating mobile dashboards:

- **Design phase**: We need to consider which KPIs should be displayed in the mobile dashboard version and how they should be displayed

- **Development phase**: We need to use supported dashboard components and connections only

- **Publishing phase**: We need to publish our dashboard and make it available for end users

- **Accessing dashboard**: We need to install the SAP BI application and configure it to connect to our SAP BO system

Next, we will discuss each phase.

Developing a mobile SAP BO Dashboard

We can use SAP BO Dashboards to develop dashboards for desktops as well as mobiles. We just need to consider the following if we are developing for mobile dashboards:

- Using only supported mobile components
- Using the recommended canvas size for iPads
- Using only supported mobile connections

Now, we will discuss each of these topics.

Using supported mobile components

To make sure that we are using only supported mobile dashboard components, we can use the **Mobile Only** filter from the **Components** panel. You can see this filter in the following screenshot:

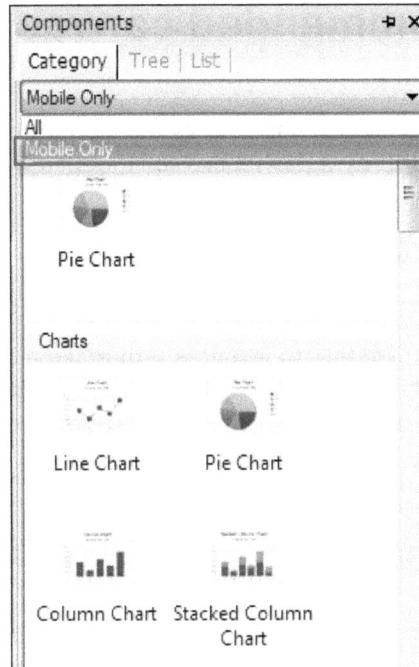

You can see a list of all supported Mobile dashboard components and connections in *Appendix 3, Supported Mobile Components and Connections*.

We can also use the **Mobile Compatibility** panel to highlight unsupported dashboard components. This panel is very useful because it is also used to highlight unsupported functions, such as **Entry Effect**. Unsupported features will simply be lost when you view the dashboard on a mobile phone. You can see the **Mobile Compatibility** panel in the following screenshot:

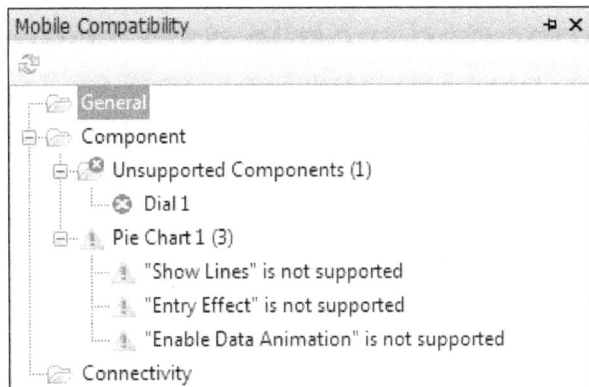

Using the recommended canvas size for iPads

We need also to take care of the canvas size, as the recommended canvas size is 1024 x 768 pixels if we are developing a dashboard for mobiles. We can change the canvas size from the following places:

- **Document properties**
- **Preferences**

Changing the canvas size from the preferences will make it the default canvas size for all new dashboards, whereas changing it from document properties will change the canvas size for the current dashboard only. If we have selected any canvas size other than the recommended one, we will get the following warning in the **Mobile Compatibility** panel:

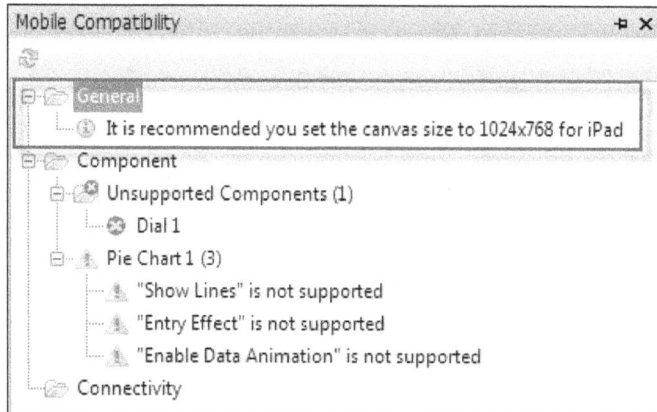

Using a supported mobile data connection

The next thing we need to take care of is the external data connection type, as only a few of them are supported by mobile dashboards. We can see a list of supported mobile connections in *Appendix 3, Supported Mobile Components and Connections*.

> We can see a * sign next to the supported mobile connection type in **the Data Manager** window, as we've already discussed in *Chapter 9, Retrieving External Data Sources*.

You can see the **Data Manager** window, selected via data connections, in the following screenshot:

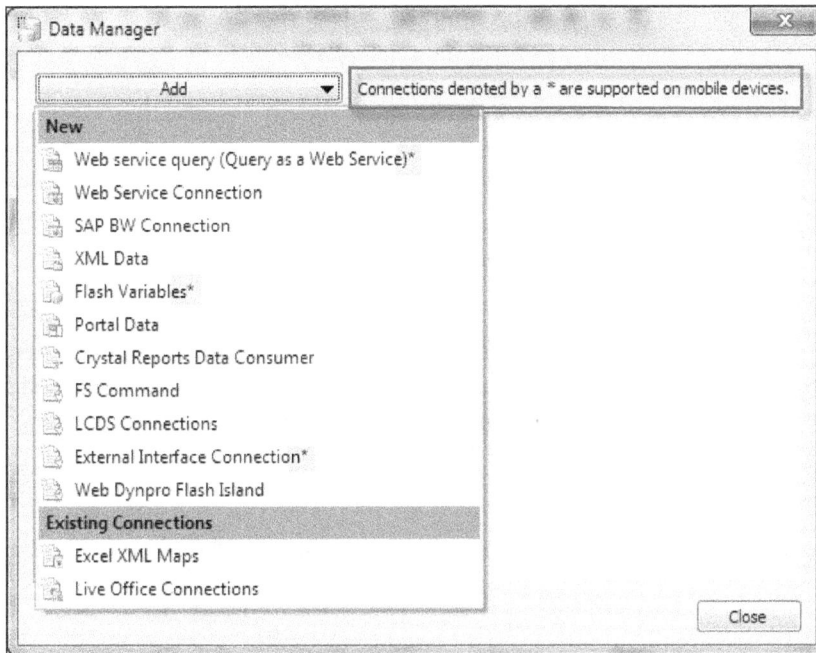

Next, we will see how to preview and publish our mobile dashboard.

Publishing mobile dashboards

Publishing a dashboard will make it available for end users. You can learn how to publish your dashboard for desktop users in *Chapter 8, Exporting, Publishing, and Importing Dashboards.*

After developing our mobile dashboard, we will need to do the following:

- Preview our dashboard to see what it will look like on a tablet
- Publish our dashboard on the SAP BO server as a mobile dashboard
- Add our dashboard to the mobile category to make it available for mobile users

Previewing our mobile dashboard

There are two modes for previewing mobile dashboards:

- **Mobile (Fit to Screen)**
- **Mobile (Original Size)**

You can see the three available options in the following screenshot. We have already explained how to use the first one.

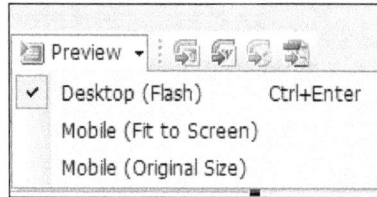

The main difference between the other two options is that **Mobile (Fit to Screen)** will fit the dashboard to the screen size, and the other will display the original size. We need to note that the previewing option will affect only the preview mode. It will not affect the mobile dashboard after it is published.

> A mobile preview exactly simulates what we will see on the iPad.

You can see a preview of a mobile dashboard in the following screenshot:

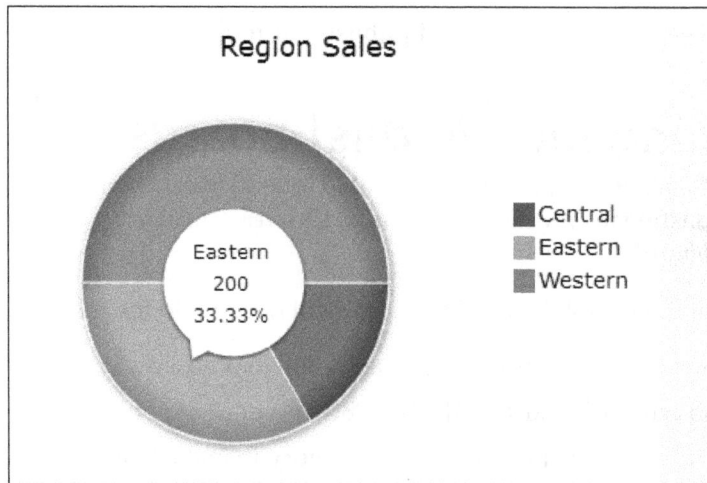

You may notice that some components, such as a pie chart for example, will create a different user experience on the mobile preview compared to the desktop preview. This is because a desktop preview generates a flash file, whereas a mobile preview generates an HTML5 file.

Publishing our mobile dashboard

The next step is to publish our dashboard on the SAP BO server. We have the following options:

- **Save to Platform | Mobile Only**
- **Save to Platform | Desktop Only**
- **Save to Platform | Desktop and Mobile**

We can access the **Save to Platform** menu from the **File** menu and see these options:

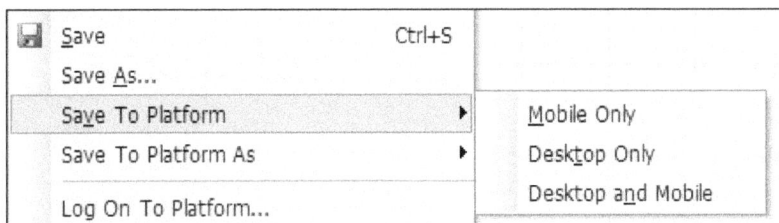

💾 Save	Ctrl+S	
Save As...		
Save To Platform ▶		Mobile Only
Save To Platform As ▶		Desktop Only
		Desktop and Mobile
Log On To Platform...		

The options are self-explanatory. The **Mobile Only** option will publish the dashboard as an HTML5 object only and can be accessed only from mobile devices. The **Desktop Only** option will generate a flash file and can be accessed only by desktop clients. Finally, the **Desktop and Mobile** option will generate both HTML5 and desktop, and can be accessed by both clients.

Publishing a mobile dashboard will be exactly the same as what we discussed in *Chapter 8*, *Exporting, Publishing, and Importing Dashboards*. We will select a location to publish our dashboard, and that's it!

Adding our dashboard to the mobile category

After publishing our mobile dashboard, we need to make it available for mobile users. By default, any dashboard or report under the **Mobile** category will be displayed for mobile users. To do this, we should follow the steps:

1. Access the BI Launch Pad (the URL will be `<SAP_BO_SERVER_NAME:8080>/BOE/BI`).
2. Navigate to the folder that we used to publish our mobile dashboard.
3. Right-click on that dashboard and add it to the **Mobile** category.

You can see these steps in the following screenshot:

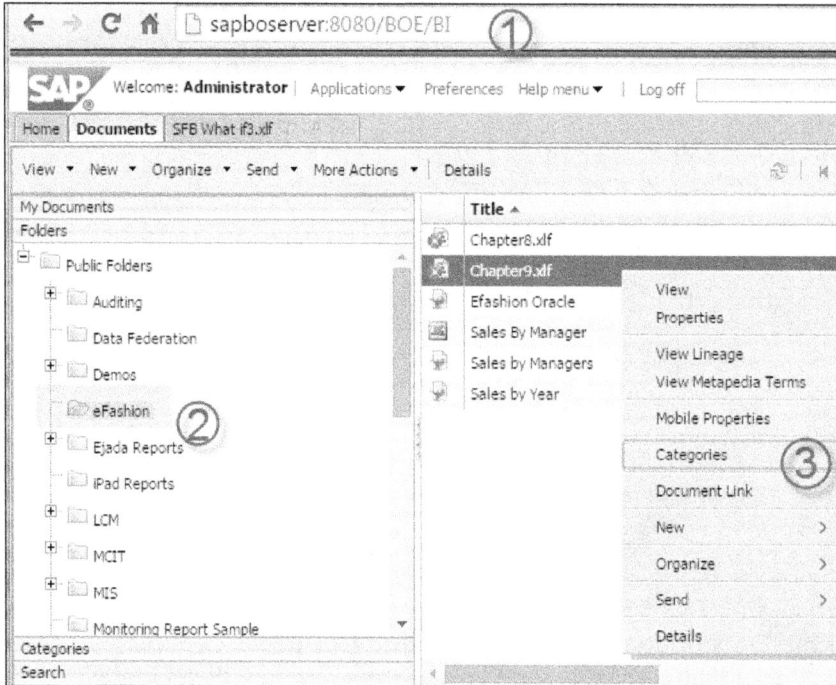

You can see the last step here:

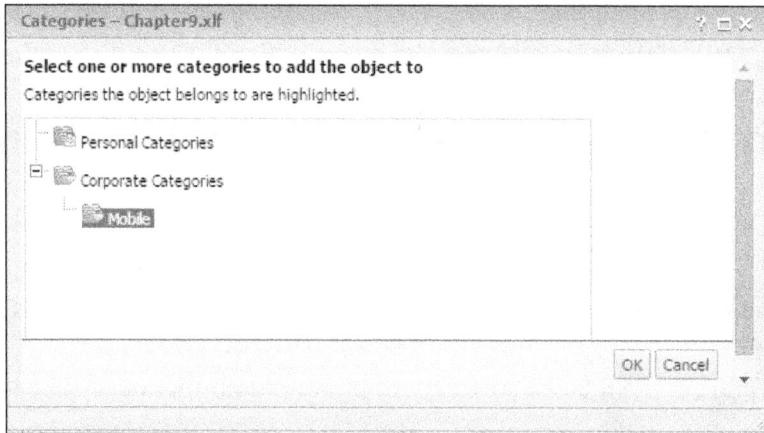

You may need to refer to the SAP BusinessObjects administrator guide to get more information on how to set up and configure a mobile server on the SAP BO server. We used the default configuration settings here.

Next, you will learn how to access it from an iPad or an Android tablet.

Accessing and using mobile dashboards

The first thing we need to do before accessing our mobile dashboard is to download the SAP BusinessObjects BI mobile application from the following links:

- **Android**: `https://play.google.com/store/apps/details?id=com.sap.mobi&hl=en`

- **Mac OS**: `https://itunes.apple.com/en/app/sap-businessobjects-mobile/id441208302?mt=8`

> The most strongly recommended mobile device for displaying SAP BO dashboards is the iPad.
>
> Starting from SAP BO BI platform 4.1 SP1, we can also view SAP BO dashboards on Android tablets.

Then, we need to configure SAP BO mobile application to connect to our server by following these steps:

> You may need to create a VPN, if you want to access your mobile dashboards from outside your organization.

1. Open the SAP BO Mobile application (SAP BI).

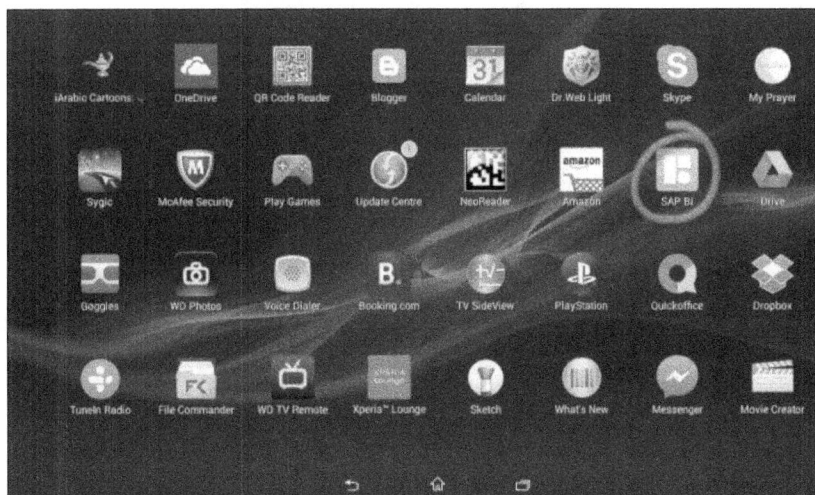

2. Tap on **Connect** and select **Create New Connection**.

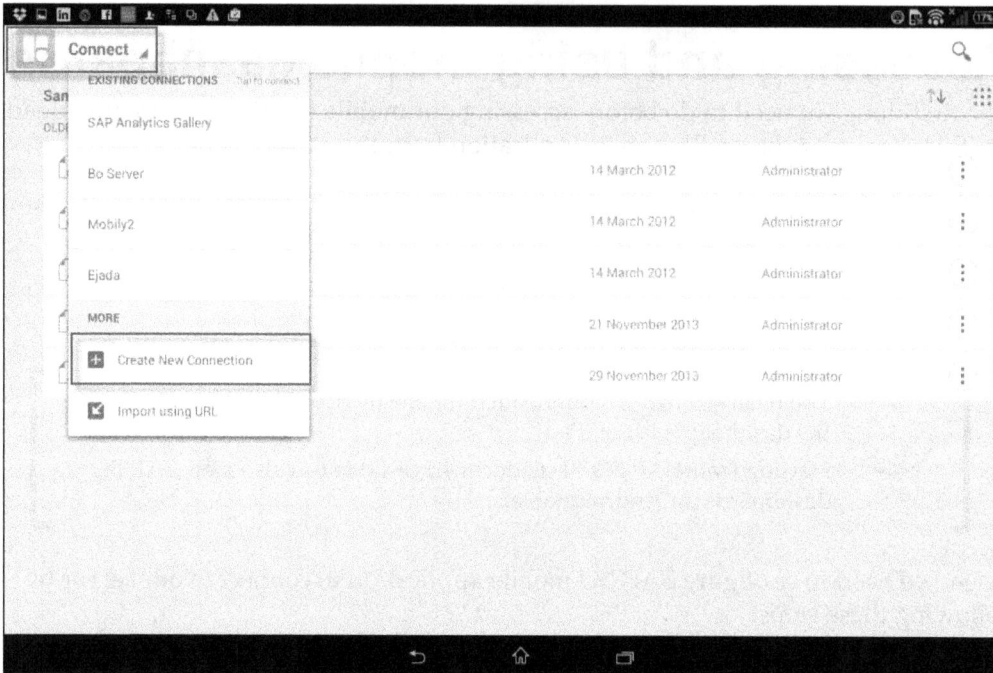

3. Enter **BO Server** in the connection name.
4. Enter **Mobile Server URL** and **CMC** in the connection details (this information will depend on your SAP BO server information).
5. Fill in **Authentication Details** (username and password).

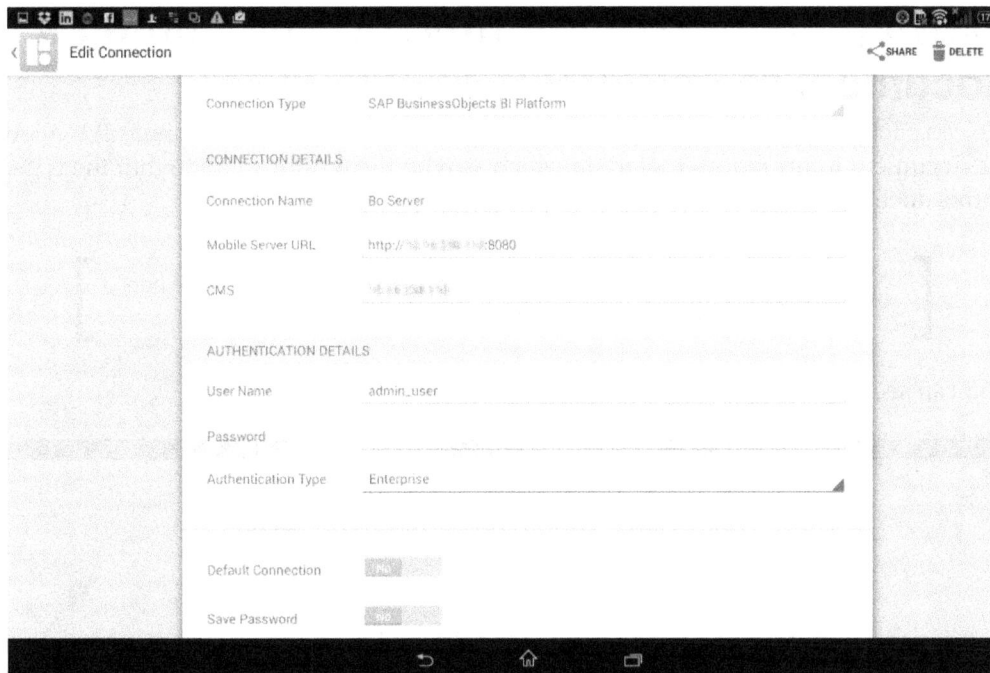

6. Establish the connection that you've already created. You should be able to see our eFashion dashboard. Tap it to display it on your tablet.

Introducing the main features of the SAP BI application

We can use the SAP BI application as a master place to view SAP BI content produced by different SAP BI tools, such as Web Intelligence, dashboards, Lumira, and so on. We can perform the following actions:

* Viewing document information and adding it to favorites
* Annotation
* E-mail

> For a complete user guide to SAP BI applications, refer to the following links:
>
> * Mac OS: http://help.sap.com/bomobileios
> * Android: https://help.sap.com/bomobileandroid

Viewing document information and adding a document to favorites

We can click on the three dots beside any BI document (report or dashboard) to view the document information (metadata), such as who the author is, and what the type of this document is.

> A small yellow star will appear on top of the document when it's added to favorites.

You can see this menu in the following screenshot:

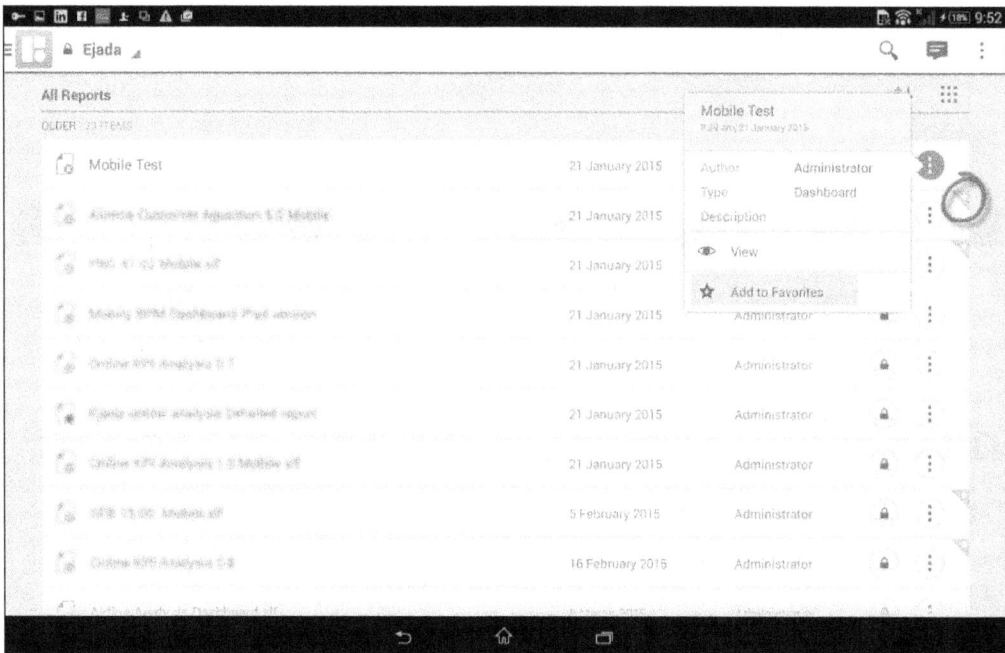

Using the Annotation feature

We can use this feature to take a screenshot of the current dashboard view and start annotating and adding our comments to it. Then, we can send it to the corresponding person. You can even add voice comments, which make it ideal to communicate results with others. This feature is shown here:

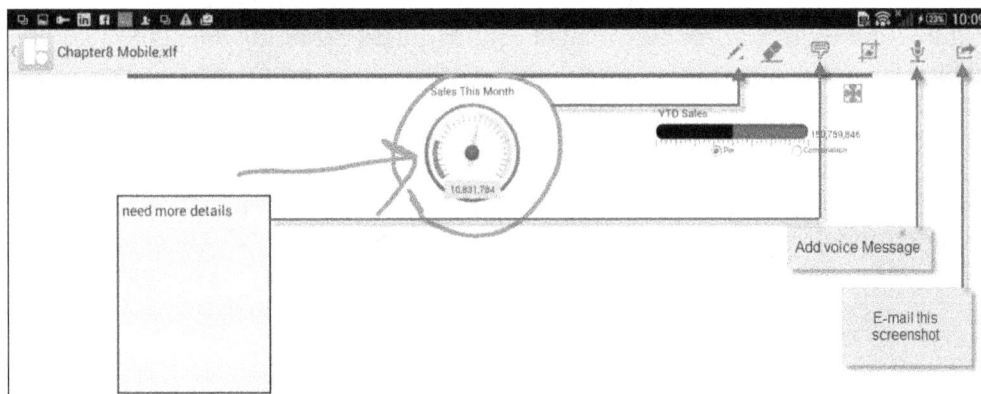

E-mailing dashboards

We can use this feature to e-mail the BI document to a specific person. It is the same as what we did in the annotation feature, except that it will send a plain image of the current view.

Summary

In this chapter, you learned how to create a mobile dashboard using SAP BO Dashboards. Then, we discussed how to find unsupported mobile dashboard components using the mobile compatibility panel. As a best practice, we should use the **Mobile Only** filter from the **Components** panel if we are targeting mobile devices for our dashboard. Next, you learned how to preview and publish your dashboard, so that it can be used and accessed by mobile devices. After that, we had an overview of the main features of a SAP BI mobile application, such as annotation and sharing via e-mails.

Throughout this book, you learned how to create a dashboard step by step, starting from the analysis phase, right up to design and development. The main challenge that you will face later is how to present your information in a meaningful way, and how to get the maximum value of your information. You may need to read Stephen Few's book *Show Me the Numbers* and *Information Dashboard Design* to learn the best way to present information. I also recommend that you read *SAP BusinessObjects Dashboards 4.1 Cookbook* by Xavier Hacking and David Lai. This book contains many great tips and tricks that every SAP BO Dashboards user should know. You may also need to take a look at other dashboard tools, such as SAP Lumira. SAP Lumira is a data discovery tool that can be used to analyze your information in the same way as Tableau and QlikView. Finally, I advise you to read more about new technologies such as SAP HANA, which is an in-memory database and is super fast. You can build a real-time dashboard that refreshes every 5 seconds to provide an online analysis of your information. You may also try to learn how to integrate SAP BO dashboards with big data providers, such as IBM Hadoop, Hive, Spark, and so on. You can even maintain a dashboard that displays your customers' satisfaction, based on their feedback on Twitter and Facebook.

I hope that you enjoyed reading this book, and I am looking forward to your input and comments.

References

Supported excel functions

A	COMBIN	E	I	L
ABS	CONCATENATE	EDATE	IF	LARGE
ACOS	COS	EFFECT	INDEX	LE
ACOSH	COSH	EOMONTH	INT	LEFT
AND	COUNT	EVEN	IPMT	LEN
ASIN	COUNTA	EXACT	IRR	LN
ASINH	**D**	EXP	ISBLANK	LOG
ASSIGN	DATE	EXPONDIST	ISERR	LOG10
ATAN	DATEVALUE	**G**	ISERROR	LOOKUP
ATAN2	DAVERAGE	GE	ISEVEN	LOWER
ATANH	DAY	GEOMEAN	ISLOGICAL	**M**
AVEDEV	DAYS360	GT	ISNA	MATCH
AVERAGE	DB	**H**	ISNONTEXT	MAX
AVERAGEA	DCOUNT	HARMEAN	ISNUMBER	MEDIAN
AVERAGEIF	DSTDEV	HLOOKUP	ISODD	MID
B	DSTDEVP	HOUR	ISTEXT	MIN
BETADIST	DSUM	**I**	**K**	MINUS
C	DVAR	IF	KURT	MINUTE
CEILING	DVARP	INDEX		MIRR
CHOOSE				MOD

MODE	P	REPLACE	SSUMXMY2	VAR
MONTH	PI	REPT	SYD	VDB
N	PMT	RIGHT	T	VLOOKUP
NE	POWER	ROUND	TAN	W
NETWORKDAYS	PPMT	ROUNDDOWN	TANH	WEEKDAY
NORMDIST	PRODUCT	ROUNDUP	TEXT	WEEKNUM
NORMINV	PV	S	TIME	WORKDAY
NORMSINV	Q	SECOND	TIMEVALUE	Y
NOT	QUARTILE	SIGN	TODAY	YEAR
NOW	QUOTIENT	SIN	TRUE	YEARFRAC
NPER	R	STDEV	TRUNC	
NPV	RADIANS	UM	TYPE	
O	RAND	SUMIF	U	
ODD	RANGE_COLON	SUMPRODUCT	UPPER	
OFFSET	RANK	SUMSQ	V	
OR	RATE	SUMX2MY2	VALUE	
		SUMX2PY2		

List of Built-in maps

Built-in maps		
Africa by country	Greece by prefecture	Russia by region
Albania by region	Hungary by county	Russia by region Mercator
Andorra by region	Iceland by province	Serbia and Montenegro by region
Armenia	India by region	Slovakia by region
Asia by country	Indonesia by province	Slovenia by region
Asia Pacific (large) by country	Ireland by region	South America by country
Asia Pacific (small) by country	Italy by region	South Korea by region
Australia by region	Japan by region	Spain by autonomous community
Austria by state	Kazakhstan by region (outdated)	Sweden by county
Azerbaijan by province	Kazakhstan by region	Switzerland by canton
Belarus by region	Kyrgyzstan by region	Thailand by province

Belgium by province	Laos by province	Turkey by province
Bosnia and Herzegovina by region	Latvia by region	Turkmenistan by region
Bulgaria by region	Liechtenstein	Ukraine by province
California by county	Lithuania by region	United Arab Emirates by region
Cambodia by province	Luxembourg by district	United Kingdom by region
Canada by province	Macedonia by region	USA
Central America by country	Malaysia by state	USA (continental)
China by region	Malta	Uzbekistan by region
Croatia by region	Mexico by region	Vatican City
Cyprus by district	Moldova by region	Vietnam by province
Czech Republic by region (outdated)	Monaco	Wales by region
Czech Republic by region	Mongolia by province	World by continent
Denmark by county (outdated)	Myanmar by region	
Denmark by county	Netherlands by province	
Denmark by county (outdated)	New Zealand by region	
Denmark by county	North America by country	
England by region	Northern Ireland by region	
Estonia by region	North Korea by region	
Europe by country	Norway by province	
European Union by country	Oceania by country	
Europe (large) by country	Papua New Guinea by region	
Europe (large) by country Mercator	Philippines by region	
Europe (small) by country	Poland by region (outdated)	
Faroe Islands	Poland by region	
Finland by province	Portugal by province	
France by region	Romania by county	
Georgia by republic	Russia by region (outdated)	
Germany by state	Russia by region	
Gibraltar	Russia by region (outdated)	

Supported mobile components and connections

The supported mobile components and connections are as follows:

- Web service query (query as a web service)*
- Flash variables*
- External interface connection*

Index

A

Adobe AIR
  URL, for installation 210
Adobe Flash Builder
  URL, for installation 210
advanced menus
  Accordion Menu 144, 145
  label-based menu 140-142
  picture fisheye menus, sliding 142, 143
  using 139
alerts, using
  about 166
  with charts 166-172
  with Combo Box selector 180, 181
  with maps 177-179
  with scorecard selector 181-184
  with Selectors 180
  with single-value component 173-177
application level security
  applying 260-262
art and background components
  examples 201
  image component, using 202-205
  resize image to component option 205
  using 201

B

bar chart 66, 67
basic art components
  using 201
BI platform 4.x, SAP BO
  Crystal Reports 2
  Explorer 2
  Lumira 2

  Web Intelligence (Webi) 2
BI reporting tools, SAP BO
  Crystal reports 271
  Dashboards 271
  Design studio 272
  Explorer 272
  Lumira 272
  Web Intelligence (Webi) reports 271
built-in map dashboard components
  adding 86-89
  region keys 89
  USA maps, adding 87
  US maps, adding 87
bullet chart
  about 77
  metrics 77
Business Explorer (BEx) 223
business requisites
  gathering 35
  KPIs 35
  sales and quantity per product analysis 36
  sales by state analysis 35
  sales trend analysis 36
business user categories
  analysts 37
  executives and top management 37
  operational 37

C

calendar dashboard component
  using 100-103
calendar functionalities
  calendar default date 103
  date/day insertion type 103
  enable calendar limits 103

Candlesticks charts 76
canvas containers
  using 160-165
capabilities, SAP BO Dashboards
  about 10
  samples, accessing 10-12
  samples, using 10-12
  templates, accessing 15
  templates, using 15
Central Management Console (CMC) 249
charts
  using, with alerts 166-172
charts types
  about 65
  bar chart 66-72
  bubble chart 73-75
  bullet chart 77
  Candlesticks charts 76
  column chart 66
  column line charts 66-72
  line chart 66-72
  OHLC chart 76
  Radar chart 77
  Scatter chart 73-75
  Tree Map 73-75
checkboxes
  click label to change selection option 133
  data insertion 133
  using 130-133
CMap plugin
  Address Data mode 93
  configuring 90-96
  Labels and values field 94
  Shape Data mode 93, 94
  URL 90
  using 90-97
colors and themes
  Appearance tab, using 192-195
  color binding feature 196, 197
  color scheme, using 197-199
  dealing with 192
column chart 66, 67
column line chart 67, 68
comboboxes
  using 128-130
Combo Box selector
  using, with alerts 180, 181

Components panel 22-25
containers
  about 158
  canvas container, using 160-165
  panel container, using 159, 160
  tab set, using 165
  types 158
  using 158
Crystal report document
  dashboard, linking to 187

D

dashboard
  about 117
  canvas size, changing 50, 51
  creating, process 42
  Dashboard Object to Replace Flash
    Object 215
  document properties 55
  exporting 208
  importing 215
  preferences 52
  prerequisites 50
  previewing 208
  publishing 211-214
  Save To Platform 214
  single value component, adding 78
  workspace, preparing 43-46
dashboard components
  basic art components, using 201
  formatting 205
dashboard creation, process
  data, importing 42
  model, building 42
  model, publishing 43
dashboard file
  AIR, exporting to 210
  block content warning, allowing 211
  data connections 211
  export option 210
  import option 210
  secured https servers 211
dashboard samples
  accessing 10-12
  Accordion menu 12, 13
  Accordion menu, components 13

Chart Drill Down 14, 15
Chart Drill Down, components 15
file, exporting 207-210
using 10-12
dashboard templates
accessing 15, 16
using 15, 16
US Sales Map 17-19
dash printer
URL 112
using 111-113
dimensions
about 34
geographical dimension (region) 34
product line 34
time 34
direct query
about 217
using 218-228
drill-down (Insertion) feature
using 184-186
dynamic visibility feature
using 152-156

E

Export toolbar 28

F

Format toolbar 28

G

grouping components
actions 156
using 156-158

I

image component
using 202-205
Information Design Tool (IDT)
used, for creating row level security
data profile 264-266
inheritance types
inherit from parent folder option 260
inherit from parent group option 260

installation
SAP BO Dashboards 4-10

L

line chart 66
list boxes
using 128-130
Live Office
using 236-245

M

maps
about 85, 86
built-in dashboard components,
adding 86-89
CMap plugin, configuring 90-96
CMap plugin, installing 90-97
CMap plugin, using 90-96
using 86
using, with alerts 177-179
Micro charts
using 113-116
mobile dashboards
accessing 274, 281-283
adding, to mobile category 279-281
creating, for smart devices 273, 274
design phase 274
development phase 274
previewing 277, 278
publishing 277-279
using 281-283
mobile SAP BO Dashboard
developing 274
recommended canvas size, using for
iPads 276
supported mobile components,
using 274, 275
supported mobile data connection,
using 276, 277
month to date (MTD) 82

O

Object Browser panel 25, 26
object level security
applying 251-260

open price, high price, low price, and
    closing price chart (OHLC chart) 76

P

panel containers
  URL 160
  using 159, 160
pie chart
  adding 56-59
  best practices 57
  linking, with data 60, 61
  main properties, configuring 62-65
Preferences
  about 51, 52
  Document tab 53
  Excel options 54
  Grid tab 53
  tabs 51
project management office (PMO) 33
project phases
  closing phase 33
  control/testing phase 33
  execution/implementation phase 33
  initiation phase 32
  planning phase 32
Properties panel 21, 22
prototype
  about 41
  building 41, 42

Q

Query Browser panel 26
quick views 29

R

Radar chart
  about 77
  types 77
radio buttons
  enhancements, applying 122
  insertion types 124-127
  Insert On 123
  Interaction Only option 123
  orientation 123
  selected item 127, 128

  using 118-123
requisites
  business requisites, gathering 35
  dashboard, sketching 38-40
  devices, determining 36, 37
  dimensions 34
  prototype, building 41, 42
  target audience, determining 36, 37
row level security
  access restrictions, creating with
    UDT 267-269
  applying 263
  data profile, creating with IDT 264-266

S

SAP BI application
  Annotation feature, using 285
  dashboards, e-mailing 285
  document, adding to favorites 284
  document information, viewing 284
  main features 283
  on Android, URL 284
  on Mac OS, URL 283
SAP BO
  about 1
  BI reporting tools 271
  official user guide, URL 260
  security model 249
  URL 250
SAP BO Dashboard components
  calendar dashboard component,
    using 100-103
  history component, using 107-111
  Print button, using 106
  Reset button, using 107
  Scenario button, using 106, 107
  source data component, using 107-111
  trend analyzer, using 104-106
  trend icon, using 103, 104
  using 97-99
SAP BO Dashboards
  about 2, 3
  BI platform 4.x 2
  capabilities, exploring 10
  design history 3
  downloading 5-7

installing 4-10
interface 19
prerequisites 4, 5
quick views 29
URL 3
SAP BO Dashboards, interface
about 19
canvas 20
Excel model 20
menus 20
panels 21
panel's area 20
properties panel 20
quick views 29
toolbars 27-29
SAP BO Dashboards, panels
about 21
Components panel 22-25
mobile compatibility 27
Object Browser panel 25, 26
Properties panel 21, 22
Query Browser panel 26
SAP BO Dashboards, toolbars
about 27
Export toolbar 28
Format toolbar 28
Start Page toolbar 29
SAP BusinessObjects. *See* **SAP BO**
scorecard
about 136
Allow column sorting option 137
Enable case-insensitive sorting option 138
Rows are selectable option 138
security best practices
applying 269, 270
customized access level 269
inheritance 270
row level security 270
security matrix 269
security model, SAP BO
about 250
access level 250
Administrator group 251
authentication 250
authorization 250
deny access 251

grant access 251
inheritance 251
rights 251
single sign-on (SSO) 250
User Group 251
selectors
about 151
Filter, using 147, 148
icon, using 146
push and toggle buttons, using 149
third-party selectors, using 149
using 145
using, with alerts 180
single-value component
adding, to dashboard 78
dial, adding 78-81
gauge, adding 78, 81
play dashboard component 83
progress bar 82
sliders 82
spinner 82, 83
using, with alerts 173-176
value 82, 83
smart devices
mobile dashboards, creating 273, 274
source data component
Insertion Type 110
Selected Index Item 111
Standard toolbars 28
Start Page toolbar 29

T

tab set
using 165
tabular data
displaying 134
grid 139
hierarchical table 138
list view 135
scorecard 136, 137
spreadsheet table 138
text dashboard components
Input Text Area, using 191
Input Text, using 191
labels, using 191
using 189, 190

themes
  using 200, 201
Themes toolbar 28
third-party plugins
  dash printer, using 111-113
  Micro charts, using 113-116
  using 111
traditional selectors
  checkboxes, using 130-132
  comboboxes, using 128-130
  list boxes, using 128-130
  list builder 133, 134
  radio buttons, using 118
  using 118
Tree Map chart 73-75
trend analyzer
  using 104-106
trend icon
  using 103

U

Universe Design Tool (UDT)
  used, for creating row level security
    access restrictions 267-269

W

Web Intelligence (Webi)
  about 1
  dashboard, linking to 187
web service query
  creating 229-233
  using 229
web services
  query 229
  URL 234
  using 229

X

XML data
  using 245-247

Y

year to date (YTD) 82

Thank you for buying
Learning SAP BusinessObjects Dashboards

About Packt Publishing

Packt, pronounced 'packed', published its first book, *Mastering phpMyAdmin for Effective MySQL Management*, in April 2004, and subsequently continued to specialize in publishing highly focused books on specific technologies and solutions.

Our books and publications share the experiences of your fellow IT professionals in adapting and customizing today's systems, applications, and frameworks. Our solution-based books give you the knowledge and power to customize the software and technologies you're using to get the job done. Packt books are more specific and less general than the IT books you have seen in the past. Our unique business model allows us to bring you more focused information, giving you more of what you need to know, and less of what you don't.

Packt is a modern yet unique publishing company that focuses on producing quality, cutting-edge books for communities of developers, administrators, and newbies alike. For more information, please visit our website at www.packtpub.com.

About Packt Enterprise

In 2010, Packt launched two new brands, Packt Enterprise and Packt Open Source, in order to continue its focus on specialization. This book is part of the Packt Enterprise brand, home to books published on enterprise software – software created by major vendors, including (but not limited to) IBM, Microsoft, and Oracle, often for use in other corporations. Its titles will offer information relevant to a range of users of this software, including administrators, developers, architects, and end users.

Writing for Packt

We welcome all inquiries from people who are interested in authoring. Book proposals should be sent to author@packtpub.com. If your book idea is still at an early stage and you would like to discuss it first before writing a formal book proposal, then please contact us; one of our commissioning editors will get in touch with you.

We're not just looking for published authors; if you have strong technical skills but no writing experience, our experienced editors can help you develop a writing career, or simply get some additional reward for your expertise.

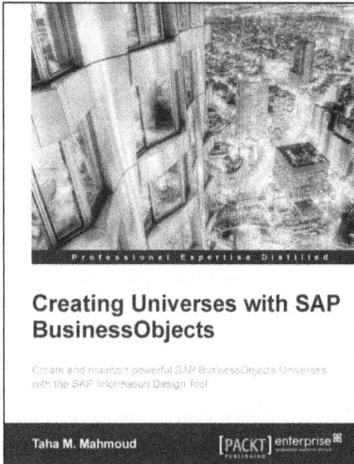

Creating Universes with SAP BusinessObjects

Create and maintain powerful SAP BusinessObjects Universes
with the SAP Information Design Tool

Taha M. Mahmoud   [PACKT] enterprise ✕

Creating Universes with SAP BusinessObjects

ISBN: 978-1-78217-090-7   Paperback: 310 pages

Create and maintain powerful SAP BusinessObjects
Universes with the SAP Information Design Tool

1. Gain all the skills needed to achieve your
    business intelligence goals by linking your
    business, data, and people using SAP
    BusinessObjects.

2. Master the SAP Information Design Tool to
    create a universe and explore its resources
    such as the connection, data foundation layer,
    and business layer.

3. Learn to use a business case supported with
    illustrated diagrams that will help you to build
    robust universes.

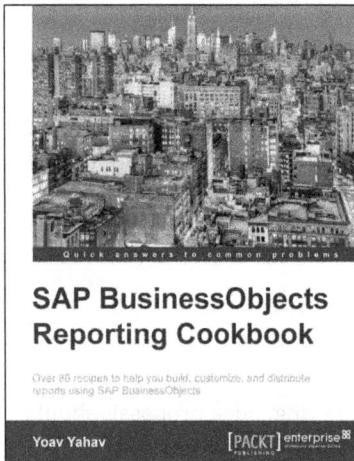

SAP BusinessObjects Reporting Cookbook

Over 80 recipes to help you build, customize, and distribute
reports using SAP BusinessObjects

Yoav Yahav   [PACKT] enterprise ✕

SAP BusinessObjects Reporting Cookbook

ISBN: 978-1-78217-243-7   Paperback: 380 pages

Over 80 recipes to help you build, customize, and
distribute reports using SAP BusinessObjects

1. Discover how to master different business
    solutions which will help you deliver high
    quality reports to your organization and clients.

2. Work efficiently in a BI environment
    while keeping your data accurate, secured,
    and easily shared.

3. Learn how to build and format reports that
    will enable you to get the most useful insights
    from your data.

Please check **www.PacktPub.com** for information on our titles

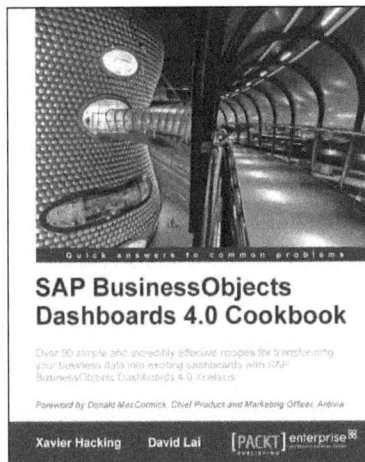

SAP BusinessObjects Dashboards 4.0 Cookbook

ISBN: 978-1-84968-178-0   Paperback: 352 pages

Over 90 simple and incredibly effective recipes for transforming your business data into exciting dashboards with SAP BusinessObjects Dashboards 4.0 Xcelsius

1. Learn valuable Dashboard Design best practices and tips through easy to follow recipes.

2. Become skilled in using and configuring all Dashboard Design components.

3. Learn how to apply Dynamic Visibility to enhance your dashboards.

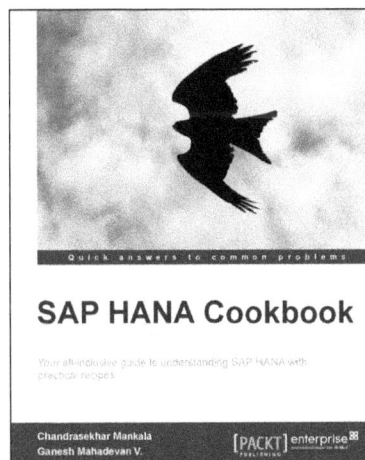

SAP HANA Cookbook

ISBN: 978-1-78217-762-3   Paperback: 284 pages

Your all-inclusive guide to understanding SAP HANA with practical recipes

1. Understand the architecture of SAP HANA, effectively transforming your business with the modeler and in-memory computing engine.

2. Learn about Business Intelligence, Analytics, and Predictive analytics on top of SAP HANA Models.

3. Gain knowledge on the process of transforming your data to insightful information using the Modeler.

Please check **www.PacktPub.com** for information on our titles